TO ARM
A NATION

BY THE SAME AUTHOR

Japan: Images and Realities

Conflict and Compromise:
The Dynamics of American Foreign Policy

TO ARM
A NATION

REBUILDING AMERICA'S
ENDANGERED DEFENSES

RICHARD HALLORAN

MACMILLAN PUBLISHING COMPANY

NEW YORK

Macmillan Publishing Company
866 Third Avenue, New York, N.Y. 10022
Collier Macmillan Canada, Inc.

Library of Congress Cataloging-in-Publication Data
Halloran, Richard, 1930–
To arm a nation.
Bibliography: p.
Includes index.
1. United States—Defenses. I. Title.
UA23.H354   1986   355′.033073   86-8717
ISBN 0-02-547540-1

Macmillan books are available at special discounts for bulk purchases
for sales promotions, premiums, fund-raising, or educational use.
For details, contact:

Special Sales Director
Macmillan Publishing Company
866 Third Avenue
New York, N.Y. 10022

10 9 8 7 6 5 4 3 2 1

Designed by Jack Meserole

PRINTED IN THE UNITED STATES OF AMERICA

DEDICATED

TO

THE HONORED MEMORY

OF

THOMAS PATRICK GREENE

FIRST LIEUTENANT, INFANTRY, UNITED STATES ARMY

KILLED IN ACTION, REPUBLIC OF KOREA, 10 FEBRUARY 1951

AND

LAWRENCE DOUGLASS GREENE

FIRST LIEUTENANT, INFANTRY, UNITED STATES ARMY

KILLED IN ACTION, REPUBLIC OF VIETNAM, 30 JANUARY 1968

CONTENTS

Let him who desires peace prepare for war.
>   —FLAVIUS VEGETIUS

If we desire to secure peace, it must be known that we are at all times ready for war.
>   —GEORGE WASHINGTON

It is an unfortunate fact that we can secure peace only by preparing for war.
>   —JOHN F. KENNEDY

PREFACE AND ACKNOWLEDGMENTS

In the New Testament, Saint Luke professes: "When a strong man armed keepeth his house, all the things that are his are at peace." From that passage comes the belief that to arm a nation in an effort to keep the peace is just. The theme of forging military power to protect a nation's citizens and to preserve the public tranquillity has echoed down through history from the Roman military writer Flavius Vegetius to George Washington and John F. Kennedy.

This book is a critical appraisal of the military power America has forged to keep the peace. It looks at the link between the American people and the armed forces that was broken during the war in Vietnam; examines the quality of the combatant commanders who would lead American soldiers, sailors, marines, and airmen into battle; tells something of the men and women in the armed forces, who they are and why they are in military service, and tries to show what the forces do every day as they train and stand guard around the world. It delves into the way the military establishment, largely in Washington, is organized and functions; scrutinizes the defense industry that produces arms and equipment for the forces; surveys the deployment of forces all over the globe; examines their readiness for sustained combat; and explores the costs of defense to see whether the taxpayers are getting their money's worth. The focus here is on conventional, nonnuclear forces because they are far more likely than nuclear arms to be needed. But the book reviews the nation's nuclear offensive forces and and examines nuclear defenses, including the scheme known as "Star Wars."

The book argues that, in the main, the nation is well served by dedicated soldiers, sailors, airmen, and marines and the leaders who command battalions and ships and air squadrons on every continent and the seven seas. But the national security has been truly jeopardized by institutions in Washington that shape military policy. The political leadership is in fundamental disarray, fluctuating between chaos and paralysis. Organization is splintered, with leaders too often motivated more by vested than by national interests, and warring factions spending more time in squabbling with each other than in deterring the nation's enemies. The defense industry, bound by excessive regulation, produces high-priced weapons of questionable quality. National leaders have pledged the United States to military commitments beyond the capacity of the forces, have failed to make the force ready for sustained combat, and have been unable to persuade allies to carry their fair share of the burden for collective security. Either the cost of defense is $100 billion too high, or the taxpayers ought to be getting another $100 billion worth of military power for their money. Only in offensive nuclear arms, the military and political value of which has come increasingly into question, does the United States have an adequate force. Defensively, President Reagan's Strategic Defense Initiative, better known as Star Wars, may be worth pursuing militarily and technically, but it has been presented with hypocrisy and deceit.

The consequence of this dichotomy between field and flagpole is that the armed forces of the United States are incapable of applying more than minimal military power with conventional arms in pursuit of American national interests. The armed forces have the power to invade the tiny island of Grenada in the Caribbean or hammer the puny forces of Libya in North Africa but not to engage in combat on the level of Korea or Vietnam in, for instance, Central America or the Persian Gulf. Moreover, the military power of the United States will most likely remain in that precarious condition for the rest of the decade and longer unless there is a sweeping, top-to-bottom overhaul.

After six years of reporting on military affairs for *The New York Times*, I wrote this book for American citizens who might be concerned about the capabilities and limitations of their armed forces. It was written for the voters who are the ultimate judges of whether and how the United States will employ military power as an instrument of national policy, and for the taxpayers who pay enormous sums every year for military protection. It is for Americans, whether they have served in the military or not, who have little connection with their armed forces beyond what they see on television or read in the press.

The book is reportage from a newspaper correspondent rather than the work of an academician or specialist. Much of the material came from my notebooks and files for *The New York Times*. Other material came from the work of colleagues at the *Times* and from friends and competitors on other publications. Instead of providing footnotes and other trappings of a scholarly treatise, useful as they are in their own setting, I have included sourcing in the text where necessary and have appended a bibliography. I should note, too, that this book is about military power. It touches only lightly on other elements of national security, such as foreign policy, international economics, arms control, or the nature of just and unjust wars.

Readers may want—and, indeed, have a right—to know the point of departure and the credentials of the writer. My perspective is implicit throughout the book but should be made explicit here, up front. As already suggested, I believe that effective military power is vital to the survival of America in a rough-and-tumble world filled with people who do not wish us well. I further believe that the only legitimate reason, ultimately, for this nation to have a military force is to defend the human rights of American citizens. The armed forces are a shield to protect Americans from threats to our freedom, political democracy, social values, and economic prosperity. The men and women who form that shield deserve the allegiance of those who are protected. But if American military power becomes aggressive, or is used for purposes other than to defend the human rights of Americans, it would not be worthy of the nation's trust. Over the last three decades, some Americans have emphasized the need for military power rather than human rights; others have asserted that human rights are more important than armed force. It is my belief that the two are irrevocably connected, that it is not a matter of military power *or* human rights but a matter of military power *and* human rights.

I believe the profession of arms to be honorable, a belief that springs from a tradition of military service that has seen members of my family serve in every American conflict since the war with Spain. It began with my grandfather, Brigadier General Michael Joseph Lenihan, the son of Irish immigrants, who graduated from West Point in 1887 and was a brigade commander in the 42nd Rainbow Division in World War I. He taught me the passage from Saint Luke that still sums up my view on military power. My late father, Rear Admiral Paul James Halloran, was a civil engineer, a career naval officer, and commander of the 6th Brigade of Seabees who built airfields on the islands of Saipan and Tinian in the Marianas in World War II. Several cousins on both sides of the family served, with distinction, in World War II. My brother was a fighter pilot in the Navy in the 1950s.

Two of my family have given their lives for our country. My cousin, Pat Greene, a graduate of West Point in 1950, was killed in action in Korea; a younger cousin, Larry Greene, was killed in action in Vietnam. It is to their honored memory that this book is respectfully dedicated.

After growing up around the military service, I enlisted in the Army, graduated from officers' candidate school as a lieutenant of infantry, and served as a paratrooper in the 82nd Airborne Division. I was sent to Korea just after the war there and to Vietnam at the start of America's involvement in Indochina, in both instances to serve in military advisory groups. In journalism, I covered military affairs in Korea, Indochina, and elsewhere in Asia and the United States off and on from 1962 to 1976, although never as a full-time war correspondent. Since September 1979, I have been a military correspondent for *The New York Times*, based in Washington, reporting on military policy in the capital and on military activities in the field.

I would like to acknowledge the many people who have contributed to this book, directly and indirectly. First among those are the hundreds of soldiers, sailors, airmen, and marines who have taken the time to talk with me. I am especially grateful to the senior noncommissioned officers—the first sergeants and sergeants major of the Army and Marine Corps, the senior and chief master sergeants of the Air Force, and the senior and master chief petty officers of the Navy—who have given generously of their time and thoughts. It is a cliché, but nonetheless true, that they are the backbone of the armed forces. I would single out for thanks the combatant commanders, the battalion commanders, ship captains, and squadron leaders who hold their people in good hands and who were patient and helpful when I visited their commands.

Thanks are also due to the public affairs officers of all services, in Washington and in the field, for their help. They are unsung heroes who get caught between the demands of skeptical reporters like me and the demands of their superiors who want nothing, or nothing but applause, to appear in the press and on television. The majority of the public affairs officers, however, understand the workings of both sides and do their best to find an accommodation because they believe that public support is essential to the mission of their services.

To Harry Zubkoff and his associates in the Pentagon's News Clipping and Analysis Service go thanks for publishing the *Current News* and its affiliates, the best reference service in the nation on current events and trends in military affairs.

I am grateful to Bill Kovach, Washington Bureau Chief of *The New York Times*, for giving me the assignment I wanted and for encouraging me in covering it. Thanks, too, to colleagues on the *Times* and on other publications whose published information I have used shamelessly but to whom I have tried to give due credit. A special word of thanks to Colonel Harry G. Summers Jr. for furnishing helpful materials.

Several people read all or parts of the manuscript at various stages. I am immensely grateful to General Edward C. Meyer, former Chief of Staff of the Army and a perceptive editor who saved me from errors of omission and commission. R. James Woolsey, former Under Secretary of the Navy, took time during an especially trying period to bring his incisive mind to bear with helpful suggestions. John M. Collins, senior specialist in national security affairs at the Congressional Research Service, badgered and berated me but deserves much credit for trying to clear up murky thinking. Timothy Seldes, my agent, had an ever-ready ear and a cheerful word of encouragement and advice. Robert Stewart of Macmillan proved to be a persuasive editor who gently nudged me in the right direction. Neil Beshers was an excellent copy editor with a keen eye and a deft touch. Robert Weil, of *Omni* magazine, encouraged this book at the beginning. Martin Tolchin, my friend at the *Times*, offered sage advice at a critical time.

My son Chris, an aspiring writer, showed previously unseen skills as an editor and critic. My daughter Laurie had perceptive comments and did yeoman work on the bibliography. My daughter Catherine added helpful thoughts to round out points of view from three young adults.

Lastly, I am grateful beyond words to my wife, Fumiko Mori Halloran, for everything she did to see me through this project. She encouraged it from the beginning, listened to ideas at the dinner table and asked questions that made me expand on them, read and reread chapters. She provided invaluable insights as an accomplished writer, as a non-American who is detached from the issues, and as a person who had not been much exposed to military affairs. Most of all, she made me explain things until she understood them.

To all of them, my deepest thanks. But they are absolved of errors of fact or judgment in this book, for I alone take responsibility for that. That is particularly true of the last chapter, with my thoughts on changes that are needed.

R. H.

Washington, DC
March 1986

TO ARM
A NATION

INTRODUCTION

The foundations of modern American military power were laid in the early 1950s, not in World War II, as is often said.

In the spring of 1950, President Truman's National Security Council produced a remarkable document known as NSC-68 that outlined the United States response to the detonation of the first Soviet nuclear device. It called for a buildup of American nuclear and conventional forces to meet the threat from the Soviet Union that had become apparent during the Cold War of the preceding three years, and set out the principles of nuclear deterrence and conventional containment that govern American military posture today.

The first military test of containment came but a few months later, when North Korea mounted a surprise attack on South Korea, then under American occupation. That lasted until the summer of 1953. The United States was basically successful in the Korean War, as the nation's leaders turned away from the heady visions of total war and unconditional surrender of World War II and went back to the tradition of limited conflicts with limited objectives that had marked most of American military history. Moreover, the United States did not demobilize after the Korean War, as it had after every war before, but built the nation's first large, standing peacetime armed force and adopted the fundamentals that make the military posture of the nation today different from anything before.

The United States had emerged from World War II, with its stirring emotions, clarity of purpose, and unusual national unity, in a position of overwhelming military superiority. The nation had an armed force of 12 million trained men, excellent armaments, a war industry that was a mighty engine of production, and a homeland unscarred by the destruction that befell Europe and Asia. With the atomic bomb, the United States had perhaps the greatest military superiority in history.

But after the victory of 1945, America rushed to return to normality. The armed forces were largely disbanded, arms were scrapped or put into mothballs, and industry turned to producing all manner of consumer and capital goods to satisfy demands held in check by the war.

In 1950, however, the armed forces began a revolution of many parts. Obviously the greatest change in warfare has been nuclear weapons and the evolving strategy for employing them. Bernard Brodie, a professor at Yale who was among the early nuclear thinkers, said shortly after the atomic bombings of Hiroshima and Nagasaki in 1945 that military forces would no longer be maintained to fight wars but to prevent wars. That concept came to be known as deterrence; it applied initially to nuclear arms but came to include conventional forces. Deterrence, however, has not always prevented armed conflict, as witness the wars in Korea and Vietnam.

Along with deterrence came containment, the most far-reaching American doctrine on national security since the Monroe Doctrine. The doctrine of containment says the United States will try to prevent the expansion of Soviet power with a combination of political, economic, and military instruments, including the posting of American military forces around the periphery of the Soviet Union. Over the years, containment has slowed but not stopped the expansion of Soviet power. Since 1950, Cuba and Vietnam have become Soviet allies, and Soviet influence is widespread in parts of the Middle East, Africa, and Latin America.

Until the Korean War, the nation's armed forces had been a small cadre of professionals around which citizen-soldiers rallied in time of need. When the need passed, the citizen-soldiers were sent home. Since Korea, the force has expanded and contracted but has never fallen below 3 million, counting civilian employees of the Defense Department who are an integral part of the total force. From 1948 until 1973, the nation relied on conscription to maintain the force; after Vietnam, the nation returned to the tradition of a volunteer force.

The surprise attack of the Korean War reinforced the lesson of Pearl Harbor, the Japanese surprise attack on Hawaii that brought America into World War II in 1941. Since 1950, the objective of American military policy has been to organize, train, and equip the armed forces to be ready at any time for the first day of war. No longer will the United States have the luxury, as it has in every case before, of mobilizing and going off to war at its own pace. This change in the way America makes war has left unsettled the constitutional issue of where lies the authority to send forces into battle. The Constitution assigns to Congress the power to declare war. Yet President Truman dispatched forces to fight in Korea, President Johnson to make war in Vietnam, and President Reagan to invade Grenada, all without congressional declarations of war. Militarily, containment has led to the strategy of forward deployment. Until the new era, American soldiers in peacetime served largely at home, and American sailors patrolled the Atlantic and Pacific moats that protected the United

States. When war came, American forces were dispatched abroad for combat, after which they came home. But with the occupations of Germany, Italy, and Japan after World War II and the dispatch of forces to other nations after the Korean War, American forces have been deployed all over the world. Today the United States has forces spread around the globe on a relative scale greater than that of any nation since the Roman Empire.

Together with forward deployment, a contemporary concept of collective security has evolved. Until the new era, American military alliances with other nations were those agreed upon to prosecute a war. Now, for the first time, the United States has committed itself to a series of peacetime alliances with foreign nations. The United States has made military commitments through treaties to nations in Latin America, Western Europe, and Asia. In addition are political understandings with nations such as Israel and Egypt that the United States will help preserve their national security. Altogether, the United States has military obligations, either by treaty or political understanding, to sixty foreign nations.

With the changes in military posture has come a fundamental change in military spending. Before World War II, peacetime military spending was a pittance. Since 1950, the military budget has been consistently a noticeable part of the national economy. During the Korean War, military spending consumed 13.8 percent of the gross national product, the total value of the goods and services turned out by the nation each year. It settled back to a range around 7.5 percent of GNP in subsequent years, then rose to 9.5 percent during the war in Vietnam. It dropped to 5 percent in the post-Vietnam period but has risen to 7 percent during the Reagan Administration. Since about one-third of the funds every year are spent to buy arms and equipment, the defense industry producing those things has become a permanent fixture.

The military forces today are incorporated within the Department of Defense, led by the Secretary of Defense. His immediate staff includes the Deputy Secretary, two under secretaries in charge of the formulation of policy and the development of weapons, and assistant secretaries for manpower, financial matters, legal affairs, legislative relations, and other specialties. Altogether, the Defense Department comprises 2.2 million men and women in four military services and 1 million civilians in administrative, technical, and support positions.

Within the department, known in Washington as DoD, are the Departments of the Army, Navy (including the Marine Corps), and Air Force. The military departments, each headed by a civilian secretary and a military chief of staff, are responsible for recruiting, training, organizing, equipping, and administering their respective forces. They are not, in theory, involved in operations, which are the responsibility of the combatant commanders, of which more below.

The Army, with 781,000 soldiers, is organized around 18 divisions that range in size from 10,000 to 18,000 soldiers each. Eleven are stationed in the continental United States, one each in Hawaii and Alaska, four in Western Europe, and one in South Korea. Armored divisions are equipped with tanks but have infantry in mechanized battalions that move in armored personnel carriers. Mechanized divisions are similar, but with more infantry and fewer tanks. The 82nd Airborne Division is a parachute unit, the 101st Airborne a helicopter assault division, the 9th a motorized division. Four new light divisions of 10,000 soldiers each have been formed. All divisions have artillery, signal, engineer, chemical, intelligence, military police, helicopter, medical, and support units. In addition are units like the Rangers, who are commandos, and the Special Forces, or Green Berets, who specialize in guerrilla warfare and counterinsurgency. The Army has 850,000 soldiers in the National Guard and Army Reserves.

The Navy, with 586,000 sailors, is equipped with 13 deployable aircraft carriers and 1,000 airplanes in 65 squadrons. The surface Navy includes 3 battleships; over 200 cruisers, destroyers, and frigates; more than 60 amphibious ships; and numerous smaller vessels and support ships. Under the seas are nearly 100 nuclear-powered attack submarines and almost 40 ballistic missile submarines to bring the total to 550 ships. The Reagan Administration's goal is 600 ships by the early 1990s. The Navy is deployed in four fleets: one on each coast, one in the eastern Atlantic and Mediterranean, and another in the western Pacific and Indian Ocean. The Navy has 66 ships and 142,000 sailors in reserve.

The Marine Corps, which is part of the Navy Department, has 200,000 marines organized in three divisions, with a fourth division in the reserves. The Marine Corps has 430 aircraft in 25 squadrons. The marines are deployed in amphibious units of 1,800 marines in a ground force, an air unit, and a combat support unit. Marine amphibious brigades are similarly organized and three times as large. An amphibious force of 50,000 marines includes a division, an air wing, and a combat support element. Other support—such as medical, supply, financial, and transport—comes from the Navy.

The Air Force of 612,000 airmen is organized into three large commands. The Strategic Air Command has 315 bombers and 1,000 intercontinental missiles tipped with nuclear warheads. (The Navy's

44 submarines armed with ballistic nuclear missiles are under Navy control, but their missions are coordinated with those of the Strategic Air Command.) The Tactical Air Command has 1,800 fighters and ground attack planes organized in 79 squadrons. The Military Transport Command has 350 long-range transport planes and 215 medium-range transports. The Air Force also has a full panoply of engineering, intelligence, medical, logistics, police, and support units. In the Air Force Reserve and Air National Guard are 188,000 airmen.

The armed forces today are deployed in operational commands that have forces from two or more services. The commanders in chief, known in military parlance as CINCs, are responsible for drawing up war plans in peacetime and for employing the forces in battle when war comes.

The chain of command for military operations runs from the President, who is Commander in Chief of all the forces, through the Secretary of Defense to each of the commanders in chief of the operational commands. It does not run through the Vice-President, to preclude the remote possibility that a Vice-President might seek to use the armed forces in a coup against the President. Nor do the Joint Chiefs of Staff have command authority. That group includes a Chairman, who may serve for two terms of two years each, the Chief of Staff of the Army, the Chief of Naval Operations, the Commandant of the Marine Corps, and the Chief of Staff of the Air Force, each of whom is appointed for one four-year term. Collectively, they are the senior military advisers to the Secretary of Defense and the President.

In peacetime operations and wartime battle, the armed forces have been divided into combatant commands, known as unified commands (if formed of forces from two or more services) or as specified commands (if the forces are from one service).

Within the United States, Readiness Command, with headquarters at MacDill Air Force Base in Tampa, Florida, has operational control over most Army and Air Force combat units. While it is responsible for the defense of the United States itself, its main task is to prepare forces to move overseas to reinforce American troops already there.

Southern Command has headquarters in Panama and is responsible for the defense of United States interests in Latin America south of Mexico, including Central America. Southern Command has few forces assigned to it and draws on forces in Readiness Command and other commands for operations such as the shows of force in Honduras in the mid-1980s. Similarly, Central Command, which also has headquarters at MacDill Air Force Base, has few forces assigned but has the vast region around the Persian Gulf as its area of responsibility.

If Central Command were to engage in hostilities, it would draw forces from other commands.

The three biggest commands are the Atlantic, Pacific, and European commands. The Atlantic and Pacific commands are primarily naval commands, although Pacific Command has Army and Air Force units assigned in Hawaii, Japan, and Korea. The Atlantic and Pacific commands control the fleets deployed in their respective oceans. The European Command is primarily an Army and Air Force command controlling forces assigned to the North Atlantic Treaty Organization to defend Western Europe.

Specified commands include the Strategic Air Command of intercontinental bombers and missiles, the Military Airlift command of transports serving the entire military service, and the Air Defense Command, whose mission is to provide warning of an air or missile attack. Their forces come almost entirely from the Air Force.

CHAPTER 1

<hr/>

THE LEGACY OF VIETNAM

WHEN the agonizing war in Vietnam was finally over and it came time to figure out what had gone wrong, General Frederick C. Weyand went to the heart of the matter. "Vietnam was a reaffirmation of the peculiar relationship between the American Army and the American people," he wrote as Chief of Staff of the Army in 1976.

The American Army really is a people's army in the sense that it belongs to the American people who take a jealous and proprietary interest in its involvement. When the Army is committed, the American people are committed; when the American people lose their commitment, it is futile to try to keep the Army committed. In the final analysis, the American Army is not so much an army of the executive branch as it is an arm of the American people.

In its finest hours, at times of national peril, the bond between the American people and their armed forces has been something of an unwritten, perhaps even mystical, covenant. The armed forces have been the shield whose sworn duty has been to defend the American people from foreign aggressors, a duty they have carried out with honor and devotion, and sometimes at the cost of their lives. The people, in turn, have given their moral support to the military forces and expressed their gratitude for the sacrifices the soldiers have made. The symbols of those emotions dot the calendar and the landscape— Memorial Day, Armed Forces Day, the monuments in the villages and cities of every state, the Tomb of the Unknowns in Arlington Cemetery, the somber and dignified wall in Washington dedicated to those who died in Vietnam.

At other, less emotionally charged times, there has been a bond between the American people and their armed forces for reasons that may be obvious but that bear repeating. It is the people from whom the armed forces are drawn, whether the citizen-soldiers are volunteers or conscripts. It is the people who pay the taxes to raise and maintain the armed forces, and the people who produce the arms and equipment to sustain the forces in battle. In the American democracy, it is the people who elect the government that decides when to apply military force. Ultimately, it is the people who give or withhold their consent for military action.

But the bond between the people and the armed forces has been tenuous throughout American history. Since the Revolution, Americans by nature have been suspicious of authority and thus skeptical of the military hierarchy and its necessarily authoritarian ways. Americans have opposed a large standing force in peacetime and have gone to war only with the greatest reluctance. "Americans have a long and proud tradition," General Weyand wrote, "of irreverence toward and distrust of their military."

During the war in Vietnam, an emotional bond between American citizens and American soldiers never developed, as American sentiments were not engaged the way they were in World War II. The first American military advisers went to Vietnam in the summer of 1954, shortly after the North Vietnamese defeated the French at Dien Bien Phu, and a handful stayed until 1975, when NorthVietnamese forces marched into the South Vietnamese capital of Saigon. For the twenty years in between, to most Americans Vietnam was a steamy jungle country halfway around the world to which American soldiers went to fight—58,000 of them to die, 153,300 to be wounded, and the rest to return home after thirteen-month tours. The only fervor Vietnam generated was vigorous dissent. Americans quarreled over the morality of the war, the need for fighting it, the tactics of bombing and counterinsurgency, the draft that sent soldiers to war. Thus was the already tenuous bond broken.

Among the myriad lessons of Vietnam, one stands out: No government of the United States can long sustain a military venture without the consent of a large majority of the American people. When that consent is withheld, or is given and later withdrawn, the capacity of the government to conduct military operations will eventually be eroded and the armed forces almost certainly doomed to failure. Another Chief of Staff of the Army, General Edward C. Meyer, was succinct in stating a principle for applying American military power in the modern world. "Armies don't fight wars," he said, "nations fight wars."

James Webb, the writer and marine who fought in Vietnam, illuminated the broken connection with a telling passage in his searing novel *Fields of Fire*. A marine sergeant reporting for his second tour in Vietnam tells his platoon leader what it's like back home:

Lieutenant, you'd hardly know there was a war on. It's in the papers, and college kids run around screaming about it instead of doing panty raids or whatever they were doing before, but that's it. Airplane drivers still drive their airplanes. Businessmen still run their businesses. College kids go to college. It's like nothing really happened, except to other people. It isn't *touching* anybody except us. (italics in original)

The sergeant had it exactly right. Vietnam never touched Americans, who lost faith in their government and their armed forces. During Vietnam, the people were deceived by the White House and the Defense Department. The Congress failed in its constitutional duty by not demanding a declaration of war, the debate over which would have either given the nation some unity or prevented the dispatch of American forces. Instead, the Congress gave President Johnson a blank check, and continued to appropriate funds for the war even after public opinion had turned against it. The administration refused to call up the reserves to signal the nation that the United States was engaged in a large military venture; instead, the government relied on a draft that was unfair and severely abused. Senior military officers in Washington failed to give their political superiors sound military advice, while commanders in Saigon made strategic mistakes, including errors in assessing the fundamental nature of the war. The press and television brought violent images of war into American homes more vividly than ever before.

But most of all the bond between the people and the armed forces was broken when the American people discovered that the war was a waste, that it didn't make any difference to their security whether the United States won or lost. Many Americans came to that conclusion during the war and had it confirmed later. The United States today is no less secure because the North Vietnamese rule in Saigon and would have been no more secure had Saigon remained in friendly hands. When the war was over, Americans were relieved that the bloodletting had ended. They were weary of the dissension that had divided the nation as it had not been split since the Civil War. They were indifferent to the defeat. Mostly they just wanted Vietnam out of their minds.

Time and the fading memory of Vietnam, however, have not restored the connection between Americans and their armed forces. After American forces were withdrawn from Vietnam in 1973, most Americans were uninterested in the armed forces, resented paying taxes for national defense, and were unwilling to serve in the military. Some interest revived in 1979, when the Joint Chiefs of Staff lamented the neglected state of the forces, Americans were taken hostage in Iran, and the Soviet Union invaded Afghanistan. More concern was generated with the news in 1980 that Army divisions were unfit for combat, Navy ships couldn't sail for lack of trained seamen, and Air Force planes were grounded for lack of spare parts. The debacle at Desert One in Iran, where an attempt to rescue the American hostages in Teheran ended in flames, caused anxiety. When Harold Brown, the Secretary of Defense in President Carter's administration, left office in January 1981, he said that a "fragile consensus" on national defense had begun to form.

That consensus was indeed fragile. But President Reagan, during his first five years in office, did little to revive a sense of trust between Americans and the armed forces, despite his political rhetoric and pledges to "rearm America." The President was unable, even within his own administration, to forge a consensus on the uses of military power as an instrument of national policy. The Reagan Administration and the Congress had no fundamental agreement on the military power needed for national defense, nor on a national strategy that would govern foreign and military policy, nor on the mission and size and composition of the armed forces. Military leaders in Washington, while applauding the Reagan Administration's efforts to obtain money for the forces, were at odds with the President and many of his advisers over the employment of those forces. Secretary of Defense Caspar W. Weinberger could have been the point man in rebuilding a consensus, but by the end of Mr. Reagan's first term he had succeeded in alienating other members of the administration, many members of Congress, and large segments of the public. Among people over forty years old, thoughts of military force only rekindled unwanted memories of Vietnam; for those under forty, military power and the armed forces seemed to have little to do with their lives.

The legacy of Vietnam therefore is that the United States spends $300 billion a year for armed forces that American leaders are unable to use effectively in the national interest. As the smoke from that long conflict has drifted away, it has become clear that Americans distrust their government's ability to apply military power prudently. It has become equally clear that most Americans feel they have no ties to their armed forces, other than paying enormous sums in taxes for their upkeep. Moreover, there is ample evidence that American military leaders, while adhering to the tradition of civilian control of the military, mistrust the motives and talents of their civilian superiors in exerting military force.

The absence of a consensus among Americans, their government, and the armed forces is the biggest single weakness in the complex of political vibrance, economic strength, foreign policy, and military power that provides for the nation's security. Strategic thinkers, military officers, scholars, and politicians in recent years have increasingly revisited the consequences of the conflict in Vietnam. Most have come to the conclusion that, as the respected *Wilson Quarterly* reported after a survey, "The disarray of the Vietnam era brought one long-term consequence: It helped to shatter the U.S. foreign policy consensus forged during the early Cold War, greatly complicating the task of later Presidents in defending U.S. interests abroad."

The covenant between a people, their army, and their government has engaged the minds of military thinkers since the Chinese statesman Sun Tzu wrote 2,500 years ago a treatise titled *On the Art of War*. At the beginning of his essay, Sun Tzu said, "The Moral Law causes the people to be in complete accord with their ruler, so that they will follow him regardless of their lives, undismayed by any danger."

In the West, the Prussian military thinker Carl von Clausewitz saw in the 1820s that the nature of European war had changed with the rise of the nation-state in the seventeenth century. Before, the people were "absolutely nothing," and military operations were the province of governments and small, sometimes mercenary armies. Clausewitz said the French Revolution was the turning point in which war became "an affair of the people," especially under Napoleon. "This military power, based on the strength of the whole nation," he wrote, "marched over Europe, smashing everything in pieces so surely and certainly that where it encountered the old-fashioned armies the result was not doubtful for a moment." Clausewitz concluded that the government, the people, and the armed forces should be joined in a "wonderful trinity."

Since the early days of the Republic, Americans have had difficulty reconciling military power with democracy. Alexis de Tocqueville, the Frenchman who wrote so perceptively about democracy in America at the same time Clausewitz wrote so incisively about war in Europe, found a natural conflict between the needs of democracy and those of the military. But Professor Martin Diamond, a specialist on Tocqueville at Northern Illinois University, has said that Tocqueville thought the democratic spirit and the military spirit could complement one another:

The great teaching of Tocqueville is that one must create in the country a general spirit of democratic liberty to temper and balance the military spirit, and one must use the soldier's martial spirit to balance off, so to speak, the flabby potential of property-loving democracy.

Tocqueville himself said the democratic spirit leavened the martial spirit:

The general spirit of the nation, penetrating the spirit peculiar to the army, tempers the opinions and desires engendered by military life, or by the all-powerful influence of public opinion, actually oppresses them. Once you have educated, orderly, upstanding, and free citizens, you will have disciplined and obedient soldiers.

A reluctance to go to war, however, has always marked the American political scene. Vietnam was not, by far, the first war in which American soldiers fought with dissent at their backs. Indeed, with the exceptions of the Civil War and World War II, both passionate battles for national survival, large numbers of Americans have long shunned entangling alliances and opposed military ventures. Vincent Davis, of the University of Kentucky, said that one fundamental fact is clear. "Americans do not like to fight in wars," he wrote, "especially and most particularly in ground forces." Contrary to the belligerence that some foreign commentators profess to see in Americans, Professor Davis pointed to "the massive unpopularity of most American wars and warlike situations that have lasted for more than about a year, or two years at most, even when those efforts appeared headed toward something resembling a clear cut-cut 'victory.' "

Even the American Revolution, depicted in high school history books as an idealistic struggle for independence, was marked with dissent. Tories opposed the break with Britain, and merchants and farmers traded with the British during the fighting. Service in the militia was fitful. Samuel Eliot Morison, the historian, said: "The young men's favorite contribution to the war was to turn out for a short campaign with the militia, then go home to plant corn, get in the hay, or harvest the wheat, according to the season."

In the War of 1812, Americans were enraged when the British Navy flagrantly violated American maritime rights by impressing American merchant seamen. But the vote to declare war was not overwhelming, 79 to 49 in the House of Representatives and 19 to 12 in the Senate. Federalists in New England and New York, both maritime regions, denounced the politicians for going to war, refused to lend money to the government, and continued to trade with Britain through Boston and Canada.

In the war with Mexico in 1846, enthusiasm appeared only in the Mississippi Valley and in Texas, where feelings against Mexicans ran deep. Henry David Thoreau protested by refusing to pay a state tax, spent a night in jail, then returned to his cabin by Walden Pond outside Boston to write his *Essay on Civil Disobedience*. The military historian T. Harry Williams noted: "For the first time, a sizable number of Americans opposed a war not for political or economic reasons but because they considered it unjust and immoral."

The Civil War was America's first total war, a conflict of desperation and bitter regional rivalries that literally pitted brother against brother. People on both sides were aroused; the economies of North and South were mobilized; the Union and the Confederacy resorted to conscription for the first time in America. Both had objectives for which there was no compromise: the North sought to crush the rebellion; the South fought for secession and the end of the Union. Even so, dissenters were found North and South. Both had peace movements that advocated a truce and a negotiated settlement. Both President Lincoln and Jefferson Davis, the Southern leader, had political opponents who sought to undermine them. In the South, said Morison, poor whites complained that "it was a rich man's war and a poor man's fight."

The Spanish-American War of 1898 was a strange interlude in American military history: it was popular. Secretary of State John Hay called it "a splendid little war," and the press whipped up a public clamor. The war began in February with the sinking of the battleship *Maine* in the harbor at Havana in Cuba and was over by August, with the relatively small loss of 385 dead. The regular army ballooned from 28,000 to 275,000 with volunteers and without a draft.

World War I returned Americans to their disagreements over foreign military ventures. At first, the nation was divided into three factions: a small pro-Allied group, a smaller pro-German group, and a large group advocating neutrality. As the war progressed, the pro-Allied faction grew, the pro-German faction shrank, but the neutrals held a majority and helped to re-elect President Wilson in November 1916 on the slogan "He kept us out of war." Once elected, Mr. Wilson led the nation into war in April 1917 "to make the world safe for democracy." The President, asserting that "it is not an army that we must shape and train for war, it is a nation," obtained from the Congress the authority to regulate industry, shipping, food, fuel, and the railroads. Mr. Wilson set up the Committee on Public Information as a propaganda machine and persuaded the Congress to pass the first sedition law since 1798, even though it had been declared a breach of the First Amendment's protection of free speech.

American soldiers began to arrive in France in the summer of

1917, but they went into training rather than battle. Not until the spring of 1918 were they fully engaged in combat. Then the horrors of trench warfare began to sink in. In the few months before the armistice in November, the United States suffered 125,000 dead, of whom 50,000 were killed in battle and the rest by sickness and accidents. It was a sobering experience and may well have contributed to the postwar return to isolation, the rejection of the League of Nations, and large cuts in the Army. But the Navy, which patrolled the Atlantic and Pacific moats to prevent foreign intervention, was kept up.

Twenty years later, as war clouds again gathered over Europe and Asia, Americans clung to neutrality as long as they could. Pacifists, isolationists, and neutralists such as the famed aviator Charles Lindbergh sought to keep the nation out of foreign conflicts. The German attack on Poland, Holland, Belgium, France, and Britain in 1939 began to swing public opinion behind the Allies. The German conquest of France and German bombing of London and the small town of Coventry swung more Americans in favor of Britain. President Roosevelt got the Congress to approve a draft in 1940 and Lend Lease shipments of military equipment to Britain in 1941. Even so, a poll by *Fortune* magazine in the summer of 1941 found that 70 percent of the American people were still against going to war.

Then came the Japanese attack on the United States naval base at Pearl Harbor in Hawaii on Sunday morning, December 7, 1941. Americans were aroused as rarely before or since, and, as Arthur Krock of *The New York Times* wrote, "unity clicked into place." During the winter of 1942, America was frightened and pessimistic. Soldiers guarded the beaches looking for spies. Coastal cities were darkened as aircraft spotters watched for air raids. Rationing began and the economy was geared for all-out war. American support for the war effort, despite black markets and draft evasion, was almost total. The stakes were the very existence of the nation and a way of life; the political and military objectives were clear and accepted by the public; the bond between the American people and their armed forces was unquestioned.

With victory in 1945, Americans sought to return to normality as quickly as possible. The forces surged home from overseas and were swiftly demobilized, troop strength dropping from 12.1 million in 1945 to 1.5 million in 1947. Military budgets were slashed from $614 billion in 1945, if that had been measured in the value of the dollar in 1985, to $71 billion in 1948—and much of the 1948 appropriation was for mustering soldiers and sailors out of the military services.

Despite a desire to get on with their lives, Americans were at war again less than five years after World War II. In June 1950, North Korea mounted a surprise attack against South Korea, then under American occupation as a former part of the Japanese Empire. President Truman decided to intervene immediately under the flag of the United Nations, without asking Congress for a declaration of war. The American public initially supported the President, given fears of communism at the time and a perceived need for collective response to aggression. But public support gradually wore off, partly due to war weariness that remained from World War II. More important, the armed forces of the United States were, by any measure, ragged from demobilization and unfit for combat. Because the forces were caught unprepared, many reservists who had served in World War II were recalled, which they and many citizens thought unfair.

Shifting objectives further confused the public as President Truman first sought to reunify Korea, then said the United States would settle for the previous dividing line along the 38th parallel in Korea. Some Americans, savoring the unconditional triumph of World War II, wanted an all-out war against North Korea. President Truman and General Douglas MacArthur, the American field commander, disagreed on strategy and objectives, causing the President to relieve the general.

When it was over, the Korean War had left an imprint on the military posture of the United States that is clearly visible today. The Korean conflict marked a return to traditional concepts of limited rather than all-out war but led to the formation of the first large standing force in peacetime. Military alliances with other nations became part of national security as the Truman and Eisenhower administrations built a ring around the Soviet Union. American occupation forces in Germany and Japan became guards on the ramparts, and other United States forces were deployed to bases abroad to reassure allies. There was another, unspoken reason: New conflicts would be fought as far from American shores as possible. Americans generally supported these fundamental changes in the nation's military posture because they were brought about gradually, they were explained by the administration in office, and, until Vietnam, they worked without bloodshed.

When the United States first got deeply involved in Vietnam, the reason given was to close the ring intended to contain the Soviet Union and communism. At breakfast one morning in Saigon in 1962, a senior official of the American Embassy contended to a news correspondent that the North Koreans had been stopped, NATO had deterred a Soviet attack on Western Europe, and the Russians had been foiled in the Middle East and South Asia. "This," he said, "is where we slam the gates on them."

But that was not to be, for many reasons.

The policy of containment of communism, the basis of American foreign policy since 1950, had become so ingrained that President Johnson and his senior advisers did not question whether fighting in Vietnam was necessary to maintain that policy. They seem, in retrospect, to have decided that Vietnam was vital to American security without ever asking themselves whether that was really true. The President, moreover, committed American forces to battle without obtaining from the Congress the declaration of war prescribed in the Constitution. The President deceived the nation with shifting and inconsistent explanations of why the United States was engaged in Vietnam. He restricted military operations in an effort to avoid turning attention at home away from the social and political program called the Great Society. Finally, President Johnson failed to mobilize the economy for war or to raise taxes to pay for it, causing inflation that took years to bring under control. Eventually, the public discovered what Mr. Johnson had done, turned against him, and forced him to abdicate. That was the effect of his announcement on March 31, 1968, that he would not seek re-election.

The Congress contributed to the tragedy of Vietnam by abdicating its constitutional responsibilities instead of demanding that the President obtain a declaration of war. To the contrary, Congress adopted the Gulf of Tonkin Resolution in 1964 without really examining the consequences, permitting President Johnson to wage unfettered war. Congress continued to fill the administration's war chest even after the public demanded a stop. The War Powers Resolution voted by the Congress in 1973 to restrict the President's authority to conduct military operations was a congressional afterthought to atone for mistakes during the war in Vietnam and to recover a portion of the Congress's warmaking authority. That law requires the President to obtain congressional approval if American forces are in a hostile situation for sixty days.

The Joint Chiefs of Staff, the nation's military leaders, did not present the President or the Congress with sound military judgments about the war. The chiefs did not urge that clear political and military objectives be set, and acquiesced in presidential decisions they knew to be unwise militarily. They failed to persuade the President to let field commanders fight the war and silently allowed him to run the war from the White House to the extent that he personally assigned bombing targets. It would have been improper for the generals and admirals to have criticized the President in public or in the councils of government, or to have refused to carry out his orders. But they could have tried to persuade him privately and, failing that, they could have resigned.

General Weyand said later, "the major military error was a failure to communicate to the civilian decisionmakers the capabilities and limitations of American military power." Consequently, he said, the military force was "called upon to perform political, economic, and social tasks beyond its capability." At the same time, he said, the American force in Vietnam "was limited in its authority to accomplish those military tasks of which it was capable." The general went on: "Another military error was our failure to communicate to the American people the harsh realities of war. Although it might sound paradoxical to civilians, the most 'humane' way to fight a war is by the violent and overwhelming use of military force. Attempts to use force sparingly, to hold back, to gradually put pressure on the enemy, serve only to prolong the war and to ultimately increase casualties and suffering."

Beyond that, American commanders in Vietnam made several strategic mistakes. In his book, *The 25-Year War: America's Military Role in Vietnam*, General Bruce Palmer Jr. said the United States "Americanized" the war instead of training the Vietnamese to fight for their own country. American commanders put too much faith in air power, which was gradually applied to North Vietnam to make that government quit. Moreover, he said, "we were fatally handicapped by a strategy of passive defense and could not decisively erode the enemy's forces." Colonel Harry G. Summers Jr., an Army officer who has written extensively on the lessons of Vietnam, said that commanders in Vietnam mistakenly assumed they were fighting only a counterinsurgency against South and North Vietnamese guerrillas instead of both that conflict and a war of maneuver against regular units trained, led, and supplied by North Vietnam.

To raise forces to fight the war, President Johnson relied on the draft rather than call up reserves. Calling the reserves to active duty would have warned the public that the nation was becoming engaged in a full-scale war, a political development the President sought to avoid. He hoped the draft, in which individuals were conscripted from all over the nation one at a time, would cause less opposition. But the inequities of conscription, in which thousands of white, middle-class young men managed to evade service through exemptions to stay in college or through medical or other subterfuges, soured the American public. That left the burden on those who lacked the means to evade the draft, notably black Americans and the poor.

The role of the press and television in Vietnam has been long disputed. Political and military leaders of that era have asserted that public support was undermined by critical reports. Television, in particular, has been accused of bringing death into American living rooms. But analyses such as those by Lawrence W. Lichty of the University of Maryland show that less than 5 percent of the reports pictured combat or dead and wounded. Moreover, Colonel Summers has written that "the majority of on-the-scene reporting from Vietnam was factual." Much showed horror, which is the nature of war. "It was this horror, not the reporting, that so influenced the American people," he said. In sum, it was the war itself, not the press, that turned Americans against it.

Finally, the United States failed in Vietnam because the vast majority of Americans saw no good reason for their country to be engaged in a war there. They rejected the argument that the war was necessary to contain communism, that a failure to hold Vietnam would lead to the fall of other nations in Southeast Asia like a row of dominoes. They dismissed the contention that Americans would have to fight on the beaches of California if they didn't fight in the jungles of Vietnam. Richard K. Betts, a senior fellow at the Brookings Institution in Washington who has delved extensively into the causes and effects of Vietnam, has written, "The American effort in 1965-72 was not subverted by moral objections (such objections remained those of a minority even to the end), but by a gradually building public perception that all the blood and treasure was simply being *wasted* to no visible end" (italics in original).

The consequences of America's twenty-year involvement in Southeast Asia have been wrapped up in the slogan "No more Vietnams." Since 1973, when American combat forces left Vietnam, the United States has shown little stomach for military ventures. President Nixon, understanding that, sought to avoid military force in his foreign policy by pursuing détente with the Soviet Union, opening new relations with China, and formulating the Nixon Doctrine. In that doctrine, Mr. Nixon declared that America's allies must be responsible for their own first line of defense, with the United States continuing to provide the nuclear umbrella and conventional forces in a strategic reserve force. At home, Mr. Nixon ended the draft in 1973 and returned the military to the volunteer force it has been through most of the nation's history. The attention of Americans to military issues was further diluted when the nation became engrossed in the throes of Watergate, which led to the resignation of President Nixon in 1974.

President Ford was not in office long enough to change the policies of Mr. Nixon. But Mr. Ford dismayed the nation with his handling of the *Mayagüez* mission in 1975. After Cambodia had seized the American cargo ship *Mayagüez* in the Gulf of Siam, a hastily assembled and inadequately informed force of Navy, Marine, and Air Force units lost forty-one men trying to rescue the ship's crew—only to find that the Cambodians had already let them go.

In his successful election campaign in 1976, Jimmy Carter capitalized on the antimilitary sentiment of the nation, an ironic tactic for a graduate of the Naval Academy and onetime naval officer. In the White House, President Carter was indifferent to military matters until his term was nearly over. But a quick succession of events in 1979 and 1980 started a shift in mood that Mr. Carter was slow to sense and that lost him support in his bid for re-election in 1980. The Joint Chiefs of Staff, as their price for backing Mr. Carter in his effort to obtain ratification for the SALT II arms control agreement with the Soviet Union, made a public issue of military spending and forced Mr. Carter to ask for higher military budgets. The rediscovery of a Soviet brigade of troops in Cuba in the summer of 1979 caused a brief flurry. The seizure of American diplomats in Teheran in November and their year in captivity held national attention. The Soviet invasion of Afghanistan in December, the first intervention by the Soviet Union outside its post–World War II sphere of influence, stunned Mr. Carter and the nation. Shortly after, the President declared that the United States would use military force if necessary to protect American interests in the oil-producing regions around the Persian Gulf. In the spring of 1980 came the fiery end to the rescue mission in Iran. Although that risky and complicated operation was not a fair test of regular forces, it enlarged the image of American military incompetence. With all that, the antipathy toward anything military was so deep that it took Mr. Carter many months to persuade the Congress to approve the relatively innocuous matter of renewing draft registration. The proposed bill required only that young men go to the post office within a month of their eighteenth birthdays to sign a card. After heated debate, Congress voted for the plan in the summer of 1980.

In his campaign against Mr. Carter in 1980, Ronald Reagan played on fears of military impotence and won large numbers of votes with promises to renew American military strength. Once in the White

House, President Reagan showed himself to be different from his immediate predecessors and moved into the front ranks of those Presidents who, since World War II, have been willing to use military power as an instrument of national policy. Over the next five years, Mr. Reagan ordered marines and warships to Lebanon; deployed combat forces to Central America for maneuvers and shows of force; and ordered the invasion of Grenada in the Caribbean. Libya was a particular target: The President sent air forces to Egypt and naval forces to the Mediterranean several times to warn Libya against attacking Chad and the Sudan. On the violent side, he dispatched air and naval forces to the Gulf of Sidra, where they downed two Libyan fighter planes in 1981 and sank two patrol craft and hit a radar site in March 1986. Mr. Reagan ordered a stronger attack against Libyan terrorist and military bases the following month, striking harder with land-based and carrier-based bombers. Altogether, in ordering those actions, Mr. Reagan took his place alongside President Truman, who sent forces to fight in Korea; President Kennedy, who dispatched forces to Thailand when Laos was threatened in 1962; and President Johnson, who deployed forces to the Dominican Republic in 1965 and embroiled the United States in Vietnam. (In contrast, the President most reluctant to employ military power was President Eisenhower, perhaps because as a former general he knew more about the consequences of military action than any other President in the post–World War II era.)

But President Reagan did little to renew the bonds among the trinity of the people, the armed forces, and the government. The President proposed enormous military budgets to "rearm America" but, beyond trying to sell that plan, left Americans unprepared to back military ventures unless there was a distinct and overwhelming danger to the nation. By the first year of the second term, it was clear that only an immediate threat so striking that no American could avert his eyes would arouse Americans to sustained military action. As Professor Davis of the University of Kentucky observed, only then would there be "no doubt that Americans would once again rise to the call for national defense—*if* a dramatically provocative event aroused them, and *if* it allowed time for effective security responses" (italics in original).

President Reagan has been unable to build a consensus on military power because he appears to have little understanding himself of the uses and limits of that power. When he arrived at the White House, Mr. Reagan brought with him little experience in military matters and a scant record of thinking about military issues. During his eight years as Governor of California, he shunned the war in Vietnam. When he sought the Republican presidential nomination in 1976, he spoke about military issues only in passing, criticizing the détente that President Nixon had sought with the Soviet Union and the military parity that implied. Instead, Mr. Reagan suggested he would seek military superiority. During the 1980 election campaign, Mr. Reagan ran on a platform calling for "military and technological superiority over the Soviet Union" and asserted that the war in Vietnam had been "a noble cause." But he offered no cohesive, comprehensive program of military policy.

Once in office, Mr. Reagan spent the first year concentrating on domestic issues and left to Secretary of Defense Weinberger the formulation of the administration's $1.5 trillion, or $1,500 billion, plan for armaments. During that period, Mr. Reagan delivered at West Point a lackluster speech that showed no insight into military matters. The President was left uninformed for several hours, because he was asleep, when the Navy shot down two Libyan fighter planes over the Gulf of Sidra. He jarred Europeans after an interview with European journalists in which he suggested that a nuclear conflict might be confined to Europe without expanding to the United States. On television, he showed himself ignorant of his administration's $180 billion plan for MX missiles, B-1 bombers, Trident submarines, and the command and control apparatus to revitalize the nation's nuclear deterrent. The President's comments at news conferences and addresses on Central America and Libya were ambiguous and left viewers wondering what the policy of the administration really was. James Reston, the columnist for *The New York Times*, wrote in March 1986: "President Reagan is not making his purpose clear. He is pretending that if only he could get $100 million out of Congress for the opponents of the Sandinistas in Nicaragua, all would be well in Central America. And he is pretending that he has a battle fleet strolling through the Mediterranean off the coast of Libya merely to defend the right of passage through the international seas. This raises a recurring question here: Why can't we get a plain and honest answer out of this administration about what it's trying to do?"

Perhaps most illuminating, the presentation of the Strategic Defense Initiative during a televised address in March 1983 underscored the ineptitude of the administration in getting a message across to the voters and taxpayers. The speech was vague, leaving many viewers puzzled when the President said he wanted to build a shield against ballistic missiles that would make "nuclear weapons impotent and obsolete." Staff work was slighted and there was little evidence that the proposal had been carefully thought out. On the day of the speech, few people in government outside a close circle of advisers and speech-writers knew the President would make the proposal. Officers in the Pentagon who had been supervising research into technology that might lead to a defense against missiles were left in the dark. All they knew, said an official there, was that a blank space had been left in the text of the speech for a last-minute insert. No thought was given to persuading Congress and the public to support the initiative. Instead, it was sprung without briefings to members of Congress or to key scientists or to the press to enlist their help in explaining the proposal to the public.

Moreover, the President, having earlier called the Soviet Union an "evil empire," baffled many Americans by suggesting that the United States would be willing to share the new defensive technology with Moscow. Mr. Reagan's first Secretary of State, Alexander M. Haig, later blamed the President for the confusion surrounding the proposal, saying the issue was so complicated that it should have had "months of preparation" before being made public. "I thought the President's speech was ill-timed, ill-advised, and created the problems we have today," Mr. Haig said. "I wish he hadn't made it."

The President and his advisers, so eager to have their surprise, left the political field to their opponents. The administration didn't even have a name for the proposal, a void promptly filled by Senator Edward M. Kennedy, Democrat of Massachusetts, who derisively dubbed it "Star Wars" after the imaginative science fiction film. *The Boston Globe* reported that when Senator Kennedy was called for a comment on Mr. Reagan's proposal, he "criticized what he termed 'misleading Red-scare tactics and reckless Star Wars schemes.' " The name stuck, much to the chagrin of the President, who later named his program the Strategic Defense Initiative. "I wish whoever coined that expression," he said more than once, "would take it back."

Instead of displaying genuine leadership, Mr. Reagan occasionally indulged in heady rhetoric about military power. After the invasion of Grenada, the President attended a dinner in New York for 125 winners of the Medal of Honor, the nation's highest decoration for valor in battle. When a red-coated fife-and-drum corps had finished playing patriotic tunes, the President stood before a giant portrait of the pale blue ribbon and the five-pointed star of the Medal of Honor and spoke glowingly of the invasion of Grenada. "Now the world knows that when it comes to our national security," the President said, "the United States will do whatever it takes to protect the safety and freedom of the American people." He drew cheers and applause when he concluded: "Our days of weakness are over. Our military forces are back on their feet and standing tall."

But there was not much more than that. The President delivered no perceptive addresses, sent no memorable messages to Congress, made little effort in news conferences or other forums to educate the voters and taxpayers on the need for military power. He made no attempt to show where military force might be necessary to protect the national interest, especially in relatively small and messy pre-emptive actions intended to avert a bigger conflict. In his second inaugural address, Mr. Reagan sought support for the Strategic Defense Initiative but otherwise limited his remarks on military power to this paragraph: "We've made progress in restoring our defense capability. But much remains to be done. There must be no wavering by us, nor any doubts by others, that America will meet her responsibilities to remain free, secure, and at peace." A little more than a year later, Mr. Reagan's televised plea for a larger military budget was a recitation of his 1980 campaign against President Carter, a patchwork of generalities about his own military program, and little vision of the future. The administration's security program "is in jeopardy," Mr. Reagan said, "threatened by those who would quit before the job is done." He asserted that "American power is the indispensable element of a peaceful world—it is America's last best hope of negotiating real reductions in nuclear arms. Just as we are sitting down at the bargaining table with the Soviet Union, let's not throw America's trump card away." About the same time, in a message to Congress on foreign policy, the President had only a bland comment on military power: "The defense forces of the United States are crucial to maintaining the stable environment in which diplomacy can be effective, in which our friends and allies can be confident of our protection, and in which our adversaries can be deterred."

On the other hand, President Reagan's perhaps finest hour came in his brief televised address to the nation in April 1986, when he justified the attack he ordered against Libyan terrorist and military bases in retaliation for terrorist acts directed by the Libyan leader, Colonel Muammar Qaddafi. "Today we have done what we had to do," the President said. "If necessary, we shall do it again." Mr. Reagan said: "Tonight, I salute the skill and professionalism of the men and women of our armed forces who carried out this mission. It's an honor to be your Commander in Chief. We Americans are slow to anger. We always seek peaceful avenues before resorting to the use of force, and we did. We tried quiet diplomacy, public condemnation, economic sanctions, and demonstrations of military force—none succeeded. Despite our repeated warnings, Qaddafi continued his reckless policy of intimidation, his relentless pursuit of terror. He counted on America to be passive. He counted wrong. I warned that there should be no place on earth where terrorists can rest and train and practice their deadly skills. I meant it. I said that we would act with others if possible and alone if necessary to ensure that terrorists have no sanctuary anywhere. Tonight we have."

The long-term consequence of the administration's approach was that support for the President's program didn't last and the skepticism rooted in Vietnam and American history soon surfaced. A majority of Americans, and their Congressmen, initially approved the huge increases in military spending sought by the President, then became dubious, and finally turned against them. By 1985, the President had obtained from the Congress a five-year total of $1.1 trillion for the armed forces. But the scale of increases after the first two years dropped off and by fiscal year 1986 was down to zero, or no real growth. In poll after poll, moreover, Americans expressed doubts about the President's military program. Louis Harris, the pollster, reported that during the 1980 election campaign 71 percent of the public thought that military spending should be increased. After that, the polls showed a steady decline in support for large increases, except for a brief upturn in late 1983 when a Soviet fighter plane shot down Korean Air Lines flight 007 over the Sea of Japan, sending 269 people on board to a sudden death. Beyond that, antiwar, antinuclear, and antimilitary activists captured headlines—and contributions of money. Church leaders, notably the Roman Catholic bishops, published tracts condemning reliance on military power and especially the administration's plans for expanding nuclear forces.

James Schlesinger, a Republican who was Secretary of Defense from 1973 to 1975 under Presidents Nixon and Ford, pointed out the failure of the administration to cultivate a national consensus to support the armed forces. In an interview with *The Washington Times*, he said:

Government itself must be more effective in making clear what our interests are and how they are distorted by our opponents. To arouse the American public, to create a consensus with regard to our foreign policy responsibilities will require sustained and unremitting effort—not only an occasional speech by the President but an all-hands-on-board order to the entire Administration.

In the waning months of the first Reagan Administration and the early days of the second, the issue of military power as an instrument of national policy was joined in open and vigorous debate at the highest level. At first, the argument was seen as another of those policy differences that constantly reverberate through Washington. But it soon became evident that the crux of the matter was a fundamental disagreement over the very uses of military power.

The Secretary of State, George P. Shultz, a quiet, aloof man who was painfully cautious in public appearances, opened the debate in the spring of 1984 by suggesting that the United States should be more assertive. He told the Trilateral Commission of prominent Americans, Europeans, and Japanese that diplomacy not backed with military power would fail.

Power and diplomacy are not alternatives. They must go together, or we will accomplish very little in this world. . . . There will always be instances that fall short of an all-out national commitment on the scale of World War II. The need to avoid no-win situations cannot mean that we turn automatically away from hard-to-win situations that call for prudent involvement. These will always involve risks, we will not always have the luxury of being able to choose the most advantageous circumstances. And our adversaries can be expected to play rough.

Secretary of Defense Weinberger, an outgoing, engaging politician who occasionally relished public dispute, disagreed but waited until after the presidential election to "sound a note of caution." Mr. Weinberger, an Army captain during World War II, told the National Press Club in late November that "employing our forces almost indiscriminately and as a regular and customary part of our diplomatic effort would surely plunge us headlong into the sort of domestic turmoil we experienced during the Vietnam war." In his most thoughtful speech since taking office in 1981, Mr. Weinberger said he had six major tests when considering the dispatch of American forces: (1) The United States should commit forces only to defend a vital national interest. (2) That commitment should be made only with the intention of winning. (3) "We should have clearly defined political and military objectives," he said. (4) The relationship between the objectives and the composition of the forces must be continually assessed and adjusted. (5) "There must be some reasonable assurance we will have the support of the American people," Mr. Weinberger said, without defining "reasonable." (6) "The commitment of U.S. forces to combat should be a last resort."

Mr. Shultz came back several weeks later with a rebuttal that focused on terrorism.

The public must understand *before the fact* that there is potential for loss of life of some of our fighting men and the loss of life of some innocent people.

The public must understand *before the fact* that some will seek to cast any pre-emptive or retaliatory action by us in the worst light and will attempt to make our military and our policy makers—rather than the terrorists—appear to be the culprits. The public must understand *before the fact* that occasions will come when their government must act before each and every fact is known—and the decisions cannot be tied to the opinion polls.   [Italics in original.]

A leading Democrat weighed in. Representative Les Aspin, then the newly elected Chairman of the Armed Services Committee, spoke about the policy toward arms negotiations with the Soviet Union. "We do not have a consensus in the country as to what constitutes a good agreement, about what we are trying to achieve, or how to get there," said Mr. Aspin, an affable man from Wisconsin. "Consensus does not mean taking the middle ground on every issue. It means a package that makes sense to the common sense middle."

Next the new chairman of the Senate Foreign Relations Committee, Richard G. Lugar, Republican of Indiana, said the United States was uncertain about the use of force in national security. "It does seem to me that the United States has not yet fully recovered from the Vietnam War," he said. "Nor has the United States fully adjusted to the role which its values, its economic strength, its geography, and its interests define for it in the world today."

When Senator Lugar opened hearings, Secretary Shultz and Secretary Weinberger refined but did not appreciably narrow their differences. It was left to another witness, James Schlesinger, to put the debate into perspective. Since Vietnam, the professorial, pipe-smoking Mr. Schlesinger said, it had become difficult to foster a consensus to support American troops engaged abroad. Having done more strategic thinking than most Defense Secretaries, he leaned toward Mr. Shultz's view. "I cannot concur with the emerging belief that the United States must only fight popular, winnable wars," he said. "The role of the United States in the world is such that it must be prepared for, be prepared to threaten, and even be prepared to fight those intermediate conflicts that are likely to fare poorly on television." He pointed out the essential failing of both Mr. Shultz and Mr. Weinberger. "A national consensus cannot simply be wished into being," he said. "It can be restored only gradually over time, if at all. It will come about only through the development of mutual trust, reasonable success, and the sustained credibility of the executive branch."

Behind the scenes, President Reagan's national security adviser at the time, Robert C. McFarlane, tended to agree with Mr. Shultz. But he believed the American people would not support a long war. "Five years is simply incompatible with American values and the American attention span," he told an interviewer from *The Wall Street Journal*. "The most relevant lesson I learned is what is and what isn't sustainable by the American people."

The absence of an agreed national strategy underlay much of the annual dispute between Secretary Weinberger and the Director of the Office of Management and Budget, David A. Stockman, during the administration's first term. Because the President had not propounded a rationale for military power, Mr. Stockman and Mr. Weinberger could not agree on military spending. Mr. Stockman was charged with preparing the administration's budget and, in accord with the President's wishes, with paring spending to reduce the federal deficit. Mr. Weinberger was to provide for the common defense and, equally in accord with the President's wishes, sought funds to do so. But they shared no common ground and fought each other every year until the President decided.

The disparity between the administration and the Congress over military spending has been even greater. By 1985, those differences had degenerated into a name-calling contest. The majority leader of the Senate, Robert Dole, Republican of Kansas, suggested that Mr. Weinberger had used deceptive estimates of the inflation rate in his proposed budget. Senator Mark O. Hatfield, Republican of Oregon and Chairman of the Appropriations Committee, asserted that the military budget must be cut to help reduce the federal deficit, and declared that Mr. Weinberger could not be "a draft dodger" on the issue. Mr. Weinberger, apparently exasperated, suggested through a spokesman that those seeking to cut the defense budget were guilty of "weakening the security of the country." Senator John Glenn, Democrat of Ohio, the former marine and famed astronaut, declared that statement "offensive, ill-considered, and totally unacceptable." He told Mr. Weinberger to his face, "There is such a thing as a loyal opposition in this country." Mr. Weinberger did not apologize.

Editorial writers and columnists chimed in. Some applauded Mr. Shultz, others Mr. Weinberger; a minority criticized both, and blamed Mr. Reagan for not resolving the issue. William Safire of *The New York Times*, a conservative, backed Mr. Shultz, saying that "power and diplomacy must be used in tandem." On the other side of the political spectrum, Tom Wicker, also in *The New York Times*, said Mr. Weinberger's view was "highly useful." Joseph Kraft asserted in *The Washington Post* that "the use of force is not a fit subject for public debate by senior officials." *The Miami Herald* liked Mr. Weinberger's thinking but wondered what would constitute "victory." The Louisville *Courier-Journal* said Mr. Shultz "is surely correct."

Another, more subtle disagreement over military power took place out of public view between senior civilian officials of the Reagan Administration and top military leaders. In almost every instance in which the President and his advisers wanted to exert military force, the military officers advised against it or, at least, urged extreme caution. The officers were motivated by two factors. One was their innate caution. Contrary to popular myth, the vast majority of American military officers are not warmongers. Quite the opposite—experience on the battlefield and knowledge of the lethality of modern weapons, conventional and nuclear alike, has made them cautious about applying force. The other factor was the legacy of Vietnam. Most officers sense that the American people will not support a military venture except under extreme duress. Those who served in Vietnam don't want to be hung out again to twist alone in the wind.

Eliot A. Cohen, a political scientist at Harvard, has written that military officers who served in Vietnam "were seared by the experience of public repudiation by large segments of society, including the intellectual elite." Professional officers were not only angered by what they felt was a lack of appreciation for their heroism but found themselves pilloried as murderers or incompetents or both. "In reaction to this brutally unfair treatment," Mr. Cohen said, "the military leadership has determined never again to fight a war without public backing of the fullest kind."

Even more serious has been the lack of trust of civilian officials by military officers. Mr. Cohen has asserted that "American civil-military relations are in a state of profound but hidden crisis." In his view, "the military has developed an acute mistrust of its civilian masters." William J. Taylor, of Georgetown University's Center for Strategic and International Studies, and Major David H. Petraeus, an instructor in political science at West Point, came to the same conclusion:

The military has traditionally regarded their politicians and political appointees with some apprehension. Vietnam heightened this feeling, leaving America's senior military leaders with a more deep-seated suspicion of their civilian leaders. . . . While the military still emphatically accept the constitutional provision for civilian control of the armed forces, there remains from Vietnam a certain doubt about the abilities and motivations of politicians.

Mr. Taylor and Major Petraeus also said, "Vietnam was a painful reminder for the military that they, not the transient occupants of high office, generally bear the heaviest burden of military conflict," and they quoted a retired general, William A. Knowlton: "Remember one lesson from the Vietnam era; those who ordered the meal were not there when the waiter brought the check."

Against that backdrop, senior military officers in recent years have frequently resisted the administration's plans to dispatch troops to troubled areas overseas. Military officers have repeatedly advised the President against sending American combat forces to Central America, except on maneuvers. General Meyer expressed the private view of many officers when he told reporters in 1983 it would be wrong to deploy "soldiers at the end of the string without having the support of the American people." He repeatedly came back to this point: "You can't send soldiers off to war without the support of the American people."

Similarly, the Joint Chiefs of Staff were reluctant to execute the President's plan to invade Grenada. Said an administration official, "Jack Vessey was the last one to jump aboard on Grenada," referring to General John W. Vessey Jr., then Chairman of the Joint Chiefs of Staff. With their advice overridden by the President, the chiefs insisted that overwhelming American force be employed to ensure success quickly, before the American public could question the operation. Fear that the public would not support the invasion was among the reasons the administration and the military chiefs agreed to exclude press and television coverage.

The deployment of marines and a naval task force to Lebanon made the issue more intense. The Joint Chiefs of Staff vigorously opposed that deployment, asserting that the issues were political, not military. They contended that American troops might be forced to fire on Arabs, which would harm the standing of the United States in the Middle East. Most important, as one officer put it, "Let's not get involved in something without public support." At that time, General Vessey, ever cautious when speaking in public, expressed the feeling of the Joint Chiefs: "I think one has to think through very carefully putting American troops in any kind of operation where we're using them as a political lever." He went on to tell an interviewer: "I think it's fair to say that everyone in the military, and the Secretary of Defense, and everyone in the government urged caution and was concerned about what we're doing in Lebanon." Later, as he prepared to retire in 1985 after forty-six years of service, the general was asked again about deploying the marines to Lebanon. His reply: "I wish we hadn't."

The general appeared to have in mind the terrorist truck bomb at the Beirut airport that left 241 marines, sailors, and soldiers dead in October 1983 and confirmed the fears of senior officers. Along with air losses in a raid on Syrian missile batteries and ineffective naval gunfire from the battleship *New Jersey*, that attack led to an ignominious withdrawal in early 1984. An unidentified administration official told Michael Getler of *The Washington Post*: "The implications of what has happened in Lebanon are very, very profoundly felt and they will surely condition the way we tackle other problems. We've had a clear setback there . . . a terrible loss."

In sum, after five years of the Reagan Administration, there was no agreement within the administration, or between the administration and Congress, or among political leaders and senior military officers on basic principles governing the use of military force. There was, therefore, no agreement on national strategy to defend the fundamental interests of the United States, and no agreement, beyond a vague fear of the Soviet Union, on the threat to the United States. There was little consensus on the proper size of the armed forces, on the contingencies for which they must be prepared, or on the priorities with which those forces were to be acquired, trained, and deployed. While the debate between Mr. Shultz and Mr. Weinberger and everyone else was good in a robust democracy, it never led to a resolute conclusion. Rather than defining national interests and determining a political, economic, and military strategy to defend them, almost everyone involved argued solely about how much money to spend. That argument concerned only trees and ignored the forest. As Senator Lowell Weicker Jr., Republican of Connecticut, said, "The national security debate has become more of a matter of defending budget levels than defending the nation."

Secretary of Defense Weinberger could have been the point man in building a new consensus behind the armed forces, but was not. Mr. Weinberger, an energetic man with a quick wit and a self-deprecating sense of humor, showed more interest in the troops than many of his predecessors had and often arranged his travel so that he could drop in on them. Moreover, he was seemingly tireless in going around the country trying to rally support for the President's program to rearm America. But the Secretary displayed little vision in his testimony before Congress, in speeches, news conferences, televised interviews, or other presentations in public. His demeanor was uninspiring as he recited memorized statements on whatever issue was at hand. While persistently advocating ever-higher military spending, Mr. Weinberger rarely presented a persuasive analysis of what it was for, save that the United States had to match the Russians whom he saw coming over every hill. As the second term opened, Representative Aspin, Chairman of the House Armed Services Committee, suggested that the administration lacked a coherent strategy to justify its large military budgets. "We've spent a trillion dollars," Mr. Aspin told Mr. Weinberger. "Before we give you a few hundred billion more, tell us what you did with the trillion."

Not until his speech before the National Press Club in late November 1984, after nearly four years in office, did Mr. Weinberger speak of the need for consensus. "The single most critical element of a successful democracy is a strong consensus of support and agreement for our basic purposes," he said. "Policies formed without a clear understanding of what we hope to achieve will never work."

But many of Mr. Weinberger's actions during the first term contradicted his words. Secrecy, not communication, became paramount as Mr. Weinberger ordered a reduction in the flow of information to the public, whether it had to do with routine operations, the threat from the Soviet Union, proposals for the military budget, or technical matters. The clampdown was so indiscriminate that the following paragraph, taken from a Navy document in its entirety, was classified "secret," meaning that its release could cause "serious damage" to national security:

The Navy must continue to attract and retain sufficient numbers of high-quality, skilled and motivated people. Compensation and quality of life improvements must be competitive in the job market. Ways must be found to reduce requirements for administrative functions, reduce personnel turbulence and permanent change of station moves.

The tightening of the noose around the flow of information began with a small item: Pentagon press officers were instructed to withhold information that had been previously available on the routine deployment of warships. Information on military exercises, formerly announced as a matter of course, was withheld. Pentagon press officers were cut off from the daily flow of information on operations around the world and were thus unable to explain them to the press or public. More serious, in an unsuccessful attempt to find a news leak, the Pentagon resorted to lie detector tests on senior military officers who had served honorably for more than thirty years. In an earlier day, officers whose word was doubted would have resigned on the spot.

The lie detector tests failed to find the leak but put enough fear into military officers that they became more reticent than ever.

Mr. Weinberger's annual report to Congress, which previously had been a useful reference on the posture of the military services, contained less and less factual information. The same was true of other publications, including one entitled *Soviet Military Power*. A greater number of weapons and technical programs were carried in the "black budget," meaning they had been made secret so that budget information that had once been in the public domain could be withheld.

The policy regulating the release of information was inconsistent and more influenced by politics in America than by the security of the forces. In Lebanon, for instance, an assessment of damage caused by American Navy bombers was almost immediately available after they struck targets behind Beirut. But similar reports on naval gunfire were withheld several days later because the sixteen-inch guns of the battleship *New Jersey* had done little more than break windows and kill sheep. Everyone in Lebanon knew that, but the administration didn't want the American people to know. Assessments on lessons learned by American forces in Lebanon were not available after they had been withdrawn because, according to officers in the Pentagon, the administration wanted to avoid drawing more public attention to the disaster there.

The press and television were excluded from the invasion of Grenada until most of the operation was over. In addition, neither the administration nor the Joint Chiefs of Staff made provision for military press officers to accompany the forces to send information back home. Further, a final assessment of the Grenada operation done by the Atlantic Command in Norfolk was heavily censored, evidently to cover up mistakes.

The Air Force clamped new and stricter controls on information about the space shuttle when it carried military cargo, reversing a long-standing policy of the National Aeronautics and Space Administration that had built strong support for the space program. Over the years, NASA had built a wide following among the public and the Congress by publicizing most of its activities. Only the details of military cargoes had been kept secret. In 1985, however, details of when the shuttle would lift off, when it would return, and other operational details were withheld until the last minute. Broadcasts from space were precluded. The press, notably *The Washington Post*, was criticized for publishing details of the mission even though most came from public sources.

While complaints from the press over restrictions on information were to be expected, strong criticism came from vigorous supporters of the administration. The Heritage Foundation, a conservative research organization in Washington, pointed with dismay in 1983 to declining public support for military spending. Polls showed, the foundation said, that "respondents fail to indicate they perceive any substantive correlation between the size of the defense budget and the corresponding strength and capability of the U.S. military." The foundation asserted:

Nearly everyone dealing with defense problems must share the blame for this increasingly perplexing defense–public relations conundrum. The Defense Department, the White House, members of Congress and their staffs, the news media, and traditional supporters of defense in the private sector are all responsible in varying degrees for the flood of misinformation and distortion that has resulted in a confused and ill-informed public.

About the same time, the *Armed Forces Journal International*, a monthly magazine that advocates strong military forces, published a detailed analysis of what it called "the failure to defend defense." Citing reductions in useful information from the Pentagon about the military balance between the United States and the Soviet Union, the *Journal* said: "With almost Orwellian timing, the Secretary of Defense has made '1984' the year in which the truth about the balance is missing from his defense of the nation's defense budget." The same was true, the *Journal* contended, of annual reports submitted by the Army, Navy, and Air Force.

The service budget statements this year fail to give the taxpayer any feel for how much of a gap in equipment or forces their record budget requests are designed to bridge, or of how much better America might stand against its principal adversary even if Congress were to approve those budgets in full.

William V. Kennedy, a perceptive commentator on military matters, applauded Mr. Weinberger's speech about restraints that should be applied to the use of military force but faulted him for not defining America's vital interests.

They have never been spelled out to the people whose sons and daughters must do the fighting and dying, because of the military penchant for locking up everything it writes and its dread of open discussion and debate. The public that pays the bill and that must ultimately pay the price in lives for the calculations or miscalculations of government has a right to know just what Weinberger is talking about when he uses the term "vital interests," and it has a right to know just where in the catalog of U.S. interests from "vital" to "minor" any particular foreign involvement stands.

Beyond the political arena, many senior military officers say they see the need for a national consensus behind the armed forces and for a public understanding of their duties. Many feel personally misunderstood and unappreciated, resenting what they see as ingratitude for the sacrifices they make and the liabilities they accept. But many senior officers in Washington flounder when it comes to articulating what it is they do, and how, and why the armed forces should be backed by the American people. Those officers, with a few exceptions, rarely appear in public beyond testifying before congressional committees or making speeches before the converted in friendly audiences of reserve associations or defense contractors.

While those officers yearn for the support of the people they have sworn to defend, many believe they are not accountable to the voters and taxpayers. It is the job of the nation's political leaders, the officers say, to foster a national consensus on military power. Still other officers believe that public support is their due, and that they need not cultivate it. Admiral James D. Watkins, the Chief of Naval Operations, delivered a reflective graduation address at a civilian college on the theme "I am a moral man." It was well received, and the admiral followed it with other addresses and articles in which he developed the thesis. But another admiral said privately he was "disappointed" that Admiral Watkins felt it necessary to assure American citizens that military officers are moral men. "Everyone should have understood that," the other admiral said. That admiral, who had served with distinction, did not realize that most Americans do not understand and that Admiral Watkins was right in making an effort to explain himself.

In contrast to the military penchant for secrecy, some officers have urged that more information, especially on what they see as the threat from the Soviet Union, be made available in an effort to win public backing. General Bernard W. Rogers was outspoken on that issue as the commander of all American and allied forces in Europe, wanting to release satellite and other photographs of Soviet military forces aimed at Europe. But the intelligence agencies refused, citing potential compromise to their sources and methods. A retired Army major general, Henry Mohr, who writes a column for the *St. Louis Globe-Democrat*, criticized the Defense Department for withholding that information.

An informed public will reach the right decisions. One of the best ways to secure public support of the national security budget is to make sure Americans are given credible information as to why the money is needed. When the security of the United States is threatened by a foreign power, keeping information secret never has succeeded in generating public support.

Perhaps a real test of the willingness of Americans to have their government exert military power as an instrument of national policy will come in Central America. The Reagan Administration has contended that a long-range threat to the United States has been mounted by the leftist Sandinista government in Nicaragua, which the administration has portrayed as an ally of the Cubans and the Russians. In that view, the communists, once having consolidated their foothold on the American mainland, will make it only a matter of time before they push south toward the Panama Canal and north to Mexico and the border of the United States. Then, administration officials suggest, for the first time since the War of 1812, the United States may be threatened with a foreign invasion or at least a flood of Central American refugees.

During President Reagan's first term, however, that prospect had little credibility among the majority of Americans. The absence of public support for direct American military action was notable. News about any ripple in developments either in Washington or in Central America often produced trumpeting headlines or television reports, both of which reflected public nervousness. Indirect support for opponents of the Sandinista government was bitterly disputed in the Congress. Privately, middle-ranking military officers expressed the belief that the problems in Central America were basically political and economic and that therefore the United States should search for political and economic, not military, solutions. Government reports about growing support from Nicaragua and Cuba for leftist guerrillas in El Salvador were passed off as the same sort of propaganda produced by the United States government during Vietnam. In particular, President Reagan, like President Johnson before him, seemed to lack a well-defined objective. Mr. Reagan addressed the nation on television in March 1986 in an effort to persuade Congress to approve $100 million in economic and military aid for the "contras" fighting the leftist Sandinista government in Nicaragua. But the President had no word about his basic goal, saying only that the insurgents sought "to recapture their betrayed revolution" and that he wanted "a negotiated peace and a democratic future in Nicaragua." In sum, the Central American issue in the United States began to seem more and more like the issue of Vietnam twenty years ago even though the geographic, political, economic, and military realities of Central America were utterly different.

When Lawrence S. Eagleburger, the Under Secretary of State for Political Affairs, prepared to retire from the Foreign Service in 1984, he was asked why the American public was so worried about the possibility of military action against Nicaragua. The reply from the respected diplomat and veteran of crises for three decades appears to have stood the test of time: "There is a real national interest in terms of what the United States might have to face, should people like the Sandinistas succeed. We have to talk more about what we may be called upon to do if we fail to achieve our objectives now through a limited involvement."

But he asserted that the main difficulty in making American policy was the legacy of Vietnam. "There is a lot left of the Vietnam syndrome," he said, "the concern that we will become directly involved militarily, and that it's a bottomless pit."

CHAPTER 2

~~~~~~~~~~~~~~~~~~~~~~~~~~

COMBATANT COMMANDERS

I N A CONVERSATION about the possibility of using American military forces in Central America, the Army colonel shook his head. No, he said, all the generals or admirals he'd heard talk about it in Washington for the last six months, plus middle-ranking officers like himself, were dead set against it. Why? "You have to understand the thinking of those of us who were in Vietnam," he said. The colonel, who was in a position in which he might be called upon to give briefings in the White House, spoke as if he were addressing the President. In a deferential but firm tone, he said:

"Mr. President, don't send us to war again unless you have clear-cut political goals and attainable military objectives.

"Sir, don't send us unless you give us sufficient forces and the freedom of action to use them according to the principles of war.

"And, Mr. President, you'd better have a helluva lot of public support."

The armed forces are commanded today by a generation of officers tempered in the fires of Vietnam. The legacy of Vietnam has profoundly etched the minds of those officers and has laden them with emotional baggage that shapes their judgments on military power and operations. Many of those officers believe the elected leaders of the United States during the Vietnam era failed to define the nation's political objectives and therefore gave commanders in the field a constantly shifting set of military objectives. Many think they had sufficient forces to win but were restricted by extensive and intricate rules under which they engaged the enemy. They are vehement in charging that they were abandoned to twist alone in the wind without the support of the American people, and they blame this predicament on the press and television. They are determined not to go through that again.

It is this generation of officers who will lead the armed forces for the next decade, influencing military policy with attitudes formed not only on the battlefields of Southeast Asia but by perceptions of political leadership and public support at home. At the top are the generals and admirals who are among the makers of national military policy. In Vietnam from 1965 to 1972, most of these officers were the battalion commanders, squadron leaders, and ship captains in the thick of the war. Today, they are the chiefs of staff of the four services, the commanders of the combatant commands in the United States, the Atlantic and Europe, the Pacific and Asia, the Caribbean and Latin America. Below them are the younger brigadier generals and Navy rear admirals who will move into the leadership of the military establishment within the next ten years. They served as military advisers and company commanders, fighter flight leaders, and ship's officers during the Vietnam conflict.

Among the middle-ranking officers of today are the colonels and Navy captains, the lieutenant colonels and Navy commanders who were young officers leading platoons, flying fighter planes, and serving as junior leaders in the "brown water Navy" in Vietnam. Some are mid-level combatant commanders now. Others are key staff officers, the "worker bees" or "iron majors" or "action officers" serving the Joint Chiefs of Staff, the chiefs of the four services, and the commanders of the large combatant commands. After the next ten years, some will rise to the top to continue the Vietnam generation's leadership of the armed forces.

The officers of the Vietnam generation constitute, by and large, an admirable corps of professional, competent, dedicated men and women. Especially impressive are the commanders of the Army brigades and battalions, Marine regiments and battalions, Navy ship squadrons and ships, Air Force wings and squadrons—the tactical leaders who would bear the brunt of any extensive military operation. They have assumed enormous military, human, and moral responsibilities and carry them well. Overall, the officer corps is loyal to the nation and to the American tradition of civilian control of military forces. The officers are well educated and well trained, and they subscribe to the ethics of the military brotherhood. Contrary to a widely held myth, they are, for the most part, believers in deterrence, not in warmongering. Indeed, today's officers are perhaps the most cautious of all Americans when it comes to exerting military force to resolve an international dispute. They understand better than most politicians and people the lethality of the modern battlefield, the ultimate danger of escalation to human survival, and the limits of military power.

Moreover, contrary to another myth, there is no "military mind." The officer corps comprises as vast a diversity of personalities, talents, ambitions, and styles of leadership as there is in America. Some officers are given to daring and bold ventures, others to tried and true methods by the book. The military profession has fostered styles that have ranged across the ego of Douglas MacArthur, the bombast of Curtis LeMay, the imagination of Elmo Zumwalt, and the "effective anonymity" sought by Jack Vessey. The demeanor of officers has run from the steely calm of a George Marshall to the open good humor of a Jim Watkins to the soft-spoken reserve of a Charles Gabriel.

Altogether, the Vietnam generation appears to have come a long way from the time when the ethics of military officers were in question because of atrocities in Vietnam, rigged reports on accomplishments, promotions put ahead of duty, and financial scandals. That is particularly true for the Army, which bore the burden of much of the fighting in Vietnam and lost the most in self-esteem and public respect. The Army and the other services have purged most of the unprofessional and the incompetent in the tough competition for promotion. A new sense of pride has sprouted. "We've stopped apologizing to ourselves for Vietnam," said Lieutenant Colonel Richard P. Dacey, an Army battalion commander at Fort Hood in Texas, "It's more of an Army looking to the future than to the past."

To help new generals sharpen their skills for command, the Army has employed the Center for Creative Leadership in Greensboro, North Carolina, to assess those officers much the way they develop business executives. A psychologist at the center, David P. Campbell, subjected a group of new brigadier generals to a battery of tests to compare them with their peers among corporate executives. Mr. Campbell said he found the generals to be better educated, brighter, more self-confident, more competitive, and more forceful than businessmen, but less cooperative and harmonious. Presumably, much the same would have been said about Navy, Marine, and Air Force officers.

"I doubt that any major military power in history has had such a well-selected, well-educated, effective, experienced, honest, loyal group of career general officers, hundreds deep, as the U.S. Army does now," Mr. Campbell said in a report.

The fact that they do not quite fit my definition of perfection should not blind us to the fact that these people are not only maintaining a world-class defense organization, they are also running a remarkably effective social institution, one that is handling racial relations better than most of the rest of society, an institution that is grappling more with the new role of women than are most civilian institutions, an organization that appears to be making the volunteer army work, and a military organization that has never strayed from proper civilian control, even when it felt it was being irrationally restrained.

The officer corps, however, is not without fault, Mr. Campbell continued.

I do have some concerns. While this pattern of personal characteristics seems excellent for the officer corps of a combat oriented army, I am less sanguine about the prospects of such individuals understanding the concept of achieving world peace without bloodshed. I wish I saw more evidence here of leaders who understand the broad scope of history, who value the world of ideas, who respect the value of unproductive beauty, and who have some sense of the interlocking nature of human aspirations. I wish I felt that softness and gentleness were occasionally valued by these military executives.

While the officer corps today is generally first class, it most assuredly has its share of deadwood, as does any large organization or bureaucracy. There are incompetent officers who have managed to survive the selection process. Others are, as the saying goes, "retired on active duty," waiting out their twenty years so they can retire on half of base pay for the rest of their lives. The military services have self-servers who would be a match for the best in corporate life. Yes-men, apple polishers, and bootlickers can be found fawning on many staffs. There are officers whose sole purpose is to look good on annual reports, inspections, and other statistical measures of military prowess that may or may not have anything to do with reality, all with the aim of getting promoted. Such officers care hardly a whit for their subordinates, their troops, or the training of their units, but use anyone and everyone to get ahead. Martinets, although rare, still exist. For some officers, the military is not a calling but a nine-to-five job like any other. Still others are lazy and spend more effort getting out of work than it would take to do it. Buck-passing for some has been refined to a high art. Some are haughty, others arrogant, and a few still act like tin gods.

The Army, in a remarkably candid self-evaluation in 1985, found that half the officers surveyed thought "the bold, original, creative officer cannot survive in today's Army." Some 68 percent said "the officer corps is focused on personal gain rather than selflessness," with the selfish officer considered unlikely to make a good military leader. One-third of the officers thought "most officers are promoted before becoming competent at their existing grade levels." Finally, nearly half the generals queried in a separate questionnaire concluded that "senior Army leaders behave too much like corporate executives and not enough like warriors." In sum, the findings suggested the Army officer corps had not entirely recovered from the dark days of Vietnam.

Several other issues trouble the officer corps. Between the Vietnam and the post-Vietnam generations are differences in attitude arising from the younger generation's roots in the dissent of the 1960s. After that is coming another generation of officers, now in the military academies and the Reserve Officer Training Corps in civilian universities, for whom Vietnam is only an era in a history book.

The military services, seeking to be representative of the people they defend, have been more successful than most institutions in assimilating black Americans. For black Americans, like the Irish and other minorities before them, military service has been a road out of the ghetto and into full-fledged citizenship. But there is still far to go. Overt discrimination has been abolished, but black officers contend that they have experienced a subtle discrimination by getting less desirable assignments or not being selected for key military schools, thus having less chance than their white peers for promotion. In addition, the services have not been able to attract large numbers of black Americans as officers. The relatively small number of black college graduates and the competition from industry, civil government, and the professions make it difficult for the services to recruit.

Even more of an issue is the increasing presence of women in what has been the world's most masculine preserve. When General Vessey was Chairman of the Joint Chiefs of Staff, he told the House Armed Services Committee:

The greatest change that has come about in the time I've been in the military service has been the extensive use of women. That's even greater than nuclear weapons, I feel, as far as our own forces are concerned. . . . I want you to know I'm not against it. We've got some absolutely wonderful servicewomen doing some extraordinary things and doing them very, very well. But we've taken a male institution in a very short period of time and turned it into a coed institution, and it has been a traumatic exercise for us.

Lastly, military officers in recent years have been criticized for separating themselves from the rest of American society. They have also been accused of embracing the values of business managers rather than retaining those of warriors. The officer corps is said to have failed to produce strategists able to render sound military advice to the nation's political leaders.

Vietnam is ever in the background of the public utterances and private conversations of most officers who served in that era. General Vessey, who fibbed about his age to enlist in the Minnesota National Guard in 1939, spanned the era from World War II until the post-Vietnam period. The general—who won a battlefield commission in World War II and the Distinguished Service Cross, the Army's second-highest combat decoration, in Vietnam—was asked by young visitors what he had learned from his years in service. A straightforward man given to spare, declarative sentences, General Vessey said: "Don't send military forces off to do anything unless you know what it is clearly that you want done. Like you, I am absolutely, unalterably opposed to risking American lives for some phoney sort of military and political objectives that we don't understand." Later, just before he retired, the general reflected over breakfast one morning about the uses of military force: "Don't go if you don't have to; that's a cinch. But if you have to go, go in the fashion that's going to get public support for what you're going to do. Do it quickly." He added: "Americans are not patient with long, drawn-out, protracted wars, wars that dribble away our public support and strength."

Admiral James D. Watkins, the Chief of Naval Operations until mid-1986, served as executive officer, or number two in command, of the cruiser *Long Beach* off the coast of Vietnam. He remembered the time "we had to self-destruct one of our missiles aimed and fired at a North Vietnamese MiG aircraft, retiring back to Hanoi after raiding our forces in the south, because predicted missile intercept was slightly north of a certain Vietnamese parallel—an arbitrary political restriction." The admiral lamented: "For us in the military, Vietnam was a confusing and ever changing maze of rules of engagement and policy. . . . Political considerations here at home often dictated military operations to a debilitating extent."

In a private conversation, an Army lieutenant colonel who fought in Vietnam alluded to the lack of well-defined objectives. "If I have to go again," he said succinctly, "I want an ironclad understanding of what it is you want me to do." A Navy commander said that military professionals should be given guidelines by political leaders, then allowed to do their jobs. "I hope the people who are responsible for the care and feeding of the country," he said, "don't again commit young men to a cause that they proscribe us from winning."

Middle-ranking officers contended that four-star generals and admirals have a responsibility to protest when political leaders ignore sound military advice. An Army lieutenant colonel said generals and admirals should be candid in their reports and advice to the President and the Secretary of Defense. "Those guys sit on the board of directors," he said, "and they should speak up." A Navy commander agreed: "I hope the next time, the four-star generals and admirals find some way to register a protest if they see the political leaders doing something militarily unsound. The guys who wear four stars have a commitment to the nation itself, not just to the President." Another lieutenant colonel in the Army said that, because of Vietnam, "I lost a lot of faith in general officers." He was critical because no general resigned to protest the way the war was being fought. "God," he said, "we wasted so much over there in the way of human life."

Many middle-ranking officers bear the scars caused by the split between the armed forces and the American public over Vietnam. A lieutenant colonel in the Marine Corps, having done a study of public opinion in World War II, the Korean War, and Vietnam, warned against sliding into a conflict. "Don't get into a war incrementally," he urged, "and don't try to have guns and butter at the same time." Other officers expressed frustration over the distance between the armed forces and the rest of the nation. "If you didn't get drafted," said an Army officer, "Vietnam didn't exist." After returning to the United States in 1968, he felt so out of place that he ended a leave sooner than necessary to report to his new duty station. "I was escaping back into an environment where I understood people, and where I could communicate and where I could feel part of a group," he said. "There was nothing left in civilian life with which I could identify." Many officers lamented the absence of a tie between the armed forces and the middle class because smaller numbers from middle America have served in the military over the last twenty years. They worried because few elected officials, educators, and journalists under forty years of age have served in the armed forces. "Those three elements," said an Army officer, "are made up of people whose experience with the military is a flat zero."

The experience of Vietnam has reinforced the natural caution of military officers. The officers are wary about applying military force for a simple reason—they would be the first to go, to bleed, and to die. General Vessey once said: "If we think that military power is the supreme power, we are kidding ourselves. We see every day the limits of military power in solving the problems of the world." Admiral

Watkins told the Baltimore Council on Foreign Relations: "Military options are no panacea, and should never substitute for aggressive diplomatic or other measures to implement a strategy."

Nuclear weapons in particular give officers pause. Today's senior leaders were young men during the Korean War and matured as officers in an era in which the United States had a nuclear monopoly, then lost that superiority, and finally accepted a rough nuclear parity with the Soviet Union. They have lived through a time when Britain, France, and China have produced nuclear weapons, when India has demonstrated a capability to do so, and when other nations such as Israel and South Africa may have done so secretly.

The senior officers, with access to secret technical studies, nuclear war games, and nuclear war-fighting plans, are aware of the devastation that nuclear weapons could cause. General Charles A. Gabriel, until mid-1986 the Chief of Staff of the Air Force whose bombers sit on runways armed with nuclear bombs and whose missiles tipped with nuclear warheads are always on alert, dealt with nuclear issues in advising the Secretary of Defense and the President. "You have to be very careful," he said, "that whatever it is you're recommending doesn't right away risk a sudden escalation."

General Gabriel said he had been struck by the differences in attitude toward the use of military force between political officials and military officers. In war games, civilian political appointees simulate the President, the Secretary of Defense, and other top officials; military officers play themselves. As the group is confronted with a crisis, the political leaders, with advice from the military officers, decide a course of action; computers and war-game specialists calculate the consequences and present new situations for decision. "I think you'd find in all the war games we run that the military are by far the most cautious of any of the players," General Gabriel said. "The civilians are more aggressive than the military when it comes to playing a scenario involving escalation."

On the conventional level, most officers are wary of military intervention intended to resolve political and economic issues. Among middle-ranking officers, a Navy captain said, "there's a real appreciation that you can't solve every international problem by throwing military force into it." A colonel on the Army staff said his associates would be reluctant to have American forces deployed to Central America. "The problems down there are not military, they're political and economic. You shouldn't send soldiers to solve political and economic problems. That's not what I signed up for."

While Americans have been concerned with the issue of civilian control of the military since the earliest days of the Republic, rarely have there been military challenges to political leaders. Civilians have retained a firm hand not only by law and tradition but by holding and allocating the financial resources of the armed forces. There is little danger, over a long run, that American soldiers could capture the government unless civilian leaders fall sound asleep at their duties. That a group of military officers could attempt a coup is always a remote possibility, but it would be an aberration so unpopular and out of American tradition that the vast majority of officers and troops would oppose it vigorously, and perhaps violently.

The only real challenge to civilian control in modern times erupted when General MacArthur disagreed with President Truman over the conduct of the Korean War. The President was determined to limit the war to Korea and to prevent it from spreading to China, which had troops fighting alongside the North Koreans and Russia, which was arming and supplying the North Koreans. General MacArthur wanted to bomb a Chinese sanctuary in Manchuria and to open a second front against China by having Chinese Nationalist troops invade the mainland from the island of Taiwan. The differences between the President and the general became public and, in Mr. Truman's eyes, were intolerable. In April 1951, President Truman abruptly removed General Mac-Arthur. General Matthew B. Ridgway, who succeeded General Mac-Arthur, approved of the President's decision. "No man in uniform, be he private or five-star general, may decide for himself whether an order is consonant with his personal views," he wrote. "While the loyalty he owes his superiors is reciprocated with equal force in the loyalty owed him from above, the authority of his superiors is not open to question."

General Weyand, the former Chief of Staff of the Army, wrote that the loyalty of the military to properly constituted civilian authority cuts many ways and that the American soldier cannot take things into his own hands. Officers should refrain from politics and obey legitimate orders, even when they disagree.

During the Vietnam War, there were those—many with the best of intentions—who argued that the Army should not obey its orders and should refuse to serve in Vietnam. But their argument that soldiers should obey "the dictates of their own conscience" is a slippery slope indeed. At the bottom of this slope is military dictatorship.

A more immediate question is the relationship between civilian officials and military officers on national security. Particularly, under what circumstances should a military officer speak up when he believes the President or the Secretary of Defense is making a mistake?

The vast majority of officers believe that senior officers should speak freely on military matters within the councils of government. Once a decision has been made by the President or another political authority, generals and admirals should cease debate, salute, and do as they are told. Some officers believe that if a general or an admiral thinks political leaders are making fundamental mistakes that would harm the nation, and will not change course, he should resign. "Every once in a while," said one officer, "you have to be willing to put your commission on the line." Other officers note little precedent among American soldiers for falling on their swords. The officer who has resigned would get little attention once he lost his platform, they argue, and the officer named to replace him would most likely agree with the views of the civilian superior. Thus, those officers argue, no good purpose would be served by resigning in protest.

General Bruce Palmer Jr., who was the Army's field force commander in Vietnam and later Vice Chief of Staff of the Army, has contended that the Joint Chiefs of Staff erred during the war in Vietnam by failing to speak up to President Johnson.

They were unable to articulate an effective, workable strategy for the war that the President and our civilian leaders would support. Moreover, there was a profoundly significant omission in the advice provided by the chiefs. Not once during President Johnson's tenure, 1963–1969, did the chiefs tell their commander-in-chief that the strategy was not working and would fail to achieve U.S. objectives. . . . In hindsight, a strong case can be made for the resignation of one, several, or all the chiefs on the grounds they could not in good conscience support the dispatch of more and more young Americans to Vietnam to fight a war with such dubious chances of success. Such resignations in protest might not have done much good and the resignees might have been accused of disloyalty or worse, but they would have gotten the attention of many thinking Americans in and out of government.

General Vessey ruminated over the same question just before he retired in 1985 as Chairman of the Joint Chiefs. Choosing the time and place for employing military force, he said, was a political decision. "We have some ideas about whether it's right or wrong," he said. "We ought to make those ideas known but recognize that it's a political decision." If a senior officer sees the President about to make what the officer considers to be a mistake, the general said, "you have to tell him." But he immediately qualified that: "He's commander in chief. It's our business to advise him and tell him; then, when he makes his decision, to carry it out." The general asked himself the next question: "Suppose you know that he's absolutely wrong and that it won't work. What do you do?" An officer could resign, but General Vessey didn't think much of that idea. "You have to set your 'shove-it' tolerance someplace. But you also have to recognize that you, too, may be wrong, and that in two weeks time you'll be 'old what's his name' and won't be able to influence the situation at all."

Every now and then, an officer oversteps the mark and is brought up short, often by his military colleagues. Vice Admiral James A. Lyons told an audience at the Naval War College in Newport, Rhode Island, in 1984 that the War Powers Resolution should be repealed. (That measure was passed by Congress after the Vietnam conflict to restrict the President's authority to employ forces in hostilities.) "We need to remove this impediment to the President's power to carry out our national policy," Admiral Lyons said. "The impact of the War Powers Resolution is insidious in that it encourages our adversaries and it also influences the decision-making process at every level of command. It is clear we need to limit the impact of this resolution on our national policy-making machinery and the sooner the better, in my view."

Admiral Lyons was immediately condemned by political leaders for trespassing beyond his competence. But among the sharpest words were from Admiral Stansfield Turner, a retired officer:

If Admiral Lyons is campaigning for Ronald Reagan's re-election, it is against the law for him to do so while on active duty. The admiral needs to be reminded that the American people want their military to stay clear of domestic politics. We see enough of military meddling in politics in the rest of the world. The United States military has far too deep a tradition of following civilian control and remaining aloof from domestic politics to be swayed easily by indiscretions such as were rampant in Newport.

A related question is the protocol within the military service under which a subordinate may disagree with a superior. The leader of a well-run military organization encourages suggestions and ideas from below. Despite the authoritarian nature of military service, good officers are not robots or yes-men. On operational staffs, vigorous debate goes on until the commander makes a decision. Then discussion stops and orders are executed. Moreover, even after a decision, effective subordinate officers advise their superiors on courses of action and warn them if they see the senior officer about to make a mistake. When Captain F. L. "Skip" Bowman was captain of the submarine *City of Corpus Christi*, he encouraged, even demanded, what he called "back-up" in which all hands warned superiors before something went wrong. He tested the crew one day by ordering the periscope to be raised when the submarine was speeding under the sea. To have raised it then would have risked having the long slender shaft bent by the pressure of onrushing seawater. A split second after giving the order, the officer of the deck snapped: "Urgently request you rescind that order, sir," then explained to the captain why. Captain Bowman countermanded his order, and smiled at the quick reaction. "Many submarine force accidents could have been avoided if someone in the watch party had professionally questioned the ordered action," he told every newcomer to the ship. "I never want to hear: 'I could have told him that was going to happen.' "

Altogether, the officer corps in the mid-1980s is about 280,000 strong. The Air Force has the largest number, 104,500 officers; the Army has 90,750, the Navy 65,450, and the Marine Corps 18,500. Officers, especially in the Army, tend to come more from the South than from other regions, probably because of military traditions and the location of many military bases in the South. Relatively fewer officers, for reasons unknown, come from the West. Defense Department reports showed that almost all officers had college degrees and that many earned master's degrees. A *Newsweek* survey in 1984 reported that 57 percent of the senior officers said they had grown up in middle-class homes but that 80 percent considered themselves upper-middle-class now. The same survey said 52 percent of the senior officers were Republicans, 43 percent independents, and only 4 percent Democrats—figures that may reflect the shift toward a conservative mood in America as well as the political bent of military officers.

Although the armed forces are trained for war, they employ not only infantry troop commanders but nuclear physicists, fighter pilots and speakers of Russian and Chinese, ship navigators and journalists, planners of amphibious assaults and lawyers, artillery gunners and financial advisers, engineers of every description, intelligence specialists, doctors of all sorts, communicators, tank and aircraft designers, historians, mapmakers, policemen, and practitioners of nearly every other professional or executive skill in America. The officer corps is, in short, a cross section of the nation.

At the same time, the military community appears to stand apart from the rest of American society, a perception that has drawn criticism from those who see the military as an elite not responsive to democratic controls. Part of that distance is emotional, a vestige of Vietnam. But even without Vietnam, military people are distant because they live and work on remote Army posts or Air Force bases with their officers' clubs, commissaries, and recreational facilities. The Navy is especially distant; while naval bases are surrounded by civilian communities, the long months at sea when naval officers are confined in defined spaces breeds a mentality of separation.

Further setting military people apart are hazards, not just in combat but in everyday training. Roaring across the desert in a tank, thundering off the deck of an aircraft carrier in a fighter plane, parachuting with 800 men out of transport planes 1,000 feet above the earth, lifting off the deck of a pitching assault ship in a helicopter, plunging in a submarine to a depth of 1,000 feet, and a thousand other dangerous tasks give military people a sense of shared values. Not all officers experience those adventures, but the ethos rubs off. The codes of truth, loyalty, and honesty by which soldiers strive to live are more demanding than those elsewhere, making military service at its best a calling not unlike that of the ministry or priesthood.

A profile of the officer corps looks more like an art deco building than like a pyramid: solid at the bottom but with sharp cutbacks from the rigorous selection process, and split into Vietnam and post-Vietnam generations. The competition for promotion to colonel or Navy captain and especially to the ranks of general and flag officer is among the toughest in American life. While the distribution shifts slightly every year, the structure of the officer corps looks like this:

Army, Air Force, Marine Corps Ranks	Numbers	Navy Ranks
VIETNAM GENERATION		
General	34	Admiral
Lieutenant General	122	Vice Admiral
Major General	366	Rear Admiral (upper half)
Brigadier General	525	Rear Admiral (lower half)
Colonel	14,500	Captain
Lieutenant Colonel	32,500	Commander
POST-VIETNAM GENERATION		
Major	51,500	Lieutenant Commander
Captain	98,000	Lieutenant
First Lieutenant	43,000	Lieutenant (junior grade)
Second Lieutenant	38,500	Ensign

With Vietnam dominating the attitude of the officer corps, there are but few shadings from World War II and the Korean War. General Vessey and a few other senior officers were the last on active duty to have experienced World War II. Gone from the military memory is the experience of massed armies that maneuvered in the crusade that freed Europe from Nazi Germany. Since World War II, no naval officer has experienced the vast surface and aerial naval engagements, the submarine campaigns, the amphibious island hopping that led to victory at sea over Japan. With the brief exception of bombing North Vietnam, no aircraft pilot has flown in aerial armadas like those that pounded Germany and Japan. Indeed, young generals and Navy admirals today have no personal memory of World War II. A small point illustrates the difference: No officer on the ground or at sea today has experienced prolonged attack from the air. Consequently, said a retired general who fought in World War II, "Nobody today thinks to look up."

Officers who were young at the time of the Korean War were, in mid-1986, a thin layer at the top of the officer corps. The Chairman of the Joint Chiefs of Staff, Admiral William J. Crowe Jr., was commissioned shortly after World War II. General Wickham, the Army Chief of Staff, Admiral Watkins, the Chief of Naval Operations, General Gabriel, the Air Force Chief of Staff, and General P. X. Kelley, the Commandant of the Marine Corps, were commissioned at the time of the Korean War, although only General Gabriel saw action, flying 100 missions as a fighter pilot.

But those officers also belong to the Vietnam generation. General Wickham commanded a battalion in the 1st Cavalry Division and was wounded in action; Admiral Watkins's cruiser, *Long Beach*, provided naval gunfire to support forces ashore; General Gabriel flew another 152 missions and was the leader of the 452nd Tactical Reconnaissance Wing; General Kelley commanded a battalion in the 4th Marines and, on a second tour, was regimental commander of the 1st Marines.

From the Vietnam generation, the workaday leaders of the forces today are between forty and fifty years old and have fifteen to thirty years of military experience. Brigadier General Ward M. LeHardy represents the early part of the generation. He was a captain and a general's aide in Japan in 1962, when only American advisers were in Vietnam. As a young officer, he told his boss, "Sir, I want to leave you and go to war." The first two American advisers had just been killed in Vietnam; Captain LeHardy took the place of one. Later, he did a second tour in Vietnam, winning two Bronze Stars. Since then, General LeHardy has been a battalion commander, brigade commander, chief of staff of a division, and, after being promoted to brigadier general in 1985, an assistant division commander. He summed up his attitude toward his career: "I want to serve with soldiers."

In the Navy, Rear Admiral William A. Dougherty, Jr., has combined flying attack planes with analyzing nuclear strategy. During two tours in Vietnam, he flew more than 200 missions in A-4 Skyhawk attack planes. By 1983, he was captain of the aircraft carrier *Independence* when she took part in the invasion of Grenada and the air attack on Syrian forces in Lebanon. On other assignments, he has been a staff officer analyzing nuclear forces, doctrine, and arms control.

At the mid-level, Lieutenant Colonel Samuel W. Floca Jr., who commanded a battalion of heavy artillery in West Germany in 1985, is among those combatant commanders on whose shoulders would ride the outcome of a conventional war in Europe. Colonel Floca, a Texan, dropped out of Southern Methodist University to enlist in 1963. After a year as a rifleman, he went to Officer Candidate School in the artillery and was commissioned in 1965. He went to Vietnam in 1966 as a forward observer in the First Infantry Division's artillery, calling in gunfire to support long-range reconnaissance patrols and Special Forces, or Green Berets. After several months, he was badly wounded and was evacuated back to the United States. But he returned to Vietnam, again to serve with the "Big Red One" in the May offensive of 1968, where he was the forward observer for an infantry battalion. He was wounded slightly three more times and won the Silver Star, the Army's third highest combat decoration, on Friday, September 13, 1968. During a North Vietnamese attack, Captain Floca ran through enemy fire to a vantage point from which he called in artillery fire, once only twenty-five yards from his own position, to beat off the attackers. A short time later, he was wounded again seriously when a Vietcong sapper placed a demolition charge under the floor of the hut where he was sleeping and literally blew him, atop his mattress, through the roof. A tree broke his fall, but that was the end of the war for Sam Floca.

Colonel Floca relished his assignment in West Germany. "Like any other lieutenant colonel of artillery," he said, "I wanted more than anything in the world to command a battalion." The colonel considered himself a teacher of the 600 officers, sergeants, and soldiers in the battalion, saying that "my responsibility is to pass on everything I can about how a field artillery battalion should be ready to go to battle." As each new soldier reported to his battalion, Colonel Floca wrote a letter home to his family promising them that "if we are ever called upon to meet the enemy on the field of battle, your son will be well-trained and well-led."

Another combatant commander is Commander Charles Beers, a submariner who has shown a different kind of courage and sacrifice. Several years ago, as a lieutenant commander and executive officer of a submarine, Commander Beers stood deep in his ship explaining the maze of pipes, gauges, electric cables, and machinery that made the long, black, cigar-shaped vessel work. Gradually the conversation shifted from ship to officer; Commander Beers had graduated from the Naval Academy thirteen years earlier. Since then, he had served continuously at sea in attack submarines or ballistic-missile submarines.

At that time, the Navy was short of nuclear-trained submarine officers, so that they were rarely permitted to take shore billets that would have given them a break from the arduous duty at sea. Instead, attack submarines spent six of every fifteen months on patrol, plus shorter training cruises. All but a few hours of each patrol would be submerged. Commander Beers had thus spent more than a third of his adult life literally under water, with long separations from his wife and two children. The commander, who was later captain of an attack submarine, was asked why he did it. "I guess," he chuckled, "I just like submarines." A minute later, he became serious. "I think what I do is important," he said quietly, "and I think that if I don't do it, then maybe nobody will."

Between the Vietnam generation and the next generation is a subtle gap that comes from the younger officers' not having fought in Southeast Asia. The post-Vietnam officers—who are majors and captains in the Army, Marine Corps, and Air Forces, and lieutenant commanders and lieutenants in the Navy—joined the service in the 1970s as American participation in the war ended. It was a time when young people were taking to the streets to protest the war, and those officers came from the ranks of people caught up in that turmoil.

The post-Vietnam officers appear to respect the officers who bore the brunt of the battle in Vietnam. "The military did well in Vietnam," said a captain at Fort Benning. "It wasn't the military who lost the war." But the younger officers don't necessarily hold up the Vietnam generation as heroes. Indeed, they tend to be skeptical of what they hear from their superiors, to be less impressed by authority, and more impressed by ability. The younger officers sometimes resent the attitude of Vietnam veterans. "When I argued with a colonel one day," said another captain at Fort Benning, "he said he didn't see any overseas patch on my shoulder." The younger officers also differ from the older generation in their attitudes toward military service. An older officer may be willing to accept something he doesn't like because he is looking forward to his retired pay after serving for twenty years. The younger officers seem ready to leave if they are not given the assignments that provide the satisfaction they seek.

Senior officers said they noticed the difference. Major General John W. Foss, the commanding general at Fort Benning, said that if a subordinate questions an order, "no longer can I say to some major or captain 'well, young man, that's the way it is.' They want to know why." General Foss approved of that attitude as a healthy contribution to the Army. But he made clear that he expects officers to obey orders once a decision had been made, adding with a chuckle, "and I don't expect them to come in here and call me a dummy." Similarly, younger officers were being taught at the Infantry Center at Fort Benning that they must rely more on persuasive leadership than on direct orders to lead volunteer soldiers. "We are getting away from telling soldiers to listen to what I say and getting more toward saying 'what do you think?'" said Major Thomas Dyne, an instructor. "Today we have to tell soldiers why we want something done because we have smart soldiers."

Military service has surprised some of the post-Vietnam generation by being not nearly so monolithic as they had expected. Major Raymond C. Gagnon joined the Air Force though the Reserve Officer Training Corps at the University of New Hampshire in 1970. He had drawn a low number in the draft lottery, meaning he could have been drafted. So he joined the Air Force ROTC to stay in school and graduated from college in 1974 intending to do the three years of active duty for which he was obligated. "I am achievement oriented," Major Gagnon said, "and I thought there was no way in the military I would be allowed to do that—no room for innovation, or for individual action." After several months, he changed his mind. "I found it was entirely different from what I had thought. There's room for individual creativity, for loyal dissent until a decision is made. The whole process before a decision is open. If you do it right, people will be responsive. I've never been a super-patriot, but I found in the military that I was able to be myself." Major Gagnon, a relaxed, outgoing officer, has been an administrative officer, a political-military analyst, and executive officer to several senior officers. He said that so long as the Air Force continued to give him interesting assignments, he would stay.

In contrast, Major Peter W. Chiarelli, an Army officer, represents probably a minority of the post-Vietnam generation. He considers himself to have been patriotic when it was not fashionable, and supported the war in Vietnam. He planned to enlist after finishing high school but his father urged him to go to college instead. A tall, slender, intense man, Major Chiarelli was a student at Seattle University from 1968 to 1972, which he said was "the worst four years to go to college, because of Vietnam." He joined the ROTC, which was difficult when students were demonstrating in front of the armory and breaking windows in ROTC classrooms. Secret formations had to be held, with members called at 5:30 in the morning to meet for a drill at 6:00, each time in a different place. When the lottery was held, Majory Chiarelli prayed for a low number so that he could justify his ROTC membership to his friends. When he drew number 323, out of 365, he said, "it was a black day."

After graduation, Major Chiarelli was assigned to an armored unit at Fort Lewis, Washington. "But the cavalry was coming home from Vietnam then, telling war stories that showed it was not what I thought it had been like," he said. "I was disillusioned by what they had done; it was not the same kind of fervor that I had." Major Chiarelli planned to leave the Army after completing his obligation but changed his mind when the Army offered to send him to graduate school and then to West Point, where he spent four years teaching political science. He studied for another year at the Naval War College, then returned to the Army as executive officer of a tank battalion in West Germany. "I will stay till the day I'm no longer moving," Major Chiarelli said. "I want to have a chance to affect things. I've learned how the system works, but I've been down in the trenches, too."

Among the youngest officers, Vietnam is but a hazy memory of childhood. First Lieutenant Stephen Tibbets, an F-16 pilot at Shaw Air Force Base in South Carolina, graduated from the University of California at Santa Barbara in 1979 with a degree in geology. Because he couldn't get a job in his field, he worked in construction and thought about flying, "but that was something somebody else did." One day he walked into a recruiting station, filled out the papers, found himself accepted, and reported to the Officer Training School at Lackland Air Force Base in Texas. Later, he did well enough in flight school to have his choice of assignments and picked F-16s. Among other young pilots at Shaw, one had joined the Air Force because his father had been in the Air Force, another because he went to the Air Force Academy, and a third just because he wanted to fly airplanes. Each had a five-year obligation after finishing flight school, and each said he would decide later whether to make a career of it. Vietnam and its aftermath loomed on their horizons hardly at all.

A new generation of officers with no memory of Vietnam is forming among the young men and women at the military academies, in the Reserve Officer Training Corps, and at officer training schools. At a time when civilian colleges are experiencing a drop in applications, the numbers of young people applying to the service academies have been running at a high. For the class of 1988, the Military Academy at West Point, New York, received 14,000 applications, second only to that for the class of 1980, the first class to accept women. Fewer than one in ten applicants entered the academy. The same was true for the Naval Academy at Annapolis in Maryland and the Air Force Academy in Colorado Springs, Colorado.

Coming from a cross section throughout the nation, the young men and women at the military academies and in the ROTC have been of higher quality than ever before. The director of admissions at West Point, Colonel Manley E. Rogers, said academic records and extra-curricular activities presented for admission by the class of 1988 were better than those of any class before. And the Military Academy ranks fourth among American colleges in graduates who have won Rhodes Scholarships. At the Naval Academy, the average Scholastic Aptitude Test score in mathematics was 665 in 1983, compared with 467 nationwide on a scale of 800. The Air Force Academy, in a survey of the class of 1986, found that 92 percent had graduated in the top quarter of their high school classes; 72 percent were in an honor society. In the National Merit Scholarship program, 20 percent had been finalists or semifinalists, or had won letters of commendation. In athletics, 83 percent had won one or more letters in high school, and 36 percent had been either in the Boy Scouts or Girl Scouts.

On a spring day in 1983, several cadets at the Air Force Academy gathered to discuss their reasons for being there. Thomas M. Webster Jr., of Mountain View, California, could have had scholarships to two civilian colleges but decided on the Air Force Academy because he felt that he had not been challenged in high school and that the academy would do so. Jeffrey J. Kubiak, of Green Bay, Wisconsin, had been offered scholarships to play football in civilian universities but chose the Air Force Academy because he thought it would be academically more satisfying. But he disagreed with a suggestion that young people came to the academy, with its rigorous discipline and full military schedule, for a free education. Some had entered with that in mind, he said, but found that "the price was too high and left." Gregory W. Wheeler, of Rockville, Maryland, said he had come to Colorado Springs to become an Air Force officer but thought that most people would wait until they have served part of their five-year obligations before deciding whether to make it a career.

At the Army ROTC's exhausting six-week basic summer camp at Fort Knox, students who had finished their sophomore years in college were competing for scholarships that would pay for tuition, books, and laboratory fees in the junior and senior years, plus $100 a month for living expenses. There were other reasons. "The leadership training gives you a background for dealing with people," said John F. Kope, of Ohio State; "they teach us to handle anything that comes along." Daniel E. Campbell, of Towson State in Maryland, said that "lots of people here are career oriented" and that the ROTC would lead to an immediate job after college. He wanted to go into military intelligence because "that would be more useful than the infantry in the real world" and hoped to be promoted to captain in four years as "that will look good on a résumé." A few came for the discipline. Robert W. Hayworth, of East Carolina University, said he'd done "too much partying" during his first two years of college and was out of condition. The physical training, he said dryly, was "very challenging." But, he said, "I feel more confidence in my physical shape now and I feel more confidence in myself." Still others wanted to see what military service was like, never having been exposed to it before. "I haven't worn a uniform," said Joseph N. Gaines of Salisbury State in Maryland, "since I was in the Boy Scouts."

In the Army's ROTC program, national enrollment more than doubled from 1973, the year the draft ended, to a peak of 72,700 in 1984. Then it dropped off to 61,500 in 1986 as the Army, flooded with applications and hampered by tighter budgets, raised standards. Of all the officers in the Army today, 75 percent earned their commissions through the ROTC, 14 percent from the Military Academy, and 11 percent from officer candidate schools that train men and women from the enlisted ranks. Similarly, the Air Force ROTC has experienced a steady increase in enrollment and has provided 40 percent of the Air Force's officers. In the Navy, six of seven new officers come from the ROTC or an officer candidate school.

The resurgence of the ROTC, a prime target for protesters during the Vietnam war, has begun to restore the ties among the military, the middle class, and the universities that were among the leaders of the antiwar movement in the 1960s. ROTC graduates who follow military careers may improve those ties as they rise. Of the sixty-four Army colonels promoted in late 1984 to brigadier general, forty-three had come from the ROTC. The grip of the Naval Academy on the top rungs of the Navy has slipped enough that more than half the captains selected for rear admiral in 1983 and 1984 were from the ROTC or officer candidate school or received direct commissions as specialists. In 1958, only 3 of 248 line admirals, those eligible for command, were not from the Naval Academy.

In one sense, black Americans have done well as officers in the military services. The proportion of blacks in the officer corps rose from 2.5 percent in 1973, after the war in Vietnam, to 6.4 percent in 1985. But measured in another way, blacks have lagged: the ratio of black officers has not come close to the proportion of blacks (12 to 13 percent) in the national population. Of 18,400 black officers in 1986, moreover, 17,100 were concentrated in the four lowest grades. Only in the Army's three lowest grades of officers did blacks, at 12.5 to 14.5 percent, reach a level proportionate to the black population.

In general, black officers seemed to find military life more rewarding and less discriminating than civilian life. At the same time, many black officers suggested that the services had not lived up to their own standards of offering an equal opportunity to all.

Lieutenant Colonel Melvin P. Smith Jr., an adjutant general officer at Fort Dix, New Jersey, said "the Army has been better than anything I saw growing up in the South." He had come into the Army in 1964 after graduating from Virginia State University, a predominantly black university, where he had been in the Reserve Officers Training Corps. A big, athletic man, he had served in Vietnam, lived through the days of racial turmoil in the services in the 1970s, and was one of the few black officers to have been selected recently for promotion to colonel. He said that the Army had done a "more positive job" than the civilian sector in "solving an American problem" but that subtle discrimination still existed. "A lot of ideas haven't changed, they've just gone underground." He cited the few black officers who had been promoted to colonel. In early 1986, there were 4,864 colonels in the Army; only 240, or 4.9 percent, were black. Colonel Smith said some of the lag was due to the "faint praise" found in reports in which senior officers rated junior officers. White officers writing the evaluations, he said, often lacked enthusiasm and produced a "bland word picture" of the black officer he was rating.

Lieutenant Colonel Paul Lewis Jr., the provost marshal at Fort Dix, agreed: "The system has gone from overt discrimination to subtlety in the same things." Moreover, relatively few black officers held what he called "meaningful jobs," such as battalion commander, where a good performance would mean promotion. He said the "movers and shakers" have been white officers, and their natural racial affinity had led them to select other white officers for the better assignments and schools. "Fifteen years ago, that was conscious. Now it's subconscious." Colonel Lewis added another subtle dimension: competition. To white officers, he said, "I am an aggressive, articulate officer—and I am threatening."

At McGuire Air Force Base, also in New Jersey, Lieutenant Colonel John D. Hopper was one of five blacks who had graduated from the Air Force Academy in 1969, had become a pilot, and had flown C-130 combat transports in Vietnam. A soft-spoken, thoughtful officer, Colonel Hopper said: "The Air Force has done a better job of providing a structure that allows a person to do his best. It hasn't been a perfect opportunity. But as much as can be mandated by public law, the chance is there." Colonel Hopper found nuances that were negative in the evaluation reports by which officers are judged. "If the right things aren't said," he noted, "that sends a signal."

Black naval officers gave their service mixed reviews. "The black Navy officer is still looked on as a novelty," said Lieutenant Marvin E. King, a graduate of the Naval Academy, where he was one of 44 blacks in a class of 800 commissioned in 1978. "It's impossible to get definitive answers on what you need to do to break out of the middle of the pack. If you're white, you can be one of the boys. But blacks are different; you still have something to prove."

Lieutenant Edwin D. Dawson, who got his law degree from the University of Wisconsin, differed. "I've had more legal experience in one year than I probably would have gotten in several years outside," he said. He planned to leave the Navy when his five-year tour ended, however, to teach and practice law in the Middle West because "the opportunities to get into new areas of law are limited in the Navy." He said whatever conflicts he had in the Navy were not racial but differences in personalities. "Would I do it again? Yes, I would."

For First Lieutenant Joe L. Winbush of the Marine Corps, the service has been a way out of rural southwestern Virginia. He enlisted in 1967, served in Vietnam as a radioman, then was a drill sergeant at Parris Island. "That was the most rewarding duty," he said, "because you could see the end product." Promoted to warrant officer in 1977, he was with marine contingents in Beirut in 1982 and 1983. Meantime, he completed a degree at Eastern Carolina University while serving at the Marine Air Station at Cherry Point and was commissioned a first lieutenant in 1984. "It would be naive to say that you have not run into someone who is prejudiced," he said. "But you have to learn to work with them and eventually he will look at you as an individual. In the Marine Corps, we don't look at you as black or white, we look at you as green."

Personnel officers in the Pentagon said recruiting black officers has been slowed by a drop in the number of black college entrants, which made recruiting into the ROTC harder. In addition, competition for able black graduates was fierce as industry, the professions, universities, and journalism were actively seeking young black men and women. Said a harassed Army officer in late 1985, "Have you tried to hire a good black college graduate lately?"

The personnel officers asserted that standards would not be lowered to meet a racial quota. "You're competing for a quality product with all of society," said an Air Force officer. A Marine officer said, "we don't have enough black officers," but saw little prospect the Marine Corps would reach its goal of 11 percent soon. A Navy personnel officer said his service, which had long been less receptive to black officers than the others, had set a "realistically attainable" goal of 6 percent. "We're really out there actively recruiting," he said, "but we're competing in a rough marketplace."

Blacks were not joining or staying as officers for another reason. Throughout the services, ambitious officers find mentors to teach them how to succeed in the military culture. With the senior officer corps predominantly white, junior black officers have not found mentors. Said a young black naval officer, "I'm running out of people ahead of me who I want to emulate." As more black officers reach senior ranks, that is slowly changing. Colonel Smith, at Fort Dix, said he tried to mentor all younger officers under his command, adding:

But I owe that black officer something more. He has to be the best guy, not one of the boys but the best among them. I tell them, when you put on a uniform, make it look good. When you speak, be sure it's something everyone is going to get something out of. Don't just open your mouth.

Colonel Hopper at McGuire offered this advice to black officers: "You are a member of a minority in a majority world. When you are faced with a choice of jobs, take the tougher job. When you have a social commitment you don't want to attend, do it anyway."

Another drawback to black officers has been a lack of technical training to qualify for some jobs. Only small numbers of Air Force and Navy pilots have been black. The attrition rate for black student pilots has been higher than that for white student pilots in the Air Force. That has not been so in the Navy, but fewer blacks have applied for Navy flight training. Among the Army's helicopter pilots, black flyers did better but were still below the ratio for American society.

The end of the draft and a consequent drop in the number of men seeking to be officers opened up opportunities for women in the military services. At the same time, women seeking equal rights and opportunities led them to look at military service with a pioneer spirit. In short, the services needed people, and jobs for women in civilian life were hard to get. In 1973, when the volunteer force began, the four services had 12,600 women as officers, which was 3.8 percent of the officer corps. That figure rose steadily to 30,000 and 10.4 percent in 1985, with the Army, Navy, and Air Force around 10 to 11 percent each and the Marine Corps at 3.3 percent. For the three big services, the numbers of women officers seemed likely to rise further before leveling off.

Ultimately, the central issue on which the place of women in the military will turn is what part they may take in combat. It is a question of profound political, moral, constitutional, and practical implications. The law today prohibits the Navy, Marine Corps, and the Air Force from sending women into combat; Army regulations preclude women from duty in which they might be directly engaged in combat.

The critical question: What constitutes combat? Clearly, carrying a rifle in a jungle while searching for an enemy is combat. Is a radio operator in a headquarters several tens of miles behind the lines in combat? Probably not, but what about the danger of a commando raid or an air attack? Is cruising aboard a submarine armed with nuclear missiles to be considered combat duty? If an order comes to fire the missiles, the firing is likely to be over within a few minutes, with the submarine fleeing for survival or, if discovered, being destroyed in a sudden death for all hands. The Air Force has decided that standing watch in an underground capsule controlling intercontinental nuclear missiles is not direct combat and has assigned women officers to two-woman crews in Minuteman capsules. In sum, are there ways to employ women in some combat for which they might well be suited? At the same time, should they be excluded from other combat, especially that in which they might risk capture and sexual exploitation by their captors, such as being raped or tortured in an interrogation?

Few of those questions have been answered in perhaps the most difficult and extensive social experiment ever undertaken by the American armed forces. Women officers seem to believe that they are ahead of their sisters in civilian life because they get equal pay for equal work, because all officers of the same rank and length of service get the same base pay. Women officers also say they get more responsibility faster in the armed forces than they would in the civilian sector. But few women believe that the services have yet done all they could have to make the best use of women, to give them every opportunity, or to erase the discrimination against them.

The unresolved issues in the experiment with women officers show up daily as male and female officers search for ways to deal with each other. Senior male officers with more than twenty years of service, rooted in the days when military women were mostly nurses, have difficulty in coping with women officers. The attitude of some: "You shouldn't be in the Army, you should be back home cooking and having babies." Others see women, particularly newly commissioned officers, as daughters. A Marine colonel, asked whether he would treat a young male lieutenant and a young female lieutenant the same if each made a mistake, thought for a minute. "No," he said slowly, "I would brace that young man, but I would counsel the woman." Senior male officers may be diffident about correcting the appearance or behavior of young women officers. Said a Navy admiral, "How do I tell a woman that her skirt is too short or her hair is too long, or that she had too much to drink in the club last night?" Some senior male officers ask a woman officer to correct the offender. On the other hand, women report that slowly but steadily, senior male officers are coming to treat them as they wish to be treated, as officers in the United States armed forces. Still, social life has to be handled with care. Dating an officer of equal or nearly equal rank who serves in a different unit is okay; dating a senior officer, particularly one who supervises the female officer, is not.

At McGuire Air Force Base in New Jersey, Lieutenant Colonel Suzanne Phillips is the public affairs officer, or the spokesman for the commanding officer, and the senior female officer. She had come into the service in 1968, after having worked on newspapers in California, because a male subordinate was being paid more than she was. "I kept hearing that if a female joined the military," she said, "she got the same pay as a male."

Colonel Phillips has seen great changes in attitudes toward women. When she entered, women could not be married; now they can. After they were permitted to marry, they could not be mothers and remain in the service; now they can. At first, she was often the only woman on the base; now there are many, and career fields have widened. In her career, she had not experienced sexual harassment but had encountered officers who thought she should not be in the service. Even today, she has problems with male officers who look on her as a token female. "About 10 percent really look at you as a token lieutenant colonel. I have trouble with the perception of being a token and not being taken seriously." She said that was particularly true when she reported to a new assignment until she had proved herself and won the confidence of her commanding officer. In dealing with female subordinates, Colonel Phillips differed from some female officers, saying she expected more of women. "In correcting a junior, I don't think sex should make a difference," she said. "But I would be harder on a female who has potential and wasn't using it or was making a bad name for women in the service."

Lieutenant Commander Dana S. Koch came into the Navy in February 1973, in the first wave of commissioned women in the volunteer force. "I was always the one who did the off-the-wall stuff," she said of her childhood in Texas. "Mothers didn't want their daughters to play with me." After she graduated from Angelo State University, she walked into the Navy recruiting office and told the chief petty officer she wanted to enlist for officer training. "His jaw dropped from here to here," Commander Koch said, holding her hands two feet apart. But she was treated as an adult in officer training at Newport, Rhode Island. Since then, women have come a long way in the Navy, she said, but still haven't arrived, largely because of the exclusion from sea duty aboard combatants. "I used to be real angry because the Navy was not giving me the opportunity to prove I am as good an officer as my husband." But Commander Koch, a communications officer at the Naval Base in Norfolk, Virginia, suggested that she had accepted some of the restrictions because American society was not ready to permit women to serve on warships. "That's not going to happen," she said. "My folks in Texas are just not going to let that happen."

The combat exclusion regulations in the Army seemed not to bother women officers so much as they saw other chances for command and advancement. Captain Marianne F. Rowland had commanded a company at a reception center for recruits, where her subordinates in the cadre were all male. She had also been a class leader during parachute training and had been chief of a personnel section managing 14,000 records. "I've done a lot of things," she said, "and had a lot of opportunities to surpass my peers in civilian life." Captain Rowland noted that equal pay for equal work was guaranteed in the service. On the other hand, she said, "I still encounter people who are skeptical about my abilities."

Captain Ruth E. Thomas's experience in the Army has not been so fortunate. Commissioned in the Corps of Engineers in 1975, she has found male colleagues resentful. "Engineers do not like women in their corps," she said. "It hurts their macho image." The engineers would not give her command of a company, a position she needed to be eligible for promotion to major. When she heard of an opening at the training center at Fort Dix, however, she paid her own way, about $1,000, to move there from Fort Belvoir in Virginia. Her experience with senior male officers, she said, has been fifty-fifty. "Some of them treated me rotten, standing me at attention in front of their desks, screaming and yelling. They just don't like me in the Army. But others have been nice and understanding." Among her male peers, Captain Thomas said, it was the same. "They don't like the competition. I'm better at details than the men, who sometimes forget." Among male subordinates, only senior noncommissioned officers had been troublesome. "They want to see how far they can push me," she said, "and to see what I will do if I say no. It gets embarrassing sometimes; the arguing gets on your nerves."

Two first lieutenants in the Marine Corps, Lauren Brennan and Joan E. Stubbs, underscored the problems that confront women officers daily. "You are in the minority and you are on the skyline," Lieutenant Brennan siad. "Make a mistake and you stand out because you are different." Male subordinates, she added, "test you to see how much they can get away with." On the other hand, Lieutenant Stubbs said, "the older men don't know how to deal with females. Sometimes they treat you like their long-lost daughters." She recalled that a colonel had come into the office one morning, put his arm around her shoulders, and said, "Honey, you sure did a good job last week." The lieutenant had to think fast so as not to give him or other Marines the wrong idea. "Sir," she said politely but firmly, "I am not your honey, I am Lieutenant Stubbs."

At McGuire Air Force Base in New Jersey, First Lieutenant Carol Ann Jones belonged to a group of captains and lieutenants who met periodically to develop professional skills. "The women take part in that more than the men," she said, partly because the men have senior officers to teach them and the women don't. A graduate of the Air Force Academy, Lieutenant Jones had found the attitudes of senior officers ranged from not wanting her in the Air Force to acting like her father. But there seemed to be more of a blending toward the middle, with other officers respecting her for the job she did once she had proved herself. She added a new thought, that sometimes the father-daughter relationship was the doing of the woman. "I think I see some women looking for the father," she said. "They start associating the senior officers with their own fathers."

For women of college age, the military service is still a male institution. Barbara A. Huggett, who was among the 10 percent of the cadets at the Air Force Academy who were women, had gotten bored after a year of college in Michigan and enlisted in the Air Force to see the world. She became an aviation electronics technician, had a good time during two years she spent in England, and had enjoyed the Air Force. She applied to the Air Force Academy in a program for enlisted Air Force people, was accepted, and hoped to learn to fly after she graduated. "The Academy has a long way to go to give equal treatment to women," she said, "but the people here are working on it." She scoffed at the idea that women came to the academy, with its intense pressures, to find husbands: "There just isn't time for that."

In the survey of cadets at the Air Force Academy, perhaps the most revealing result was that in every case the women had done better than the men in high school. Of the 156 women in a class of 1483 cadets, 99 percent had been in the top quarter of their high school classes, compared with 92 percent of the men. The young women had done better in the National Honor Society, 90 percent to 71 percent, and had a larger participation in the Girl Scouts than did the young men in the Boy Scouts. Even in athletics, the women outshone the men in winning letters in basketball, baseball, track, and swimming.

The challenge for the 823 women among 2,807 men in the Army ROTC camp at Fort Knox was the competition. The only difference in the program was that women lived in separate barracks and were not allowed out alone after dark. "They really watch out for us," said Catherine F. Delgadillo, of Colorado State University. "But in training, they expect the same from us. They don't want us wimping out." The training was coed, including running through piney woods in the rain and mud with rifles in a drill known as "squad in the attack." She and many of the women were there, said Rebecca A. Ellingwood, of the University of New Hampshire, because the military "was one of the few fields where women haven't yet broken the barriers." Cadet Delgadillo also thought that job opportunities for women after college were not good in the civilian sector and that "in the Army, I can start out at a decent salary." Second lieutenants are paid $20,000 a year, including allowances for housing and rations.

Shortly after the last American shot was fired in Vietnam, civilians known as defense intellectuals began a running duel with military officers over the quality of American military leadership. Among the first civilian critics were Richard A. Gabriel and Paul L. Savage, who in 1978 argued in a book entitled *Crisis in Command* that officers had lost values as "gladiators" motivated by duty-honor-country. Instead, they asserted, military officers had absorbed values from the corporate world even before Vietnam.

The American military structure had already become permeated by a set of values, practices, and policies that forced considerations of career advancement to figure more heavily in the behavior of individual officers than the traditional ethics normally associated with military life.

Another persistent critic has been Jeffrey Record, of the Institute for Foreign Policy Analysis in Washington. Mr. Record has argued that after the amphibious landing at Inchon executed by General MacArthur in 1950 during the Korean War, America's military record "has been one of persistent professional malpractice." Mr. Record cited three alleged failings. First, "the American military is culturally, as well as by professional training and education, prone to disregard the fact that war remains first and foremost a human encounter—notwithstanding advances in weaponry." Second, "America's military malaise stems largely from the substitution of managerial and technocratic values for traditional warrior values that has taken place since World War II." Third, "professional dereliction and incompetence have rarely been punished since World War II."

Similarly, Edward N. Luttwak of Georgetown University's Center for Strategic and International Studies has contended that there are

plenty of engineers, economists, and political scientists in the officer corps—but where are the tacticians? There are many skilled personnel managers, logistical managers, and technical managers—but where are the students of the operational art of war? And at the top, there are many competent (and politically sensitive) bureaucrats—but where are the strategists?

Mr. Luttwak charged that American officers think strategy "is a phrase that refers only to budgets and foreign policy in the discourse of senior officers—men who think that Clausewitz was a German who died a long time ago."

Such criticism of American military officers is not new. In 1935, the question came up in the Senate Military Affairs Committee. Senator Francis Duffy, a Democrat from Wisconsin, worried that officers were not fit to command in battle. But General Douglas MacArthur, the Army's Chief of Staff, told the committee, in effect, not to worry.

There is really no measure in time of peace which can determine who are the brilliant combat officers. As a result, you find in every war, in every nation, in every age, the phenomena of apparently young and unknown men that rise suddenly to the top. That is because you have an unfailing and infallible measure in time of war. . . . You pick a man for a division commander or a regimental commander. . . . His method may be his own but in battle, if he does not fight, you have his measure. . . . You will find that men, like water, under battle conditions seek their own level.

Colonel Summers, the Army officer who has stimulated interest in the lessons of Vietnam, echoed General MacArthur a half century later. The colonel partly agreed with the critics, saying the armed forces had fallen under the "Tyranny of the Clerks." But, referring to Clausewitz, Colonel Summers noted the difference between "preparation for war," which is the administrative and logistical side of the military, and "conduct of war proper," which is operational.

The administrative side of the military is normally the province of clerks—military and civilian bureaucrats in both the best and worst senses of that word—who budget for, procure, and supply the material needs of the military and administer the various programs thus involved. In peacetime, there is a tendency for these clerks to dominate the soldiers who fight our wars, but in wartime the balance normally shifts from the bureaucracy to the battlefield.

Many officers argue, moreover, that they manage resources but lead people. Military officers today have been made responsible for enormous sums of money and are under constant scrutiny by Congress. The officers contend that managers are found in the Washington bureaucracy but that leaders are in the field and at sea with the forces. When General Meyer, then Chief of Staff of the Army, named new division and corps commanders in the summer of 1981, he pointed to their extensive combat and command experience. "I think this counters, in my judgment, the continuing statement that the Army is growing a group of managers as opposed to leaders," General Meyer asserted. "If you went to war, those are the kinds of guys you want out there leading soldiers." The general acknowledged a need for managers. "The Army in Washington is going to have to be more adept in how it manages the resources than it has ever been if we are going to convince the American people that we're effective and are applying those resources properly," he said. "So I don't need a flamboyant, swashbuckling guy charging down the halls of the Pentagon."

The charge that American military officers are not strategists is partly true; it is also mostly irrelevant. The critics fail to distinguish among grand or national strategy, military strategy, operations, and tactics. In the American way of war, national strategy is the responsibility of the President, the Secretary of Defense, the Secretary of State, and the National Security Council, not of military commanders.

The role of senior military officers in national strategy is to render sound military advice, if they are consulted, to the President and his civilian aides before a decision is made. The decision to seek, accept, or reject that advice, however, is unequivocally the President's. That the United States has floundered in recent years without a national strategy is a valid criticism. The fault, however, lies with those who wear business suits, not those in Army or Marine Corps green or Navy or Air Force blue.

After a strategic decision has been made by civilian leaders, the task of military commanders is to take that decision as a guide for devising military strategy. That strategy, particularly in the limited wars fought since the end of World War II, is also strongly controlled by political leaders who have not hesitated to dictate to senior military officers. That was especially true during the war in Vietnam, when President Johnson tried to run the war from the White House to the extent that he personally selected targets for bombing runs.

Even without politicians dipping their hands into military strategy, it has not been a strong point with Americans ever since the Revolution. Military strategy has been improvised, mostly by following the Civil War adage of "git thar fustest with the mostest." The study of military strategy, to the detriment of the nation, has been left to a lonely few thinkers in Washington and the war colleges. Moreover, American officers have not really been tested in planning military strategy for a sustained campaign since the end of the war in Vietnam.

On the other hand, military operations and tactics run by officers in the field have been an American forte. The record, while not unblemished, has shown more successes then failures since the landing at Inchon on the west coast of Korea in September 1950. Moreover, the operational art of war has been emphasized in recent years in the curricula of the Army War College at Carlisle Barracks, Pennsylvania, the Naval War College in Newport, Rhode Island, and the Air War College in Montgomery, Alabama. Tomorrow's generals and admirals are educated at those senior service schools and at the National Defense University in Washington, D.C.

After the Chinese intervention in Korea in late 1950, American and South Korean forces were driven halfway to the southern tip of the peninsula. But Lieutenant General Matthew B. Ridgway began a well-planned and well-executed drive to the north in January 1951. In operations code-named Killer, Ripper, Rugged, and Piledriver, his forces recaptured Seoul on March 15. By June 15, they were well above the thirty-eighth parallel, which had divided North and South Korea before the war. On July 10, the North Koreans and Chinese agreed to negotiate. General Ridgway's forces continued to attack, taking objectives around the Punchbowl and Heartbreak Ridge in the eastern sector until he ordered them, on November 12, to go over to an active defense. Negotiations plodded along until a truce was signed in July 1953. Measured by World War II's exhilarating unconditional surrender or General MacArthur's fiery slogan, "in war, there is no substitute for victory," the outcome of the Korean War was not a clear-cut triumph. But measured in limited objectives, American operations were a success.

During the most dangerous episode in the nuclear age, the Cuban missile crisis in October 1962, military operations were carried out with precision and skill in perhaps the best demonstration of active deterrence to date. When Air Force reconnaissance planes discovered Soviet nuclear missiles in Cuba within range of American cities, President Kennedy ordered more reconnaissance by U-2 aircraft to gather proof of the Soviet deployment. That order was executed effectively despite the danger; one pilot was shot down and died during a flight over Cuba. The President ordered a buildup of naval forces in the Caribbean and the Atlantic approaches to Cuba and a quarantine of ships that might carry missiles to Cuba. The Navy evacuated American dependents from the United States Naval Base at Guantanamo, on the eastern tip of Cuba, brought in marines to reinforce base defenses there, and swiftly had 180 ships at sea or on alert. The quarantine was executed without mishap. Navy antisubmarine forces tracked and harassed six Soviet submarines, forcing them to surface where they could be brought under the trained guns of Navy warships. The Strategic Air Command dispersed its B-52 bombers, loaded several with nuclear bombs on fifteen-minute alert, and flew a few on airborne alert. Polaris submarines bearing nuclear missiles put to sea to join others with missiles aimed at the Soviet Union. To prepare for an invasion of Cuba, the Army moved 30,000 troops into the southeastern United States and put five divisions on alert. The Tactical Air Command ordered twenty-four reserve fighter and attack squadrons to duty.

Later, Robert F. Kennedy, the President's brother and confidant, said in his book *Thirteen Days* that "President Kennedy was impressed with the effort and the dedicated manner in which the military responded." But the President

was distressed that the [military] representatives with whom he met, with the notable exception of General [Maxwell] Taylor, [then Chairman of the Joint Chiefs of Staff], seemed to give so little consideration to the implications of steps they suggested. They seemed always to assume that if the Russians and the Cubans would not respond or, if they did, that a war was in our national interest.

"When we talked about this later," Robert Kennedy continued, "he said we had to remember that they were trained to fight and to wage war—that was their life. Perhaps we would feel even more concerned if they were always opposed to using arms or military means—for if they were not willing, who would be?" (A telling observation, especially when compared with the Vietnam generation's caution in applying military power.)

Two decades after President Johnson ordered American forces into Vietnam, a new appraisal has emerged to suggest that American operations and tactics there were better than was realized at the time. American forces more than held their own in almost every battle during that war. To cite but a few: Troopers from the 1st Cavalry Division took on three regiments of North Vietnamese in the Ia Drang valley in 1965, killing 1,300 and driving the rest into Cambodia, with a loss of 300 American soldiers. In the summer of 1966, American troops broke the Vietcong hold on the coastal provinces. Later, the First Infantry Division defeated the Vietcong in two separate campaigns north of Saigon. In Operations Cedar Falls and Junction City in 1967, American and South Vietnamese forces formed a giant horseshoe to envelop a large Vietcong force, killing 2,700 over a period of several months and forcing the rest into Cambodia. Even the Tet offensive of 1968, seen by many at the time as an American defeat, has been reassessed and seen to have been a draw at worst, an American and South Vietnamese victory in all probability. The North Vietnamese and Vietcong lost 32,000 killed and 6,000 captured; the Americans and the South Vietnamese lost 2,000 each. The American bombing of North Vietnam around Christmas of 1972, an operation called Linebacker II, was poorly planned at first, with B-52 bombers flying in cells of three planes that were vulnerable to North Vietnamese surface-to-air missiles. After taking losses, the Air Force switched to World War II aerial armadas that were effective enough to persuade the North Vietnamese to return to the negotiating table in Paris.

Since Inchon, American Presidents have employed the armed forces frequently in smaller operations in pursuit of American interests. In their 1978 study, *Force Without War*, Barry M. Bleichman and Stephen S. Kaplan of the Brookings Institution in Washington examined 215 incidents in which the United States employed the armed forces between 1946 and 1975 to achieve political ends. Extrapolating from that figure, by early 1986 the number would be around 275 episodes, especially since President Reagan has shown that he is willing to use military power more freely than have his immediate predecessors.

Among those smaller incidents, President Kennedy dispatched marines and soldiers to Thailand in the spring of 1962 in a show of force that was successful in getting the Pathet Lao communists in Laos to back off from an offensive that threatened the Lao government. American warships in the Sea of Japan in 1967 defeated, with superior seamanship and steady nerves, Soviet ships whose captains played reckless games of "chicken." After North Koreans tried to kill the president of South Korea and seized the American intelligence ship *Pueblo* in 1968, United States ground forces in Korea went on alert, air squadrons flew into Korea, and the carrier *Enterprise* and other warships showed up. The net effect was to dissuade the North Koreans, who may have been planning a new invasion across the demilitarized zone. Two Libyan planes shot down by Navy pilots in a one-minute flight over the Gulf of Sidra in 1981 hardly exercised the well-trained Americans flying F-14 aircraft far more powerful than the Russian-built planes of their hapless adversaries. The disaster in Lebanon in which 241 Americans died in 1983 was the responsibility of the President, who put the troops into an untenable tactical position, plus poor intelligence and an absence of antiterrorist training. Planning for the invasion of Grenada in 1983 was clumsy, but it was executed with only five days' notice by well-trained rangers, marines, and paratroopers. The Navy pilots who forced down the Egyptian airliner carrying the hijackers of the Italian ship *Achille Lauro* in 1985 executed a touchy mission with skill. Naval aviators dodged Soviet-built missiles fired from Libya in 1986 and retaliated without a loss.

With all that, there is no gainsaying the American weakness in strategy. The new assessment of the American role in Vietnam holds that the war was lost for lack of a United States national strategy, for lack of an effective military strategy in Vietnam itself, and for lack of national resolve and public support at home. Both military officers and civilian analysts contend that those failures were caused by politicians in Washington and senior officers in Washington and Saigon. But American operations and tactics in Vietnam were creditable. Soldier for soldier, unit for unit, the Americans were more than a match for their adversaries. In the end, however, the North Vietnamese prevailed because their leaders plotted a political and military strategy that was applicable to the situation and were able to command popular support even though they ruled in a dictatorial regime.

Colonel Summers likes to tell the story of the time he went to

Hanoi on a negotiating trip in 1975. Standing at the airport, he got into a conversation with a North Vietnamese colonel. "You know," Colonel Summers said, "you never defeated us on the battlefield." The North Vietnamese pondered a minute. "That may be so," he replied, "but it is also irrelevant."

CHAPTER 3

~~~~~~~~~~~~~~~~~~~~~~~~~~~~

THE CALIBER OF TROOPS

O N A CRISP SPRING DAY at Fort Hood, Texas, Command Sergeant Major Ronald J. Hammer, a huge man with a barrel chest and the arms and fists of a prizefighter, pulled himself up in his chair and leaned across his desk. "I'm telling you," he said, "we are so damn much better today than we were a year ago. We're better because we've eliminated so many problems that sucked up so much of the time before." In his small, wood-paneled office surrounded by pictures, plaques, and mementos of thirty-three years in the Army, Sergeant Major Hammer said the Army in 1983 was bringing in men "with the willingness and the ability to perform." Beyond that, the senior noncommissioned officer in III Corps said, the Army was purging soldiers who did not measure up. In the previous year, 17,000 soldiers have been denied re-enlistment or given "expeditious discharges."

Sergeant Major Hammer's outlook was shared by other sergeants major in the Army and Marine Corps, master chief petty officers in the Navy, and chief master sergeants in the Air Force. The optimism of those senior noncommissioned officers, who know more about what's going on in their services than anyone and who render the most honest judgments, was evidence that the volunteer force was succeeding. After a long struggle from the end of the draft in 1973, the volunteer force by 1985 was on a firm footing despite widespread predictions— and not a few hopes—that it would fail. The young men and women volunteering were, by all measures, the best since World War II. The services had been weeding out or retraining noncommissioned officers who enlisted ten years before, when recruiters would take almost anyone who walked into their offices.

The top noncommissioned officers had twenty to thirty years of military experience, had been hardened by combat and a rigorous life in the field or at sea or in air bases, and had accumulated a deep knowledge of human nature in the raw, all of which made them superior leaders. Advocates of a return to the draft grumbled whenever a flaw appeared, but there was little public support for a peacetime draft and much opposition, not the least that of President Reagan. The Assistant Secretary of Defense for Manpower, Lawrence J. Korb, stated in 1985, "The volunteer force is here to stay."

Not everything was perfect, by any means, nor the future without uncertainty. Race relations were perhaps the best of any large institution in American life, but with a long way to go before blacks were fully accepted and their allegiance unquestioned. The military services, previously nearly all-male organizations, had difficulty in absorbing increasing numbers of women. More young soldiers and sailors married while still young, causing changes in everything from billeting to medical care and putting new demands on leaders who had to consider families in every decision. Demographic projections were troubling, as predictions for more civilian jobs coincided with projections of a decline in the number of young men of military age. In 1985, enlistments fell off slightly, the number of young men and women signing up for delayed entry fell, and the proportion of high school graduates slipped. "It is clear that we have entered a different and more demanding recruiting climate," Mr. Korb told Congress. "We anticipate that recruiting will become increasingly difficult."

Even so, problems in military personnel appeared to be manageable so long as the Congress and the American people were willing to pay competitive and fair wages. A draft would be necessary only if the United States got into a war the size of those in Korea or Vietnam. The Chief of Staff of the Army in 1985, General Wickham, said that "I don't really see a need for a draft in the near term," meaning the foreseeable future. But he immediately qualified that, saying the Army could continue to fill its ranks so long as Congress provided decent pay, educational benefits, re-enlistment bonuses, family programs, and retired pensions. Mr. Korb agreed and added that, contrary to a widely held contention, returning to a draft would cost more than a volunteer force. Training costs, for instance, would go up if soldiers served for two years instead of the current four years.

There was one striking fact: The improvement in military personnel had cost the taxpayer the smallest relative increase in the military budget since President Reagan began his military buildup. In 1980, the last full year of President Carter's administration, military personnel cost $69.4 billion in 1986 dollars. In 1985, the Congress approved $80.3 billion for military personnel, measured in the same dollars, a 15.7 percent increase over five years, including pay for retired military people. In contrast, procurement of arms over that period had gone up 91.9 percent, to $99.6 billion.

Fort Hood, which sprawls across the rolling plains of central Texas, is home for the 1st Cavalry Division, the 2nd Armored Division, and 38,000 soldiers. As the Army's largest post, it fairly reflects the mood and trends of its parent service.

Sergeant Major Lawrence J. Holley, the top soldier in an infantry battalion there in 1983, had recently gone to Fort Knox in Kentucky to escort back twenty-seven soldiers who had completed basic training. Of those, twenty-six were high school graduates; the other had finished the eleventh grade and would get a high school diploma while in the Army. "Five years ago," the sergeant major said, "a soldier was someone who couldn't make it on the outside. But that trend is reversing now. These guys are trainable."

The armed forces have found that a high school diploma is the most reliable indicator of ability and willingness to learn the rudiments of military life. The high school graduate has shown that he or she has the determination to stick to something and thus is more likely to complete not only basic training but the entire enlistment. The diploma shows a beginning of discipline because it has taken some discipline to get through high school—though not so much as recruiting sergeants would like. The diploma usually means that the young man or woman can follow instructions—to use a compass, to read a map, to calculate ranges for mortars, to assemble a machine gun.

In addition, young people in the Army demonstrated a desire to serve. Sergeant Major Malachi Mitchell had asked each of the 2,000 soldiers who had come into an artillery battalion over the last two years why they had joined the Army. The main reasons, he said, were the lack of jobs in the civilian economy, pay that compared well with that outside, an opportunity to learn a skill that could be carried back into civilian life, and a chance to save money for college. Beyond that, Sergeant Major Mitchell said, were individual reasons: "He wanted to get away from home, he'd just broken up with his girl friend, he didn't know what to do with himself." The sergeant major, who had spent more than twenty years in the Army, added, "One thing you don't hear anymore is that old standard: ' I came in the Army to keep from going to jail.' "

At Camp Lejeune in North Carolina, the 2nd Marine Division was on the same upbeat. "We're getting a better caliber troop today," said Sergeant Major Arthur R. Cowan in the spring of 1984. "It's getting harder and harder to get into the Marine Corps," he said. "And if a kid comes to the 2nd Marine Division without a high school diploma, he must get it in night school. The smarter the kid, the easier it is to train him." In addition, Sergeant Major Cowan said, "we've put a lot of marines out of this division over the last couple of years." He estimated that 4,000 had failed to measure up. Company first sergeants had been instructed to tell new marines, "If you deviate from the rules of the road, you'll be instantly unemployed."

Deep in the Atlantic aboard the attack submarine *City of Corpus Christi*, the chief of the boat, Master Chief Petty Officer P. J. Melher, pointed to a boatload of capable young men. The crew was small but highly trained, with twelve officers and 115 chief petty officers and sailors. In a crew whose average age was twenty-three, all but a few had earned ratings as radiomen, electricians, machinist mates, and a dozen other skilled specialists. Many had qualified for the dolphins, the badge that takes a year to earn and signifies wide knowledge of the ship. Those who operated the nuclear propulsion system had been to a year-long nuclear school.

But it takes more than training to get the best out of the advanced technology in the ship. The innate intelligence and skills of the crew made it work. Petty Officer First Class Thomas Clouthier, who operated an electronic panel to plot torpedo runs, said his work was 90 percent instinct. "You have to be smarter than the machine," he said. "You can't follow blindly because the machine makes mistakes." Quartermaster Second Class Ronald Peterson waved his hand at the inertial navigation equipment behind his chart table. "I can sit here and sometimes I can just feel where we are," he said, "and I'll be closer than all that stuff."

Aboard the aircraft carrier *Independence* at the naval base in Norfolk, Virginia, the average age in the crew of 5,000 officers and sailors was twenty-two. Their task was to run an 85,000-ton ship and nearly 100 aircraft that altogether cost $8 billion. It was dangerous work, making medical care essential. Senior Chief Hospitalman D. J. Dupuis said he had people "with a good, basic medical background." Many of the young medics had come into the service after having taken first aid courses in high school, been in a volunteer fire department, or worked in a pharmacy. The senior chief thought the Navy had little trouble getting corpsmen "maybe because we're a little bit more cushy and comfortable than the others."

At Shaw Air Force Base in South Carolina, Chief Master Sergeant James B. Hall, who had been working on aircraft engines for more than twenty years, said, "It takes three to five years to train technicians who can check and repair engines to where you can be sure they are ready to fly." But he said he had those people. Senior Master Sergeant Gerald G. Arruda, in charge of the maintenance shop on the flight line, had most of the trained people he needed, with young airmen coming in from technical school soon working up to a level where they could do their jobs with a minimum of supervision.

In 1973, after thirty years of conscription, the United States returned to its tradition of volunteers for military service in peacetime. When the draft ended, however, the armed forces went into a long slide, hitting bottom about 1980. Recruiters could fill enlistment quotas only by taking young men who barely qualified. Only half of the Army's recruits that year were high school graduates, and large numbers fell into the lowest acceptable mental category, as determined by entrance examinations. Nor could the services retain skilled and experienced people. Pay had fallen behind wages in civilian life, morale was low, and discipline suffered. The Army was short of infantry and artillery sergeants, computer operators, and programmers; the Navy had a shortage of 23,000 technicians and petty officers; the Air Force lacked electronic technicians, air controllers, and communicators; the Marine Corps lacked fire controllers, radar operators, and computer programmers.

On a hot July day in 1980 at an Army recruiting office in a downtown Baltimore shopping mall, Sergeant Robert T. Parham got up from his desk to shake the hand of a young man as he walked in. The stocky, soft-spoken sergeant asked a few questions; within a minute, the young man turned on his heel and walked out. "Burglary," the recruiting sergeant explained. "Besides, he went to a high school for problem kids and he dropped out after the tenth grade. There was no way I could put him in the Army."

Asked how he found out so fast, Sergeant Parham said: "We call it APPLE-MD—age, prior service, physical, legal, education, and marital status and dependents. If he's got problems somewhere in there, there's usually not much point in going on." Turning to the larger question of recruiting, Sergeant Parham said: "I really got chewed out the other day by the first sergeant of an infantry company, a guy I've known for a long time. He was really sore and said we were sending him scum." The sergeant shrugged: "Maybe we are. Or maybe first sergeants always talked like that. All I know is that we're sending him the best we can get out of the system here."

First sergeants were indeed critical of their troops at that time. In an infantry battalion of the 101st Airborne Division at Fort Campbell in Kentucky, first sergeants said many soldiers were immature, poorly educated, and unwilling to accept discipline. First Sergeant Joseph A. Robinson, the senior noncommissioned officer in a combat support company, grumbled: "We're getting a lot of people not educated enough for what we need. The kids can't understand what's going on even though we've reverted to comic book training manuals." The first sergeant of a headquarters company, Thomas S. Loving, said he had recently had a hand in discharging six medics, who are usually handpicked. "They were unsuitable," he said. "They should not have been in the service in the first place."

In addition, noncommissioned officers and technicians were leaving the service in droves. At the Norfolk Naval Base in Virginia, Petty Officer First Class Gregory A. McCann, an electronics technician aboard the destroyer *Radford*, said he was leaving the Navy for two reasons: family separation and money. "I like the Navy," he said, "but I love my family and you can't have both at once." He made about $12,000 a year and expected to get $20,000 after leaving the service—and that for a five-day, forty-hour week instead of a sixty-hour week with a watch on the weekend, even in port.

During 1980, senior officers in Washington marched up to Capitol Hill to lament what the Chief of Staff of the Army, General Edward C. Meyer, called his "hollow army." The Chief of Naval Operations, Admiral Thomas B. Hayward, said the Navy was experiencing a "hemorrhage of talent" and was close to a point "where we may have no realistic alternative but to consider standing down some ships and aviation units." General Lew Allen Jr., Chief of Staff of the Air Force, testified, "Our manpower situation has never been more critical than it is today."

A turnaround began in 1981, after President Reagan took office, with two big jumps in pay and a new acceptance by young people that the service was, as the recruiting ads said, a good place to start. The upswing became breathtaking: In 1984 the services enjoyed the best recruiting year in numbers and quality since the end of World War II. Enlistments were so good the services turned people away; in July, the Army stopped taking recruits and made them wait until the new fiscal year began in October. More than 90 percent of those who enlisted had high school diplomas, a sign to gladden the eyes of drill sergeants. Scores on the entrance tests were equally impressive.

Generals and admirals stumbled over themselves with superlatives as they reported to Congress. Said the Joint Chiefs of Staff in a written report, "The men and women of today's armed forces are better led, better equipped, and better prepared than ever before." General John

A. Wickham Jr., the Army's Chief of Staff, said, "It is the best Army I have seen in thirty-four years of service. We have high quality soldiers, noncommissioned officers, and officers." The Chief of Naval Operations, Admiral James D. Watkins, reported, "The talented youngsters who are now volunteering to serve are well matched to our modern weapons."

Fiscal year 1984 has become the benchmark against which future years are being measured. Recruiting and retention were excellent despite the truck bombing that took the lives of 241 Americans in Beirut and the invasion of Grenada, where 19 were killed—both occurred in October 1983. Among enlistments, the rise in the percentages of high school graduates between 1980 and 1984 looked like this:

| | 1980 | 1984 | | |
	Combined	Combined	Men	Women
Army	54	91	89	100
Navy	75	93	92	99
Marine Corps	78	95	95	100
Air Force	83	99	99	99

The results were equally cheering in the Armed Forces Qualification Test, which tested recruits on reading, mathematics, logical reasoning, and mechanical aptitude. Scores were in five categories: I for well above average, II for above average, III for average, IV for below average, and V for well below average. In categories I–III, the improvement was this:

| | 1980 | 1984 | | |
	Combined	Combined	Men	Women
Army	50	90	88	100
Navy	82	92	92	98
Marine Corps	72	96	96	100
Air Force	91	99	99	99

Moreover, those who enlisted in the armed forces were a cut above their civilian contemporaries. The figures below show the percentage of civilians of military age in each of five mental categories compared with those in military life:

	Civilian	Military
Category I	4	4
Category II	33	37
Category III	32	52
Category IV	24	7
Category V	7	0

In addition, re-enlistments of first-term and career military people jumped in 1984, making the force more experienced, less costly to recruit and train, and better disciplined, with fewer cases of unauthorized absence or courts martial. The Army, which had been re-enlisting about 35 percent of those eligible through the late 1970s, jumped to 52 percent in 1980 and was up to 61 percent in 1982. As standards tightened and more career soldiers re-enlisted, the percentage of first-termers who re-enlisted dropped to 45 percent in 1984. During the same period, re-enlistments of career soldiers rose from 70 percent in 1980 to 83 percent in 1984. The other services, which had not fallen off so much during the trying days of the late 1970s, also improved but not so noticeably.

The recruiting and retention of qualified men and women continued after 1984, although there were bumps in the road. The Army, for instance, missed its recruiting quota by 2 percent in the first quarter of fiscal 1986 while the other services were filling or going over their quotas. But high standards continued to be met. On an average for all four services, 90 percent of the recruits were high school graduates and 94 percent were in categories I-III in mental ability in that quarter. In retention, 49 percent of those eligible to re-enlist after the first term did so, while 84 percent of the career force signed up once again.

A steady decline in the use of illicit drugs is evidence of improved discipline and morale in the armed forces. Surveys done for the Pentagon showed that the percentage of military people who used drugs dropped from 27 percent in 1980 to 19 percent in 1982 to 9 percent in 1985. Much of the drop, according to specialists on drug problems inside and outside of the government, has been due to a vigorous program of education, random urine tests, and stiff penalties. A young member of the service found to have used illicit drugs may be punished and rehabilitated but allowed to remain in the service after the first offense. A second offense brings dismissal, as does a first offense for a noncommissioned officer or officer. The surveys, done by a private research firm, asked 20,000 men and women in the service around the world whether they had used illegal drugs within the past thirty days. The replies were confidential to encourage candor.

In contrast, the National Institute of Drug Abuse reported that 37 percent of the seniors in civilian high schools admitted to having used illegal drugs in 1978, with that figure dropping to 25 percent in 1984 and remaining the same in 1985. High school seniors are a year or two younger than the largest number of the people in the armed forces, the young military people considered the most likely to have used drugs. The comparison, while not exactly parallel, is considered by the specialists close enough to be reasonable.

Young men and women seemed to have clear ideas about why they enlisted. In the recreation room of a quartermaster battalion at Hunter Army Air Base in Georgia, thirty male and female soldiers were asked why they had joined the Army. By far the most common answer: "I needed a job." Not far away, at Fort Stewart, Specialist Fourth Class Ronald D. Colley said he could find only odd jobs in his home town of Savannah and recalled thinking, "Anything has got to be better than this." Sergeant LeRoy Reid had worked as a bricklayer in Charleston, South Carolina, but joined up because "I wanted to do something different."

The pay increases of the early 1980s and the more modest increases of the mid-1980s were attractive, although no one would get rich in the military. Income included base pay and tax-free allowances for quarters and rations, plus medical and dental care, commissaries, clubs and recreational facilities, insurance, and retirement benefits. Bonuses for enlisting into specialized fields and hazard pay for parachuting or demolition disposal attracted some young people. An unmarried recruit in 1986 earned $10,500 a year in base pay and allowances. After four months, that went up to $11,200. A married private first class with a year's service was paid $13,800.

Another reason for enlisting was to learn a skill. At Camp Lejeune, Private First Class Scott Turner, son of a state trooper in New Jersey, enlisted to become a military policeman so that he could eventually join the New Jersey state police or the New York City police. Aboard the destroyer *Scott* in Norfolk, chief petty officers were wary about discussing their technicians. "We had tech reps from General Electric come right on the ship and try to hire our guys away," said a chief. Technical representatives supervised the repair of equipment made by their companies—during which time they could identify and try to recruit able Navy technicians.

To further his education, Sergeant Paul A. Bartolomeo, at Fort Stewart, planned to leave the Army for college within a few months. "They offered me educational money," he said, "and I took it." At that time, a soldier could save $15,000 in four years. A new plan started in 1985 gave a person enlisting for three years a basic benefit of $9,600 but provided another $14,400 for learning a needed skill.

Travel was another inducement. Private Allen W. Hart, of the 24th Division at Fort Stewart, said, "I got tired of living at home; I wanted to get out on my own and I wanted to travel so I thought I would latch onto a traveling organization." He had already been to several posts in the United States and to maneuvers in Egypt. Several months later, his unit went by ship through the Panama Canal to an exercise in California. Most of the thirty soldiers at Hunter Army Air Base had been to Honduras on a training exercise and to Grenada during the invasion there.

Some military officers said young men and women enlisted because they were more patriotic that those of ten years ago. Others pointed to the new conservatism in the 1980s that made military service more attractive. But few young people brought that up; neither patriotism nor politics was likely to be uppermost in the minds of youngsters nineteen years old. The young people did say, however, that the service had become acceptable, even desirable, to many of their peers. Private David A. Nelson, of the 24th Division at Fort Stewart, said that he had enlisted "to meet people and go places" and that many of his friends from high school in Rome, Ohio, had done the same. Specialist Fourth Class Bruce J. Dutton said that when he went on leave to his hometown of Miami, Florida, "people look up to me."

While the young people didn't talk much about patriotism, some said they thought they were contributing to the security of the nation. Submariners aboard *City of Corpus Christi*, asked why they endured three- to six-month separations from families, plus working and living conditions cramped beyond the ken of landlocked mortals, spilled out a litany of reasons. Adventure, a fascination with life under the sea, and pride in the dolphins awarded only to accomplished submariners were all on the list. Liberty in American and foreign ports, admittedly rare, counted. The chance to learn about submarines or machinery and the heavy responsibility put on young men figured heavily. Camaraderie ranked high, as submarine crews are tightly knit from a sense of shared danger. Petty Officer Clouthier pointed to that as he stood in the control room lit only by the glow from red gauges and green monitors. "Every one of the guys on this ship knows he holds 127 heads on a platter," he said. "If any one of them screws up, we could all die."

But most of all, the submariners seemed to have a clarity of purpose, a sense that their duty had genuine meaning. Maybe more than most military people in peacetime, submariners are often operational and live in the real world where they stand guard against a threat from Russian submarines that they frequently encounter through sonar under the sea. The skipper, Captain Bowman, said he sometimes reminded the crew, "What we do is so blasted important, whether the general populace recognizes it or not, that you should be proud."

In a wider sense, young people in the service appeared to understand the purpose of military forces. Charles C. Moskos, a sociologist at Northwestern University who specializes in military personnel, did an extensive survey in 1984 of what soldiers thought about combat. They worried about whether their weapons would work properly and whether their units were well trained, but they had no qualms about defending the American homeland or about rescuing Americans in danger. They were not keen, however, about defending West Germany or South Korea, or intervening in the Middle East, especially if opposition arose at home.

"Soldiers' understanding of the utility of force is firmly anchored in the viewpoint that military commitment should be clearly related to America's defense and requires the support of the citizenry at large," Dr. Moskos wrote. "In their own artless manner, the GI's may be showing more sophistication about the use of force than some of the nation's political leaders."

Among the shortcomings of the services have been certain middle-ranking sergeants and petty officers who enlisted from 1975 to 1980, when the services took barely qualified people. Some of them have managed to stay on even though they have not been so effective as the younger people in their charge. That has caused disciplinary problems because the younger people quickly sense that they are more capable than their immediate bosses. To overcome this difficulty, the services have purged noncommissioned officers who haven't met the new standards. "We probably haven't gotten rid of all the bad ones hiding in the woodwork," said Sergeant Major Hammer at Fort Hood, "but they show up faster than they did before."

The services have been retraining those who have ability and stepping up the training of younger people so they can be promoted faster. The Non-Commissioned Officer's Academy at Fort Hood in 1983 offered retraining for sergeants who missed that schooling earlier; it was mandatory for promising but inexperienced soldiers on promotion lists for sergeant. Under the eye of Sergeant Major E. L. Byrum, the senior sergeant at the academy, and his instructors, the prospective sergeants were taught how to talk to soldiers, to manage time, to drill troops, to inspect a squad, to teach a course in weapons. Sergeant Major Byrum said a student might not be sure of himself when he came to the month-long school. "But when he goes back to his unit," the sergeant major said, "he can take it whether it comes from up above or down below."

To keep young people who have the potential to be noncommissioned officers, the services offered new duty, schooling, and bonuses. Master Sergeant Norman H. Thibault, the 2nd Marine Division's re-enlistment sergeant, said that by the end of a three-year hitch, a good marine had done his turn as a rifleman and had made corporal. When it came time to re-enlist, job security was an important reason for staying in, especially for marines who were married. The Marine Corps offered a change of duty, say to security guard in an American embassy abroad, or to a school for advanced training. If the marine picked a specialty in which there was a shortage, he might be eligible for a bonus up to $16,000. After the second tour, with seven or eight years in the service, retired pay of one-half of base pay for life appeared on the marine's horizon. "Marines today look at that a lot sooner than I did," said Master Sergeant Thibault, who had been in the Marine Corps for twenty-two years. "Marines are also buying insurance a lot faster than we did when we were young." Finally, he said, many marines admitted sometime in a re-enlistment interview, "I do like the Marine Corps."

Aboard the aircraft carrier *Independence*, Senior Chief Dupuis said many Navy corpsmen re-enlisted for job security, to make a job change within the Navy's medical field, or to continue traveling. But the travel often had the opposite effect, with family separation still among the reasons petty officers left. *Independence* had been on a long deployment in which she took part in the invasion of Grenada, supported the marines in Lebanon, and went through winter manuevers with NATO ships in the North Atlantic. By the time the ship reached home port in Norfolk, she had logged 176 days away, of which 158 days had been at sea. Even with that, Senior Chief Dupuis said, "I didn't see one of my forty people want to be somewhere else."

Pay comparable to that outside was another reason people gave for staying in the service. After four years, a soldier, sailor, airman, or marine promoted to sergeant in the Army or Marine Corps, petty officer second class in the Navy, or staff sergeant in the Air Force would earn an annual base salary of $12,110. Added to that would be a tax-free allowance for rations of $1,900 and a tax-free quarters allowance of $3,710 if he or she was married, for a total of $17,720.

Senior noncommissioned officers are a special breed, especially in the combat arms. Men like Command Sergeant Major Hammer, Division Sergeant Major Cowan, Chief Master Sergeant Hall, and Master Chief Petty Officer Melher have survived a rugged competition to reach the top. Of the 1.8 million enlisted men and women in the four services, only 14,000 have made it to the top grade of E-9 and 38,000 to the second-highest rank of E-8, which altogether is the top 3 percent of the enlisted force. Most have had between twenty and thirty years of service, a few even more. Some are veterans of the Korean War; the majority, veterans of the war in Vietnam. They have learned how to get things done and are responsible for the actual training and care of troops, whether in a camp, a school, or on the job. They have acquired a knowledge of human nature and dealing with people that comes almost purely from experience and only slightly from books.

Master Chief Melher, the chief of the boat aboard *City of Corpus Christi*, had risen to a senior position ashore as master chief of a group of submarines after twenty-four years in the Navy when, at the age of forty-two, he asked to return to sea. He had been in submarines armed with ballistic missiles and wanted a tour in an attack submarine. Besides, he said, "I wanted to work with the young guys again." The chief of the boat, addressed as "Cob" by officers, chiefs, and sailors alike, was disciplinarian and counselor, detective when sleuthing was needed, and barber if a young sailor neglected to keep his hair cut. At battle stations, as the most experienced submariner aboard, he was the diving officer.

But mostly the Cob was responsible for keeping the ship squared away. "If the boat is dirty, if the dungarees are dirty," he said, "it's the Cob's fault, not the captain's fault." At the same time, Master Chief Melher, a soft-spoken, self-confident salt, was old enough to be father to the young sailors, many of whom were away from home for the first time—and sometimes acted as such. In port, he had posted on the ship's bulletin board a sign saying "Dial-A-Cob," with his home phone number listed underneath, inviting sailors to call him if they needed help.

In the time-honored manner of master sergeants and chief petty officers, they can be gruff. The first sergeant of an infantry company at Fort Campbell in Kentucky one Monday morning braced a soldier in front of his desk for five minutes of relentless, withering criticism delivered in decibels considerably above that of normal conversation. It ended with the first sergeant lowering his voice to a growl: "If you think you can go out and get drunk on the weekend and then come in here and try to go on sick call on Monday morning, you are sadly, miserably mistaken. Now get out of my sight, I'll deal with you later."

They can also be paternalistic. A platoon sergeant in the field said sometimes, when his troops are fouling up, "you have to stop what you're doing and take 'em in your arms and love 'em a little bit." A first sergeant, hearing that a young soldier had asked for emergency leave because his wife wanted a divorce, told the young man: "Before you go, you come see me. I've seen some trouble in my life, and I can help you."

Many senior noncommissioned officers have acquired an intangible quality known as command presence that comes from experience, knowledge, and ability. It leaves little doubt in anyone's mind, whether a junior enlisted person or a senior officer, about who is in charge. The top noncoms are, as the cliché holds, the backbone of their services, and they know it. That makes them outspoken and unafraid, within the bounds of military courtesy and discipline, to speak their minds to officers or people outside the service.

Not all senior NCOs are paragons of military ability, by any means. As in all bureaucracies, some have risen because they are fast talkers, or have shrewd minds that have figured out how to manipulate the system. Nay-sayers who can find seven different reasons for not doing something, or for getting out of work, have survived. The comic-page image of the master sergeant or chief petty officer with the round beer belly is still a reality. But their ranks are thinning in today's competition.

Senior noncommissioned officers lost some authority during the war in Vietnam and more during the turbulent period after Vietnam when soldiers were products of an era not given to discipline. Officers often took on tasks ordinarily left to sergeants and petty officers. But that has been reversed, with the noncoms resuming their supervision of individual and small-unit training. At an infantry brigade at Fort Campbell in Kentucky, the colonel turned over to the sergeant major and other senior sergeants responsibility for running the firing range when soldiers went out to qualify as riflemen each year. Sometimes the noncoms have to be the nudged. Aboard *Corpus Christi*, a petty officer brought a personnel problem to an officer. The officer listened, offered a word of advice, and said, "You handle it." When the petty officer suggested maybe it would be better if the officer took on the problem, the officer was firm, "Petty Officer Smith, you handle it." As Sergeant Major Byrum, the head of the NCO Academy at Fort Hood, said, "We're getting our credibility back."

Among the successes of the armed forces in the last decade has been the integration of black Americans into the mainstream of military life. It has not been easy: many episodes have been bitter, some violent, and there are still inequities. But the armed forces have done more than most institutions in America to achieve racial equality.

Black Americans have fought for America since Crispus Attucks led a crowd in Boston jeering at British soldiers until the redcoats turned and fired, killing Attucks and several others on March 5, 1770. Later, about 5,000 blacks fought in the Revolution. After that, slavery and racial prejudice prevailed, but Andrew Jackson enlisted the Battalion of Free Men of Color during the battle of New Orleans in the War of 1812. After the Emancipation Proclamation during the Civil War, the Union Army recruited 180,000 black soldiers while the Confederates, in desperation, planned to draft 300,000 black slaves. But the war ended before the Confederacy could do that.

After the Civil War, the Army formed four regiments of black soldiers, who garrisoned posts in the West. The Indians called them "buffalo soldiers," probably referring to the blacks' curly hair. Those regiments fought in the Spanish American War in Cuba, including one battle in which black and white soldiers, mixed up in the confusion, charged up a hill shoulder to shoulder. But in World War I, the four regiments, the most experienced troops in the Army at the time, were not sent overseas. Instead, 400,000 blacks were drafted, mostly as labor troops. A division of black soldiers, the 92nd "Buffalo" Division was formed but was badly trained and led by white officers and did not perform well. Other black Americans were assigned to French divisions, where the 369th Infantry spent 191 days in the trenches, the longest of any American regiment in the war. Over 170 soldiers in that regiment were decorated by the French with the coveted Legion of Honor.

In World War II, some units in the 92nd Division fought well, others did not. But smaller black units fought with distinction, notably the 761st Tank Battalion, which was in combat for 183 days consecutively and won the Presidential Unit Citation. In the Army Air Force, the 99th Pursuit Squadron, and the 332nd Fighter Group distinguished themselves in Europe. But the majority of the 909,000 blacks in the Army were relegated to the quartermaster, transport, and engineer corps as laborers. The Navy, which had enlisted blacks only as mess stewards, and the Marine Corps, which had enlisted none, opened their ranks slightly for blacks as the war progressed.

After World War II, President Truman in 1948 ordered the armed forces to desegregate: "There shall be equality of treatment and opportunity for all persons in the armed services without regard to race, color, religion, or national origin." It was a courageous political decision, coming shortly before an election when Mr. Truman was behind in the polls. The Navy, the Marine Corps, and the newly formed Air Force slowly executed the President's order, but the Army resisted, arguing that white soldiers did not want to associate with black soldiers. Not until 1950 did the Army begin to break up all-black units, sometimes known as "black battalions."

In the Korean War, black soldiers won "the right to fight" in integrated units, although not until 1954, after the war was over, did the Army abolish all of its black units. From then until the war in Vietnam, racial relations were quiet. Black and white soldiers lived and ate together in garrison and trained together in the field. But some discrimination against blacks remained in military justice and in clubs and recreational places. Outside the bases, blacks and whites split into racial groups when they went home or into town on pass. Black servicemen often had difficulty in finding places to live, getting children into schools, and eating in restaurants in the South.

The war in Vietnam stopped progress on race relations in the services, as it did elsewhere in America. Relations between whites and blacks were often tense, openly antagonistic, and sometimes violent. The exception was blacks and whites under fire—the fight for survival wiped out color lines in the foxholes and rice paddies. Racial relations deteriorated so much that, by the end of the war, the Army was in a crisis. The same was true in the Navy, where racial clashes broke out aboard warships. Admiral Elmo R. Zumwalt said in his book *On Watch* that racial relations were much worse than he expected when he became Chief of Naval Operations in 1970. Racial clashes were fought around Marine Corps bases.

An Air Force study in 1971 was devastating. After a tour of training bases, a team of officers and noncommissioned officers submitted a report to their commanding general: "One thing has to be taken and understood by everyone in the Air Training Command: There is discrimination and racism in the command and it is ugly." The team found that unequal treatment is manifested in unequal punishment, offensive and inflammatory language, prejudice in the assignment of details, lack of products for blacks in the base exchange, harassment by security policemen under orders to break up five or more blacks in a group, double standards in enforcement of regulations.

The report concluded, "The cause of this is blatant supervisory prejudice in many cases, but for the most part it was the supervisory indifference to human needs."

The military services, unlike most institutions in civilian life, can regulate behavior, if not attitudes, and thus could enforce orders to rectify wrongs. As Major General R. C. Oaks, a senior personnel officer in the Air Force, said later, "Because we are a controlled society, the Chief of Staff can say 'we are going to do this' and it will happen." Beginning in the 1970s, many units of all services required members to attend classes in which they were taught to avoid racial offense. Racial slurs were forbidden, and whites were made aware of unintended slurs. Evidence of racial bias damaged chances for promotion. Housing was integrated, as were clubs and recreational facilities. Food in mess halls included dishes that appealed to blacks. Post and base exchanges carried magazines and products that blacks wanted. Music in clubs included that favored by blacks.

In 1984, the benchmark recruiting year, 13 percent of the American population between the ages of eighteen and twenty-four was black; 23 percent of the Army's recruits, 17 percent of the new marines, 15 percent of the Navy's seaman recruits, and 13 percent of the Air Force's airman basics were black men and women. The higher proportion in the Army reflected the historical connection between the Army and black Americans and the Army's greater number of positions that could be filled by men and women of lesser skill and education, whether black or white. But the proportion of high school graduates among blacks entering the Army consistently exceeded that of whites.

Black soldiers, sailors, marines, and airmen generally gave the services good marks for their efforts in racial relations and in providing equal opportunities. But they made clear that room for progress was still there.

For Yeoman First Class Gregory D. Lewis, the Navy was a way out of the Deep South. Brought up in Mississippi, he didn't have the money for college and so enlisted in the Navy, intending to stay only for two years. Thirteen years later at the Naval Base in Norfolk, Virginia, he said, "Here, I can make this work. I would not have done any better on the outside." But Yeoman Lewis suggested that life in the Navy had been a struggle: "I've had to prove myself to my superiors—I can read, I can spell, I can run this office." He and other black sailors said there was a difference between what their superiors told them about their work and what was written in their evaluation reports. "A lot of times," Yeoman Lewis said, "I've been told: 'Outstanding job. Attaboy.' But the written markings were a lot lower. All the ghosts in the closet come out."

Gunnery Sergeant William V. Brown of the Marine Corps grew up in a town of blacks, Mexicans, and whites in Kansas where there were no real problems among the ethnic groups. He was drafted during the war in Vietnam; at the induction station, draftees with even numbers went to the Army while those with odd numbers went into the Marine Corps. "I didn't know a thing about the Marine Corps," he said, "other than that's what they said I was in." After fighting in Vietnam, he decided to stay in the Marine Corps because "it was something I could grow into—no one was telling me that this was something I couldn't do." He found the Marine Corps, as have other Americans for 200 years, "something of a cult." Sergeant Brown, on duty at the Marine Air Station at Cherry Point, North Carolina, said that wherever he went in uniform, a former marine would identify himself, "even if he was the biggest bigot in the world."

At Fort Stewart, Georgia, a black soldier promoted to sergeant and given command of a tank asked why he had come into the Army. He chuckled: "To tell you the truth, I was just your basic neighborhood thug." Then he became serious: "I came in the Army to straighten myself out. The Army has taught me a whole lot. It's changed my way of thinking. It's challenging and it feels good when I conquer that." The sergeant's officers hoped he would stay in the Army. "I'd take a kid like that into combat with me anytime," said one officer. The sergeant asked that his name and hometown not be used because "my momma'd kill me if she knew what I just said about being a thug."

Among senior noncommissioned officers, Chief Master Sergeant Johnnie E. Charles of the Air Force grew up in Oklahoma and Detroit and enlisted in 1957 when he was seventeen years old. "It was the first time," he said, "that I was away from a predominately black environment." But a white sergeant took him in hand, advised him to get the equivalent of a high school diploma, taught him how to qualify in his job, and told him that "I want you to be the sharpest man in supply." The chief said he had lived through the days of blatant racism, when base clubs would not accept blacks and barbers refused to cut blacks' hair. Added to that was his marriage to a white woman he met while on duty in England. During the war in Vietnam, Chief Charles was a sergeant in an air transport unit at Da Nang. "That's when I got my real education about the black movement," he said, citing a lack of discipline and bitter tensions that people brought back to the United States. Consequently, he went into the social action program in the Air Force, where "people talk about their hostilities in a controlled environment." Slowly, over time, things changed, especially on bases where blacks were a relatively small number and were absorbed into the life of the unit. Today, he said, "we are head and shoulders above civilian life in avenues to get justice."

Another senior noncommissioned officer in the Air Force, Senior Master Sergeant Titus Andrews, agreed. During his service in pararescue in Vietnam, he said, many blacks were "angry people" who sneered at other blacks who were not militants. "You're still colored," was the jeer directed at him, the senior master sergeant said, "but we're black." Since then, he said, many little things have been corrected, one at a time. "There will always be an underlying current of racial tension, but most of the outdated ideas are out of the Air Force. It's gotten more sophisticated; it's not a missile fired right at you." He noticed slights in the NCO club, at lunch, and at Christmas parties and felt that blacks were sometimes unfairly not selected for schools that would mean faster promotions.

Both Chief Master Sergeant Charles and Senior Master Sergeant Andrews, who were on duty at McGuire Air Force Base in New Jersey, said that camaraderie among blacks and whites of the younger generation was much easier than among their generation. Both said they tried to advise younger black airmen how to succeed in the Air Force, with mixed success as sometimes the younger people elect not to take their advice. Senior Master Sergeant Andrews had a problem with a particularly recalcitrant young man. "There are two things wrong with you," he told the younger airman. "One you can't help, and that is that you're black. The other is that you're not listening to me."

A Marine, Staff Sergeant Jacob I. Wills, came from a family of six girls and nine boys; of the boys, seven had served somewhere in the military except the Marine Corps. But the Marine Corps, Sergeant Wills thought, offered the most discipline, on which he said he thrived. Moreover, he said, "I have a real sense of belonging." Sergeant Wills's experience, however, has not been free of prejudice. When he enlisted in 1973, "it was 'nigger this' and 'nigger that.' But now the letter of the law is enforced and that's stopped." There were also isolated incidents. When Sergeant Wills was a drill sergeant at the marine basic training camp at Parris Island in 1980, a white recruit from Georgia took one look at him and said, "What's this, a nigger in charge?" Then he spat in the sergeant's face. Sergeant Wills said he had to restrain two other drill sergeants, both white, from beating the recruit. But the authorities were notified, and the white was thrown out of the Marine Corps the next day.

Black noncommissioned officers said they sometimes had trouble working for white superiors who didn't like blacks, or in getting white subordinates to obey orders. In the Navy, according to Signalman First Class Wayne E. Bursey, of Texarkana, Texas, "You can't let being in a minority handicap you. But sometimes you have to fight to be accepted." He also said black sailors occasionally asked him for preferential treatment: "They'll say: 'We're both black, so give me a break.' When I don't give them a break, they hate me."

Despite the problems, black Americans have increasingly made careers in the armed forces. While black Americans comprised 12 to 13 percent of the nation's 1985 population, 30 percent of the Army's enlisted soldiers were black, while 20 percent of the Marine Corps, 17 percent of the Air Force, and 13.5 percent of the Navy were black men and women. Over the years, black soldiers have risen steadily in rank. In 1964, only 3 percent of the Army's sergeants major were black; by 1986, that figure had risen to 30 percent; in the Marine Corps, 17 percent of the sergeants major were black. In the middle ranks, 39 percent of the Army's sergeants were black, compared with 13 percent twenty years ago. Blacks, however, have not done so well in the Air Force, where in 1986 only 11 percent of the chief master sergeants were black, and in the Navy, where only 6 percent of the Navy's master chief petty officers were black.

Even with the steady resolution of racial issues, questions about the racial composition of the armed forces continue to be raised by northern liberals who contend that more middle-class white young men should serve and by southern conservatives who question, albeit in euphemistic terms, the wisdom of arming large numbers of blacks.

The questions, summed up, run like this:

- Can blacks, who often have less education that whites and score lower on qualifying exams, learn to operate and maintain highy technical weapons?
- Will units be cohesive and effective in battle if they include large numbers of blacks?
- Is it fair that black Americans form a higher proportion of the military service than of American society as a whole? What will

be the political reaction if, in a future war, blacks suffer casualties at a rate greater than that for whites?

- Will an integrated force lessen the confidence of American allies in the military power of the United States? Will it cause the Soviet Union, which openly distrusts the ethnic minorities in its armed forces, to consider the United States weaker?
- Finally, the most pernicious question of all—will black American soldiers retain their allegiance to the United States and obey orders if ordered to fight against nonwhites at home or abroad? That's the same question asked of Japanese-Americans—but not of German-Americans or Italian-Americans—in World War II. It is a question that some white Americans ask about black Americans today, but not about Russian-Americans or East European–Americans.

Martin Binkin and Mark J. Eitelberg, analysts of military personnel issues, raised the question in their book *Blacks and the Military*, published by the Brookings Institution.

Suspicion that black troops might be unwilling to carry out their assignments in certain domestic situations—a suggestion that is understandably reprehensible to many members of the black community—cannot be dismissed out of hand. The deployment of troops that share a racial or ethnic bond with an adversary poses difficulties. Less serious is anxiety about foreign involvements since, with the unlikely exception of an American intervention on the side of whites in a conflict against blacks (for example, to support the South African government). It is difficult to conceive of a situation in which black allegiance would be tested.

Black Americans, many of whom see military service as a road out of the ghetto, have not lamented what some whites consider to be racially imbalanced forces. But some have criticized whites for raising the question. Carl Rowan, who is black and a longtime newspaper columnist and television commentator, wrote in 1980, "Few Americans will come right out and say these blacks are too uneducated or too cowardly or too anything else to entrust the nation's defenses to them, so many take the tack of pretending great concern that blacks not wind up bearing an unfair share of the burden."

Army officers have answered questions about the allegiance of black soldiers partly by pointing to their performance in 1967 during riots in sections of Washington that were inhabited largely by blacks. About 30 percent of the soldiers ordered to Washington to help control the civil disturbances were black. Officers who served with the black soldiers said they performed well and there was no question about their allegiance, discipline, or obedience to instructions.

More recently, Lieutenant General Maxwell R. Thurman, chief of Army personnel in 1982 and later a general and Vice Chief of Staff, said the large percentage of blacks in the Army "doesn't cause me any problem at all." General Thurman, a North Carolinian, disputed the assumption that black soldiers would suffer a higher portion of the casualties in combat. Much would depend, he said, on the kind of fighting, whether largely by infantry units, in which black soldiers were about the same ratio as in the rest of the Army, or artillery duels, in which a relatively larger number of black soldiers would be exposed to danger. He said the number of blacks and whites in a unit varied from month to month, making predictions difficult. The general further said no evidence had been produced to support the contention that large numbers of black soldiers in a unit eroded its cohesion. Imbalances in various career fields were due to computers matching the needs of the Army with aptitude tests to select soldiers for specialized training. "The computer," General Thurman said, "is color blind." As to whether black soldiers would perform well against non-whites, General Thurman said flatly, "We don't have any evidence percolating up through the chain of command that would substantiate those allegations."

The trauma about women in the service—to which General Vessey, when he was Chairman of the Joint Chiefs of Staff, referred in testimony before Congress—arises from the obvious issue of whether women will distract men from their duties. The question is unanswered even though men and women in the services have been seeking for ten years to find ways to deal with each other fairly, without paternalism or sexual harassment by men and without women seeking special treatment by offering sexual favors. Another obvious question is whether women have the physical strength and stamina to endure military life; the answer appears to be yes, except in a few cases. In some fields, women have demonstrated more skill than men, such as electronic repair work that takes dexterity and patience. A less obvious question, far from answered yet, is whether women have the psychological and emotional capacities to handle the stresses of miltary duty. There is a cultural issue: Western civilization, at least in ideal and theory, has accorded women a protected and privileged place. Does that mean women should be shielded from military service or, in a modern world of women's rights, obligated to undertake military service? At its deepest, the basic instinct for human survival may lie beneath these questions: If men go off to die in battle, some will survive to perpetuate the species, but women must be preserved to bear children. Whatever the case, America is in the midst of an extraordinary social experiment, the outcome of which is far from determined.

The most troubling problem for day-to-day operations is sex. Military traditionalists contend that having women serve alongside men will inevitably cause men to neglect their duties, sometimes to assist women, other times to engage in sexual dalliance. At worst, they argue, it will lead to dating, sexual encounters, and possibly rape. In response Jean Ebbert, a columnist for the *Navy Times* who was once a naval officer, asserted that while some of those relationships could be romantic or erotic, others would be of a sibling nature. She pointed to men and women who share dormitories on college campuses or group houses as young adults. "Fall in love with good ol' Phil?" she wrote. "Preposterous—why, he's just like my brother."

Nonetheless, marriages between male and female members of the service have become more common. Some say their marriages are strong because both partners share values and both understand the nature and demands of military duty. The big problem is transfers, and whether the service can accommodate sending both spouses to new posts at the same time. Senior officers say their services are trying, but caution that the needs of the service must come first.

Beyond that, pregnancy has been a difficult issue. Initially, all services required women who became pregnant to resign on grounds that they could not perform their duties and raise a child at the same time. Under pressure from women's groups, pregnant women have been allowed in many cases to remain in the service. The Army treats pregnancy as a "temporary illness" unless the mother seeks a discharge. The Air Force and Navy decide case by case, while the Marine Corps was the last to permit pregnant women to stay in the service. A study in 1984 showed that 45 percent of the 2,300 women who had enlisted in the Marine Corps in 1979 had dropped out, half leaving because they were pregnant. The others left because of disciplinary problems, medical disabilities, or inability to adjust to life in the Marine Corps. The other services had lower rates of dropout, but pregnancy was still among the leading causes.

Single parents, most often women, are equally troubling. An attorney in New York at the National Center on Women and Family Law, Phyllis Gelman, has asserted: "The number of single mothers has more than doubled in the past 10 years, and they form the poorest part of our population. . . . Service in the armed forces is a way out of poverty, a way to support their children, to have full and proud lives as Americans." The opposing position of the armed forces was summed up in a statement by the Army and Air Force in a legal dispute:

Neither the Army nor the Air Force nor their reserve components are federal jobs programs, child welfare agencies, or "social experiments" in opportunities for married or unmarried parents. The services' sole mission is to have ready and available human resources prepared to fight wars in defense of the United States.

The outcome of that issue is far from settled.

American women have been in military service since the earliest days of the Republic. Women fought alongside men in the Revolution, in the Civil War, and on the plains of the West. They served as military nurses in World War I and World War II, and in the latter conflict were inducted into the armed forces to free men for combat. At the end of the war in 1945, there were 266,300 women in the services, half of them in the Army and Army Air Force. The Women's Armed Services Act of 1948 provided that women could be regulars but were limited to 2 percent of personnel strength. Only 18,000 women were on active duty the following year, again about half in the Army. During the Korean War, that jumped to 45,000; later the number fluctuated between 30,000 and 35,000 until 1967, when the 2-percent ceiling was abolished.

The beginning of the volunteer force in 1973 opened new doors for women. In June 1973, six months after the end of the draft, 55,400 women were in uniform, 20,700 of them in the Army. Over the next ten years, the number of women in the services more than tripled and reached 203,300 in 1984.

But in the early 1980s, the services paused to review the role of women, closing some fields for fear women would be in combat. In July 1983, Secretary of Defense Weinberger issued a directive:

It is the policy of this department that women will be provided full and equal opportunity with men to pursue appropriate careers in the military services for which they qualify. This means that military women can and should be utilized in all roles except those explicitly prohibited by combat exclusion statutes and related policy.

After that, the Air Force opened all but 5 of 230 enlisted fields to women, blocking out aerial gunnery and para-rescue. In the Army, 302 of 351 military occupational specialties are open to women. The Navy has opened all but 17 of 99 enlisted ratings to women, 13 closed because of combat restrictions and 4 more because they require extensive sea duty.

Without doubt, the armed forces have been recruiting qualified women. Almost all female recruits have been high school graduates, and nearly all have scored in the top three categories on the Armed Forces Qualification Test. Once in the service, women have been promoted at the same rate as men in the lower-ranking grades and slightly faster than men in the higher grades. But the number of women in the services leveled off in the mid-1980s, with 9.8 percent of the enlisted force being women in late 1985. Projections showed little growth, presumably because large numbers of women do not see the armed forces as offering good job opportunities.

The proportion of enlisted women in each service in 1986 varied, from 11.8 percent in the Air Force to 10.7 percent in the Army and 9 percent in the Navy down to 5.1 percent in the Marines Corps. The Air Force, with its emphasis on high technology, has a large supporting element and thus has many duties that women can perform out of the combat zone. The Marine Corps, on the other hand, is heavy with combat forces and draws much of its support from the Navy, and so has relatively few places for women. The Navy has a different problem, known as sea-shore rotation. Sailors assigned to ships for, say, three years, are then due an assignment ashore. But if women, whose billets at sea are limited, have filled the positions ashore, male sailors must then do longer tours at sea. For that reason, the Navy has sought to open up billets for women on noncombatant ships.

Women in the services give mixed reviews on what has been done so far. Senior Chief Petty Officer Joan F. McErlean, a legal assistant at the Norfolk Naval Base in Virginia, liked the opportunities for promotion. But she found male officers unsure of themselves when directing female subordinates and said they often asked her to correct junior female sailors rather than do it themselves. Chief Air Traffic Controller Linda Dunn, at the Naval Air Station in Oceana, Virginia, was married to a Navy chief petty officer and had three children. She said she had been treated fairly. "I think the attitude toward women in the Navy has improved quite a bit," she said in an interview with *Navy* magazine. "Women with families are accepted better now."

Dealing with men, as superiors or subordinates, has troubled many women. Carol L. Denson, an aviation maintenance administrative mate first class at the Norfolk Naval Base, said: "I am really being treated by the men as if I don't know much. Some of the men are afraid of having women in positions of authority. It's hard to assert your authority because the men will go around you to a male superior, and he'll take their side." Karen I. Castro, a data processing technician second class, agreed: "I can't say you're treated equally. The older men look down on women as being dumb." She also said: "I've been getting a lot of flak from the men about sea duty, who say: 'You take our shore billets.' " But the prospect of sea duty on a noncombatant ship caused other concerns for Petty Officer Castro, who was the single parent of a two-year-old daughter. "I'm up for sea duty," she said, "and I don't know what I'm going to do."

At the Marine Air Station, Cherry Point, North Carolina, two female sergeants liked the Marine Corps but said they resented the attitude of men toward them. Sergeant Alicia D. Thompson, who is black, said, "I haven't suffered any prejudice because of my race but I've experienced prejudice for my gender." Male subordinates tried to take advantage of her in an earlier day. "Not any more," she said, emphatically. "When I give an order to a PFC, I say 'please' but there's no doubt about what I want done. And if it's not done, we're going to have a little talk." Sergeant Graciela M. Nollner agreed, saying that "the men will try to put one over on us, but we're not that gullible."

Sergeant Nollner, like many women in the service, had been troubled by gossip. When she worked in the motor pool, she invited fellow marines to her backyard on a Saturday afternoon for a picnic of Mexican food and beer. The next week, the master sergeant in charge of the motor pool said he had heard rumors of "an orgy" at her place. Sergeant Nollner said she bristled. "You know me better than that, Top," she told him. "Yes," said the senior sergeant, "but I had to make sure." Sergeant Nollner said she paid more attention to appearances after that, and invited a married couple when she asked people to come over to her apartment until she herself was married.

The Marine Corps has changed its rules about arming women and now requires women to learn to fire rifles and pistols to protect themselves if necessary. Sergeant Thompson thought that a good idea. "If it ever comes to war, and we get overrun," she said, "what are we going to do, throw pencils at them?" Sergeant Nollner added: "We're taught combat, but we're also taught to be ladies." Women marines take classes in etiquette and personal appearance. Sergeant Thompson said on Okinawa one day, a sergeant major let out a stream of curses with every four-letter word she'd ever heard and some she hadn't. She stopped him. "Don't you cuss at me, Sergeant Major," she said, "I'm a lady."

The base sergeant major at Cherry Point, William R. Boggs, a veteran of the Marine Corps and combat in Vietnam, said that the presence of women had disturbed some of his contemporaries and their officers. "Some of the guys," he said, "are intimidated by the girls. And a lot of the officers don't know how to mark a woman marine." He and Sergeant Major Maurice R. Parent were vigorously critical of another senior sergeant, whom they did not name, for demanding sexual favors from a young woman marine. "That man," said Sergeant Major Boggs, "has disgraced the noncommissioned officers corps." To avoid gossip, and to avoid having a disgruntled woman marine charge sexual harassment, the sergeants major said, many senior sergeants would not talk with a woman marine in their offices without a third person present. Sergeant Major Boggs said he had enough confidence in his reputation not to do that—but made sure the door to his office was open whenever a woman marine came in to see him.

A senior master sergeant in the Air Force, Ruth A. King, said the role of women in the Air Force had improved steadily during her nineteen years of service. "We are looked at today as professional women," she said, "and we are earning respect. We are their equals in job responsibility." Senior noncommissioned officers expected more of their female subordinates, and there was less need for a woman to prove herself before she was given responsible work. Because she had been in the Air Force for so long, Senior Master Sergeant King said, some young female officers occasionally asked her for advice on how to deal with male superiors. On the other hand, male officers asked for advice because they were not sure of regulations about women and were uncertain as to whether, for instance, a woman should be assigned to duty at night.

A younger noncommissioned officer, Staff Sergeant Debra J. Coffey, had enlisted in 1978, three years after she had graduated from high school, to get away from her small hometown in Pennsylvania. Her first years had not been happy in the Air Force as she had been sent to an American base in Turkey, where she was homesick. In addition, "they treated me like a little girl." After she returned home, however, and became a noncommissioned officer, things got better. "I seem to be treated fairly now," she said. In dealing with her subordinates, Sergeant Coffey thought the men competitive with her while the women saw her as a "mother figure." In response, she said, "I tend to be a little harder on the females" in the quality of their work and in discipline.

Both Senior Master Sergeant King and Sergeant Coffey said that gossip about women was often irritating but that they had to pay attention to appearances. When she had been on duty for a year at

Sondestrom Air Base in Greenland, Senior Master Sergeant King was the top-ranked female noncommissioned officer. She and the senior male noncommissioned officer met regularly to devise ways to bring gossip out in the open where it could be quashed. At McGuire Air Force Base in New Jersey, they said they were careful when counseling a male subordinate or in going to see a male superior that a third party was present, or that they met in a public place, or that they took some other precaution to make sure no one misunderstood.

Mr. Moskos, of Northwestern University, interviewed Army women on temporary duty in Honduras in 1984. The work was hard and the living conditions primitive but he found "the morale and commitment of the American soldiers, male and female alike, were remarkably high." At the Honduran air base at Palmerola, American soldiers lived in segregated wooden huts that had electricity for lights, stereos, and television.

The females' huts were cleaner, more decorative, and more likely to have family photographs than the males' huts. Members of the opposite sex were forbidden to visit each other's huts at any time. Latrines were outdoors, screened, and sexually segregated. Menstruation did not seem to be a worry and apparently was not invoked as an excuse from work.

At an aviation battalion at Cucuyagua, men and women shared large tents, with a blanket hung between male and female sections, which offered only minimum privacy. Showers were only partly screened, so women took turns standing watch while others showered. Because the men and women worked together, most men respected the women's need for privacy. "The women's concerns with personal privacy rather quickly eroded over the course of the field experience," Mr. Moskos said. "Within a time span of a week or so, the prevailing female attitude developed into one of 'let 'em look.'

"Women worked as effectively as men," he said.

Over the course of an extended field deployment, the women were increasingly being judged as individuals, not by their sex. The person universally regarded as the most outstanding driver of heavy vehicles over treacherous mountain roads was a woman. When really strenuous labor had to be performed (such as heavy lifting), men would help the women. That was no more begrudged than when a stronger male would help a weaker male in a similar situation.

Before the volunteer force, there was an old saying: "If the Army wanted you to have a family, they would have issued you one." The

Navy's variation was: "If the Navy wanted you to have a wife, she would have been in your seabag."

That attitude has changed. As General John A. Wickham Jr., the Army's Chief of Staff in 1983, said,

The Army's willingness to acknowledge the critical role families play in its mission has moved from studied neglect through ambivalent and selective inclusion of families in the military community to a sense that the development of a family philosophy is an institutional imperative.

The reason is the large number of young married soldiers, sailors, marines, and airmen today. Before, senior noncommissioned officers were almost the only enlisted people who had families. Today, about one-third of the first-term enlisted men and women are married. Some officers have speculated that decent wages have made it possible for young enlisted men and women to marry earlier. Others have suggested that people who marry at a young age are more likely to come into the service because they are eager for jobs.

Whatever the reason, the presence of thousands of young married men has caused profound changes in the responsibilities of leaders, from small units to large commands. Leaders today must concern themselves with the welfare of the families of their troops because a soldier in the field or a sailor at sea will be distracted, and thus will detract from readiness, if he is worried about his family.

Corporal Randal L. Kaster of the Marine Corps typified the young married man in the service today. In the spring of 1980, he married a girl he'd known since grammar school in his hometown in Indiana. Two weeks later, he graduated from high school, and five days after that he went to boot camp, or basic training, at Parris Island, South Carolina. His wife remained at home with her mother and worked at two jobs to save money to fly to South Carolina to see him graduate from boot camp. Then they drove to his new duty station in Meridien, Mississippi, where they had a difficult time living in a trailer on his pay as a private first class because she couldn't find a job. A transfer to Camp Pendleton in California was equally difficult because housing was so expensive. But after eighteen months they were able to move into base housing that was less expensive. When his four-year enlistment was over, the Marine Corps offered him a $16,000 bonus to reenlist as an aviation operations clerk. At Cherry Point, they had to wait only a month for base housing for themselves and their baby.

With finances better, Corporal Kaster said, their main problem was the possibility he would be sent to Okinawa for a year. That would be an unaccompanied tour, where the corporal would leave his wife and baby behind. "She doesn't mind it when I go off for two weeks or even a month," Corporal Kaster said. "But the unaccompanied tour, she's really scared about that. The single guys want to go, but they weren't picked. That's the big thing she doesn't understand." He was thinking of taking his wife and child with him even if he had to pay their way and find housing for them on Okinawa.

Young married people have caused changes in housing and eating arrangements, control over troops, unit cohesion, and discipline. Housing is a severe problem in many places. Some young married people live on base, where often the only housing available is temporary housing, some of it built in World War II. Others must live off base, where housing can be expensive. At Fort Ord, California, sergeants were asked what their biggest problem was. The unanimous answer: housing for their soldiers. Housing on the post was insufficient, even with old houses refurbished, forcing many to live around Monterey, an affluent resort where rents started at $800 a month. "Man," said one sergeant, "those are New York and Washington prices." Solutions included having soldiers live in Salinas, which a sergeant said was a "good working-class town" but was more than thirty minutes' drive from Fort Ord. Post staff officers had asked local businesses to build a trailer court on government land where soldiers could live in low-cost mobile homes and had persuaded landlords to reduce deposit requirements.

First sergeants expressed mixed feelings about troops living out of the barracks where they could not be reached so easily. An Army first sergeant lamented that "it cuts into my control over the troops," but a marine first sergeant shrugged it off, saying that "the world changes and you have to change with it." When a unit is on alert and must be ready to move within hours, soldiers are either kept on post or must be reachable within minutes by telephone. Frequent drills test the ability of a unit to assemble.

Noncommissioned officers in ground combat units worried about cohesion, that intangible bond of soldiers or marines to one another that comes from living, eating, and serving together. With large numbers of troops going home at night instead of being in the mess hall and barracks, leaders were concerned the bonds would be weakened. But so much time is spent in the field or at sea or deployed on operations that the effect of married people on cohesion seemed less than the turbulence churned up by constant transfers.

On the other hand, married people caused fewer disciplinary problems. The young trooper who goes home to his wife and family is not downtown with his friends drinking and getting into fights. All of the traditional measures of disciplinary problems, from drinking to un- authorized absence to venereal disease, have dropped as the number of married people has gone up.

Confronted with the needs of families, battalion commanders, squadron commanders, and ship captains have established volunteer networks of wives of officers and noncommissioned officers to help families of younger people. Lieutenant Colonel Harry W. Mohr, an infantry battalion commander at Fort Ord, puts out a newsletter and holds regular meetings with soldiers and their wives. He sends a letter to each wife before the battalion goes overseas for maneuvers to explain who will be available to help them while their husbands are gone. Like other commanders, he designates an officer as "stay-behind com- mander" to look after families while troops are away. Mrs. Mohr, who teaches English to Hispanic Americans and foreign wives of sol- diers who married in Europe or Korea, has given her telephone num- ber to everyone in the battalion. A telephone network keeps the battalion's wives informed about the soldiers while they are abroad.

At an ever-widening number of bases, commanders have set up family service centers to help young married couples. The commander remains responsible for the welfare of his people, but the family service center, staffed with military and civilian specialists, takes on the bur- den of the day-to-day work.

Outside the Norfolk Naval Base, a family service center seeks to provide the social support of family and friends that young people leave behind when they go away to join the service. "We're trying to build a network to sustain people," said a social worker there. That means giving information that will help youngsters to find housing, assist wives to find jobs, and tell young families what Navy or private medical facilities are available. In that Navy community of 90,000 people, 400 babies a month are born to couples in which the father's average age is 21 and the mother's 19.

Social workers in family service centers report that many of the problems facing young people are financial. At home and in high school, they have not been taught how to balance a checkbook, to make a budget so that expenditures do not exceed income, to pay credit installments when they are due. The centers, either individually or in classes, give instructions on financial management. Specialists also warn newcomers to beware of unscrupulous merchants who offer things they cannot afford or who take advantage of their inexperience to sell cars, stereo equipment, and furniture at inflated prices or high interest rates. The centers give legal advice on drawing up wills or powers of attorney, or signing leases with landlords. Day-care centers for small children are set up because so many military spouses work.

The center helps with two problems that can be traumatic for young people: the absence of the husband at sea or in the field and the transfers that are an inevitable part of military life. Young wives away from home the first time feel physically vulnerable in a strange place, so the center teaches them how to make their homes secure and how to move around the community safely. On moving, which can be frightening for the inexperienced, the center provides information about how to make the move and what to expect on the other end. Many centers have storerooms with pots and pans, sheets and towels, and other household necessities for a young military couple to set up housekeeping until they can get their own things.

For much of American history, the nation has obtained soldiers by relying on citizens who volunteered. But conscription has several times been a contentious issue. When Secretary of War James Monroe proposed during the War of 1812 that a draft be instituted, Representative Daniel Webster of Massachusetts rose in the House on December 9, 1814, to thunder:

The Constitution is libelled, foully libelled. The people of this country have not established for themselves such a fabric of despotism. They have not purchased at a vast expense of their own treasure and their blood a Magna Carta to be slaves. Where is it written in the Constitution, in what article or section is it contained, that you may take children from their parents, and parents from their children, and compel them to fight the battles of any war, in which the folly or the wickedness of Government may engage it?

Webster's view prevailed until the Civil War, when both the Union and the Confederacy resorted to conscription. After that, the draft was not revived until May 1917, a month after the United States entered World War I. The Supreme Court ruled in January 1918 that the power of the Congress to raise and maintain armies permitted conscription. The court said that a citizen could be required to undertake "his supreme and noble duty of contributing to the defense of the rights and honor of the nation" without "the imposition of involuntary servitude in violation of the prohibitions of the Thirteenth Amendment."

The first peacetime draft was enacted in September 1940, after World War II had started in Europe, but was limited to 980,000 men, to one year of service, and to duty within the Western Hemisphere. A year later, the draft was extended for eighteen months by a margin of fifteen votes in the Senate and one vote in the House, a measure of the antipathy for conscription even when war threatened.

As World War II drew to a close, President Truman, General George C. Marshall, and, later, President Eisenhower favored universal military training for all young men. But political opposition was too strong, and the draft was allowed to lapse briefly until the Cold War began. It was resumed under a new law in 1948. That law was in effect through the Korean War and the war in Vietnam, when abuses were widespread. President Nixon, recognizing that any post-Vietnam consensus would require an end to the draft, ceased conscription in 1973.

Hardly had the volunteer force begun, however, than calls for a return to the draft came from some military officers, northern liberals, and southern conservatives who contended that the services needed a continuous influx from a cross section of America. They asserted that the poor quality of volunteers, in a day when pay and benefits were less than those in civilian life and the distaste for military service evident, could be avoided with a return to the draft. The draft was seen as a way to build up the reserves in the event the United States was again engaged in combat abroad. Conscription was further considered a way to maintain racial balance. Critics of the volunteer force contended that military service fostered patriotism and should be required as a civic duty. An unspoken reason was that officers had gotten accustomed to leading conscripts, or people who had gone into the Navy or Air Force to escape being drafted into the Army. A drafted force was considered easier to control because compulsory service meant officers could give orders knowing that enlisted men could not evade.

After the Soviet invasion of Afghanistan in late 1979, President Carter proposed that draft registration be resumed; Congress agreed in the summer of 1980, after a long, bitter fight. President Reagan, during his campaign for the presidency, said he opposed both draft registration and peacetime conscription. Once in office, he reversed himself on draft registration under pressure from the Joint Chiefs of Staff, who asserted that registration could speed conscription if the United States got into a war—and if Congress approved a draft.

By the middle of the 1980s, calls for resuming a peacetime draft had largely subsided because the volunteer force was attracting large numbers of well-qualified young men and women. But there were warning signs for the future.

The Bureau of the Census has predicted that the number of young men between the ages of eighteen and twenty-one, the primary source of recruits, would decline from 7.8 million in 1985 to 6.6 million in 1995. One-quarter of those young men would be mentally, physically, or morally unfit; another quarter would probably be in college. In 1990, for instance, 3.7 million young men would be available for military service. Since 28 percent of the armed forces are between the ages of eighteen and twenty-one, the Defense Department would need 616,000 of those men, or one of every six. When 65,000 women of the same age are included in the calculation, the requirement for men would drop to one in nearly seven.

The arguments against returning to the draft are powerful. Among the most salient: No draft would be fair unless all young men, except those mentally, physically, or morally unfit, were inducted.

So long as the peacetime force remains between 2 million and 2.5 million men and women, the services cannot absorb all available young men of military age. The needs of the services for the future, even if projections for recruiting turn out to be optimistic, would require only a small fraction of those eligibile. In 1990, for instance, nearly 1.7 million young men wil become eighteen years old. Of those, 1.3 million would be eligible for a draft with no deferments. The services have projected a recruiting quota of 278,000 for that year. If all were drafted and none allowed to volunteer, the services would take about one of every five eighteen-year-olds. No matter how random a lottery or fair any other system might be in selecting that one young man, four others would stay home without being required to serve. The inequity of that is inescapable.

If, as is sometimes argued, drafted men were to be required to serve for two years at salaries lower than those in civilian life, or than volunteers were paid in the military service, they would be doubly taxed, once for their time and again for their money. In contrast, paying men and women in the military service fair wages spreads the burden more evenly over the entire population.

The military effectiveness of a conscripted versus a volunteer force has been long debated, without resolution. There is evidence that soldiers who serve because they want to serve make better soldiers, as did British volunteers against Argentine conscripts in the Falklands in 1982. There is no evidence that a drafted force would be more effective than a volunteer force. General Vessey, when he was Chairman of the Joint Chiefs of Staff, said he preferred a volunteer to a conscripted force. "I have looked at those nations with compulsory military service," he said, "and I want to tell you that our armed forces are far better."

Racially, a return to the draft would presumably include an attempt to bring about a force in which blacks and other minorities would serve in the same proportion as their numbers in American society. But a total draft could deny a young black or a young white volunteer the position he wanted, while others would be compelled to serve against their will. If volunteers were permitted alongside conscripts, as during the wars in Korea and Vietnam, the services would have a less-than-cohesive mix of those who wanted to be there and those who didn't—not a combination destined for high morale.

Advocates of a return to the draft assert that conscription is necessary to enlarge the armed forces. But the size of the armed forces and how those forces are to be raised are separate questions and should be addressed apart. The nation should first determine the size of the force needed, then decide whether to build that force with volunteers, with conscripts, or with a combination.

Politically, an effort to revive military conscription in peacetime could regenerate the dissent of the Vietnam era. Many military officers, including some that might otherwise favor a draft, are not willing to risk jeopardizing already tenuous public support by returning to conscription. Some advocates of conscription argue that a draft would foster patriotism and a sense of service to the country. But opponents contend that the armed forces have been instituted to deter and to fight wars and should not be teaching civics, a responsibility that belongs in the home and the schools.

Lastly, the absence of a peacetime draft places a check on the power of government, a basic principle on which the United States was founded. Nearly all students of military affairs agree the United States could not sustain a prolonged, large-scale war without enlarging the armed forces with a draft. But there is no law now that would permit a President to resume the draft. Conscription could be revived only by an act of Congress. Legislation proposing a draft would therefore become the focal point of a debate over the national interest at hand and the threat to it. If the nation approved a draft, it could be unified to go to war. If the nation decided the threat was not enough to go to war, the people and the Congress could apply a strong brake to whatever an administration had in mind. The absence of conscription restricts a President more than the War Powers Resolution, which permits the President to send American forces into hostilities for sixty days but requires him to obtain the consent of Congress to continue. With the War Powers Resolution, the President can only engage the United States in ventures on the scale of the invasion of Grenada. Without the draft, a President cannot engage the nation in another Korea or Vietnam.

Daniel Webster, as he argued against peacetime conscription in 1814, railed,

Who will show me any constitutional injunction, which makes it the duty of the American people to surrender every thing valuable in life, and even life itself, not when the safety of their country and its liberties may demand the sacrifice, but whenever the purposes of an ambitious and mischievous Government may require it?

CHAPTER 4

~~~~~~

STANDING WATCH

LIEUTENANT WILLIAM MILES, piloting an F-14 jet fighter 22,000 feet above the aircraft carrier *Constellation* in the Gulf of Oman, picks up on radar two large planes 200 miles away heading toward the carrier. The Navy pilot and his wingman in another supersonic F-14 turn to meet two Soviet IL-38 long-range transports and circle around to come up behind them. The wingman eases into position just behind the two Soviet planes while Lieutenant Miles guides his fighter to the right and slightly to the rear, the computer-controlled swept wings of his F-14 Tomcat inching forward as he slows down. "The Russians looked out and waved," the compact, soft-spoken lieutenant says later. "I didn't wave back."

Meantime, two more F-14s on alert on the carrier's flight deck, their pilots in the cockpit and missiles slung under the wings, are trundled to the steam catapults and launched with a bellow of jet blast. As the planes shoot over the edge of the flight deck, they dip out of sight for an anxious moment, then pick up airspeed and climb swiftly to intercept the Russians and to relieve Lieutenant Miles and his wingman. As a matter of course, the carrier puts up F-14s with full loads of fuel to "escort" intruders so that fresh planes can sustain a watch if the Soviets loiter or start something hostile; it thus avoids having the F-14s run low on fuel in a tense situation. This time, the four-engine Soviet planes lumber steadily to the north, heading over Iran to the Soviet Union. The F-14s follow them for 200 miles, then turn back to resume their "cap" over the carrier. An operations officer says afterward the Soviet aircraft had come from a base at Aden on the Red Sea, had flown over the American carrier *John F. Kennedy* to the southwest, "then came to check us out."

Lieutenant Miles and his wingman, having been relieved, return to land on the carrier. Each thunders in at 130 miles an hour, chops back on the throttle to drop onto the flight deck and to catch a tailhook on an arresting cable as thick as a man's wrist stretched across the deck. As soon as he touches down, the pilot shoves the throttle forward in case the plane misses the hook and he has to bolt back into the air. Otherwise he would roll forward to pitch off the flight deck into the sea. But Lieutenant Miles catches the hook and comes to an abrupt, gut-wrenching halt, throttling back to complete what carrier pilots call the "controlled crash."

The episode over the Gulf of Oman, where the carrier *Constellation* steamed to maintain a United States military presence close to the troubled region around the Persian Gulf, was a small piece of the action in which American forces are engaged every day. The basic mission of the forces afield is to deter the Soviet Union or other possible adversaries from military aggression against the United States or its allies. They maintain a presence at home and abroad to reassure Americans and allies that forces in being are committed to their defense. Most of all, the armed forces train hard every day, much the way an athletic team practices, with a critical difference—the forces hope they don't have to play in a real game. Often, the functions of standing watch, providing a presence, and training are accomplished at the same time, as when marines practice amphibious landings on a beach in Kenya to demonstrate that the United States can bring military power to bear in that region. From time to time, the forces are ordered to engage in open hostilities, as in Lebanon, Grenada, or the Gulf of Sidra and Libya.

American forces operate today in what President Kennedy once called a "twilight that is neither war nor peace." They march and sail and fly in a real world that is sometimes just short of a shooting war, a world in which many of them, like Lieutenant Miles, are in frequent contact with potentially hostile forces. It is a world in which soldiers, sailors, marines, and airmen are in constant jeopardy, sometimes from adversaries but more from dangerous weapons and training regimes. It is a world of long, tiring hours with weeks and months of separation from families in inhospitable jungles or deserts or icy waters far from home.

To prepare for war and to keep the peace, the forces have been charged with spanning what military people call the spectrum of conflict. That encompasses getting ready for:

- Protracted nuclear war, which requires bombers, missiles, and submarines that could survive a nuclear attack and strike back repeatedly over weeks or months as ordered by the President.
- Nuclear strikes launched in reaction to an unambiguous warning that the Soviet Union had launched a nuclear attack, or launched

under attack as Soviet missiles begin striking the United States but before the full force of the blow has been felt.

- All-out, spasmodic nuclear exchange, which requires that American nuclear forces survive a nuclear attack in sufficient strength to fire back on presidential order to inflict massive destruction on the Soviet Union.

- Massive war around the globe fought with conventional weapons under the shield of a nuclear standoff, which requires forces armed, trained, and provisioned to fight for many months while industry gears up to replace weapons and ammunition expended in battle.

- A full-scale conventional war on the central front in Europe, where the massed Western European and American forces would try to prevent the Soviet Union and its allies in the Warsaw Pact from driving across the continent to the English Channel.

- Limited war, such as that in Korea, fought within geographic and military boundaries set by political authorities, with limited military force, and with limited political and military objectives.

- Counterinsurgency, such as that during the war in Vietnam, where American advisers and American forces sought to devise operations and tactics that would defeat guerrillas.

- Defense of the sea lines of communication between the United States and its allies and between the United States and its sources of supply and markets for exports.

- Quick reaction strikes, such as those into Grenada and Libya or, possibly, a movement of American forces into the region around the Persian Gulf to prevent a takeover of the oil sources vital to Western nations.

- Shows of force, such as those in Lebanon in 1982 and 1983 and in Central America starting in 1983, which require troops carefully trained and tightly controlled to handle volatile operations.

- Special operations, including commando raids and guerrilla warfare or the rescue mission into Iran that tried but failed to free American hostages held by Moslem fanatics.

- Antiterrorist operations, inside or outside the United States, with American forces operating alone or with United States law enforcement agencies or counterterrorist forces of another nation.

- Military training and sales of weapons to allied or friendly nations, which can be effective as a "force-multiplier." Such training and sales can add to the common defense with a minimum of expenditure in funds and time by the United States.

Whether in standing watch or in shows of force or in battle, the extensive training and personal courage of officers and troops has caused them to perform well in almost every instance. Like American troops throughout history, they have risen to meet the challenge and have been ingenious in improvising and in overcoming obstacles as they came up. There have been not a few acts of individual heroism in the field even when the operations themselves were poorly conceived at the highest political levels in Washington.

Back on the carrier *Constellation*, the pilot of another F-14 and the naval flight officer, or weapons officer, in the back seat sit in their flight gear sweltering in the cockpit under a hot sun and hazy sky.

"How long do you stay up there?" shouts a visitor over the din of engines, tractors tugging planes around, and orders barking from the public address system.

"About two hours," the pilot shouts back.

"What do you do?" the flyer is asked.

"Read a book," he shouts again, holding up a paperback.

A while later the pilot, Commander Lawrence Ernst, and the weapons officer, Lieutenant Commander James Santangelo, clamber down from their sweaty perch and shrug off the boredom as part of the job. Commander Ernst says the alert is necessary so that "we can be off the deck in five minutes ready to shoot people down." In recent weeks, he and Commander Santangelo had intercepted three Soviet bombers, plus several Iranian planes that ventured out to look them over. Sometimes, Commander Santangelo says, the Russians come down over the carrier. "They're taking pictures of us," he says, "just like we're taking pictures of them." Was there any trouble? Commander Ernst, talking with his hands in the manner of flyers since the Wright brothers, says that once in a while a Russian pilot tries to drive an American plane into the sea by flying low and going into a sudden turn. The F-14 fighters have to scurry to get out of the way because they are designed for high-speed turns at high altitudes and have mushy responses at low speeds at low altitudes. "It does make life interesting," says the pilot, drily.

Life on *Constellation* can be harsh. The work day often runs to twenty hours, day after day, in a tempo close to that of wartime. The need for maintenance is constant as grit blows 200 miles off the Arabian peninsula and gets into everything—electronics systems, air conditioning, hydraulic gear. It chips away at paint and turns yellow foam-rubber filters black in two days. Keeping morale up is hard because nations on the littoral of the Indian Ocean are not keen about being identified with the United States; thus, port calls are rare. On one voyage, *Constellation* spent 110 days at sea without liberty for the sailors. When the captain senses the crew of 5,000 is tiring and becoming inattentive on the hazardous flight deck, he stands the ship down, stopping all but essential operations. One time, the captain had the cooks broil steaks for a picnic on the flight deck and allowed the sailors, especially those from the bowels of the ship who might not see the sun for days on end, to loll on what they called "the steel beach." Sometimes the ship calls at Diego Garcia, a tiny island 2,000 miles to the south in the middle of the Indian Ocean. The British have allowed the United States to turn the island into a supply depot, communications center, and staging area for cargo ships loaded with arms and supplies for American ground forces that might be deployed to that region. Sailors from *Constellation* can go ashore, but there is nothing much to do on what they call "Fantasy Island." Occasionally, the ship visits Australia, on the other side of the Indian Ocean. An officer, asked when the next liberty had been scheduled, says ship movements are classified secret. But a sailor in a radio shack marks off the days on a calendar, with a sign announcing, "Perth, 16 days."

The flight deck of a carrier, with high-powered aircraft taking off and landing, steam catapults and arresting cables in operation, tractors towing airplanes, and fuel pumps dispensing jet fuel, is among the most dangerous pieces of real estate in the world. During a training cycle, the carrier *Nimitz* suffered a tragedy of flaming death and destruction as an EA-6B electronics plane veered off the center line during a landing, smashed into parked planes, and plowed forward to explode. Firefighters battled the ball of flame on the flight deck for seventy minutes before dousing the blaze. In all, fourteen men were killed, including the four-man crew of the plane and sailors on the flight deck, and forty-eight more injured. The electronics plane and two F-14s had to be pushed over the side as they were beyond repair, but still a hazard. After the ship had returned to her base in Norfolk, Rear Admiral Byron Fuller, commander of the *Nimitz* battle group, said, "There was a lot of courage up there on that flight deck."

As tugs pushed the ship alongside the pier, there was another kind of courage among the anxious relatives who waited. Dagmar Green, the young, dark-haired wife of a crewman on the flight deck, had heard the news on the radio while visiting her parents. She rushed back to reach the pier just before the ship arrived, not knowing whether her husband was dead or alive. As she stood bewildered, one of the older wives, seeing her shaking and weeping, put her arm around the young woman and took her to an officer who had a list of the dead and injured; it was still confidential since not all of the next of kin had been notified. The officer scanned his papers, looked up, and said, "He's not on the list." As relief flooded over the young woman's face, she broke down a bit but got control again a few minutes later. "He never told me that things like this could happen," she said. "This is peacetime, not war."

As sailors and petty officers streamed off the ship to seek out wives or girlfriends and parents, there were long hugs and quick kisses and looks in the eyes without much being said. Some women fought back tears; others tried but didn't quite make it. Mrs. Joanne Clarke, whose son operated a catapult and could have been in the path of the stricken aircraft, said it had taken a while before she heard he was okay. "The last twenty-four hours," she said, "have just been hell." Eric Herman's parents walked along the pier toward the stern of the ship with a sign bearing his name until they spotted him waving from a small porthole. "It's such a relief," his mother said. "But I'm really sorry for the sixty other families who don't have the same relief." Nor was Mrs. Green's wait over, although she had spotted her husband on the flight deck. "He has the duty, and can't get off the ship until tomorrow morning," she moaned. "I wish they'd give me just a few minutes with him, just to hold him, just to be sure."

USS *Cincinnati*, a nuclear-powered attack submarine, is a sleek, black, tapered steel cylinder 360 feet long, the length of a football field from end zone to end zone. Even moored to a pier in Norfolk, she looks forbidding, sinister, mean, bearing no identifying marks, no name, no number. Led by her captain, Commander Robert E. Hawthorne, the crew prepares her for a five-month patrol at sea. They load torpedoes and provisions, work on equipment to prevent breakdowns at sea, and train. The Navy calls the submarine fleet the "silent service" both for the way the undersea boats operate and for the curtain of secrecy about where they go and what they do. True to that tradition, Commander Hawthorne talks about his ship but not about her forthcoming mission.

Life aboard *Cincinnati* is not for a sailor with claustrophobia. The forward half of the ship is filled with sonar, navigation equipment, communications gear, the control room, the torpedo room, and living quarters for the crew of 130 officers, chief petty officers, and rated seamen. The aft portion of the ship is taken up with the nuclear reactor and propulsion plant. Working space is so cramped that in no passageway can two sailors pass shoulder to shoulder; they must turn sideways. In the torpedo room, a sailor lies on the deck to check a 3,500-pound torpedo as the hydraulic lift eases it into a torpedo tube— only three inches above his head.

In the crew's quarters, three-deep bunks are shelves with thin mattresses. Each sailor has barely enough headroom in which to roll over. No one can sit up in a bunk. Since there are not enough bunks for every man to have his own, junior enlisted men must "hot bunk," with three men sharing two bunks on different schedules. Storage space is a wide tray under each bunk; in that goes clothing, toilet articles, candy bars, cigarettes, and whatever else sailors might want for three to six months at sea. A small locker above the bunk holds valuables. In the stainless steel head, or bathroom, the shower stall is smaller than a telephone booth. "To get clean," says a sailor, "you soap the walls and turn around."

Sailors bring little extra clothing with them, Commander Hawthorne says, pointing to a washing machine that "goes twenty-four hours a day, almost, when we're under way." A stationary bicycle that can be stowed behind pipes is the ship's gym. The only open space in the submarine is the crew's mess, a dining room with half a dozen booths like those in a drug store. The mess is also the recreation center, where closed circuit television and movies are shown. If the captain wants to hold a meeting with members of the crew, he can do it there.

Beneath the sea, *Cincinnati*'s sister ship, USS *City of Corpus Christi*, is a blind leviathan from which nothing outside can be seen. But in a sea full of sound, she relies on her sensitive sonar ears to stalk Soviet submarines and surface ships. Standing in the dim sonar room, Petty Officer Second Class Donald Cox supervises three other operators listening to sounds from the sea on headphones and scanning green monitors where those noises have been translated into squiggly lines that flow down the screens. "Sonar is a combination of hearing, seeing, and thinking," Cox says. "But the most important thing is thinking and deciding." The sounds coming through the sonar are distinctive. Chicka-chicka-chicka is a merchantman. Chug-chug-chug is a diesel. Squeals, whines, and noises like the rattling of teacups are what sailors call "biologicals," or creatures in the sea. A long, pleading moan, Cox says, comes from a whale nearby.

Conversely, to evade detection, *Corpus Christi* depends on quiet. An admonition from Captain Frank L. "Skip" Bowman is posted: "Our acoustic sonar advantage over the Russian submarine is very small. Our shipmates who mindlessly slam doors and hatches, drop tools, and otherwise make unnecessary noises are giving away that small advantage—they can hear us before we hear them." Thus the sounds of silence are the door that is eased shut, the hatch lowered slowly, the wrench placed softly on the steel deck of the torpedo room. When a potentially hostile submarine or ship is encountered, the word is passed to "rig for ultra-quiet." The water evaporator is shut down. Garbage is stowed because the disposal device would make a dull thud. Soft drink and ice cream dispensers are turned off. All hands not on watch climb into bunks. During a training run, an engineering officer tells the captain he has heard a ticking in the drive shaft. Captain Bowman curses and rushes to the engine room, coming back an hour later, relief on his face. "They found it with a stethoscope," he says. A bushing had been improperly lubricated by shipyard workers. How far could the ticking have been heard? "Thousands of yards," he says, grimly.

One day at lunch, Captain Bowman takes a glass of fresh milk and says: "We run out of this pretty fast; then we have to drink that powdered stuff. It's the thing the crew misses most." A young officer down the table demurs. "No, captain," he says softly, "it's the thing the crew misses second most." Long separations from wives or girlfriends and family are a difficult part of submarine duty. At sea, submariners cannot communicate with the outside world. Sailors leave birthday and Valentine's Day cards with the base chaplain to drop in the mail when they're due, and florists take orders for Easter flowers months in advance. On a long deployment, wives can send forty-word "family-grams" once a month, giving her message to the Navy, which flashes it by satellite. Bad news is a dilemma; some sailors tell their families and the captain they don't want to receive bad news while at sea because there's nothing they can do about it.

Day to day, the versatile attack submarines roam under the seven seas searching for Soviet submarines armed with nuclear ballistic missiles aimed at targets in the United States, or for Soviet attack submarines that might threaten American warships or cargo ships, or gathering naval intelligence. *Corpus Christi*, for instance, sailed in 1984 from her home port in New London, Connecticut, down the Atlantic and around the Cape of Good Hope into the Indian Ocean, spending eighty-three days submerged. After taking on supplies at Diego Garcia, she returned to sea for more operations, gave the crew a week's liberty in Perth, Australia, then sailed under the Pacific to the Panama Canal and home. She was gone for seven months.

In an era of air power and submarine warfare, duty aboard cruisers, destroyers, and frigates is perhaps not so glamorous as that on carriers or submarines. But those surface ships are the workhorses of the Navy and are driven by old salts of long tradition. In peacetime, they patrol the seas with the carriers or picket the choke points through which Soviet vessels must pass to reach the high seas of the Atlantic or Pacific. In wartime, they would protect carriers with their antiaircraft missiles and anti-submarine helicopters and weapons, convoy amphibious landing teams of marines, and protect the sea lanes across which American troops and supplies would be shipped.

Aboard the destroyer *Scott*, Commander A. R. Brittain, Jr., a big, hearty man known on the waterfront as a good skipper, puts his crew through "sweat week," slang derived from the acronym SWTW, or surface warfare training week. A computerized simulator on shore in the Norfolk Naval Base sends signals, information, and battle descriptions to several destroyers tied up along the piers, telling them they are under attack by aircraft or submarines. As each ship responds, orders sent electronically to its weapons are registered on the simulator, which judges whether the ship has warded off the attack, or partly met it but suffered damage, or has been unsuccessful and is sinking. Those assessments are relayed back to the ships for further decision by the officers and crew. In the combat information center, the focal point of the drill, a sailor hunches over a radar scope. "It's good training," he says, "but it's not the same thing as being under way at sea."

Scott is a guided missile destroyer, one of four ships known facetiously as the "Ayatollah class." They were built for the Shah of Iran but that regime was overthrown by the Ayatollah Khomeini before they were delivered, and thus they were absorbed by the American Navy. *Scott* is powered by four gas turbines, designed for large aircraft, that can accelerate the ship from a standing start to better than thirty knots in about a minute, making her a 9,300-ton speedboat. "*Scott*," says her captain, "is a destroyerman's dream."

In the piney woods of North Carolina not far from the Atlantic Ocean, Camp Lejeune is home for the 2nd Marine Division, including its eleven maneuver battalions of 870 marines each. On a given string of days, three of those battalions are training at the camp while a fourth, just back from a deployment, rests and regroups. Two battalions are on temporary duty with the 3rd Marine Division in the western Pacific, one on Okinawa, the Japanese island south of Japan proper. The northern half of that island is rugged, jungle-covered terrain where the battalion trains in small-unit tactics, combat marksmanship, and survival in living off the land. The other battalion is afloat on amphibious ships, practicing landings in Korea one week and the Philippines the next. A seventh battalion from Camp Lejeune is in the North Atlantic aboard amphibious ships for a training assault into Norway. The eighth is afloat in the Mediterranean or, for a time, ashore in Lebanon. Another battalion is at the Marine Corps combat training center at Twenty-Nine Palms, in the California desert. The tenth battalion is in the Caribbean for a naval, air, and amphibious exercise called Ocean Venture, while the eleventh is back at Camp Lejeune preparing to deploy to California for maneuvers at Twenty-Nine Palms. Says an operations officer: "We don't have too many people just sitting around here."

In the woods is a computerized training center set up in vans to simulate a battalion command post, in this case the 2nd Battalion, 6th Marines, which was getting ready for training at Twenty-Nine Palms and six months on Okinawa. The program feeds information about an approaching enemy onto screens in the command post, where intelligence officers interpret it and pass it to operations officers to draw up battle plans for the battalion commander, Lieutenant Colonel Edwin C. Kelley Jr. His decisions are fed back into the computer, which presents new situations to confront the battalion staff and commander. "The whole idea," says an officer running the training, "is to train a battalion battle staff. We can train troops in the field, and train platoon leaders and company commanders in the field. But there was no good way before this to train staff officers to make combat decisions." After the terrorist bombing of the marine landing team in Beirut in October 1983, Colonel Kelley was the officer ordered to assemble a replacement unit of battalion staff and headquarters company, to load onto long-range transport aircraft, and to fly to Lebanon. They were moving within twenty hours of getting the word.

The 2nd Marine Division in 1984 and 1985 was revitalized with a reorganization in which the number of marines in combat battalions was reduced by 10 percent but new weapons were added to increase firepower by 25 percent. Each squad, the smallest unit in the infantry, was cut from thirteen marines to eleven—a squad leader and two fire teams of five marines each. Each fire team was given a new light machine gun, new versions of the M-16 rifle, and a new grenade launcher. Antitank missiles and launchers were added to each regiment. Light armored vehicles increased mobility and protection for marines. New 155-millimeter howitzers replaced the 105-millimeter howitzers to give the artillery more punch and range. A battery armed with the new guns got themselves T-shirts inscribed in earthy marine humor, "Reach Out and Touch Someone." Said Lieutenant Colonel

Donald F. Anderson, the training officer, "This year, the Marine Corps is picking up more new weapons than at any time since World War II."

At Shaw Air Force Base, a well-trimmed base in South Carolina, the 17th Tactical Fighter Squadron of F-16 jet fighters was a hot-shot outfit in 1984 even though it was then the newest squadron of its kind in the Air Force. Of its thirty pilots, Captain Charles Simmons and sixteen others are rated as "experienced," Captain Simmons having flown for 2,000 hours, 700 in the F-16, the Air Force's versatile fighter. His wingman, First Lieutenant John Brandon, and twelve others are rated "inexperienced." Even so, Lieutenant Brandon, who had been a civilian pilot with 1,500 hours of flying time before joining the Air Force, has logged 450 hours in the F-16 over the past eighteen months and needs only fifty more to be rated "experienced." Lieutenant Colonel Scott W. Pilkington, the squadron's operations officer and second in command, says that "the inexperienced guys we're getting now are the best I've ever seen."

Proficiency in flying a fighter plane is much like gymnastics; it takes hours of concentrated practice to hone skills. The Air Force has tried to raise flying time steadily; in the 17th, the pilots fly twenty-two sorties a month, or one every duty day, but a senior officer says, "we'd have more, if we had our way." On a spring afternoon, in weather that Captain Simmons jokingly describes as "severe clear," he and Lieutenant Brandon sit at a table in a small briefing room to run through the drill for that afternoon. It is important to do that each time they fly, Captain Simmons says, "to become accustomed to the nuances of working together." Their mission: To fly down low on a circular route away from the base, to come in toward a gunnery range at tree-top level, to pop up and fire a simulated Maverick missle at a bunker on the ground, then to go around for a strafing run. Captain Simmons cautions that at a certain point on the flight they have to climb to avoid making too much noise over a village. If something goes wrong during the drill or if either pilot sees a threat to safety, the call would be "knock it off," when both are to cease the exercise and head for home.

As Captain Simmons climbs into the F-16's single-seat cockpit, which is close to the nose of the plane and on top of its engine, he says that "flying this thing is like riding on the end of a broomstick." Thirty minutes later, the two planes can barely be heard as they come up on the gunnery range just above the treetops, their jet engines muffled by the hills and the foliage. They fly in one at a time, jumping up and then nosing down to get an angle on the target in the simulated missile run. On the next run, each lets go with bursts of machine gun fire at old trucks and oil drums. Later, back in the briefing room, they run a videotape in slow motion to study their moves, each commenting on his own and his partner's performance. At the end, Captain Simmons pays Lieutenant Brandon fifty cents—the wingman had outshot his leader on the strafing runs.

Colonel Pilkington says the squadron of twenty-four aircraft must prepare for four missions. One is to attack airfields to reduce an enemy's ability to mount air attacks against American forces. In a second, they would fight enemy aircraft trying to penetrate friendly air space. The third is to interdict enemy supply lines. Lastly, the squadron could provide close air support for Army forces on the ground. The squadron, Colonel Pilkington says, must be ready to move on twelve hours' notice, possibly to Europe, to Southwest Asia around the Persian Gulf, or to Central America.

Vital to the mission of the squadron is the unending job of maintaining the planes, the task of 275 airmen. The Air Force demands that 75 percent of a squadron's aircraft be ready for a mission on any given day. The 17th Fighter Squadron ranges from 83 percent to 90 percent, largely due to the efforts of several senior noncommissioned officers and a flock of young but skilled technicians. Under the eye of Senior Master Sergeant Gerald G. Arruda, "wrench-turners" troop in from the flight line to get parts, then go back out to install them. When each pilot returns from a flight, or when a crew chief inspects his airplane, deficiencies are noted and recorded in a log book. Some are serious, such as a leaking hydraulic line, and ground the plane until fixed. Others, such as a light out in an instrument, are not serious enough to keep the plane down if the pilot is aware of it before he takes off. But little things count, especially in how fast they get fixed. "The number of delayed discrepancies," says a senior officer, "tells about the attitude toward maintenance."

Even in peacetime, flying military aircraft is risky and far more dangerous than flying civilian planes. Military flying is hazardous because the margins for error are so slender. Pilots in an F-15, a heavier and more powerful plane than the F-16, hurtling through the sky at twice the speed of sound, can be knocked unconscious in ten seconds if they get careless during a tight turn.

Yet military flying has become gradually safer, with 1985 the safest year yet. The Air Force, for instance, lost 38 pilots, 40 crewmen and passengers, and 51 aircraft that year. In 1943, during World War II, the Army Air Force lost 5,603 airmen and 20,389 airplanes in accidents unrelated to combat.

At Langley Air Force Base near Newport News, Virginia, Lieutenant Colonel Paul V. Hester sat in his olive-drab flying suit and explained why pilots in his 94th Tactical Fighter Squadron had not suffered a serious accident in three years. The commander of the squadron once led by the fabled Eddie Rickenbacker in World War I attributed the safe flying to discipline, attention to detail, specific goals for each training sortie, and strict obedience to the rules of engagement.

The cigar-chomping colonel, whose F-15s sport the Hat-in-the-Ring emblem of their World War I ancestors, said that in a practice dogfight, for instance, his squadron would fly above 5,000 feet in blocks of air space 4,000 feet high between five and nine—15,000 to 19,000 or 25,000 to 29,000 feet. The simulated adversaries would fly in similar blocks but between zero and four—10,000 to 14,000 or 20,000 to 24,000 feet. Perhaps most important, Colonel Hester said, the pilots went into a briefing room after each sortie to view video tapes and to point out each other's mistakes, regardless of rank. "We don't gloss over mistakes I made," the colonel said, "just because I'm a lieutenant colonel."

The military services define a serious mishap as an accident in which a flyer is killed, an aircraft is lost, or $500,000 worth of damage is done. Those accidents are measured in mishaps per 100,000 hours of flying time. For the Air Force that year, the rate was 1.5 compared with 3 in 1978, the lowest that anyone then thought could be achieved, given the inherent dangers of military flying. The rate for the Army, which flies helicopters and small fixed-wing aircraft, was 3 while the combined rate for the Navy and Marine Corps, in which pilots land on aircraft carriers heaving in an angry sea, was 3.4. In comparison, the National Transportation Safety Board said the accident rate is .22 per 100,000 hours in scheduled airliners and 1.8 in chartered planes.

Another commander at Langley, Lieutenant Colonel John W. Rutledge of the 27th Tactical Fighter Squadron, said that giving more responsibility to majors who commanded flights of four F-15s had helped to keep mishaps down. The majors were particularly charged with training new pilots who joined the squadron out of flight school. In addition, the colonel said, the cockpit of the F-15 was "user friendly" compared with older planes, as vital instruments and controls had been placed where the pilot could easily see or feel them. Assigning a crew chief to maintain a specific aircraft, instead of switching him around among different planes, had improved maintenance—especially as he or she had his name stenciled outside the cockpit.

Like Colonel Hester, Colonel Rutledge pointed to the mutual criticism among the pilots. "Before, we equated being aggressive in the air with being obnoxious on the ground," he said. "But there's been a revolution in the attitude of fighter pilots. There's less ego and more learning from the other guy." Both squadron commanders asserted that increased flying time had been especially important in cutting the accident rate. "Flying is a perishable skill," Colonel Rutledge said. "If you don't fly regularly, your skills deteriorate." Younger pilots flew about twenty hours a month, or almost once a duty day, while "older heads" got in about fifteen hours.

A flight surgeon, Major Thomas H. Nelson, said the tremendous stress put on a pilot by swift turns in the F-15 was a real threat. In the tightest turns, centrifugal force could cause the blood to drain out of a pilot's head so fast that he could lose consciousness in ten seconds. Dr. Nelson said pilots were taught to contract the muscles in their abdomens and to grunt, forcing the blood back to the heart so that it could be pumped to the brain. A pilot with high blood pressure had an easier time of it, he said. Complacency was another threat. "These pilots have done everything well all of their lives," the doctor said. "They're smart, they're good athletes, they were the best in flight school. The first thing we teach them is the possibility they could make a mistake."

Another flight surgeon, Captain Guy M. Newland, said "we teach respect for crew rest, not to get so tired that they don't care and make mistakes." Before they fly, pilots are required to get at least eight hours of sleep. Pilots taken ill must see a doctor and are not allowed to medicate themselves, except for an aspirin for a headache. The reason for all this, Dr. Newland said wryly, "is that fighter pilots cost a lot more than doctors." It takes $100,000 to get through medical school but $1.5 million to train a fighter pilot.

In drills, the forces try to simulate real life as much as possible. The 60th Military Airlift Wing at Travis Air Force Base in California is alerted on a Thursday morning that "war" is imminent between the fictional countries of Sikap and Steivos. The President, in response to a request from Sikap, might order American forces into action. The 60th Wing is told to prepare to transport those forces, which requires servicing planes, getting crews filled out if people are away on leave, bringing personnel and inoculation records up to date. By Saturday afternoon, that has been completed.

On Sunday at 9:18 A.M., the 60th Wing is put on full alert, and at 9:50, Colonel William B. Kehler is assigned to pick up a mechanized infantry battalion of 800 soldiers from Fort Carson; they will assemble at nearby Peterson Air Force Base in Colorado Springs, Colorado. At 10:30, Colonel Kehler finds out that his planes and crews are to fly forty-five sorties in C-5 Galaxies and C-141 Starlifters, the long-range four-engine jet transports, from Peterson to Mountain Home Air Force Base in Idaho, where the infantry will maneuver. At 5:55 that Sunday afternoon, the first plane takes off from Travis with Air Force crews to provide liaison with the Army logistics group that will load the planes. By midnight, the first wave of the Air Force unit has arrived at Peterson. At a briefing in a cavernous hangar, Colonel Kehler tells a meeting of Air Force and Army officers, "We are here to move you, and we will move you on time."

Air Force and Army officers inspect armored personnel carriers, trucks, jeeps, boxes of weapons, and equipment to be loaded, working through the night. At sunup, loading begins, and at 8:29 Monday morning, the first plane lifts off. Through the rest of Monday, airmen and soldiers sweat under an unseasonably warm spring sun to load aircraft. Getting a sixty-ton tank into a huge C-5 Galaxy is easy, since it is the entire cargo for that sortie. In real life, the C-5 would carry two tanks, but only one is lifted on this exercise as a safety precaution. Loading a smaller C-141 transport plane with a jeep, a water tank, an armored personnel carrier, a 2½-ton truck, and another jeep, plus assorted smaller items, takes time, skill, and a bit of imagination on the part of the loadmaster and crew.

About midday, Murphy's law (anything that can go wrong will go wrong) strikes. A C-5 is cleared to start engines, but the pilot can't get an outboard engine to turn over. A mechanic climbs a three-story scaffolding, inspects the engine, announces that an igniter box isn't working and that it will take several hours to fix. An hour later, the crew and passengers of a second C-5 scurry to evacuate the plane when a hydraulic line begins leaking flammable fluid over the tank in the cargo bay. In a third C-5, the engineer informs the pilot that the landing gear might not retract once they are aloft. The pilot, after a quick conference with the navigator, decides they will fly anyway as they have enough fuel to handle the drag the extended landing gear would cause. Colonel Kehler, exasperated by this time, can only sigh, "Well, that's what happens in the real world and that's why we train like this."

After the C-5 with the suspect landing gear takes off, the gear retracts properly, which the pilot announces to the crew amid cheers.

The flight is uneventful, and the landing in the plane loaded with a sixty-ton tank is the softest imaginable. The plane halts at the edge of an arid plain of sagebrush, lifts its nose, and with engines screaming at a pitch so high that human voices cannot be heard, discharges the tank. The plane turns and takes off for Travis. At Peterson, troubles with the three C-5s slow the flow to a trickle, but other planes are loaded faster and a surge through Monday night gets things back on schedule. The movement ends late Monday night an hour ahead of time.

On the Upper Peninsula of Michigan near the town of Gwinn is K. I. Sawyer Air Force Base, one of more than a dozen bases in the United States for B-52 long-range bombers of the Strategic Air Command. Their mission, should the President so order, would be to fly north over Canada and the Arctic to drop nuclear bombs on the Soviet Union. At K. I. Sawyer, six of those bombers are loaded and standing on alert twenty-four hours a day. "When the Russians rattle their sabers," says Major Geoffrey H. Smith, "we can get the B-52s in the air to show them that we mean business and then we can call off the fireworks and come on home."

Technical Sergeant David Demmon, a tail gunner on one of the B-52s, is required to spend one of every three weeks on alert "inside the fence." The alert compound stands close to six armed and ready B-52s and six KC-135 aerial tankers that would refuel the bombers, once on the way to the Soviet Union and again on the way back. At another part of the base, behind another fence, this one topped with barbed wire, are rows of concrete bunkers. The sign outside said "Weapons Storage Center," but everyone knows that's where the nuclear weapons are kept when not on the planes.

Sergeant Demmon says he believes in his mission but doesn't like being on alert. "It's the most excruciating boredom," he says. "I mean, all we're doing is waiting for the klaxon to ring telling us it's time to fly off to Armageddon." The alert crews of six men each can go outside the fence on limited forays to the base exchange, the hobby shop, or the movie theater, where the last two rows are reserved for them. But they must stick together in blue vans called "six packs." If the bell rings, the vans race back to the planes past signs warning other drivers that the "six packs" have the right of way over everything. "This whole thing in the middle of nowhere," the sergeant says, "is really set up to support the 180 men who fly the bombers and their tankers."

To train for a nuclear air strike against the Soviet Union, a B-52 bomber thunders down an icy runway at Grand Forks Air Force Base and lifts off over the North Dakota prairie just as dawn breaks. The pilot, Captain Randall W. Spetman, climbs above the fields dusted with the winter's first snow and levels off at 29,000 feet to look for an aerial tanker that will practice filling his plane for the long flight. As the KC-135 tanker appears a thousand feet overhead, Captain Spetman drives slowly up until the fueling boom under the tanker's tail looms a few feet above his head. He watches the signal on the underside of the tanker that tells him whether to move forward or right or left and, with his peripheral vision, keeps an eye on the engines and wings of the tanker. "The biggest thing," the pilot says, "is to sense movement as you get close." Gently, he inches the plane up until the boom locks with a light thump into a receptacle in the bomber's shoulders. The bomber is less than forty feet from the tanker, close enough so that the pilot can read the lips of the boom operator lying on his stomach and looking out of the tanker's bottom window.

After twenty minutes of taut flying at 320 miles an hour, Captain Spetman breaks off and heads for the practice bombing runs. The bomber carries no weapons; strikes will be simulated and scored by radar. The B-52's mission, which has changed since it was designed as a high-level bomber in the 1950s, is to penetrate hostile territory a few hundred feet above the ground in an attempt to escape detection by the vastly expanded radar network of the Soviet Union. In wartime, the plane with a crew of six flyers would carry three kinds of nuclear weapons: twelve air-launched cruise missiles, which are flying torpedoes with a range of 1,500 miles that would be hung under the wings; eight short-range missiles carried in the bomb bay; and four bombs, also carried in the bomb bay. That heavy load, plus the low-level flying and the long distances to targets, make the B-52 consume huge amounts of fuel. On a wartime mission, the plane would load as much fuel as possible without losing its ability to get off the ground, then meet up with a tanker to complete filling the tanks. The commander of the 319th Bombardment Wing, Colonel John T. Jaeckle, the unit to which Captain Spetman and his crew belong, says that "refueling is the name of the game anymore."

On this eight-hour sortie, Captain Spetmen and the copilot, First Lieutenant Michael E. Walker, fly a twisting course over North Dakota, South Dakota, Nebraska, Wyoming, Montana, and North Dakota again. The B-52 costs an average of $10,000 an hour to fly, counting fuel, spare parts, and maintenance; thus this training mission takes $80,000.

As the plane glides down to 7,000 feet, the electronic warfare officer, First Lieutenant James M. Tinnesz, and the tail gunner, Staff

Sergeant William J. Pangborn, seated behind the pilot's cockpit facing aft, test their jamming gear and guns. The bomber skims over a layer of clouds, then drops over the edge to fly through the Big Horn Mountains at 600 feet. With the plane flying at 450 miles an hour, the meandering valley below seems to scroll under the plane, like one of those driving games in a video arcade. Snow-covered ridges rise to within 400 feet of the plane, canyons drop off to 1,000 feet. A few houses are scattered in the valley and an occasional car wends along a lonely road, its driver perhaps startled to see the behemoth roaring over him. In the distance, a mountain peak rises to 13,000 feet. Captain Spetman guides the plane over the changing contours by watching not only the ground but the television monitor immediately in front of him; a radar trace tells him the altitude directly below and the terrain three miles ahead. He thus has ample warning to pull up.

Keeping the plane within an eight-mile-wide training corridor and getting to the targets is the job of the navigator, Major Joseph L. Olenoski, who sits with the bombardier, Major Frank A. Greenwood Jr., on the deck below the pilot and copilot. Their operating space, like that of the pilots and the defensive aviators, is no bigger than the inside of a Volkswagen. Because this mission calls for simulating the loss of the inertial navigation system, Major Olenoski must rely on headings and radar readouts of the terrain to determine where they are. When it comes time to change course, the navigator gives the pilot a new bearing, then says in crisp cadence, "coming up on left turn—ready—ready—now." Close to the target, Major Greenwood, who is also called the radar navigator, takes over and seeks to keep the cross hairs on his radar screen on a series of simulated targets— a prominent piece of terrain, a grain silo, a water tower. As the plane approaches a target, Major Greenwood opens the bomb-bay doors, switches on a radar tone to signal the scoring team on the ground that the bomber is coming up on the target, and "releases" the bomb by stopping the tone. As soon as he says "bomb away," the pilot pushes the throttles forward to get the plane away from the detonation.

About fifteen miles north of Grand Forks Air Base, through a concrete capsule sixty-five feet underground, will run the front line of the United States if nuclear war comes. In that capsule controlling ten Minuteman III nuclear missiles will be two young Air Force officers like Captain Randal T. Russell and Second Lieutenant Melvin S. Lockett who are standing watch here this particular day. Should the order come from the President, they may be among the first to launch missiles aimed at the Soviet Union. The drill would be precise and would take less than a minute to execute. Once the message from the President had arrived and been authenticated, they would spin dials to insert code numbers, flip switches to arm the missiles, and turn launching keys at the same time. In the capsule behind an eight-ton blast resistant door, Captain Russell's post is in front of a control panel at one end, Lieutenant Lockett's at a panel beside the long wall. Before the lieutenant is a panel of red and green lights reporting the status of each missile in the unit of ten. The two officers have been separated so that neither could turn both launch keys. Ten miles away, as a safety precaution, another pair of officers would have to do the same thing for the ten missiles to fly.

The young officers seem to take their awesome task in stride. "I don't suppose I feel any different about my job than any other officer performing any other duty in the U.S. military," said Captain Russell, the capsule commander. "I don't believe that a global conflict will ever take place," he said, but added, "Should a need ever arise, I will carry out any authorized launch orders to the best of my ability."

The Minuteman missiles will continue to be the mainstay of the United States intercontinental ballistic missile force into the next century, despite the deployment of the much-disputed MX missiles. In 1986, even with fifty Minuteman missiles retired to make room for the new MX, 950 remain on duty—500 Minuteman IIIs with three warheads each and 450 Minuteman IIs with one warhead apiece. Around Grand Forks, the 321st Strategic Missile Wing commanded by Colonel Kenneth B. Van Dillen has 150 Minuteman IIIs scattered over 7,500 square miles, an area the size of New Jersey, with the northernmost only seven miles from the Canadian border. Each of the warheads could be aimed at any one of 2,400 targets, with the capsule commander sending target orders to the computers in the missiles with a few strokes on a typewriter keyboard.

The missiles themselves are miles from the control capsule, in concrete silos buried in government land surrounded by farms. They are unattended but are guarded by fences and sensors so touchy that they can be set off by rabbits wandering into the site. When an alarm is triggered, security guards from a support building on the surface above the control capsule speed over to check for intruders. "The security police," says Colonel Michael R. Denington, the wing's operations officer, "soon learn to hate rabbits."

Farm families sometimes provide additional security because, in that sparsely settled region, they know who is supposed to be around the silos and who are strangers. In one case, officers from the Strategic Air Command showed up for a surprise inspection, only to find themselves looking down the barrel of a shotgun held by a farmer who told them to stay put until the security police arrived.

The crews of the B-52s and Minuteman missiles are part of the Strategic Air Command, with headquarters in Omaha, Nebraska. Underneath that headquarters, better known as SAC, down a ramp watched by a dozen armed guards, is a war room two stories high for a battle staff of fifty officers and noncommissioned officers. On one side are six screens, each a story high, on which can be flashed maps, information about incoming missiles, and a running summary of the status of every American missile, bomber, and submarine in the nuclear triad. Red, gold, black, and gray telephones connect the command center to the White House, the Pentagon, command centers in the Pacific and Europe, and the airborne replica of the command center known as Looking Glass. In that plane, twenty-four hours a day for thirty years, a general and a battle staff have been flying at random over the United States so that a command post will survive if Omaha is knocked out. Says an officer in Omaha, "We'll never have another Pearl Harbor."

In the event of a Soviet missile and bomber attack, SAC in turn would get a warning from the North American Aerospace Defense Command, or Norad, in a vast cavern deep inside Cheyenne Mountain in Colorado. Neither Norad nor SAC has the authority to order the planes to strike; that order may come only from the President or his designated subordinate, such as the Secretary of Defense. Norad's function is to warn the President that an attack has been launched and to give him its best assessment of where the attack has been aimed, when it will hit, and how much damage it might do.

Inside Cheyenne Mountain, the operations center of Norad occupies several buildings three stories high mounted atop huge coiled shock absorbers intended to lessen the impact of a nearby nuclear explosion. Three shifts of 250 people from the Air Force, mostly officers and skilled technicians, operate the center twenty-four hours a day. In a darkened room the size of an ordinary living room, technicians watch for evidence picked up by satellites and radar and flashed to their green screens that the Soviet Union has launched an attack. In another room, technicians monitor every man-made object in space, more than 14,000 of them since the Russians put up Sputnik in 1957. There are 5,800 satellites and pieces of debris up there now. Norad watches those objects because the trace of a decaying space object as it hurtles into the atmosphere is almost identical to that of an incoming missile. When that trace appears, Norad must be able to tell whether it is a piece of space junk or a Soviet missile. Another crew keeps a constant check on the weather, since sunspots and other solar disturbances can affect the workings of the sensors. An intelligence team monitors developments around the world to preclude surprises from events that could lead to war. (Most strategic thinkers believe that no conflict would begin with a "bolt out of the blue," or surprise attack, but only after a period of rising tensions.) In another room, two stories high, is the command post with large screens along one wall. Information about incoming missiles, disposition of enemy and friendly forces, and other data can be flashed on the screens. Telephones connect Norad directly to SAC headquarters, the National Military Command Center in the Pentagon, and the White House.

There have been several false alarms at Norad, when the system signaled that the Soviet Union had launched missiles aimed at the United States. In each case, the alarm was declared false within minutes. But that raised a nervous question: Could a mistake cause an accidental nuclear war? An officer inside the mountain shakes his head. For all the machinery that looks like it came out of a science fiction movie, he says, "people are the key." They make the system work, he says, and they prevent it from making mistakes. "The people here," he says, "are trained to be suspicious." For an alarm to be given, there must be evidence of a strike from at least two different kinds of sensors. An infrared sensor on a satellite in space must pick up the heat trail of a missile that has been launched, and that finding must be confirmed a few minutes later by a radar on the ground. In addition, all other information coming in from intelligence and weather must fit into place before an attack can be confirmed with a high level of confidence. To ensure discrimination, people selected to work in Norad are carefully screened and are frequently given psychological tests to ascertain that they have remained stable. The operations center is heavily guarded against saboteurs or intruders who might damage the system, with sensitive areas posted, "Use of Deadly Force Authorized."

The complex inside Cheyenne Mountain was originally built to withstand the blast of nuclear bombs dropped by Soviet aircraft, and later was found sufficiently protected to withstand all but a direct hit by the most lethal nuclear missile. But as Soviet warheads have become more explosive and missiles more accurate, the operations center has become vulnerable. No matter, said General James V. Hartinger, who was in command at Norad in 1983: "Our system would have detected them and we would have performed our main mission."

When 900 soldiers from the 101st Airborne Division at Fort Camp-bell in Kentucky land in Egypt on Operation Bright Star, they are stunned by the vast, barren spaces in the desert. They soon find that sand, driven by relentless winds, gets into everything, gumming up rifles and machine guns, eroding blades on helicopters, clogging filters in jeeps, jamming radio switches, and causing diarrhea because it seeps into food. But they learn to cope. "We learned a thousand new things, mostly little things," says Major David H. Ohle, an operations officer. "We could spend months, or a year, in the desert out west and not learn as much as we did in Egypt."

Perhaps the most important lesson during the exercise, intended to train soldiers for rapid dispatch to the region around the Persian Gulf, is that helicopters are suited for war in the desert against tanks. "We found that we can kill tanks on our own terms as long as we have ammunition," says another operations officer, Lieutenant Colonel W. W. Hunter. "The guy with the most mobility and who uses it best will win." Both helicopters and light trucks on which antitank missiles have been mounted can fight well in the desert. "We could shoot at 3,000 meters, then move back and shoot again," the colonel says, "We could eat up enemy tanks as long as we had room."

The commander of a troop-carrying helicopter company, Major William A. Glennon, says the desert at first appears flat. But his pilots see that the desert has gullies through which choppers can fly and still stay hidden. By tilting their helicopters at a certain angle, the pilots fly a few feet off the ground at forty-five miles an hour without leaving a "signature" of swirling sand that would give away their position. But the terrain of undulating sand and rock, without trees or other visual clues, looks all the same in the haze of bright sunlight and floating dust. "You really had to concentrate to pick out the terrain features," Major Glennon says, "and with all that concentration, the pilots got tired faster."

Lieutenant Colonel H. D. Kuhl, the infantry battalion com-mander, finds he can disperse his troops much more than he could during his two tours in the jungles of Vietnam, making it harder for an enemy to hit and easier for his soldiers to cover more ground. Despite that, "it gave me a sense of security because I could see everyone," he says. Colonel Kuhl discovers that in the desert the avenues of enemy approach came from 360 degrees, making leaders shift tactics from a linear to a circular front. Constant maneuvering is the key to success in the desert. "Holding ground is not the name of the game out there," Colonel Kuhl says. "It's to shoot and move. If you don't move, you might as well stay home and watch TV."

When digging in the sand, Sergeant Karl D. Keeler's squad figures out that it's better to put their equipment upwind and throw the sand downwind, no matter where the enemy might be. In other terrain, a soldier puts his equipment behind him and throws the dirt to the front. "I was surprised at how quickly we acclimated over there," the sergeant says. "But the breeze was deceiving. It was hot but dry and you didn't feel hot or sweaty." For that reason, soldiers drink less water than expected, and some become dehydrated and sick. In the ancient ways of armies, squad leaders line up their soldiers and order them to drink water three times a day, by the numbers.

Water is a different problem for soldiers from the 5th Infantry Division when they deploy from Fort Polk in Louisiana to Belgium and West Germany on Operation Autumn Forge. This time it is too much rain bogging down tanks and other vehicles and causing the Army to cut back on the annual exercise for fear of tearing up farms and private property. "The problem," says Specialist Fourth Class Jeffrey Hargrave, a mechanic, "seems to be getting to the place we're supposed to be fighting." But Staff Sergeant Jerome Gregg, an artilleryman, has been here before. "We expect things like this to happen," he says. "By going through this, we get a chance to see and operate in the real world, with all the problems we'd have to overcome."

It is not all working in the mud and eating rations from a tin can. "It's a good way to see Europe, a cheap way to see Europe," says Airman Mark Darby, who had flown with an Ohio Air Force reserve C-130 air transport. "We rented a car yesterday and went all over the place." Having 17,000 Americans barge in upsets many Europeans, but others are bemused. In the village of Lier, in Belgium, children swarm over a motorized artillery howitzer that has broken down. "People here like Americans." says a villager, "and the children are crazy about it." A Belgian newspaper, reporting on the exercises, says later that they took place "under the amused and often interested eyes of the local populace."

Back in the United States, in the Smoke Bomb Hill area of Fort Bragg, North Carolina, the Special Forces that figured so prominently in Vietnam have made a comeback. Better known as the Green Berets, they came out of Vietnam with a poor image. "We were seen as either snake-eaters or Mafia in uniform," says a Green Beret officer. "We've had too much macho." With a new rise of insurgency and terrorism around the world and particularly in Central America, the Green Berets are back in demand for their brains and their brawn.

Major Thomas J. Kuster Jr. is among the new breed of Green Berets. A lean, red-haired, and sunny man from the Bronx in New York, he speaks fluent Spanish, is a serious student of guerrilla warfare, and can quote from strategists such as Che Guevara of Cuba, Carlos Marighella of Brazil, and Vo Nguyen Giap of Vietnam. Major Kuster and a dozen other young officers work in the Institute for Military Assistance, scrutinizing guerrilla and terrorist operations from the maquis in France in World War II to the Nicaraguan Sandinistas aiding insurgents in El Salvador. At their disposal is a steady flow of intelligence, plus perhaps the best research library on guerrilla warfare in the United States. But Major Kuster cautions that strategy and tactics for fighting insurgencies must be tailored. "There is no immediate, automatic response," he says, "where you just plug in and go."

Besides planning for potential counterinsurgency operations, the Green Berets are teachers, primarily of foreign armies. Captain Bradley W. Miller and Captain Thomas W. Grace spend nearly five months in Liberia with ten sergeants on an "A Team," the basic unit of Special Forces, training a battalion of 600 Liberians. The Green Berets improvise everything at the abandoned air base where they do the training. They set up living and dining quarters, a medical room, areas for instruction, and firing ranges. "When we got there," Captain Miller says, "all we found were empty buildings and a big rock pile."

During the training, Captain Miller, the team leader, advises the Liberian battalion commander while Captain Grace works with the battalion's executive officer and second in command. "We kept it simple," Captain Grace says. "Shoot, move, and communicate." Two sergeants teach marksmanship, two more teach tactics, and a third pair teach radio operation. Two engineering sergeants instruct the Liberians in field fortifications while two medics teach first aid and the operation of a medical platoon and a battalion aid station. They also treat families of Liberian soldiers and deliver a baby. Since the Liberians speak a different brand of English and many of the junior soldiers cannot read well, the Green Berets teach by example. "They're going to do what they see you doing," Captain Grace says. "You always make sure that you can do it better than they can."

Colonel James H. Morris, the director of the school in which the Green Berets are trained, emphasizes the teaching role of the Special Forces. "Every Special Forces individual who goes through our training," he says, "from the very first day is put in a position where he must tell or demonstrate something to everyone else." The colonel says the Green Berets are taught to work through interpreters, to understand the difficulties of cross-cultural communication, and to deal with foreign officers who are almost always senior in rank to the American instructor. "We tell them to be sensitive," Colonel Morris says. "Our business is sensitive in nature."

In a dense patch of jungle only a few hundred yards from the Panama Canal, American paratroopers in full battle gear pull themselves through green slime hand over hand on a rope, only their helmets and rifles sticking out of the water. Close by, more paratroopers rig waterproof rafts of ponchos and pup tents, then ease them into the murky backwater to swim to the other side, one trooper towing the raft with a string in his teeth, the other pushing from behind. Still other paratroopers of the 2nd Battalion, 187th Infantry lash field packs into an eleven-man rubber boat and, after chasing off a couple of nosey alligators, slide the boat into a muddy pond and paddle away in a stealthy crossing.

Those troopers, members of the 193rd Infantry Brigade, train to help Panamanian forces defend the Panama Canal against a threat of guerrillas that United States authorities fear may infiltrate from Cuba and Nicaragua. Along with an infantry battalion, a battalion of Green Berets, and artillery, the troops also prepare for contingencies anywhere in Latin America. They are the only American combat forces on long-term duty in Latin America and are, in effect, the fire brigade of the Southern Command, which has its headquarters in Panama. For veterans of Vietnam, the jungles of Panama recall younger days. "After you walk around here for a while," says Lieutenant Colonel George B. Utter, who commands the paratroop battalion, "the smells start coming back to you. It seems like I've been here before."

Soldiers in the 193rd Brigade spend a good bit of time in waterborne training. Defending the canal doesn't mean standing guard next to the locks that lift and lower ships as they transit the isthmus, which is the responsibility of the government of Panama, but going out into a countryside filled with streams and ponds. "We want to engage the guerrillas as far away from the canal as we can," says an operations officer. Outside of Panama, troops of the 193rd Brigade have served in El Salvador, guarding a radar station on Tiger Island, and in Honduras, where they have taken part in maneuvers with Honduran and other American forces. On one occasion, an infantry battalion from the 193rd took the part of the opposing force that resisted a marine amphibious landing. It was good training, says the battalion commander, Lieutenant Colonel Thomas K. Sewell, adding with a chuckle, "I really liked going up against those marines."

Far into the lush Aguan valley in northern Honduras, United States Army combat engineers are carving a dirt road through the green brush and across shallow streams. Under a blazing hot sun, an engineer on a bulldozer scoops gravel from a creek bottom while another rides a grader touching up the side of the dusty road. Nearby a squad of soldiers smooths the concrete on a spill shield intended to keep a culvert from being washed away. An Indian peasant sits in the saddle on a lean pony, watching impassively, as do several cows lying in the middle of the road. The commander of the engineers, Colonel Paul Y. Chinen, relishes the experience for his troops because "we couldn't do this kind of training in the U.S." That would be precluded, he says, because of environmental restrictions and lack of space outside military reservations. But environmental considerations apply here as well. "We have to put everything back, except for the road itself," Colonel Chinen says, "just the way we found it."

The road-building project is among the diverse exercises that American forces have been undertaking in Honduras in recent years. Infantry and artillery units have trained here, as have units working on counterinsurgency, medical teams giving shots to Hondurans, and more engineers building airstrips. The exercises have also been shows of force intended to caution the leftist Sandinista government in Nicaragua not to meddle in Honduras. And they have been intended to reassure the Hondurans of American support. "For the American image," says an officer, "that road is worth ten divisions." In cases like this, the Honduran government picks the project site and furnishes fuel and construction materials. The road will give people in this remote valley a link to the outside world that they could reach before only on foot or horseback. "The immediate economic benefit," Colonel Chinen says, "is providing access out to the main road."

The project, however, underscores the logistical difficulties of operating in Central America. For this sixteen-mile dirt road, the Army brought in 850 soldiers, forty-three of them women, and 530 pieces of equipment for a project that took three months. Three cargo ships and several airplane flights carried people and equipment from the United States and Panama. Most of the troops were flown into La Cieba, a port twenty-five miles north of the construction site, and were trucked in over an old access road that an advance party had widened and straightened in a dozen places. Even so, a truck tipped over, injuring eight soldiers.

The work is hard and the living primitive. Troops are up at 4 A.M., start maintenance chores on the trucks and bulldozers at 6 A.M. and are at work on the road from 7 A.M. to 6 P.M. But the summer heat has presented few problems because the soldiers are in good condition. "There is a direct correlation," Colonel Chinen says, "between physical training and the ability to withstand heat." The soldiers live in tents, with a separate tent for the women and hours in the shower divided between men and women. Cots are covered with air mattresses and sleeping bags that the soldiers sleep on, not in, protected by mosquito nets. Recreation is limited to a few movies, as the camp is too remote to receive the American radio station in Palmerola, the Honduran air base that serves as a field headquarters for American forces here. A bag of paperback books brought in on a helicopter draws a round of applause. But officers here said disciplinary problems have been rare, except for instances in which male and female soldiers violated regulations by fraternizing. "It's been okay," says the camp adjutant, "except for a couple of cases of sex in the motor pool."

Deep in the rugged mountains of South Korea, Lieutenant Colonel Bobby R. Harkins had his battalion of light infantry dig ill-disguised foxholes, then led them on a visible retreat as the mock enemy advanced. During the cold of a March night, however, Colonel Harkins ordered his four companies to split up and slip away to circle around to the flanks of the South Korean "aggressors" and hide for twenty-four hours. They were so well concealed that the advancing Koreans came within fifty yards of one company and never saw them.

For five days after that, the battalion of 575 soldiers were marauders on a rampage through the "enemy's" rear area, hiding and resting by day but attacking headquarters, cutting communication lines, and blowing up ammunition dumps by night. In the move that the light infantrymen liked to tell about later, one company filtered into a helicopter parking area and fanned out silently to chalk graffiti and paste their 7th Infantry Division bumper stickers on the choppers to simulate blowing them up. The soldiers were in and out in ninety seconds.

That exercise in 1985 was the first overseas test of the Army's new light infantry divisions, four of which have been formed by the Chief of Staff, General Wickham, "to make the Army more relevant to the times." After the American engagement in Vietnam ended in 1972, the Army started building heavy armored and mechanized divisions intended to fight the Soviet Union in Western Europe. But General Wickham's predecessor, General Meyer, and General Wickham thought the Army also needed to be ready to respond to contingencies in the

Third World such as Central America or the Persian Gulf. A lack of air transport for quick reaction led the way toward light divisions of 10,000 soldiers each, with lean artillery, engineer, signal, transport, and other support. Divisions like the 7th Infantry, based at Fort Ord outside Monterey on the coast of California, could be moved in 500 air transport sorties instead of the 1,500 it would take to move a large division. After the 7th Infantry became operational in the fall of 1985, one battalion was on alert and ready to move in eighteen hours, the time it would take the Air Force to get planes there, while the other two battalions in a brigade would be ready within seventy-two hours.

To train soldiers as light infantrymen, leaders at Fort Ord emphasized the skills of individual soldiers, small unit tactics, and the stealth that Colonel Harkins's battalion employed in the Korean mountains. Light infantry is also a state of mind, said Lieutenant Colonel George A. Fisher, the division's operations officer: "We want the soldier really to understand what the light division is all about." New companies of soldiers arriving from basic training were given five days, each sixteen hours long, of hardening known as the Rites of Passage to increase their physical stamina and to improve their land navigation with map and compass, their ability to infiltrate, and other battle skills. On a firing range, Lieutenant Colonel George R. Dunn Jr. put squad after squad of nine men each through a live firing exercise, with the soldiers shooting on the move as they attacked a hill. Behind them, a machine gun shot tracers at the target, then shifted fire to the flank as the squad charged through the brush.

At Fort Hunter Liggett, a training reservation in the rolling hills southeast of Fort Ord, Lieutenant Colonel Richard L. St. John led his battalion through drills to teach the soldiers to fight as platoons against guerrillas. Nearby, Lieutenant Colonel Thaddius Chapman concentrated on training his staff and officers on night operations—moving, communicating, fighting. Back at Fort Ord, Lieutenant Colonel Joseph C. Windle said that getting his battalion ready to move out required "very detailed planning," more than with a regular battalion, in deciding what to take and what to leave behind: "The battalion commander has got to take some risks and not make the soldier into a pack mule. He can't carry all that and still do what we ask him to do on the battlefield." A bit later, a group of his soldiers was asked what difference being in the light infantry had made in their lives. They hooted; a young sergeant spoke up: "The light division only means that they have taken away our vehicles and now we have to hump all that [expletive deleted, expletive deleted]."

From time to time in recent years, the President has sent the armed forces into hostilities that have included the dispatch of combat forces to Lebanon, Grenada, and Libya. In each case, good troops and capable small unit leaders, plus hard training, have stood the forces in good stead despite the handicaps placed on them from Washington.

American marines were dispatched to Lebanon in 1982 to enforce a truce between the invading Israelis and the nearly decimated forces of the Palestine Liberation Organization. The marines were withdrawn when PLO forces were evacuated but returned after massacres of Palestinian refugees in camps at Sabra and Shatila in September 1982. The 1,200 marines, supported by an aircraft carrier and other warships offshore, were put by President Reagan into a difficult position at the Beirut International Airport. They had their backs to the sea on low ground where they could be fired on from nearby mountains. Their rules of engagement, or guidelines telling them under what circumstances they could fire their weapons, were restrictive. The marines were forbidden to send out patrols to collect intelligence or protect the contingent. They knew little about the chaotic military and political situation around them and had poor liaison with the Israeli Defense Force, the dominant military power in the area. Perhaps most important, as their mission changed from peacekeeping to assisting the Lebanese government in its struggle to survive, orders under which the marines operated were not revised to take into account new dangers.

On Sunday morning, October 23, 1983, a truck loaded with the equivalent of 12,000 pounds of TNT explosive crashed through the perimeter of the marine battalion, penetrated the building that housed a quarter of the marine force, and exploded. The building was demolished and 241 American marines, sailors, and soldiers died. Specialists from the Federal Bureau of Investigation said later it was the largest nonnuclear explosion they had ever examined.

A commission led by Admiral Robert L. J. Long, a retired naval officer, soon after reported that the military people in Beirut had acquitted themselves with honor after the explosion. "The Commission has the highest admiration," the report said, "for the manner in which U.S. military personnel responded to this catastrophe." It concluded, "The speed with which the on-scene U.S. military personnel reacted to rescue their comrades trapped in the devastated building and to render medical care was nothing short of heroic."

Beyond that, the Long report had little good to say of anyone from the President down to the commanders on the scene. The commission questioned the dispatch of the marines as peacekeepers and asserted that diplomatic and political efforts should have been exhausted before deploying military forces. They found the mission of the marines had not been carefully articulated; consequently, it "was not interpreted the same by all levels of the chain of command." Political and military leaders were criticized for decisions that "may have been taken without clear recognition that these initial conditions had dramatically changed and that the expansion of our military involvement in Lebanon greatly increased the risk" to the marines. The United States and, specifically, the Department of Defense were "inadequately prepared" to deal with terrorism. In particular, the commission found that the Marine Corps, which was responsible for training its troops, had neglected to instruct them in tactics against terrorist attack: "The only instruction the commission was able to identify was a one-hour class presented to the infantry battalions by the attached counter-intelligence non-commissioned officer and segments of a command briefing by the U.S. Army 4th Psychological Operations Group."

Intelligence furnished to the commander in Beirut was voluminous but was neither timely, nor specific, nor effective, "being neither precise nor tailored to his needs," the commission said. "We see here a critical repetition of a long line of similar lessons learned during crisis situations in many other parts of the world." Security measures in effect on the Sunday morning of the attack "were neither commensurate with the increasing level of threat confronting the [marines] nor sufficient to preclude catastrophic losses." The commission asserted the age-old principle that "the responsibility of military command is absolute" and faulted the battalion commander, the overall commander ashore, the admiral in charge of the naval task force offshore, the commander of American naval forces in Europe, and the commander of American forces in Europe, General Bernard W. Rogers, for having failed to plan adequate security. That judgment was softened only by a statement that "a series of circumstances beyond the control of these commanders influenced their judgment and their actions." The commission was not specific but presumably referred to political decisions that put the marines into Lebanon.

The commission concluded with a devastating comment on lack of military preparedness, finding that the American force "was not trained, organized, staffed, or supported to deal effectively with the terrorist threat in Lebanon."

The invasion of Grenada was not subjected to the same intense public scrutiny as was that in Lebanon, although the Chairman of the Joint Chiefs of Staff, the Commander in Chief of the Atlantic Command, and the Marine Corps published carefully edited or censored accounts. The failure of the Defense Department to provide a full account left the suspicion that enough went wrong to cause the Pentagon to wish to escape embarrassment.

As in Lebanon, individual soldiers, sailors, airmen, and marines distinguished themselves during the brief invasion of Grenada in October 1983. When C-130 propeller-driven transport planes carrying Army Rangers flew toward the Point Salines airfield, they came under heavy antiaircraft fire. The planes circled and returned so that the Rangers could parachute in from 500 feet, which gave each parachute barely time to open but reduced the exposure of the Rangers to hostile fire. That was at 5:30 A.M. During the ensuing fire fight, a young Ranger sergeant, his squad pinned down by machine-gun fire, spotted a bulldozer and scurried over to "hot wire" it into starting. He raised the blade as a shield, got his squad behind it, and charged the machine gun to put it out of action. Other Rangers fought so well that the airfield was cleared by 6:30. Air Force C-130 Spectre gunships flying at low altitudes provided accurate machine-gun fire on pockets of resistance to save the lives of American soldiers and Grenadan civilians.

Elsewhere, helicopter pilots braved ground fire to protect comrades down in another helicopter, saving them but losing their own lives. In a story that may have been embellished in the telling, a group of Navy commandos, trapped in a house surrounded by enemy troops and out of communication with other units, fought off the enemy while the sailor had the wit to use his telephone credit card and call back to a base in the United States to say that his unit was pinned down. The base got in touch with the task force, which brought in an air strike to relieve the siege. Marine helicopter pilots, finding a landing zone overgrown with brush, quickly spotted one that was suitable. When a marine patrol stumbled on a Russian-built light tank, an alert marine fired one quick round from a hand-held antitank weapon to put it out of action. Another marine commandeered a bulldozer to fill in a ditch so that tanks could get across. A Ranger unit, unable to get Army helicopters, worked well with a Marine helicopter squadron to make a swift assault.

Beyond that, however, were hasty decisions by President Reagan and his staff at the National Security Council. Planning was hurried and haphazard. Intelligence on potential opponents on the Caribbean island was sketchy. Information on the location of the 1,000 Americans was almost nonexistent; not until the assault was well under way did senior officers find out there were three groups of American students to be rescued, the ostensible reason for the invasion. It took thirty-six hours to round them all up, during which time they could have been massacred. Maps were so inaccurate as to be useless or so lacking the forces had to rely on gas-station maps or those they captured. An operation that was intended to be finished in twenty-four to forty-eight hours took seven days, even with the overwhelming military force the United States was able to bring to bear against 700 Cubans and several thousand poorly trained Grenadans.

A heavily excised report from the Commander in Chief of Atlantic forces, the command responsible for the operation, confirmed that intelligence and mapping was poor. In addition, planners neglected to include enough intelligence personnel to exploit information gained during the operation. Navy pilots, having been told that a certain building housed an enemy unit, bombed it only to discover later that it had been a mental hospital, several of whose patients were killed. Inadequate planning exposed helicopters, which were vulnerable to antiaircraft fire, and several were shot down. Communications often didn't work because officers had the wrong kind of radios or because messages could not be safeguarded against being intercepted. Logistics control was cumbersome.

In March 1986, President Reagan ordered three aircraft carriers and twenty-seven other warships to maneuver in the Mediterranean near Libya. The carriers *America*, *Saratoga*, and *Coral Sea* stood outside the Gulf of Sidra, which was claimed as territorial waters by Libya but said to be international waters by the United States and most other nations. Several other warships and many fighter and attack aircraft, however, went into the Gulf or flew over it. The Libyans fired several SA-5 Soviet-built surface-to-air missiles at the Navy planes, all of which missed. In response, the President ordered the Navy to attack Libyan radar and missile sites on land and Libyan patrol boats in the gulf. Three weeks later the Navy flyers were joined by aviators from the Air Force who flew around Europe from Britain to help mount a more explosive attack on Libyan bases and barracks in what President Reagan said was intended to deter terrorist acts supported by Libya.

From an immediate military point of view, both raids were largely successful. The Navy and Air Force aviators flew with professional skill that came from years of training; most of the weapons worked, as did much of the planes' electronic gear. A Navy pilot said he was "finally doing what you've been trained to do, and doing it right." Not everything was flawless, despite the effusive rhetoric that later emanated from Washington. Targets were missed and innocent civilians were killed; an Air Force plane was lost in the second raid, and five Air Force and two Navy planes had to abort because something didn't work right. But few military operations, given the "fog of war," are ever perfect and, in the Battles of Sidra, American flyers did well.

After the Navy pilots flew back to the aircraft carrier *Saratoga*, and the pumping of adrenaline slowed down, they talked about their attacks on Libyan patrol boats and radar sites, the missiles shot at them and the missiles they fired back. For many of the naval aviators, that March raid across the Gulf of Sidra just north of Libya was the first time they had flown in combat; for a few, it brought back thoughts of Vietnam.

"Some of us here have seen surface-to-air missiles before in other parts of the world," said one flyer, "so it's not a new experience for the old hands. The new guys hadn't seen it before. It's typically a bright ball of fire coming at you and it's getting brighter and brighter. You must do something, and you must do it fast."

The Navy flyer, talking with reporters, either didn't say what he did or the correspondents didn't report it. But flyers familiar with the Grumman A-6 Intruders and the Vought A-7 Corsairs said the pilots had three choices: they could have "jinked," making swift, diving turns that the missile couldn't follow; or jammed the oncoming missile's radar; or dropped chaff to give the missile a false target. Or they could have done a combination of two or three.

On offense, another Navy flyer talked about the Harpoon missiles fired at Libyan patrol boats and the Harm missiles shot at Libyan radar sites. The $1.4-million Harpoons can be launched a hundred miles from the target, after which they drop down to skim above the surface of the sea guided by inertial navigation until their built-in radar homes in on the target. Then they pitch up to dive on the target. The $231,000 Harm missile senses the emission frequency of a hostile radar, homes in on that beam, and rides it down from ten miles away. "The weapons we shot here are very expensive," the naval aviator said, "but it is very clear to everybody that we have demonstrated without a doubt that they work."

Still another flyer talked about what it was like to fire high-tech weapons that kill people, including civilians on the ground or seamen aboard a patrol boat. He found it "regrettable that Libyans have been killed" but asserted that was the consequence of "the actions of their government." Perhaps more to the point, he said, "in the heat of action, you don't have time to think about that."

Three weeks later, Navy pilots from the carriers *America* and *Coral Sea* (*Saratoga* had returned to the United States) and Air Force aviators from bases in Britain faced more opposition than those in the first raid. Officials of the Reagan Administration had alerted the Libyans by talking openly for a week before that a retaliatory strike might be mounted. One official had even told a reporter that the United States had obtained permission from the British government for the Air Force to fly medium-range bombers from bases in Britain to attack Libya.

The second raid was different in objective and tactics. In addition to standing off and shooting missiles at radar sites, the Navy and Air Force aviators were ordered to fly in very low to drop bombs on Libyan military installations inland. Thus, said a Navy pilot aboard the carrier *America* after the raid: "As we went over the beach, all kinds of weapons were fired at us." The officer in command of the fleet, Vice Admiral Frank B. Kelso II, said that "they came at us with a wide spectrum of surface-to-air missiles, and there was antiaircraft artillery of all kinds."

A bombardier sitting in the right seat of a Navy A-6 Intruder described a missile coming at him as "a little glow trekking through the sky." But reality set in quickly. "It kind of looks surreal because how could a star be going that fast. And then you realize that it might be going for you and that snaps you right back to reality." Like those in the earlier raid, a young pilot said: "The people who saw missiles in Vietnam have told us you can't really describe what a missile looks like. You've got to see it. Now I'm gonna go around saying that, too."

The Air Force flyers in the second raid flew in F-111s, a two-engine jet with swept wings capable of flying at more than twice the speed of sound for short bursts. The bomber has a crew of two sitting side by side in a cramped cockpit, the pilot to the left and the weapons officer to the right with a radar scope before him. Over Libya, as an F-111 streaked in at less than 500 feet, the weapons officer put his face into the elongated rubber mask of his scope and saw the blurred radar image of the runway and parking ramp of the military airfield in Tripoli. As the plane got closer, he flipped a switch to bring up the runway and ramp on the infra-red, a picture that was remarkably clear for 2:06 in the morning. A delivery system called Pave Tack coordinated the laser spotting of the target, the release of bombs, and the swiveling of a pod underneath the plane that gave the bombardier a picture of where the bombs went.

The primary target, a Russian-built transport plane on the ramp, was caught in the cross hairs and spotted by the Pave Tack's laser.

At the moment dictated by the computer, nine 500-pound bombs were released, their descent slowed and guided by fins that caused enough drag that the plane was able to escape the blast of its own bombs. As the plane passed over the target, an electro-optical pod underneath the plane swiveled to show nine dark blobs hurtling toward the target in what appeared to be an upside-down image. An F-111 bombardier explained later: "It's like bending over and looking back through your legs to see where they went." Other F-111s dropped 2,000-pound laser-guided bombs on a military barracks and on what the Reagan Administration said was a terrorist training camp. In eleven minutes, all but the lost F-111 had cleared the target area and were back over the sea. They formed up, took on fuel from waiting tankers, and flew back to Britain the way they had come because France and Spain had refused to allow them to fly through their air space.

Altogether, it was a fifteen-hour flight that made exceptional physical demands on the Air Force aviators. Each ate a high-protein meal before taking off and took a standard box lunch with him—sandwiches, fruit, cookies, and juice, plus small bottle of water. For bodily functions, the flyers urinated into plastic "piddle packs" that they sealed and stowed in whatever cranny was handy. Before the mission began, they made sure to move their bowels; otherwise, they had to wait until they got back to relieve themselves.

In standing watch, in training, and under fire, American soldiers, sailors, marines, and airmen do well today, as they almost always have in the past. Americans in garrison sometimes lack discipline, perhaps a reflection of the permissive nature of American society about which Tocqueville wrote a century and a half ago. But in adversity, the American GI has no equal; his shortcomings in garrison become virtues in the field or at sea or at a forward air base when the going gets rough. He is unsurpassed in taking initiative and at getting things done with ingenuity. Whether in the humid jungle, the freezing tundra, or the dry heat of the desert, the GI copes, and copes well. He is easily the best in the world at shifting for himself to find a way to get comfortable. The American in the armed forces responds to good leadership; the teamwork he learned on the high school playing field translates into a cohesion with others in his infantry platoon, his shipboard watch, his section on the flight line. In the face of bombs and bullets, his courage sustains him and his comrades.

But there is a discouraging contrast between the forces in the field and the high command around the flagpole in Washington. The soldiers and sergeants and combatant commanders who lead battalions and ships and air squadrons guard the nation well. The same cannot be said for those who plan and finance the forces, who are responsible for arming and equipping them, and who dispatch the forces to far corners of the world where they put their lives on the line every day.

CHAPTER 5

~~~~~~~~~~~~~~~~~~~~~~~~~~~~~

FEUDAL DOMAINS

THE INDICTMENT of the way the United States conducts its military affairs was scathing. General Edward C. Meyer, the Chief of Staff of the Army, declared, "If we were trying to convince an enemy that we were able to go to war with a system that works like this, he would laugh."

General Meyer, nicknamed "Shy" in his West Point days as a tall man might be called "Shorty," lamented the absence of a rational approach to provide for the common defense. After four years as a member of the Joint Chiefs of Staff advising the President and the Secretary of Defense, General Meyer felt free to speak his mind before he retired in 1983. "There is a total, absolute disconnect between the Administration and the Congress as to what the armed forces are to do and as to whether or not they are the right forces," he said in a wide-ranging interview in his unpretentious Pentagon office. "If you start out with nobody having any general agreement as to what the forces are supposed to do, it's no wonder that we don't have a rational approach." The general, who had fought in Korea and Vietnam, was particularly critical of the Congress for meddling in the details of military matters. "Every one of those committees is looking at individual weapons systems to cut, to stretch out, to do something," he said. "There is no continuity in programs, there is no incentive to industry. Nobody in Congress looks at what the purposes of the forces are." He chuckled: "This is Meyer's personal view but I don't mind telling Congress how to do business since they've been telling me how to do business for the last few years."

Indeed, General Meyer may have been gentle in his criticism, for a close look at the defense establishment discloses a structure in fundamental disarray. That establishment comprises elements in the White House, the Defense Department, other agencies within the executive branch, the Congress, the defense industry, and a mixed bag of intellectuals, dissidents, and reformers. That complex, however, is not a unified, cohesive institution dedicated to the national security. Rather,

144

it is a confederation of feudal domains, each struggling to preserve and to enlarge itself. The fiefs within the confederation do not work together for the common good but struggle to advance their own causes. They battle each other over concepts, responsibilities, weaponry, and, most of all, money. Those intense conflicts are not debates over how best to defend the nation but deadly feuds that sap military strength.

In a robust democracy, healthy competition in most institutions provides the checks and balances that prevent any one segment from becoming too powerful. But the military institution is different. It is, by nature, intended not to be democratic but to be an authoritarian, effective, and efficient war machine dedicated to defending the nation. The military institution, regimented and disciplined internally, is intended to be held accountable externally to the American people and their elected representatives. Americans rightfully are concerned about civilian control of the military, but that is not the main issue today. Rather, the issue is that the military establishment, which is responsible for deciding military policy and for building military power sufficient to defend the nation, is so riven with dissension and infighting that no one is in charge. American today is defended by a creaky war machine that lumbers along without coherence or direction.

The feudal domains in the executive branch of government begin in the White House. The two most prominent fiefs there are the National Security Council, which is supposed to draw together military, foreign, and international economic policy, and the Office of Management and Budget, which prepares and supposedly coordinates the President's annual budget, including that for defense, for submission to Congress. Elsewhere in the executive branch, the Secretary of State has his own views on military matters and State's Office of Political-Military Affairs is deeply involved with arms control, military assistance, and foreign bases. The Central Intelligence Agency runs covert operations and often influences the work of the military forces, especially those in special operations. The Department of Energy makes nuclear warheads for the Defense Department.

Within the Department of Defense, obviously the single biggest collection of feudal domains, the Secretary sits atop a bloated bureaucracy he cannot control. The Office of the Secretary of Defense, supposedly the executive center of the department, is badly organized, with far too many immediate subordinates reporting to the Secretary. The Departments of the Army, Navy, and Air Force are fiercely competitive, and each is subdivided into factions of political appointees, career bureaucrats, and military staff officers. The Joint Chiefs of Staff, the nation's top military body, violates the sound military principle of unity of command; it is a fractured committee. It functioned from 1982 through 1985 because the chairman, General John W. Vessey Jr., of the Army, was an exceptional leader, but it is the only place in the United States military service where decisions are made by a committee, not by a commander.

Within each service are separate, competing fiefs. The Navy has its submarine, surface, air, and amphibious communities, the latter including the Marine Corps. The Air Force has the Strategic Air Command (SAC), with bombers and long-range missiles; the Tactical Air Command (TAC), with fighters; and the Military Airlift Command (MAC), for transport. The Army is less split because combat divisions have elements from all branches. But there are still rivalries among officers who advocate heavy armored forces, light mobile forces, and unconventional forces.

Still other fiefs are the combatant commands, each headed by a commander in chief, or CINC (pronounced "sink"). The Atlantic and Pacific Commands are Navy fiefs; the European Command and Southern Command, for Central and South America, are Army fiefs. Within the supposedly unified commands are smaller fiefs of Army, Navy, Marine Corps, and Air Force components, each more loyal to its own service than to its operational commander. The Air Force, frozen out of the unified commands, has its fiefs in single-service, or "specified," commands at SAC and MAC. The Readiness Command within the continental United States is an Army fief with Air Force participation but without naval forces. The Central Command, whose responsibility is to defend United States interests around the Persian Gulf, started with a Marine Corps general in command, then had an Army general, then went back to a Marine Corps general, always with an Air Force officer second in command.

Congress is the site of dozens of fiefs, each more concerned with its own turf than with the national interest. There are Budget Committees in both the House and Senate that set basic levels for the military budget. The Armed Services Committees on either side of Capitol Hill, each with half a dozen subcommittees, control specific programs in authorizing force levels and funding limits in the Pentagon's annual budget, and they oversee the Defense Department. Members of the Appropriations Subcommittee on Defense, again in each house, determine levels of spending for each program. The Committees on Foreign Relations, the Committees on Government Operations, and most of the other committees and subcommittees on both sides of the Capitol sooner or later find ways to concern them-selves with defense. The primary reason is simple—money. The military budget is so immense that everyone seeks to get as much of it as possible spent in his home state or election district.

Still another set of fiefs are the defense industries, whose lobbyists and associations in Washington gather information to influence policy and legislation. Since Congress votes funds that the Defense Department translates into contracts, Capitol Hill is an important target. But lobbyists also cultivate officials of the executive departments who draw up budgets and who make decisions about where money will be spent. Altogether, about 300 defense companies or associations have representatives in Washington in offices that range from two persons to forty or more. Most of the large companies and associations have experienced public relations specialists who seek to influence press and television coverage either in their own favor or to the disfavor of a competitor by furnishing information overtly or by "leaking" it covertly to reporters.

Around the edges of the feudal domains are specialists in military matters known as "defense intellectuals." They inhabit the universities from the Massachusetts Institute of Technology to the University of California, the research organizations called "think tanks," and the consulting firms that are called "beltway bandits" because many of their offices are located close to the highway that circles Washington. The think tanks and beltway bandits survive and often thrive on lucrative contracts from the Pentagon or other government agencies. Others around the edge who can be influential on particular issues are the dissidents, who sometimes refer to themselves as "closet patriots." They leak information to congressional aides and to the press in hopes of causing a revision in a policy they consider to be erroneous. The Project on Military Procurement led by a woman named Dina Rasor and supported by Stewart Mott, a financier who often underwrites political activists, is among the chief dissidents. Much information on cost overruns, excessive prices, and other abuses that have become public knowledge has come through groups such as Ms. Rasor's. They act as brokers between dissenters inside the government, who don't want to be identified, and the public, the press, and the Congress.

Finally, the Military Reform Caucus in the Congress comprises about 100 Democrats and Republicans of diverse political persuasion who seek to cut military spending and to reshape the armed forces. Senator Gary Hart, Democrat of Colorado and a candidate for his party's presidential nomination in 1984, was active in the early days of the reform movement. That congressional caucus, along with other self-styled reformers, operates in a loose coalition favoring conventional arms over nuclear weapons, proven hardware over high technology, testing and warranties for weapons, more economical purchasing of spare parts, and tactics that emphasize maneuver over attrition. They assert that the cost of defense could be cut without damaging national security but tend to focus more on weapons programs and tactics such as maneuver warfare than on the strategic policies of the United States. Representative Jim Courter, Republican of New Jersey, a leader of the reform movement in 1985, included Congress as a target for reform. "When we speak of bureaucracies that should be shaken up, we shouldn't forget Congress," he said. "Congress places unnecessary burdens on the Pentagon through its highly disorganized budgets, appropriations, and oversight practices."

President Eisenhower gave the nation the name and concept of the military-industrial complex when he delivered his famous peroration a few days before he left the White House in 1961. In retrospect, that part of Mr. Eisenhower's farewell address seems a profound judgment that bears repeating:

A vital element in keeping the peace is our military establishment. Our arms must be mighty, ready for instant action, so that no potential aggressor may be tempted to risk his own destruction. [That is true today and is an essential ingredient of deterrence.]

Our military organization today bears little relation to that known by any of my predecessors in peacetime, or indeed by the fighting men of World War II or Korea. [That continues to be true, and Vietnam could be added.]

Until the latest of our world conflicts, the United States had no armaments industry. American makers of plowshares could, with time and as required, make swords as well. But now we can no longer risk emergency improvisation of national defense; we have been compelled to create a permanent armaments industry of vast proportions. Added to this, three and a half million men and women are directly engaged in the defense establishment. We annually spend on military security more than the net income of all United States corporations. [That, too, is uncannily true twenty-five years after Mr. Eisenhower spoke.]

This conjunction of an immense military establishment and a large arms industry is new in American experience. The total influence—economic, political, even spiritual—is felt in every city, every state house, every office in the federal government. We recognize the imperative need for this development. Yet we must not fail to comprehend its grave implications. Our toil, our resources and livelihood are all involved; so is the very structure of our society. [Undeniable, twenty-five years later.]

In the councils of government, we must guard against the acquisition of unwarranted influence, whether sought or unsought, by the military-industrial complex. The potential for the disastrous rise of misplaced power exists and will persist.

We must never let the weight of this combination endanger our liberties or democratic processes. We should take nothing for granted. Only an alert and knowledgeable citizenry can compel the proper meshing of the huge industrial and military machinery of defense with our peaceful methods and goals, so that security and liberty may prosper together.

Yet, even though Mr. Eisenhower was right about so much, the greatest threat from the military-industrial complex today is not to the workings of constitutional democracy. Rather, it is that the divided complex is neither effective nor efficient nor economical and thus does not provide well for the common defense. The complex wields enormous economic influence because of the huge sums it spends and extensive political influence as each fief seeks to enlarge its power. But the military budget has become a public trough at which the hogs of special interests feed and the struggles for power within the complex are fierce.

The military forces themselves lack unity, which leads to duplicated missions, lack of mutual support, different weapons made to do the same job, and excessive costs. American taxpayers, for instance, pay for three—some say four—separate tactical air forces in which many of the missions are similar. But all fly different aircraft, none of which is produced at an economical rate. The Air Force has its Tactical Air Command of fighters and ground attack planes; the Navy its carrier-borne fighters and attack planes; the Marine Corps its air wings of fighters, close air-support aircraft, and helicopters. Some critics have asserted that the Army developed helicopters as gunships for close air support because it did not want to rely on the Air Force fixed-wing aircraft. Defenders of the Army contend that the helicopter gunships are more like low-flying artillery and that the Army needs both them and the longer-range Air Force support. Whatever the case, a conference report of senators and representatives who had reconciled differing versions of the 1983 military budget reached this stunning conclusion: "The Defense Department is currently procuring aircraft from more than 25 production lines, not a single one of which is operating at the most efficient production rate."

Similarly, American taxpayers support two armies—and were almost asked to pay for a third—with their overlapping missions, double staffs, and lack of coordination in planning and weapons. The United States Army, with 781,000 soldiers, is the first army; the United States

Marine Corps, with 200,000 marines, is the second. The Marine Corps is among the twenty largest armies in the world—bigger than the British Army plus the Royal Marines, bigger than the army of any nation in communist Eastern Europe save that of Poland, bigger than the combined armies of Belgium, the Netherlands, Norway, and Denmark. The third army, an Air Force ground unit intended to provide security for air bases, was stopped by an agreement between the Army and the Air Force under which the Army would provide that security.

Moreover, each service has acquired weapons and equipment with little regard for the need to support other services. Perhaps the most glaring example is the lack of sufficient sea and air transport. The Navy has bought warships rather than less glamorous transports; the Air Force has built the B-1 bomber, aerial tankers, and fighter and attack planes but not so many cargo planes. The result: mechanized and armored Army divisions in the United States cannot get to most potential battlefields in time to be effective.

How is it that officers who are capable in the field as colonels and captains become such parochial advocates of their own services' interests when they go to Washington? In the field, most officers spend much of their careers within their own services, not on the staffs of joint commands. As they mature as officers, they tend to think in Army or Navy, Air Force or Marine terms. On those relatively few occasions when they must work with the forces of another service, face-to-face discussions among professional military officers steeped in the American tradition of teamwork solve the problems of a joint operation, and often with ease.

But in Washington, money is the root of all discord. An Army colonel summed up in one word the effect of the Pentagon on otherwise good officers: "The budget." Two Air Force colonels who had served in responsible command positions in the field threw up their hands. "The budget just drives you up and down," said one. "Around here," said the other in his Pentagon cubicle, "there are only two things that count, the politics of this building and the politics of Capitol Hill."

The military and civilian staffs of each service are geared toward one overarching enterprise each year, which is to get as much money as possible from the Congress, often at the expense of another service. Those officers are not selfish; indeed, they are dedicated to the mission of their service and the defense of America. But the system of budgeting and scrambling for money is corrupting. Those who had been upright officers in the field lose sight of their roles as soldiers or sailors when they gather around the flagpole and become bureaucrats hustling for funds. The point of nearly everything they do is not so much to defend the nation but to defend the turf, prerogatives, and funds of their services.

Many officers seem not to realize what happens to them and how pervasive the interservice rivalry becomes. Officers of one service often tease officers of another over football rivalries among the service academies and the like. But it is rare, in a conversation in which officers from only one service take part, that biting, sarcastic criticism of another service are not heard. The comments are incessant and the antipathy persistent—so much so that it has become a subconscious part of the Pentagon routine. As an Army officer once said: "I guess you haven't heard about my retarded brother?" No, said his visitor, he was sorry to hear that. "No, it's okay," said the Army officer, "he's a Navy captain." Or as a Navy officer said, "Be dumb, be a Marine."

The greatest potential for disaster from the lack of unity among the armed forces lies in operations, as seen in the attempt to rescue American hostages held by terrorists in Teheran in 1980 and the invasion of Grenada in 1983. The lack of coordination in those relatively small operations raises the obvious question: If the armed forces couldn't operate well together there, what would happen in a bigger conflict?

On the rescue mission, the operation ended in a flaming disaster at Desert One in Iran after one Navy helicopter flown by a Marine pilot had turned back, another had gone down in the desert with a cracked rotor blade, and a third had a mechanical problem that made the pilot consider it unsafe to go on. Another helicopter flown by a Marine, while trying to refuel to go back to the aircraft carrier in the Arabian Sea whence they had come, collided with an Air Force tanker plane on the ground and exploded, killing eight men. An investigation later blamed much of the failure of the mission on the lack of thorough, full-dress rehearsals by all hands, on excessive secrecy that kept each unit from knowing what the others were doing, on poor intelligence, and on a strange chain of command that left unclear who was in charge and who was responsible for what.

Colonel Charlie Beckwith, the commander of the Army's Special Forces unit that was to have carried out the attempted rescue in Teheran itself, was asked in testimony before a congressional committee what had gone wrong. He replied:

If Coach Bear Bryant at the University of Alabama put his quarterback in Virginia, his backfield in North Carolina, his offensive line in Georgia, and his defense in Texas, and then got Delta Airlines to pick them up and fly them to Birmingham on game day, he would not have had his winning record. In Iran, we had an ad hoc affair. We went out, found bit and pieces, people and equipment, brought them together occasionally and asked them to perform a highly complex mission. The parts all performed, but they didn't necessarily perform as a team.

After-action reports on the Grenada operation, whose objective the Reagan Administration said was to rescue American medical students, were laced with examples of how the services failed to work together. A heavily censored report from Admiral Wesley L. McDonald, the commander of Atlantic forces, to General Vessey, the Chairman of the Joint Chiefs of Staff, made the following points:

Tactical aircraft from the Air Force, Navy, and Army "were not always properly coordinated." The report said, "This created a number of problems which, while surmountable under the circumstances, could have proven more serious in the face of hostile air," meaning if the Americans faced a real enemy in the air. The specific problems were blacked out in the report, but it became known later that Navy pilots, unable to communicate with Army forces on the ground, had attacked positions held by American soldiers.

Army helicopter pilots evacuating wounded were not allowed to land on a Navy ship with hospital facilities. Said the report:

MEDEVAC [medical evacuation] operations at night became a great concern because Blackhawk [an Army helicopter] pilots had not been trained to land on seaborne helicopter platforms and were denied permission to land. This reduced the number of MEDEVAC helicopters that could bring wounded personnel to the USS *Guam*, the primary medical facility for the operation.

During URGENT FURY, the code name for the invasion, "as many as four different grid systems on three different maps were being used by operational forces," the report said. "The confusion caused by these multiple grids was considerable." In another case, a Marine detachment known as Anglico, which stands for "air naval gunfire liaison company," were forward observers who went ashore to spot targets and, over the radio, to direct naval gunfire against those targets. Part of the Anglico team was assigned to the 82nd Airborne Division's fire-control center to coordinate naval gunfire with artillery and air strikes. An Air Force forward observer was also assigned to the 82nd Airborne's fire-control center to coordinate air strikes with the artillery. But, the report said, the Air Force's forward observers didn't know what the Anglico team did. The report further cited several instances where forces from one service could not communicate with those of another, either because the radio equipment was not compatible or because the two units did not know each other's procedures. A Marine report also noted problems with communications, both within Marine units and between the Marines and other services.

But the Marine report found at least one instance in which two services worked together. An Army Ranger unit was ordered to rescue American students at a campus discovered only after the invasion had begun. Army helicopters were not available, and a Marine helicopter unit was ordered to move the Rangers. "The prime reason for this smooth execution," said the Marine report, "was the face-to-face meeting between the Ranger and squadron commanders on the ground at Point Salines before the attack."

After the operation, the Army general who took command of American forces as the operation came to a close, said in an interview with the *Navy Times* that the Army must learn to operate better with the Navy. "It's too late in exercises and actual operations to have misunderstandings or disagreements over doctrine," said Major General Jack B. Farris, the Deputy Commanding General of the 18th Airborne Corps at Fort Bragg, North Carolina. "It's too late in these situations not to be able to effectively employ all of your resources, which are always scarce, because you don't have joint procedures and techniques to employ all of those systems along functional lines." General Farris said that difficulties in communications arose not so much from incompatible equipment as lack of common procedures: "It's a matter of sitting down before you have an operation like this and having an understanding about how you are going to proceed and what communication system, for example, is for talk between the Navy joint task force and the Army ground commander."

The general noted there had been no single ground commander during the fighting.

When you don't have a common commander, then what happens is that people have some disagreements and then they bicker and then argue. And it takes time to do all that and to debate things and to decide what's going to be done. You don't have time for that in combat. With an operation like Grenada where it's not a big operation, it wasn't a violent operation, there wasn't a lot going on at any one particular time. You have time to cooperate, to discuss, to argue and to debate and to reach a consensus if that's necessary. If you get in a very hot, fast-moving situation, you don't have time to fool around with that kind of crap. Decisions need to be made and you need to move.

The disarray among the services is rooted in the period between the Civil War and World War II, when the small Army guarded the interior, watched the borders, and was the cadre around which citizen-soldiers rallied for the Spanish-American War and World War I. The Navy guarded the coasts and the sea lanes and carried the Army to war. Beyond that, each went its own way, with little need to work with the other.

World War II changed that, but not so much as it might have appeared. In Washington, the forerunner of today's Joint Chiefs of Staff worked, but not so well as it could have. General George C. Marshall, the Army's Chief of Staff during the war, said that "lack of real unity has handicapped the successful conduct of the war." The Secretary of War, Henry L. Stimson, wrote that the Joint Chiefs as a high command was "an imperfect instrument of top level decision because it remained incapable of enforcing a decision against the will of any of its members." Overseas, the Army predominated in the land war against Germany and Italy while the Army and the Navy split the Pacific region in the war against Japan. The Air Force in those days was the Army Air Force. Rivalries among the services were barely papered over, most notably the differences between General Douglas MacArthur and Admiral Chester W. Nimitz, the Army and Navy commanders in the Pacific. That led, on at least one occasion, to near disaster. During the invasion of the Philippines, some naval forces were under General MacArthur's control, others under Admiral Nimitz's. The latter, rather than supporting the Army landing in the Philippines, sailed north to engage part of the Japanese fleet, leaving Leyte Gulf open to other Japanese ships. An official history reported: "Gallant, desperate action by . . . old battleships and escort carrier planes [under General MacArthur's command] turned back the Japanese in the gulf, assuring the safety of the landing forces. It had been a close thing, clearly demonstrating the dangers of divided command."

After World War II, the need for unity among the military services became evident, given the likelihood that future operations would require forces from more than one service. But that unity has never been achieved. Indeed, the splits among the services have in many ways been responsible for the splits elsewhere in the wider military establishment.

In 1947, the National Security Act authorized the establishment of the Department of Defense, separated the Air Force from the Army, and organized it as a third service and military department. That act appointed the Joint Chiefs of Staff as the senior military advisers to the President and the Secretary of Defense. But the authority of the Joint Chiefs was limited by a Congress that feared, so soon after the war, the emergence of a general staff on the German model. The authority of the Secretary of Defense, moreover, was vague; real power remained in the hands of the Secretaries of the Army, Navy, and Air Force. In addition, the three services were unable to agree among themselves on the roles and missions of each.

In an effort to achieve order, Secretary of Defense James V. Forrestal summoned the chiefs of the services to the Key West Naval Base in Florida in March 1948. There they thrashed out differences and arrived at a compromise in the manner of medieval barons. That compromise was incorporated into a tri-service treaty known as the "Functions of the Armed Forces and the Joint Chiefs of Staff." The Navy retained control of the Marine Corps and of the Navy air force based on carriers. The Army gave up airplanes to the Air Force, and the Air Force promised to provide aerial transport and close air support to the Army. But there were no binding provisions for the services to operate together, and each retained control of its own budget. In time, the independent budgets would prove to be the undoing of the compromise because the admirals and generals preferred to spend money on their own services and missions, not on equipment that would benefit another service.

The Key West compromise ensured, for instance, that each service would develop its own weapons, an agreement that is very much alive today. Thus the Air Force flies the F-15 fighter, a heavy airplane that is roughly comparable in performance and missions to the Navy's F-14. The Navy flies the F-18 fighter, a lighter plane that is roughly comparable in performance and mission to the Air Force's F-16. The two services keep open four noncompetitive production lines that cannot achieve the economies of scale, instead of two lines, one producing a heavy plane for both services and another turning out a lighter plane for both.

The "revolt of the admirals" in 1949 revealed the deep cleavages that separated the services. In that incident, the Navy came close to mutiny against civilian control. The new Secretary of Defense, Louis Johnson, a political appointee of President Truman, had come to office with two prime objectives—unifying the Defense Department and reducing military spending. Among his early decisions were to cancel the construction of an aircraft carrier for the Navy, to slice the Navy's budget more than those of the Army and Air Force, and to favor the Air Force and its strategic bombing. The Navy responded by publicly criticizing Secretary Johnson, who was an abrasive man, and seeking to discredit the Air Force's plans for the B-36 bomber. The Navy made its case in hearings before a congressional committee, after which the Army and Air Force entered their rebuttals.

A turning point came when General of the Army Omar N. Bradley, the mild-mannered and newly appointed Chairman of the Joint Chiefs of Staff, blistered the Navy for being preoccupied with the past and unwilling to see the need for unification and new strategies. He accused naval officers of being "fancy dans who won't hit the line with all they have on every play unless they can call the signals."

The revolt failed a short time later, with senior naval officers retired or sent to less-than-desirable assignments in what President Truman called an effort "to restore discipline in the Navy." The House Armed Services Committee, which had held the hearings, issued one report upholding Secretary Johnson and the Air Force and another listing thirty-three findings on what needed to be done to achieve unity among the services. The Navy was defeated, but in the long run, little was accomplished to bring about military coordination.

After that start, interservice rivalry has continued to bedevil the armed forces and the Defense Department. President Eisenhower, the former general who was in many ways his own Secretary of Defense, was dismayed by the friction and lack of coordination among the services. In a letter to a friend in 1956, he said:

What I have tried to tell the chiefs of staff is that their most important function is their corporate work as a body of advisers to the Secretary of Defense and to me. Yet I have made little or no progress in developing real corporate thinking. . . . I simply must find men who have the breadth of understanding and devotion to their country rather than to a single service that will bring about better solutions than I get now.

Two years later, the President succeeded in reorganizing the Defense Department to strengthen the authority of the Secretary of Defense over the forces, the military departments, the budget, and the management of the Pentagon. The Secretaries of the Army, Navy, and Air Force were removed from the chain of command. Further, each chief of staff was removed from the chain of command so that he would have no authority over operations. Instead, the chiefs were made responsible for the recruiting, training, and administration of their forces. In addition, the Joint Chiefs as a group were cut out of the chain of command and became primarily advisers to the Secretary of Defense and the President.

The chain of command, on paper at least, was refined to run from the President and Commander in Chief to the Secretary of Defense, his delegated officer for military matters. The Vice-President was excluded from the chain of command to avoid the remote possibility that a Vice-President might try to take control of the forces in an attempted coup against the President. From the Secretary of Defense, the chain of command ran to the combatant commanders in the field. The new law read: "Orders to such commanders will be issued by the President or the Secretary of Defense or by the Joint Chiefs of Staff by authority and direction of the Secretary of Defense."

But the new law was not so far-reaching as it might sound, for each chief of staff retained power through his control of the structure of his service, assignments of senior officers, and promotion of officers and senior noncommissioned officers. Each secretary of a military department likewise could be effective in garnering power through control of budgets as they are drafted and through alliances with committees on Capitol Hill that favor his particular service.

That reorganization opened the way for Robert Strange Mc-Namara, who became Secretary of Defense in January 1961 in President Kennedy's administration, to bring with him the ideas with which he managed the Ford Motor Company as chief executive. Mr. McNamara, an intelligent, self-confident, and hard-driving business-man, became the most vigorous and commanding Secretary of Defense seen to that point, and was to leave the most visible imprint on the Pentagon. He served the longest—through the war in Vietnam, until 1968.

Douglas Kinnard, a political scientist specializing in the study of Secretaries of Defense, has written: "From a loosely decentralized arrangement in the Forrestal days, the control of the Secretary had gradually tightened. Eisenhower's 1958 Reorganization Act provided for ever greater central control, but the act had been basically untapped when McNamara was sworn in." Mr. McNamara himself wrote later,

The direction of the Department of Defense demands not only a strong, responsible civilian control, but a Secretary's role that consists of active, imaginative, and decisive leadership of the establishment at large, and not the passive practice of simply refereeing the disputes of traditional and partisan factions.

Mr. McNamara sought to guide the department by taking hold of the budget. As each military department submitted its budget for his scrutiny, Mr. McNamara insisted on allocating funds to functional missions such as strategic nuclear focus, general-purpose or conventional forces, communications, and logistics and parceled out funds to the services to spend on those functions. He installed a budgeting system that was intended to set objectives first, then devise programs to acquire weapons and to train forces, and finally to allocate funds to execute those programs. Although the system has rarely functioned

as designed, it remains in place today. Mr. McNamara was a controversial figure through most of his tenure, largely because he drew
power away from the military departments into his own hands. He
was unpopular on Capitol Hill for the same reason, as well as for his
intellect, knowledge of the issues, and incisive manner, which offended
less acute members of Congress. "For the first time," Mr. Kinnard
concluded, "the Secretary of Defense gained real control of the Pentagon."

Even so, Mr. McNamara failed to unify the department. The
feudal barons were too strong and outlasted even that formidable
Secretary. Nor have those after Mr. McNamara been more successful
in curbing the powers of the barons. Melvin R. Laird, President
Nixon's first Secretary of Defense, came from the House of Representatives and was effective in dealing with Congress. James R. Schlesinger, also appointed by Mr. Nixon, brought to the Pentagon extensive
experience as an associate director for national security in the Office
of Management and Budget in the White House, chairman of the
Atomic Energy Commission, and Director of Central Intelligence. He
was the best strategic thinker to hold the position. Harold Brown,
President Carter's Defense Secretary, was a nuclear physicist, a one-
time Secretary of the Air Force, and the best technician to hold the
job. But none of them moved the Pentagon much further along toward
unity. The department operates today much as it did when Robert
McNamara left in 1968.

Since President Reagan took office in January 1981, his administration has done little to lead the military establishment, to unify the
operations of the services, or to provide a coherent and visible strategy
on national security. The administration, or more precisely, the Defense Department, has tried to put together a military strategy, but
many parts of it are ignored as each service goes off in its own direction.
The primary use of the Defense Department's strategy has been to
justify the military budget to pay for a bigger and better armed military
force. But the administration has not articulated a national, or grand,
strategy that would fit together foreign policy, international and domestic economic policies, and other elements of national security. Such
a strategy could persuade the public to support the government's
policy, win the approval of Congress, reassure the nation's allies in
Western Europe and East Asia, inform neutrals of America's posture,
and advise potential adversaries not to miscalculate. Altogether, there
has been little fundamental rethinking of America's national interests,
its military posture, and the role of military force as an instrument of

national policy since 1950. Each administration has attempted to formulate a plan of its own. But all have been rooted in the National Security Council document known as NSC-68, which was written to provide fundamental guidance for President Truman.

President Reagan's national security adviser in 1982, William P. Clark, sought to pull together the Pentagon, State Department, Central Intelligence Agency, United States Information Agency, Treasury, Commerce Department, and other agencies concerned with aspects of national security. He asked them to submit their basic strategies from which the National Security Council would devise a national strategy and eliminate differences among the departments. The Defense Department brushed up its *Defense Guidance*, its first annual planning document intended to set a strategy that would guide deliberations over the defense budget, and sent that to the White House. But the other agencies failed to comply, and the effort quietly died, leaving the ship of state rudderless on national security.

The staff of the National Security Council, lacking fundamental guidance, lapsed into the day-to-day management of routine affairs and lurched from crisis to crisis. The absence of continuity at the top exacerbated the lack of direction. In five years, Mr. Reagan had four different assistants for national security affairs. Richard Beal, who was a senior director for crisis management, pointed out the drift. "National security planning is a myth," he told *Science* magazine.

You may say, well, it's just this Administration. I've got news for you; I've looked at the documents; it isn't. National security planning is weak. It's even anti-thetical to the American cultural sense of how we go about things. We're very practical. When you do not have overall national security planning, crisis management is very, very difficult.

He said the response to all crises begins with a clean yellow pad.

There is no, and I repeat no, institutional memory available at the highest levels of government for crisis management. This means that in every single instance—I don't care whether it's the Falklands or Lebanon or Poland—every single one of them begins anew because you can't draw at the highest levels on institutional memory.

Across the Potomac River in the Pentagon, the bureaucracy of 25,000 people is sluggish in responding to the direction of the Secretary of Defense. "We're the 'be here's," said a civilian bureaucrat; "we're going to be here long after these people are gone," meaning whatever administration is in office. That bureaucracy, moreover, is a collection of fiefs in the Pentagon and its outlying satellites in nearby Washing-

ton, northern Virginia, and Maryland, with scores of parallel, duplicated, redundant bureaucratic factions. Since anywhere from three to
a dozen officials must agree to a proposal before it can be implemented,
veto power is the primary weapon. It takes months or years to get
anything done, and that is usually a compromise at the lowest common
denominator, because so many officials can say no.

The most striking anachronisms within the Defense Department
are the military departments of the Army, Navy (which includes the
Marine Corps), and Air Force. They are vestiges of the pre–World
War II days when the Army and the Navy had no need to depend on
each other except on rare occasion. But the service secretaries, even
after they were removed from the cabinet amid several attempts to
strengthen the Secretary of Defense, retained much authority. A strong
service secretary, such as John Lehman, Secretary of the Navy in the
Reagan Administration, could have his own political base; set his own
agenda, carefully couched in the rhetoric of the administration; dominate the budget process within his service; and have his own alliances
with key members of Congress and their staffs. Mr. Lehman, an
aggressive, outspoken man, shrewdly outmaneuvered his counterparts
in the Army and Air Force to enlarge the Navy's budget and to impose
a greater degree of maritime strategy on the administration than perhaps the President and the Secretary of Defense intended. Mr. Lehman's largely successful effort in getting the administration and
Congress to increase the size of the Navy from fewer than 500 ships
to more than 600 has left an imprint—and a bill for payments due—
on the armed forces that will last well into the next century.

The divisions among the military departments have led them to
ignore many of the decisions set by their civilian superiors. Lawrence
J. Korb, an Assistant Secretary of Defense until 1985 and an incisive
student of military affairs, said in a speech that "we have been a house
divided against ourselves." He contended that "certain groups lobby
against corrective actions because they impact on service prerogatives."
Mr. Korb verged on accusing the services of disloyalty to the Secretary
of Defense and to their civilian superiors. "It has always amazed me
how military people can expect extreme loyalty from their subordinates," he said, "and yet they do not give it to the Secretary of Defense
when it comes to issues that impact on service roles and missions."

On duplication, the number of officials dealing with personnel is
illustrative. Nine senior officials, each with large staffs, set personnel
policy. The Assistant Secretary of Defense for Manpower heads the
civilian sector. Each of the three military departments has a civilian

assistant secretary for manpower, each with an entrenched civilian bureaucracy. On the military side, the Army, Navy, Marine Corps, and Air Force each have a three-star general or admiral as the senior staff officer for personnel. The Joint Chiefs of Staff also have a small personnel office, usually headed by a brigadier general. For each service to have someone in charge of recruiting, retaining, and administering to the needs of the people in its service is reasonable. Why both civilian and military staffs are needed, and why both Defense Department and service department staffs are needed, is less clear.

But the personnel fiefs are minor compared with those in the procurement of arms, equipment, vehicles, ammunition, spare parts, and the vast storehouse of supplies for a modern military force. It is surely the most divided and conflicting set of fiefs within the military establishment, rarely developing weapons that would be used by more than one service and hence could be produced economically. The senior official is the Under Secretary for Research and Engineering, who has eight senior deputies, each with a large staff. In each of the three military departments, the under secretary of the department is generally responsible for procurement. Each department also has a civilian, politically appointed assistant secretary for developing and buying arms and equipment.

On the military side, the vice chief of each of the four services is primarily responsible for procurement, with several three-star generals or admirals directly in charge of vast staffs. The Navy, for instance, has a vice admiral in charge of research, development, and engineering and three vice admirals in charge of acquiring weapons for surface warfare, air warfare, and submarine warfare. Beyond that are vice admirals in charge of the Naval Sea Systems Command, the Naval Air Systems Command, and the Naval Electronics Systems Command, who are responsible for the contracts under which the weapons and equipment are bought. Until 1985, the Navy also had a Naval Material Command in the contracting business until it was abolished and its functions absorbed by the other commands.

James P. Wade Jr., the Assistant Secretary of Defense in charge of acquiring arms, wrote an incisive critique of the system in late 1985:

The current Department of Defense/Service acquisition organization is ponderous, inflexible and so layered as to make it virtually impossible to maintain accountability. Department of Defense initiatives to improve the acquisition process are often implemented in a fragmented and inconsistent manner, which often defeats the objectives of the improvement initiatives. Inter-service rivalries and competition among the military departments for limited resources have hindered joint planning, joint doctrine, joint training, joint acquisition, and optimal use of new technology.

If the military departments are anachronistic, the Joint Chiefs of Staff are the greatest anomaly in the military world. In a culture that prides itself on having a designated officer in charge, on defining individual authority and responsibility, and on ordering a clear chain of command, the Joint Chiefs of Staff is a fuzzy committee. The structure of the JCS violates sound principles of military organization and unity of command, and the title "Chairman" conjures up the image of the corporate boardroom, not a military headquarters manned by warriors and disciplined to decision.

The Joint Chiefs, however, were not intended to bring unity to the armed forces; the format was chosen to preserve the domains of the Army, Navy, Marine Corps, and Air Force. James Schlesinger, Secretary of Defense in the Nixon Administration, pointed to the inherent contradiction:

In all of our military institutions, the time-honored principle of "unity of command" is inculcated. Yet at the national level it is firmly resisted and flagrantly violated. Unity of command is endorsed, if and only if, it applies at the service level. The inevitable consequence is both the duplication of effort and the ultimate ambiguity of command.

The Joint Chiefs are not a high command in charge of military operations. The law precludes them, singly or collectively, from commanding forces. The line of authority from the President to the Secretary of Defense and the commanders in chief of the combatant commands leaves the Joint Chiefs in an ambivalent position. Legally, the United States has no military officer in command of the armed forces, no military officer with the authority to coordinate the operations of the combatant commands. In peace and in war, Americans have left to a politically appointed civilian, the Secretary of Defense, the responsibility for operating the forces and for fighting military campaigns. "Since the creation of the modern American military establishment in the aftermath of World War II, we as a nation have been ambivalent regarding the goals we set for that establishment," Mr. Schlesinger said.

We have been and remain ambivalent regarding the purposes of defense unification. We have sought to preserve a degree of independence of the military services that precluded effective integration of our military capabilities. We have, above all, sought to avoid the creation of a dominating general staff—reflecting a fear of a German general staff that revealed both a misreading of history and a susceptibility to our own wartime propaganda. Those concerns, whether real or invented, bear little resemblance to the conditions of today and bear all the earmarks of another era.

In reality, most Secretaries of Defense have delegated considerable control of the forces to the Chairman of the Joint Chiefs of Staff, who issues orders in the name of the Secretary. In the Reagan Administration, Secretary of Defense Weinberger and the Chairman of the JCS, General Vessey, agreed that the general would be entrusted with operational control of the forces. But that delegation of authority, even when specified in writing, leaves the chairman open to challenge by field commanders who by law report not to him but to the Secretary of Defense. Mr. Schlesinger said his greatest concern about the JCS system was with the efficient design and execution of military operations. "The existing structure does impede planning," he told Congress, "for each of the services quite naturally wishes a piece of the action in any crisis—and the existing structure assures that all somehow will be fitted in, even if a service provides less than optimal forces for dealing with that particular crisis."

Nor do the Joint Chiefs function as well as they should as advisers to the President and the Secretary of Defense, which is their main responsibility. Because each chief must retain the allegiance of his constituency in his own service, he is more concerned with protecting turf than in providing sound military advice. Secretaries of Defense and military commentators alike have criticized the advice coming from the chiefs as a compromise at the lowest common denominator.

Mr. Schlesinger, a Republican, said, "The proffered advice is generally irrelevant, normally unread, and most always disregarded." Harold Brown, a Democrat who served as President Carter's Secretary of Defense, told a congressional committee in 1982 that he had found his informal, face-to-face meetings with the Joint Chiefs "extremely helpful." He said that previous Secretaries of Defense had said they felt the same way, as did some Presidents. But, he added,

When it comes to the formal product, the papers that come up through the Joint Staff that are approved by the action officers, the planners, the various desks and the Chiefs themselves, and to which they put their signatures, are almost without exception either not very useful or the reverse of being helpful. That is, worse than nothing. I think that is the difference between the people and the system.

A comprehensive analysis done by Georgetown University's Center for Strategic and International Studies in 1985 contended that the "institutional product," meaning the formal advice that has been drafted, debated, and compromised as papers have worked their way through the staff, was next to useless: "Although civilian leaders consistently praise the advice they receive from the individual chiefs of the services, they almost uniformly criticize the institutional products of the JCS as ponderous in presentation, predictably wedded to the status quo, and reactive rather than innovative."

The Joint Chiefs, as individual leaders of their respective services, have much to say about the annual military budget that determines the kind of force each seeks to build. As a corporate body, they have far less to say because they can rarely agree on the trade-offs. They cannot bring themselves to agree, for instance, that buying an aircraft carrier for the Navy would be less important than buying more tanks for the Army plus the ships to transport them to Europe or the Persian Gulf in a crisis. Consequently, each service asks for equipment to enable it to execute its own plans but not necessarily related to the forces the other services are trying to build. Each service asks for everything it needs, often duplicating what the other services are buying but with a different piece of equipment. Because each service wants its own budget request to be approved and fears undercutting from the others, each tends to support the requests of the others. Therefore, the annual budget request for the entire Defense Department is far larger than it need be. The lack of coordination among the services and the inability of the Joint Chiefs of Staff, and the Secretary of Defense, to thrash out those issues are among the main reasons military spending is so high.

In addition to being unwilling to think collectively about the military budget, the chiefs are unable to think strategically about the national interests of the United States or about deploying military forces to protect those national interests. There is not enough time, given the effort each must expend in looking to the needs of his own service, both internally and externally, such as answering questions from Congress. Each year, the chiefs prepare for the Secretary of Defense a joint strategic planning document that scrutinizes the threat to the United States and recommends the forces needed to meet that threat. That document, the Center for Strategic and International Studies said, is of only limited help to the Secretary in the allocation of funds:

It makes no recommendations as to priorities and does not take positions on the trade-offs necessary to construct a force structure within the bounds of available financial resources. The Secretary must make those force structure decisions without benefit of cross-service military advice. Instead, he must rely on his civilian staff to ensure that service programs are balanced and consistent with national strategic priorities. In short, budgetary priorities tend to be established in separate dialogues between the individual services and the Office of the Secretary of Defense, with only minimal joint military participation.

In recent years, more military voices have been heard criticizing the system. When he retired in 1982, General David C. Jones, who had been a member of the Joint Chiefs for eight years, began to seek reform of the system. General Jones, who had served for four years as Chief of Staff of the Air Force and four more years as Chairman of the JCS, was supported by General Meyer, who was even more critical of the system. General Jones observed that he was not the first, by far, to note the shortcomings, pointing to voluminous studies and comments from military officers dating back more than thirty years. His four main criticisms:

- Responsibility and authority are diffused, both in Washington and in the field. Because of this, we are neither able to achieve the maximum effective capability of the combined resources of the four services nor to hold our military leadership accountable for this failure.
- The corporate advice provided by the Joint Chiefs of Staff is not crisp, timely, very useful or very influential. And that advice is often watered down and issues are papered over in the interest of achieving unanimity, even though many have contended that the resulting lack of credibility has caused the national leadership to look elsewhere for recommendations that should properly have come from the JCS.
- Individual service interests too often dominate JCS recommendations and actions at the expense of broader defense interests. This occurs not only within the JCS itself but in the unified commands and throughout the multi-layered JCS committee structure where joint issues are addressed.
- A service chief does not have enough time to perform his two roles as a member of the Joint Chiefs and as head of a service—and these two roles have a built-in conflict of interest. The involvement of the service chiefs and their staffs in every facet of joint actions contributes greatly to these problems. The time-demands on a service chief not only contribute to the difficulty of managing service programs and resolving such problems as procurement cost and time overruns, personnel discipline, training, morale and force readiness, they also prevent him from being fully conversant with the joint and cross-service issues he must address in the JCS forum.

The commanders in chief (CINCs) of the field commands are not much better off. They have been unable to overcome the feudal autonomy of the Army, Navy, Marine Corps, and Air Force commanders in charge of each component within their commands. On paper, the service component commanders report to the CINC, but in actuality they owe allegiance to the chief of their service. That officer controls their funds, the size and arming of their forces, the logistics vital to their operations, and, personally, their assignments and promotions. The Center for Strategic and International Studies pointed out that President Eisenhower had established a division of labor between the military services and the unified commands to ensure unity in operations. "But the distinction between maintaining and operating functions has never been achieved in practice," the report said. "The unified and specified commanders lack adequate peacetime authority over the allocation of resources to their forces and the conduct of operations to carry out their missions effectively."

The CINCs were asked to report to Congress in 1985 on the structure within which they worked. Those CINCs who commanded forces in a specified command, such as the Strategic Air Command and the Military Airlift Command, which have only Air Force units, had few complaints. Nor did the CINC of the Atlantic Command, which is basically a naval force. But the CINCs of three commands that include large forces from two or more services had plenty to say.

General Bernard W. Rogers, commander of American forces in Europe, said "there is an imbalance between my responsibilities and accountability as a unified operational commander and my influence on resource decisions," meaning money, men, and matériel. General Rogers, a onetime Chief of Staff of the Army, asserted that Washington and the four services, not the combatant commanders, control budget decisions. "CINCs have no direct authority over component commands' personnel, readiness, logistics, and administrative control," he said. "I do not have the authority, in most instances, to remedy the problems uncovered in reports and exercises."

Admiral William J. Crowe Jr., commander of Army, Navy, Air Force, and Marine Corps forces from Hawaii west to Japan, Korea, the Philippines, and the Indian Ocean, came close to accusing his subordinates of disloyalty to him. "Major service decisions, not previously coordinated with me, have affected my ability to execute United States Pacific Command strategy," said the admiral, who became Chairman of the Joint Chiefs of Staff in October 1985.

Although these decisions were often quite logical when measured against service-unique requirements and budgetary realities, they nevertheless had a direct impact on the planning and execution of my theater strategy which concerns all the services. . . . If the unified commander feels compelled to deploy his forces in a manner that varies from an individual service's doctrine, creates an unusual command arrangement, or makes a controversial tactical decision, subordinates may dispute his judgment through service channels. In sum, the unified commander works within a very complex command structure where authority is somewhat diffused and he must rely on his persuasive skills as much as a formal mandate.

General Wallace H. Nutting, until 1985 the commander of the Readiness Command with headquarters in Tampa, Florida, said the military structure was "more accurately termed federated rather than unified." He asserted that "in a very real sense, the general principle of 'separation of powers' that underlies our governmental structure has been translated into the way we organized our defense structure." He continued, "Broadly speaking, I believe that the entire U.S. government suffers from excessive organizational layering, overstaffing, transient leadership and management, and too-short tours of duty." Like General Rogers, General Nutting said, "There is an imbalance between my operational responsibilities and influence over resource decisions." General Nutting, whose mission was to prepare Army and Air Force units within the United States for deployment overseas in the event of hostilities, argued that the system had internal contradictions:

One such contradiction derives from the establishment of two potentially competing channels of authority: the service mission to organize, train, and equip their forces, and the United States Readiness Command's responsibility to exercise operational command to ensure joint readiness, joint deployment and strategic rear area protection.

Among the main examples that CINCs have cited over the years has been their lack of say in drawing up budgets. The CINCs, who would be responsible for directing the forces in a conflict, want more money spent on ammunition, supplies, fuel, medical equipment, and other things that they might need to go to war tomorrow. In contrast, the chiefs of the services in Washington have their eyes on the future and are more interested in spending money on new airplanes, ships, and tanks that will increase the size of the force and equip it with more arms.

While critical voices have been swelling in recent years, the system does have its defenders. Among its most vocal advocates during the first five years of the Reagan Administration was the Secretary of the Navy, John Lehman. Mr. Lehman reflected the Navy's traditional resistance to efforts to unify the forces when that might mean a loss of Navy control over naval forces. He asserted that demands for reform would lead to a general staff modeled on that of the Prussians. "Always the diagnosis is the same: interservice rivalry supposedly results in poor strategy and poor military performance," he argued in an article in *The Washington Post*.

Accomplishments like the 35 years of NATO deterrence and the 215 successful applications of United States military power in crisis management are ignored, while the isolated instances of failure such as the tragic Iranian rescue mission are highlighted with the JCS organization chart provided as the scapegoat.

Mr. Lehman pointed to faults elsewhere in the defense establishment. "The Office of the Secretary of Defense staff is too large and bureaucratic, the service staffs are too large and bureaucratic, the chain of command has too many layers with too many uniformed bureaucrats," he contended. "Some functions need shifting from the Office of the Secretary of Defense to the Joint Chiefs of Staff and the services. The critical integrating and cross-service functions of the Office of the Secretary of Defense need strengthening."

General Lyman L. Lemnitzer, who was Chairman of the Joint Chiefs of Staff from 1960 to 1962, has been among the few Army officers who have advocated leaving the present system alone. "The Joint Chiefs system has served the nation well for more than 40 years in war and so-called peace," he said in a commentary in *The New York Times*.

I do not know of any major civilian activity involving such complex problems in which agreement is always unanimous; while this is taken for granted in other fields, critics seem to find it inexcusable in the military. . . . The best way to give civilian leaders balanced military advice is by using the talents and broad experience of the military chiefs of all services. Each knows his own service; each is an expert in his field. Our present organization provides the checks and balances that moderate extreme views. Some criticize this system as unwieldy. I do not. It is uniquely suited to American democracy.

A military historian, Trevor N. Dupuy, did not agree:

There is no reason for the American military machine to change from being a servant of the state to being its master just because it achieves the efficiency that has been eluding it for centuries. There is absolutely no evidence that general staffs have in any way eroded civilian control of the armed forces of any nation. They have been subservient to autocrats when they have been created in autocratic societies; they have ably defended liberty when they have been implanted in democracies. The general staff most noted of all, that of Germany, twice attempted to substitute democracy for autocracy in an autocractic society, but failed on both occasions because the autocracy was too entrenched.

Another confederation among the feudal domains concerned with military matters is the Congress, which has done as much in recent years to weaken the defense of the nation as any institution in America. Members of Congress are, with a few exceptions, barely interested in military policy or strategy or national security. Instead, they are intensely interested in drawing military spending into their home states or electoral districts. According to Senator Ted Stevens, Republican of Alaska and Chairman of the Appropriations Subcommittee on Defense, "Congress has made the defense bill a jobs bill." Senator Phil Gramm, Republican of Texas, came out of his first experience in a House-Senate conference—a meeting to reconcile differences in the 1986 military authorization bill—to call the session behind closed doors "an orgy of pork."

Similarly, the Presidential Private Sector Survey on Cost Control, led by J. Peter Grace, the chairman of Grace & Co., asserted that senators and representatives were driven by a "parochial imperative." The Grace commission defined that imperative as "an excessive preoccupation with the local impact of spending decisions at the expense of the national interest." The commission found the parochial imperative affected Democrats and Republicans equally. The conservative Heritage Foundation came to the same conclusion, that taking care of constituents is fundamental. "Defense finds itself saddled with weapons systems that it would rather not have," the foundation said in a report. "It buys them, however, simply because they are produced in the district or state of a key committee member."

On the other side of the political spectrum, the liberal organization Common Cause conducted a survey of congressional aides working on defense issues. Half the aides agreed that where a weapon would be made was the critical issue in debate. "The place of manufacture and the associated jobs," Common Cause said, "rather than the cost to the taxpayers and the effect on national security is the dominant issue even though arguments center on what is good for the country." In its analysis on organizing for defense, the moderately conservative Center for Strategic and International Studies concluded, "Any serious reform of the Congressional process is difficult to achieve because in the end it means that members of Congress will have to yield some of their ability to serve individual constituent interest to the common interest of the nation's security."

The Grace commission cited a long history of Defense Department attempts to close bases and to consolidate their missions at other bases, along with an equally long record of the congressional parochial imperative that frustrated those base closings. The Congressional Budget Office had periodically pleaded for such a program, as had the General Accounting Office, both agencies of the Congress. "All to no avail," the Grace Commission said. "The intoxicating allure of the parochial imperative has been simply too seductive, and the will of Congress to resist too weak, for the national interest to triumph."

Every year during the debate over defense spending, members of Congress huff and puff about how they are going to trim the fat out of the measure. But Congress quietly adds to military spending. Among those most eager to slip in provisions to help their states or districts are the most vocal in condemning military spending. The late Representative Joseph Addabbo, Democrat of New York and Chairman of the Appropriations Subcommittee on Defense, was a critic of military spending. But he managed in many years to increase the purchase of aircraft made by Grumman Aircraft in a district near his own, in return for which Grumman contributed to his campaign fund. Representative Jim Courter, a Republican leader of the Military Reform Caucus, reported to his constituents that he was "instrumental in obtaining Defense Department guarantees that there would be no loss of jobs or programs at Picatinny Arsenal during a command reorganization." Senator Alan Cranston, Democrat of California, has often taken antimilitary positions but has been an eager supporter of the B-1 bomber built in his home state.

Similarly, Senator Howard Metzenbaum, Democrat of Ohio, has been a critic of military spending but has supported the B-1 program because components for the aircraft are made in Ohio. Senator Carl Levin, Democrat of Michigan, has almost always been among the best-prepared members of the Armed Services Committee in a hearing when it comes to asking pointed questions of officials from the Pentagon. But for several years Senator Levin guided through Congress a measure to increase the purchase of M-1 tanks from the 720 requested by the Pentagon to 840, because many are made in Michigan. Senator Sam Nunn, Democrat of Georgia and respected for his evenhanded approach, nevertheless fought successfully to have additional C-5 transport aircraft built in Georgia even though the Army and the Air Force favored a new plane. Senator John Warner, Republican of Virginia, blocked a Navy proposal to move 16,000 workers from Arlington, Virginia, where they occupied rented offices, to the government-owned Washington Navy Yard, a couple of miles away. In one of the more absurd inefficiencies, the Congress has required American forces stationed in Germany not to buy German coal mined nearby but to ship American coal from the United States at what the Pentagon calculates costs the taxpayers an extra $6 million a year.

The House of Representatives looks kindly on proposals from members to build armories for the National Guard or the reserves in a member's home district even though the Pentagon has not requested it. On the other hand, Congress has often refused an administration's request for authority to award multiyear contracts. Under such arrangements, the Pentagon and a defense contractor would agree that a certain number of weapons would be built each year for, say, five years. That would permit the contractor to plan his production, buy his materials, hire the right number of people, cut down on overhead, and achieve other economies that would be the consequence of a stable program. But that would take a lever from the hands of Congress, and Congress has been loath to allow that.

With the stakes in the defense business ever higher, congressmen have involved themselves in ever-greater detail of military matters. To assist them, they have hired more staff members, often men and women who know much about military affairs. That, in turn, stimulates even closer scrutiny and attempts to manage defense programs. "Instead of focusing on broad military policy and spending guidelines, Congressmen have become ever more involved in minutiae," the Heritage Foundation said.

Members and staff seem anxious to control every detail, the fit of fatigues, the price of hammers, the brand of tools, even the allocation of overhead costs to the price of spare parts. They have taken it upon themselves to designate which Navy ships should go to which shipyards for overhaul. . . .

By almost every measure, Congressional oversight of defense activities is mounting. The hours of Pentagon Congressional testimony have increased every year since 1980. Defense Secretary Caspar Weinberger in 1983 logged over 55 hours in 20 appearances compared with 41 hours in 16 hearings the year before. In all, the Pentagon provided 2,160 hours of testimony in 1983, up almost 50 percent from 1982. The number of formal reports has also been a drain. In 1983 alone, the Navy sent 37 formal reports to just two committees; other committees required their own. From 1980 to 1984, The Defense Department submitted over 950 different reports to Congress and responded to thousands of other demands from the Hill.

Common Cause agreed. A large majority of the staff aides who responded to its survey said that "Congressional review of the defense budget suffers from overlap and duplication of effort among committees that participate." By an equally large margin, the staff aides agreed that "the wrong questions are being asked. The debate is focusing on how much to spend rather than on what it should be spent for and why." The Center for Strategic and International Studies said, "No legislature in the world devotes as much time, energy, and talent to decision making on the defense budget as does the U.S. Congress." But, the Center added,

The Congress contributes to turbulence in the defense program and budget by focusing excessively on the details of program management. Moreover, by using its time to review virtually every line item in the budget, the Congress foregoes opportunities to address more fundamental issues of defense policy: The establishment of national strategic priorities and the broad allocation of defense resources toward those priorities.

When Senator John Tower retired from the Senate in 1985 after twenty-four years of service, the last four as Chairman of the Armed Services Committee, he unloaded some pungent observations about the performance of his colleagues in what he called "Congressionally-mandated waste." In an interview, he said, "There are few members of Congress who think in terms of overall national security." Instead, he asserted, "Congress plays a significant role here because members of Congress, even those who complain about the military industrial complex, are actually allied with certain members of it because of their constituents. That means investments and jobs in their constituencies." The Senator said many weapons "are perpetuated because powerful members of Congress dictate that they shall be beyond military need." Members of Congress sometimes argue that they are voting only to approve the requests from the Pentagon. "Sure, it's in the Department's request," Mr. Tower said, "because the Department has been blackmailed into including it."

Senator Tower called the bluff of his colleagues in 1983. In a letter to each senator, he wrote:

If Senators are truly committed to cutting the defense budget, there should be military installations or contractor operations in every state which are candidates for reduction. . . . I would invite every Senator to give me a list by March 1, 1983, of any defense-related project in his or her state where a reduction of expenditure could be made because such expenditure is not essential for national defense.

Shortly after sending the letter, Senator Tower read it aloud in a hearing. As he finished, the room packed with lobbyists, congressional staff assistants, journalists, and political buffs, all wise in the ways of

Congress, erupted in laughter. Over the following weeks, only one serious proposal came from the ninety-nine other Senators: Senator David Pryor, Democrat of Arkansas and a leader in a fight against chemical weapons, urged that funds to build a binary chemical weapons plant in his home state be deleted.

Senators Barry Goldwater, Republican of Arizona, and Sam Nunn, Democrat of Georgia, rose in the Senate in October 1985 to deliver a series of incisive summaries on the ills of the military establishment. The criticism, coming from the Chairman of the Armed Services Committee and its senior minority member, both widely respected for their knowledge of military issues and their support for a strong defense, amounted to the most searing indictment heard in decades.

The senators started by pointing at the Congress itself. "I am casting the first stone," Senator Goldwater said, "and I'm throwing it at our glass house here in the Congress." Said Senator Nunn, "As the old saying goes: We have found the enemy and it is us."

Historically, Senator Goldwater said, "the problems currently plaguing the U.S. military establishment have been evident for all of this century. Indeed, many of them first emerged during the Spanish-American War." He turned to specifics: "The budget process distorts the nature of congressional oversight by focusing primarily on the question of how much before we answer the key questions of what for, why, and how well." [Underscoring in original.] He said the budgeting, authorizing, and appropriating functions, and the committees handling each, were intended to be complementary. "But, in fact, they are largely redundant," Senator Goldwater said. "The Constitution clearly intended that there be some duplication by creating two different chambers of Congress. But this duplication is out of control. . . . More and more legislation affecting the Defense Department is reported from subcommittees with only the smallest interest in national defense."

Senator Nunn picked up the theme: "The Constitution envisioned that the Congress would act as the nation's board of directors on public policy issues. . . . Instead we are preoccupied with trivia. Last year the Congress changed the number of smoke grenade launchers and muzzle boresights the Army requested. We directed the Navy to pare back its request for parachute flares, practice bombs, and passenger vehicles. Congress specified that the Air Force should cut its request for garbage trucks, street cleaners, and scoop loaders. This is ridiculous." The Senator pointed to the number of reports Congress required from the Pentagon: "In 1970, Congress directed the Defense

Department to conduct thirty-six studies. Last year, Congress mandated 458 studies and reports of the Department of Defense. . . . The micromanagement problem is getting worse at an alarming pace."

Next, Senator Goldwater said that "the military services' inability, or unwillingness, to work together had led this nation to military disaster or near disaster. . . . I am saddened that the services are still unable to put national interest above parochial interest. The problem is twofold; first, there is the lack of unity of command, and second, there is inadequate cooperation among U.S. military services when called upon to perform joint operations." He ticked off a list that included the Spanish-American War, when the admiral and general in charge of naval and ground forces barely spoke; the Japanese attack on Pearl Harbor in 1941, when the admiral and general failed to coordinate defenses; the battle of Leyte Gulf in the Philippines during World War II, when the fleet abandoned the Army and exposed it to the threat of disaster; Vietnam, when the absence of unity of command contributed to the defeat; and the seizure of the intelligence ship *Pueblo* by North Korea in 1968, when ships and Air Force planes under other commands could not be mustered to rescue the captured vessel. "We still have situations today," the Senator said, "where a unified commander cannot tell forces under his command where to store ammunition for war—even if it is in the wrong place."

In the same vein, Senator Nunn dissected the Grenada operation: "It is sobering to look at how much went wrong, and at how many failures of coordination and communication there were. . . . the Marine and Army units were not under a unified commander. . . . The invasion was plagued by the forces' inability to communicate, a problem caused by the services' continued practice of buying radios which are not compatible. . . . The services demonstrated a remarkable lack of knowledge about how each other operates." In sum, Senator Nunn said: "A close look at the Grenada operation can only lead to the conclusion that, despite our victory, despite the performance of the individual troops who fought bravely, the United States armed forces have serious problems conducting joint operations. We were lucky in Grenada; we may not be so fortunate the next time."

Finally, the Senators examined the Joint Chiefs of Staff. Senator Goldwater said the serious problems include: (1) the inability of the Joint Chiefs to provide useful and timely advice; (2) poor performance in joint operations; (3) the inadequate quality of the staff of the Joint Chiefs; (4) the confused command lines; and (5) lack of adequate advocates for joint interests in budgetary matters. Senator Nunn focused on the field commanders: "I regret to report to you today that we have <u>unified</u> commanders but <u>divided</u> commands [underscoring in original]. . . . There is essentially no unified command below the level of commander in chief and his staff. . . . Many commanders in chief of the unified commands have complained that they are not certain whether their boss is the Chairman of the Joint Chiefs or the Secretary of Defense. In a crisis, who do they talk to?"

Senator Goldwater concluded: "You will hear over and over again the old maxim 'If it ain't broke, don't fix it.' Well, I say to my colleagues, it is broke and we need to fix it." Senator Nunn echoed that: "I agree with the chairman. The system is broke and we need to fix it."

CHAPTER 6

~~~~~~~~~~~~~~~~~~~~~~~~~~~~~

SERVING TWO MASTERS

A T THE SANTA FE BAR & GRILL on Nogales Highway, just up the road from the Hughes Aircraft plant amid the cactus and mesquite outside Tucson, Arizona, friends of George Gonzales got together several days before Christmas to celebrate his election as the union's chief steward. Someone brought in a big pan of fried chicken, a bowl of cole slaw, and a stack of paper plates. After a couple of rounds of drinks, the talk over the blare of Latin music and Christmas carols from the jukebox turned to the troubles at Hughes Aircraft. "It's the supervisors," said a friend of Mr. Gonzales. "The supervisors got to take the blame. You can't put it off on the workers."

In other pubs along Nogales Highway, more conversations rambled around the failure of managers at Hughes Aircraft to insist on good work, to listen to people who worked on the floor when they pointed out problems, to provide workers with the best machines to do their jobs. The story was told in the Big Hat Cafe, where a few Hughes workers ducked out for lunch, or in Big Red's Cafe and Vintage Tavern, where Hughes people dropped in after the second shift let out at 12:30 in the morning, or at the newly refurbished Bojangles Saloon. At Bojangles, a barkeep in that 1984 holiday season said Hughes workers thought discipline was lax. "Some of the older guys used to say that working there was like being retired," he said. "They just went in, put in their time to get paid, and went home."

The previous August, assembly operations at Hughes Aircraft, which makes Maverick air-to-ground missiles for the Air Force and Navy, Phoenix air-to-air missiles for the Navy, and TOW antitank missiles for the Army and Marine Corps, were shut down. For two years, government officials had repeatedly complained in writing and in person to Hughes executives that the Tuscon plant was badly managed, that costs were too high, that workmanship was sloppy. The missiles passed inspection and field tests, but military officers feared that the quality of the work had so deteriorated that it was only a matter of time before the missiles would prove to be unreliable. In battle, that could be disastrous.

The government's complaints, however, went unheeded. Finally, in quick succession during the spring and summer of 1984, technicians from each of the military services tore down several completed missiles and found dozens of flaws in each. The Navy was the first to tell Hughes that it would no longer accept delivery of Phoenix missiles until corrections had been made in the plant. The Army and the Air Force followed a short time later. Then, in a rare show of exasperation, the Pentagon stopped making the $40 million monthly progress payments that kept the plant operating.

It took Hughes, which does not make airplanes anymore but concentrates on missiles, electronics, and other military equipment, more than a year to straighten out its problems and to get the plant back into full production. That long pause hurt United States military readiness, as three vital missiles were not being delivered to forces in the field when they were due. The shutdown, the rehabilitation of the plant, and the inspection and repair of missiles already delivered that was required by the Defense Department cost Hughes more than $100 million. The episode was considered serious enough that it commanded attention from Tucson all the way to the White House, where President Reagan was advised of the problem so he would be ready if it came up in the election campaign. It didn't.

More important, the troubles at Hughes Aircraft were a dark reflection on the ills that have pervaded the defense industry for the last decade. Willis Willoughby, a senior civilian at the Navy's Material Command, cited widespread shortcomings. "Hughes Tucson doesn't look any different than other places," he said. "We see things that are just as badly done all over the country." An Army officer familiar with military procurement agreed: "If you went into any defense plant in the country, you would find the same thing. Hughes was not alone in this regard."

Prominent defense contractors and smaller companies alike have been charged in recent years with a dismal array of offenses. They have been accused of producing weapons that cost more than planned and later cost too much to operate and maintain. They have been charged with overpricing and delivering late. At the beginning of a weapons program, they "buy in," meaning they submit unrealistically low bids to get the contract, then demand more money from the government later in a renegotiation, saying they can't complete the contract at the original cost. The defense industry has been charged with poor design, bad engineering, and gold-plating weapons with extra technology that was not worth the added cost. Some companies have been accused of failure to test arms or components properly. The process from concept to fielding a new weapon has grown to more than ten years in many cases. In addition, much of the blame for that lies in the Pentagon and the Congress for insisting on elaborate scrutiny of development, overregulation of the acquisition process, and reams of red tape.

The defense industry has suffered from the same deterioration as the rest of American industry, and for the same reasons. Much of American industry has lost its competitive edge and fallen behind foreign competitors because of inadequate investment in modern plant and machinery, lack of innovation in research and development, thick layers of bureaucratic management, poorly trained workers, high labor costs, and stagnant productivity. As a Deputy Secretary of Defense in the Reagan Administration, William Howard Taft IV, put it,

We must recognize that the defense industry has not escaped the productivity and quality problems that plagued all American industry during the 1970s— years when our annual national productivity growth dropped to 0.9 percent, from an average of 3.4 percent during the two decades after World War II.

Allegations of mismanagement, waste, and fraud have sprung up repeatedly. The Inspector General of the Defense Department, Joseph H. Sherick, told Congress in 1985 that forty-five of the nation's largest defense contractors were under investigation for possible criminal violations. "Anyone who quotes me as saying things are good," said Mr. Sherick, "needs their bolts tightened." Mischarging the government for costs was the most frequent allegation on the list; others included alleged substitution of an inferior material or component for that specified in the contract; conflicts of interest and giving gratuities; bribery and kickbacks; and a few cases of compromising the security of the program. Representative John D. Dingell, Democrat of Michigan and Chairman of the Subcommittee on Oversight and Investigations, asserted that the violations had become "a way of life throughout the defense industry."

Most distressing, the shoddy workmanship or poor design of many new weapons have made them unreliable once they reach the field, possibly endangering military men and women in training or operations. As Mr. Taft said, soldiers could be doomed to die if those weapons proved ineffective in battle: "Shoddy workmanship, inadequate testing procedures, and other quality control problems have been haunting American industry for over a decade. But in the defense business, they do not just drive away customers and reduce profits. They can cost lives."

Not all of the fault is with the defense industry, by any means. Even those companies that strive for efficient, economic operation are hobbled by volumes of regulations, many of them imposed by Congress. Reports or tests often serve little constructive purpose other than to retain congressional influence over a particular program in which a weapon is being developed. Administering those regulations, moreover, detracts from the Pentagon's ability to monitor and supervise the production of weapons. The Pentagon, in addition, imposes its own layers of reports, tests, and other bureaucratic red tape that further impede the process. Military specifications, or "milspecs," set down in minute detail how a weapon or component is to be made, sometimes to the point of absurdity. The milspec for making Christmas cakes for the troops one year ran to nearly two hundred pages; a purchase order for athletic supporters was thirteen pages long. "Milspecs are the sum total of all our past mistakes," said an Air Force colonel specializing in procurement. "They are lists of lessons learned."

James Wade, in his critique of the system, said the Pentagon had come to accept "the minimal amount of quality" in the production of weapons. He cited a "lack of adequate high technology and general training to meet specialized needs of acquisition and logistics personnel," especially in management within the Pentagon. "We lack a cadre of seasoned, well-rounded, technically oriented acquisition professionals. We do not need more people—but we do need superior, better qualified people." Mr. Wade deplored the lack of emphasis on costs during the early stages of developing a weapon: "The current system of design and development process is not oriented to emphasize cost tradeoffs and optimizing contract requirements. There is no close, continuous association of users, developers, the research and development community, and manufacturer." In some cases, the Pentagon tries to move too fast. "There is a tendency to force state-of-the-art technology into production," Mr. Wade said, "without allowing adequate engineering time to make a product reliable, affordable, and producible." Finally, bad relations between the Pentagon and the defense industry were damaging the development and acquisition of new weapons. "There is an unhealthy tension between the Department of Defense and industry," he said, "and many people feel the current relationship is at an all time low."

The President's Blue Ribbon Commission of Defense Management, headed by David Packard, a respected former Deputy Secretary of Defense, was especially critical of the Pentagon in its initial report to President Reagan in 1986. "Responsibility for acquisition policy has become fragmented," said the commission set up after dozens of "horror stories" about military procurement. The report continued:

"There is today no single senior official in the Office of the Secretary of Defense working full-time to provide overall supervision of the acquisition system. . . . Authority for acquisition execution, and accountability for its results, have become vastly diluted. Program managers have in effect been deprived of control over programs. They are confronted instead by never-ending bureaucratic obligations for making reports and gaining approvals that bear no relation to program success. . . . All too often, requirements for new weapons systems have been overstated. This has led to overstated specifications, which has led to higher cost equipment. Such so-called gold-plating has become deeply embedded. . . . Developmental and operational testing have been too divorced, the latter has been undertaken too late in the cycle, and prototypes have been used and tested far too little. . . . The services too often have duplicated each other's efforts and disfavored new ideas and systems. . . . Common sense, the indispensable ingredient for a successful system, has not always governed acquisition strategies. More competition, for example, is beneficial, but the mechanistic pursuit of competition for its own sake would be inefficient. . . . In sum, the Commission finds that there is legitimate cause for dissatisfaction with the process by which the Department of Defense and Congress buy military equipment and material. We strongly disagree, however, with the commonly held views of what is wrong and how it must be fixed. The nation's defense programs lose far more to inefficient procedures than to fraud and dishonesty. The truly costly programs are those of overcomplicated organization and rigid procedure, not avarice or connivance.

Unlike many nations, the United States has few government arsenals to produce arms but has turned that task over to private enterprise. The defense industry, however, is fundamentally different from other industries. It not only makes instruments of war instead of consumer goods of peace but has special responsibilities. Karl G. Harr Jr., president of the Aerospace Industries Association of America, a lobby that represents the interests of the defense industry in Washington, noted the defense industry's peculiar status. "Defense and space business is paid for by the taxpayer, involves vital national security interests, and is controlled by the government customer," he said. "It is free enterprise that must serve two masters, the government customer and the corporate stockholders." What Mr. Harr did not say was that the interests of the two masters are often different. The shareholders are interested in profits, the taxpayers in effective performance. When conflict between them arises, a defense contractor usually chooses profits for shareholders over economic production for taxpayers.

Some executives in the defense industry seem to recognize that they have a moral obligation to the national security, to the men and women who may one day bear the brunt of battle, and to the voters and taxpayers. "The products of our industry are essential to the preservation of peace and freedom and the protection of America's worldwide commitments," said Roy A. Anderson, the chairman of Lockheed. "The men and women of our armed forces must be equipped with the best weapons available, and the American public deserves assurance that tax dollars devoted to military needs are prudently expended." Warde F. Wheaton, executive vice-president of Honeywell Aerospace and a graduate of West Point, echoed that sentiment:

We should be pursuing quality in our work, first because we ought to ethically and professionally. We should be providing our armed services with engines that start the first time, missiles that launch the first time, bullets that fire the first time, and computers that compute the first time. We don't build quality products simply because it makes us feel good (although it does), or because it can be profitable (because it can), but because lives depend on it.

But many executives brush off the allegations of wrongdoing and poor management. "Widely publicized abuses are anomalies, not the norm," Mr. Harr contended. "They must not be allowed to distract our attention from the main task of ensuring the efficient functioning of a process so vital to the nation's security and economy." Thomas G. Pownall, the chairman of Martin Marietta, asserted in an article on the op-ed page of *The New York Times* that the defense industry was better than most American industries: "If other industries and the government were also examined in such intimate detail, the defense industry would emerge among the best—ethically and morally and in terms of accomplishment. Never has so much money been spent by so many people with so little dishonesty."

Critics of the defense industry agree that it has special obligations but argue that those obligations have not been fulfilled. A. Ernest Fitzgerald, an Air Force cost analyst who gained nationwide recognition in the 1960s by disclosing cost overruns in the Lockheed C-5 air transport program, alleged that the "bad management has shot down more airplanes, sunk more ships, and immobilized more soldiers than all our enemies in history put together." Lieutenant General Donald M. Babers, head of the Defense Logistics Agency, told *BusinessWeek* magazine: "In our American culture, you run trucks off the production line and let the dealership structure take care of any problems. That's the commercial sector's mind-set that we have to overcome. I don't want the soldier in the field to be the final inspector." *The Philadelphia Inquirer* argued in an editorial that the industry suffered from a sickness of values and attitudes.

It is exemplified in the sentiment that so long as Uncle Sam alone is being cheated, it's not stealing. In fact, it's bigger than mere stealing. It is runaway corruption, institutionalized. In the name of providing security to the nation, defense contractors peddle shoddy goods at fraudulent prices, all the while claiming to be free enterprise patriots. . . . This is moral rot. Clearly it infests the weapons industry to its core. To the extent that the nation tolerates it, the rot afflicts us all.

Companies in the defense industry are run by business executives and look like commercial enterprises. But competition, which usually disciplines the commercial marketplace, is almost nonexistent in defense production. Many companies in the industry are monopolies, making one set of products for one customer. A form of contract known as cost-plus-fixed-fee at one time dominated much of the contracting, giving the producer the right to charge whatever it cost to make a weapon, then to add profit on top of that. The Pentagon in recent years has tried to move slowly away from that form of contract toward contracts in which both the Defense Department and the company share either the cost overruns or the savings. Another form of contract increasingly sought by the Pentagon is that with firm, fixed prices. No matter the form of contract, however, the incentive to produce efficiently is weak in the absence of competition.

Moreover, in many instances a company cannot achieve economies of scale because the Pentagon buys relatively few of the expensive weapons each year. The Defense Department is comparable to a monopoly; it is a monopsony, a sole buyer that leaves the defense contractor no one else to whom it might sell. Grumman, for instance, makes only twenty-four to thirty F-14 Tomcat fighter planes for the Navy each year but must pay for roughly the same amount of overhead and other fixed costs that would support production of twice that number. Grumman, however, cannot sell the advanced F-14, with its secret technology, to other countries except with the rarely given permission of the Pentagon. Senator Charles E. Grassley, Republican of Iowa, said he had seen Pentagon documents showing the "our defense industry on average is operating at one-third of normal factory efficiency." In addition, the defense industry is almost totally protected from foreign competition. Congress has decreed that warships will not be constructed in Korea, where they would cost perhaps half as much, nor tanks built in Germany, where quality controls are topnotch.

Edward Kaitz, of the management consulting firm of Arthur D. Little, did a report for the Pentagon on pricing in the defense industry in which he found the absence of competition a key factor in the high prices of weapons. "Unhappily," he told the trade newsletter *Defense Week*,

the report concludes that the marketplace for major weapons is not a free market in which competition generates the best possible price while motivating contractors to look for a significant production-oriented edge over their competitors. Rather, the defense industries operate much as a public utility might with the consumer; in the final analysis, the public pretty much pays the price demanded by the monopolist.

As defense is not a competitive industry, labor costs are high. The Congressional Budget Office reported in 1984 that workers in the aerospace industry, which is a large portion of the defense industry, earned 21 percent more than the average industrial worker, even taking into account the aerospace industry's greater need for trained, skilled workers. The General Accounting Office that same year found that aerospace executive salaries, including bonuses, averaged 42 percent more than the national average in comparably sized firms, while clerical and technical wages were 9 percent more than average and factory pay 8 percent more than average weekly earnings. Only professional wages, perhaps reflecting an oversupply, were lower (by 2.5 percent) than those of counterparts elsewhere.

Even with high labor costs, profits of the ten top companies in the defense industry between 1979 and 1983 were higher than those of any other industry, averaging 25.6 percent of equity, a favorite Wall Street measure. Lockheed was highest, at 85 percent, Grumman the lowest, at 12 percent. Among 1,000 corporations surveyed by *Forbes* magazine, the average was 15.1 percent. Similarly, the Washington Analysis Corporation, a private research organization, calculated that defense industries earned profits of 10.9 percent of sales during 1980–83 compared with 6.3 percent in durable manufacturing. As a percentage of assets, the defense industry's profits were calculated at 19.4 percent, compared with 10.7 percent in durable goods. The analysts concluded: "There is a very strong connection between rising defense outlays and rising profit margins."

Despite the profits, several arms producers paid little or no taxes from 1981 through 1984, having been permitted by the tax laws to delay reporting profits from weapons programs until they had been completed, which might take years. Senator Dale Bumpers, Democrat of Arkansas, made public a report from a private group, Citizens for Tax Justice, showing that five companies paid no taxes: General Electric (profit $9.6 billion), Boeing ($2.1 billion), Lockheed ($1.7 billion), General Dynamics ($1.6 billion), and Grumman ($653 million). McDonnell Douglas paid 0.4 percent on a profit of $1.4 billion, Westinghouse 0.5 percent on $2 billion, and Martin Marietta 0.6 percent on $791 million. In contrast, Raytheon paid 41 percent in taxes on profits of $1.9 billion and United Technologies 25 percent on $2.1 billion.

Thomas S. Amlie, a civilian official with the Air Force in Washington and an engineer with long experience in developing missiles, wrote a stinging critique:

Why do we pay these outrageous markups? Turn the question around—why not? The Congress ponies up the money every year and everyone is making a buck. The fact is that the taxpayer is getting hosed and the troops are getting poor equipment, and not much of it, is unfortunate, but to change the system might ruin a good thing the high rollers have going. In my own view, the major problem is that the incentives are all backwards. The big spenders are promoted and rewarded with cushy jobs after leaving the government. Those who try to do something are not similarly rewarded. In fact, they are quite frequently punished.

Curiously, Mr. Amlie's views, which were not popular in the Pentagon, were not much different from those of John Lehman, the Secretary of the Navy whose service led the tough if belated actions against Hughes Aircraft. Both said the unique position of the defense industry breeds an attitude different from that in other industries. Mr. Lehman asserted that much of the defense industry vacillates "somewhere between arrogance and complacency." Many defense contractors, Mr. Lehman said in an interview, show "a contempt for the customer" because each is the sole source for a particular weapon or piece of equipment. Complacency, he added, meant high costs, poor quality, and late deliveries.

Relations between what President Eisenhower called the military-industrial complex and what others call the "iron triangle" or the "revolving door" among defense contractors, the Pentagon, and the Congress have become cozy over the years. Many officers retire from the service after twenty or twenty-five years, then take jobs with defense contractors with whom they had been negotiating while on active duty. General Alton D. Slay, head of the Air Force Systems Command that deals with aircraft builders, retired to become a consultant to Lockheed, United Technologies, and Raytheon. Vice Admiral James H. Doyle Jr. retired as Deputy Chief of Naval Operations to become a consultant with Martin Marietta, Vought, and RCA (Radio Corporation of America). Colonel William E. Crouch Jr. commanded the Army Aviation Development Test Activity at Fort Rucker, Alabama, the home of the Army's helicopters, and retired to become branch manager for Hughes Helicopter there.

On the civilian side, the Secretary of the Navy in the Carter Administration, Edward Hidalgo, negotiated a settlement of shipbuilding claims with General Dynamics. Later, after leaving the Pentagon, he became a consultant for that company. George Sawyer, an Assistant Secretary of the Navy in charge of shipbuilding in the Reagan Administration, joined General Dynamics as a senior executive after leaving the Navy Department. Richard A. Ichord, a Democrat from Missouri and a member of the House Armed Services Committee, left Congress to join Bob Wilson, a Republican from California, in forming a consulting firm that had eleven of the biggest defense contractors as clients. Robin Beard, a Republican Congressman from Tennessee and a member of the Armed Services Committee, became a defense consultant after being defeated in a bid for the Senate. Clark MacGregor, former national chairman of the Republican Party, became head of the Washington office of United Technologies. In addition, many staff members from the Congress move across the Potomac River to take upper-middle-level positions in the Pentagon. Occasionally, a staff aide joins the defense industry. John J. Ford, who had been staff director of the House Armed Services Committee since 1977, became a vice-president of Avco, maker of engines and other military equipment, in 1984. Executives from the defense industry are regularly appointed by both parties to senior positions in the Pentagon.

Mr. Amlie was pointed in his criticism, especially in what he saw as its effect on middle-grade officers.

The major problem with having a military officer in charge of procurement is his vulnerability. It turns out that not everyone can make general or admiral and our "up-or-out" policy forces people to retire. The average age of an officer at retirement is 43 years. Counting allowances, a colonel has more take-home pay than a U.S. Senator. At the age of 43, he has kids in, or ready for, college and a big mortgage and can't afford a large cut in his income. [Officers at that point may elect to retire at 50 percent of base pay, with none of the allowances for quarters or rations they had on active duty.]

This nice man then comes around and offers him a job at $50,000-$75,000 per year. If he [the officer] stands up and makes a fuss about high cost and poor quality, no nice man will come to see him when he retires. Even if he has no interest in a post-retirement job in the defense industry, he is taking a chance by making a fuss. The "system" will, likely as not, discover a newly-opened job in Thule, Greenland, or Adak, Alaska, or some other garden spot for which he, and only he, is uniquely qualified. Thus his family, as well as his career, suffers.

To their everlasting credit, many fine officers have made a fuss anyway and suffered the consequences. My point is that, due to this quirk in the system, the overhead industry has managed to seize control of the military procurement system by spending a relatively small amount of money. To add insult to injury, they have seized control of the government using the government's own money.

The scandals emanating from defense industry have multiplied as the procurement of weapons has assumed titanic proportions. The United States spends in the neighborhood of $100 billion a year, or one-third of the military budget, on guns, aircraft, ships, tanks, boots, underwear, paperclips, and everything else needed to arm, equip, and sustain a modern military force. That $100 billion exceeds the total net income earned by all of the nation's top industrial companies on the *Fortune* 500 list. It is roughly equal to the gross national product of Argentina or Sweden or Switzerland. It is considerably more than the gross national product of South Korea or Venezuela or Egypt. Since President Reagan took office in 1981, the procurement of weapons and equipment has been the single fastest-growing element in the military budget. It rose from $51.9 billion in 1980, the last full fiscal year of the Carter Administration, to $99.6 billion in 1985. That was a 92-percent growth measured in constant dollars, with the effects of inflation removed.

Since 1980, the companies at which fingers have been pointed for a variety of transgressions have included most of the nation's prominent defense contractors. Defenders of the industry contend that the faults attracting the most publicity are only isolated cases. But there have been so many that it is hard to escape the conclusion that there is wide and deep malfeasance.

McDonnell Douglas, the largest defense contractor in 1984, combined with Northrop to turn out the F-18 Hornet fighter plane for the Navy. The plane cost considerably more than the original estimate, was unable to reach the range specified, and had cracks in its tail. The Navy stopped taking delivery of the planes for six months until the producers had corrected the design flaw in the tail. Rockwell, builder of the B-1 bomber and other weapons, pleaded guilty to twenty counts of fraud in mischarging the Air Force with improper time cards and paid the government $1 million, which was twice the amount of the loss caused by the mischarging.

General Dynamics produces ballistic missile and attack submarines, the M-1 Abrams tank, and the F-16 fighter plane, among other things. It has probably been the most scrutinized defense contractor of the 1980s. The company has been investigated for allegedly fraudulent shipbuilding claims; one executive fled to Greece to evade prosecution for allegedly taking kickbacks, and another took refuge elsewhere in Europe for the same alleged offense. The company was investigated by the Securities and Exchange Commission for withholding information on cost overruns from shareholders. The Defense Department cut off payments for five months in 1985 after discovering that General Dynamics had charged the boarding of an executive's dog, country club dues, golfing weekends, and a chili cookout to overhead. The company and four current or former executives were indicted in 1985 on charges of defrauding the government. In an ironic twist, General Dynamics was fined $676,283 for giving jewelry and other gifts worth a tenth of that to Admiral Hyman G. Rickover, the doughty father of the nuclear navy—and a vigorous critic of General Dynamics.

Lockheed, which makes cargo and patrol aircraft, was accused by the General Accounting Office, an auditing arm of the Congress, with having violated a law governing lobbying efforts. In this case, the company was alleged to have improperly sought to persuade the House of Representatives to approve the purchase of more C-5 Galaxy cargo planes. In a separate action, the General Accounting Office reported that Lockheed had overcharged the Air Force by $120 million to replace defective wings in the C-5. The company charged the Air Force $7,600 for a coffee brewer for the C-5 and the Navy $640.09 for a toilet seat in the P-3 antisubmarine patrol plane. After adverse publicity, the company cut the price of the toilet seat to $100. Boeing did likewise when it was found to have charged the Air Force $748 for a pair of pliers used to position a small pin in jet engines. The company reduced the price to $90—but added a charge for "support equipment management" to return the price to $748. A civilian engineer said he had seen similar pliers in a hardware store for $7.61. Congressional investigators found Grumman charging the Navy $659 for ashtrays for patrol aircraft and $404 for socket wrenches. In most of those cases, the contractors contended that high prices were caused by a single order or a small order from the government. They argued, in effect, that the items had to be custom-made.

General Electric was fined $1.04 million, the maximum allowable, and ordered by a court to repay $800,000 to the government after pleading guilty to 108 counts of falsifying time cards. General Electric had engines rejected by the Navy for defective parts, while the Air Force interrupted $8.5 million in monthly payments after quality problems were found in another type of engine. In still another action, the Secretary of the Air Force, Verne Orr, asked General Electric in 1985 to refund $168 million that he said were "profits significantly in excess of those negotiated by the government." In a letter to General Electric, Mr. Orr said, "National support for building military strength has been severely battered by public perception that we pay too much for the goods and services we acquire." That was borne out later when Congress sliced into President Reagan's 1986 military budget.

At Hughes Aircraft, the issue was quality control at the Tucson plant, which included poor engineering, sloppy workmanship, and inattentive management. The responsibility for the plant's long, slow deterioration was spread among the supervisors at the plant, the company's management, the Air Force that was the executive agent for the Defense Department overseeing the production of all three missiles, and the Reagan Administration's top management in the Pentagon. At a congressional hearing, Brigadier General Bernard L. Weiss, then director of contracting for the Air Force Systems Command, said that "we probably underestimated the scope of what we were seeing. . . . We should have surfaced it to top management and taken more positive, more punitive action." Merely complaining about quality, he concluded, "was a band-aid on a symptom." The chief executive at the plant, C. Blaine Shull, acknowledged that "our operating disciplines were not what they should have been." Mr. Shull, who had been vice-president for manufacturing at the parent company in California, said in an interview later, "I wish I had been more sensitive to that when it happened."

Pratt & Whitney, a division of United Technologies, was found to have charged the government $390.47 for turbine blades for jet engines after having bought them from a subcontractor for $35.38. A refund of $432,000 was given to the government. The Defense Contract Audit Agency found that Pratt & Whitney had charged the government three times as much for tools as they should have cost. "If the tools had been purchased directly from source vendors," the agency said in a report, "the cost would have been $531,000 rather than the $1,437,000 actually paid by the government." John Lehman, the Secretary of the Navy, told a congressional committee that the TF30 engine made by Pratt & Whitney was "just a terrible engine" and had accounted for twenty-four accidents in the F-14 Tomcat, the Navy's premier fighter plane. Defense Department auditors found that Pratt & Whitney had made $16 million in excessive profits on spare parts in 1983. Another division of United Technologies, Sikorsky Aircraft, which makes helicopters, was found by Pentagon auditors to have realized between $30 million and $40 million in excess profits by paying subcontractors less than the company had contracted with the Army. Later, the Army temporarily grounded 600 new Blackhawk helicopters made by Sikorsky because they had been involved in twenty-three crashes in which thirty-seven people had been killed.

The General Accounting Office reported that one-quarter of the Navy's Sidewinder air-to-air missiles, which would be used against aircraft threatening the fleet, and one-third of its Sparrow missiles with similar uses were "unserviceable" for combat. Those missiles were made by Raytheon and several other American and European contractors. Ingalls Shipyard, a division of Litton Industries, acknowledged that it had submitted false bills to the Navy and agreed to repay the Navy $137,000 that it had charged for work on commercial oil drilling rigs.

Martin Marietta caused five test failures in sixteen shots of the Pershing II intermediate-range missile because of sloppy workmanship, according to General Wickham, the Chief of Staff of the Army. The company settled a claim that it had improperly charged $200,000 to the government for models of Titan intercontinental missiles to be given away as mementos. Each had cost $1,694. Another contractor, LTV, was found by the Defense Contract Audit Agency to have charged excessive prices for spare parts for an Army rocket launcher. In a letter to the Army, Senator William V. Roth Jr., Republican of Delaware, said, "The prime contractor's proposed prices, totaling about $39.1 million, included a markup of over 55 percent on the subcontract prices quoted by the spare parts suppliers."

Sperry Corporation, which made a launch control system for the Minuteman intercontinental missile, pleaded guilty to a charge of making false statements to the Air Force and paid the government $1.8 million in double damages, interest, and disallowed costs.

Ford Aerospace, a division of the Ford Motor Company, developed an antiaircraft gun called DIVAD, for "division air defense," that didn't work well but cost $1.8 billion by 1984, a price well above the original estimate. The Pentagon's Inspector General, Mr. Sherick, criticized the testing of the weapon, which was named Sergeant York after a World War I infantry sharpshooter and hero. Mr. Sherick asserted the test data were "oversimplified and, therefore, misleading and based on a selective analysis of the results." That prompted Representative Denny Smith, Republican of Oregon, to contend, "Not only are we buying a DIVAD that doesn't work, the taxpayers are being ripped off by excessive charges." In August 1985, the DIVAD program was canceled by Secretary Weinberger.

Bell Helicopter, which made the Huey and Cobra helicopters for the Army, had a design flaw in the rotor blades that caused a series of crashes in which nearly 250 servicemen were killed over a period of seventeen years. The flaw, known as mast bumping, occurred when the chopper ran into rough flying conditions. That caused the under-arm of the rotor blade to chip into the mast that held it aloft, wearing into that mast and finally breaking loose to cause the crash. The company and the Army knew about the problem in 1973 but did little about it until Mark Thompson, a reporter for the *Fort Worth Star-Telegram*, dug out the facts and published a series of five articles in 1984 that won him the Pulitzer prize.

The General Accounting Office found that Newport News Ship-building, in Virginia, had made profits of 37 percent on one submarine and 30.6 percent on another. A 10- to 15-percent profit on many defense contracts was considered reasonable, depending on the technical and other risks involved. The same report found that United States Steel had a 27-percent profit on components for several submarines. The Cabot Corporation had a 66-percent profit on large valves that went into submarines, and Carborundum Company a 25-percent profit on material used in nuclear propulsion plants.

The Defense Department began in 1983 to investigate reports that the nation's semiconductor industry had furnished untested and possibly flawed microcircuits to the military services. Those devices, for which the armed forces paid more than $1 billion a year, were imbedded in missiles, aircraft, navigation systems, and a variety of advanced weapons and equipment. A federal grand jury returned a forty-count indictment against National Semiconductor Corporation in March 1984, on charges of mail fraud and false statements. That meant failure to test the microcircuits properly and then falsifying records to say that they had been tested. National agreed to pay almost $1.8 million in civil and criminal fines. The Defense Department stopped accepting delivery of 4,700 different kinds of microcircuits from Texas Instruments in 1984 because they had not been tested properly. That caused the Pentagon to examine 300 defense contractors to see whether damage had been done to weapons and equipment. The Navy refused delivery of a frigate from Todd Shipyards until the issue had been resolved. The plague spread: Signetics was found to have failed to test its products, as were the Fairchild division of Schlumberger Ltd. and Advanced Micro Devices Inc. By the spring of 1985, the Pentagon concluded that the problem was pervasive and demanded that each company recheck its testing procedures.

Among smaller contractors, fraud produced a steady stream of convictions announced by the Pentagon. In one case, a Navy parachute rigger named Richard F. Williamson unpacked a box of parachute cord on a hot summer day in 1980 at the Naval Air Station in Brunswick, Maine. As he worked, a green dye stained his hands. On closer look, it appeared to the rigger that either someone had tampered with the parachute cord or it was defective. The rigger called his superiors, who notified the investigative authorities.

The Defense Criminal Investigative Service and the Federal Bureau of Investigation conducted a twenty-seven-month inquiry that led to the arrest of Barry W. Splinter, president of American Cotton Yarns, of Westmont, Illinois. Investigators found that Splinter had bought a small amount of good parachute cord to submit to laboratory testing, then won contracts to sell 2 million feet of the cord to the government. After that, Splinter bought cord that was twenty-five years old, dyed it olive drab, and falsified documents to assert that it had been tested and met government specifications. In the United States District Court in Chicago, American Cotton Yarns pleaded guilty to one count of mail fraud and one count of racketeering. Splinter himself pleaded guilty to two counts of mail fraud and two counts of filing a false income-tax return. The company was fined $225,000, the amount of profit from the sale and was suspended from receiving government contracts. Splinter was fined $7,000 and sentenced to prison for two years. According to Pentagon officials, the prosecutor on the case, William J. Cook, was a former paratrooper. The judge, Stanley Roszkowski, who said it was "the most aggravated instance of white-collar crime I have seen," was a former Air Force pilot.

In another instance, Judge Marvin H. Shoob, sitting in the federal court in Atlanta, sentenced two steel salesmen each to ten years in prison for committing what the judge called "sabotage." According to court records, Jerald R. Hedden was the sales manager of the Metal Service Center in Marietta, Georgia, and Russell D. Roper was a salesman. They won a government contract to furnish steel armor plate to the Navy for the battleship *New Jersey*, the aircraft carriers *Kitty Hawk* and *Constellation*, and the destroyer *Paul F. Foster*. The Metal Service Center bought substandard steel plate for $1.25 a pound, removed the markings, and substituted markings to indicate that the steel met specifications. They sold it to the Navy for three times as much as they paid for it.

But the Navy became suspicious when $27,000 worth of steel for refitting the destroyer was hard to weld and rusted before the ship went to sea. Similar problems turned up on *Kitty Hawk* and *Constellation*. Testing showed the steel to be only half as strong as that ordered. The inquiry led to the battleship *New Jersey*, which had been brought out of retirement, renovated, and deployed off the coast of Lebanon during the crisis there in 1983 and 1984. The Navy, fearing that terrorists might try a suicide attack on the ship with a small airplane, asked that the investigation not be made public until the ship returned home. The armor plate had been installed above deck to protect sailors in what would have been a likely target for a diving attack. The two steel salesmen, after pleading guilty to five counts of fraud each, were sentenced by Judge Shoob. "I consider this type of activity," the judge told them, "on the same level as sabotage."

Many cases prosecuted on behalf of the Defense Department seem small, given the Pentagon's $300 billion annual budget. Taken together, however, they add up to a tidy sum of the taxpayer's money. Raycomm Industries, of Freehold, New Jersey, was fined $10,000 and ordered to repay the government $2 million that the company had obtained fraudulently by charging for time and material not allowed under the contract. The president of the company, Joseph Raymond, was given three years of probation, fined $8,500, and ordered to give 360 hours of community service for three years. The former president of the company, Karse Simon, was sentenced to three years on probation and fined $1,800.

In another case, a scrap dealer named Charles E. Nelson, of Lebec, California, used fifteen different aliases on at least twenty-five different occasions in trying to buy surplus goods by passing bad checks. He was sentenced to five years in prison and ordered to pay back $64,000, the value of the property he had illegally obtained. In Ohio, the president of Argus Manufacturing, Raymond H. Huffman, was given a suspended sentence of three years in prison and a $5,000 fine for attempting to bribe an undercover agent from the Defense Criminal Investigative Service to obtain technical drawings from a defense supply center. In Connecticut, James Morck, president of Brothers Machine Company, forged the signature of a government quality-assurance official to get paid for unsatisfactory machine parts. He was sentenced to a year in prison, which was suspended, plus two years on probation.

Three members of one family in Georgia were convicted of defrauding the government of $7 million by obtaining payment for work not performed on sewers at fourteen Army, Navy, and Air Force bases. David Hurt, president of Municipal and Industrial Pipe Services, was sentenced to eight years in prison and fined $10,000. His wife, Judith, who was secretary-treasurer of the company, was given six months in prison and fined $10,000. Their son, Gordon, who was vice-president of the company, was given thirty-three months in prison and fined $10,000.

Across the nation, Robert D. Lambert, of Northridge, California, was sentenced to four years in jail and fined $208,000 for paying bribes and kickbacks to officials in the Defense Industrial Supply Center in Philadelphia and to a purchasing agent at Fairchild Industries in Florida. His company, Standard Air Parts, was fined $159,000. In Michigan, Robert K. Page pleaded nolo contendere, or no contest, to a charge of falsifying labor charges on a contract to rebuild heavy-duty equipment; he was sentenced to four years on probation and ordered to make restitution of $24,404. In Grand Prairie, Texas, the president and two regional managers of One Stop Motor Parts were convicted of defrauding the Air Force by substituting inferior parts for more expensive parts and inflating the price list in its billings. The president, Robert R. Westbrook, got three years in prison and a fine of $5,000. One manager, Berton Purdy, was sentenced to six months in prison and fined $3,000 while the other, Manuel Eres, received three years on probation and a fine of $2,500.

Nor have Defense Department officials been free of taint. Thomas M. Lofgren, a buyer at the Defense Industrial Supply Center in Philadelphia, was given one year and one day in prison for accepting $27,000 from Standard Air Parts of California and other companies. At the Defense Electronic Supply Center in Dayton, Ohio, Samuel G. Foster was caught in a conflict of interest when he was instrumental in awarding contracts to ABC Electronics, a company in which he was a principal. He was sentenced to six months in prison, put on probation for three and a half years, and fined $10,000. At the same supply center, a naval lieutenant, Donald Steven Anderson, established a company called Kar-go to sell electronic components to the government, then falsified records to show that the components had been delivered when they had not. He was given a suspended sentence of four years, placed on probation for five years, fined $10,000, ordered to make restitution of $8,100 to the government, and required to give 500 hours of community service.

The poor performance of the defense industry has roots deep in American history. In the early days of the Republic, Eli Whitney, inventor of the cotton gin, proposed to Oliver Wolcott, the Secretary of the Treasury, that he make 10,000 muskets of a new design to be delivered to the Army in two years and four months. Though Whitney had no factory and little experience in producing firearms, Secretary Wolcott awarded him a contract for $134,000, of which $10,000 was paid in advance so that Whitney could build an arsenal on the Mill River near New Haven, Connecticut. Because his labor force, recruited largely from the farm country of western Massachusetts, was unskilled, Whitney made an entire set of patterns, templates, and gauges to guide the workers through the fabrication. He also wrote instructions about how to assemble the muskets, which before had been made one at a time by skilled craftsmen. But the concept of mass production was hard for the unlettered workers to learn, and it took Whitney ten years to fulfill the contract. That was perhaps the nation's first late delivery of a weapon.

But it was not the only military contract to go awry at that time. The new Navy contracted with shipbuilders along the east coast to build six sailing frigates for $688,888, including the *Constitution*, which was to become famous as "Old Ironsides" during the War of 1812. Because of delays in construction, only three of the ships were built, while the cost ran up to $945,000 in what may have been the first cost overrun in military contracting in this country.

During the Civil War, the word *shoddy*, which has been heard so much in describing arms today, came into the language. An inferior type of wool known as shoddy was shredded and rewoven into uniforms that barely hung on the shoulders of the Union Army. In addition, arms contractors in the early days of the war were given orders for $50 million worth of weapons in agreements that were later found to have included $17 million in illegal charges. A major named Justus McKinstry was court-martialed on twenty-six counts of wasting public funds by paying a friend $150 for horses that were worth $100. He bought mules that were unfit for service and overcoats from another friend for $10.50 each when he could have gotten them at $7.50.

During World War I, certain shipbuilders were able to make profits of 90 percent, prompting President Wilson to tell Congress of war profiteering that exceeded "the restraints of conscience and love of country." A congressional committee investigating rigged bids on other contracts observed, "If there were no conversations about bidding among them, there was telepathy."

In World War II, an aircraft company with $7 billion in contracts delivered faulty engines to the Army Air Force, possibly causing the deaths of student pilots. A steel company faked tests of tensile strength on steel plate that went into the construction of warships and merchant ships carrying wartime supplies. Submariners who had risked their lives to close with enemy ships in the early days of the war were repeatedly frustrated when torpedoes, made in a government arsenal, failed to run straight and thus missed their targets or, if they hit, failed to explode. There was more of the same in Korea and Vietnam. Antitank rockets from the World War II stockpile failed to stop Russian-built tanks in Korea. The M-16 rifle developed for Vietnam often jammed, and a light armored personnel carrier repeatedly broke down in the field.

While each of those incidents may have been isolated, they were the forerunners of the incompetence and inefficiency that infect much of the American defense industry today. More than twenty years after President Eisenhower cautioned the American people to beware the ills of the military-industrial complex, another general focused on the lack of reliability in weapons produced by that complex. In a thoughtful speech to a gathering of industrialists in the spring of 1984, General James P. Mullins talked about "a joint venture" between the military and private industry. "That's why the responsibility for the defense of our democracy," said the general, then head of the Air Force Logistics Command, "lies with both the military, which must be ready to fight to protect it, and private industry, which must provide the military with the wherewithal to do so." The general asserted that, given the limited financial resources of the nation, "we must find an effective way to get more combat capability for the investment we're making." That would be possible, and not some "mindless fantasy," he said, if the defense industry could only produce what he called "better system reliability."

Taking an example from the civilian economy, General Mullins pointed to American automobiles:

Just look at the well-documented new car recalls issued by manufacturers each year for problems in fuel, electrical, and cooling systems. Realize that these defects do not occur because we don't fully understand carburetion, current flow, or thermodynamics. Frankly, these defects have occurred because we haven't tried hard enough to design them out.

He found "a striking dichotomy" between the reliability of American cars and that of cars built by foreign competitors. "So it's not that it can't be done at competitive prices," he said, "it's just that we haven't been doing it even though not doing it has made absolutely no sense at all."

"That's why each year," General Mullins continued, "with energy costs as high as they are, Americans still spend about $6.5 billion on gas and oil while they spend a whopping $26 billion on auto repairs." He said: "The real question is why we've allowed this to happen. I believe the answer is that, over a period of time, we have come to accept a standard of unreliability in cars." Turning to the Air Force, General Mullins said:

The Air Force has followed suit, somehow accepting the lack of reliability as an inherent given of high technology weapons systems. We've trained ourselves not to think about unreliability, or acknowledge the impact that it has both in terms of combat capability and dollars. Like so many American car buyers today, we seem to accept the fact that our machines will break, and that such failures are simply the inevitable price we must pay for our reliance on sophisticated high technology.

Indeed, that mind-set, more than anything else, is responsible for our designing and building aircraft to go fast and high, but not to do so reliably for any length of time. That mind-set, more than anything else, is responsible for the degradations we're now seeing in weapon system readiness and sustainability, and the tremendous number of defense dollars we're now faced with allocating just to keep the systems going.

Senior civilian officials in the Defense Department and other military officers have expressed similar complaints. Paul Thayer, who was Deputy Secretary of Defense in 1983, told a group of defense industry executives gathered at the National Defense University in Washington that shoddy work in their industry added 10 to 30 percent to the cost of weapons every year. Mr. Thayer spoke with authority, as he had been chairman of the LTV Corporation, a leading maker of military aircraft and other weapons, before joining the Defense Department. (Mr. Thayer was later sentenced to prison after being convicted of improper trading in the stock market, but that was a separate issue.) Rear Admiral Frank C. Collins Jr., the director of quality assurance for the Defense Logistics Agency, agreed with Mr. Thayer's estimate, adding in an interview, "And that may be conservative." He said in some industries as much as 50 percent could be added to the cost, largely because top management didn't care about the quality of their products and because that attitude was communicated to the workers in the factory. The Under Secretary of Defense for Research and Engineering, Richard D. DeLauer, who had been a senior technical executive at TRW, asserted to another group of executives from the defense industry that "poor workmanship" was a serious weakness in the nation's defense. "What we have is just crappy, shoddy work-manship," said the outspoken Mr. DeLauer. "These are things you would not do around the house." Secretary of Defense Weinberger was more circumspect but made the same point in addressing still another gathering of defense industrialists:

America's defense needs more help from industry in productivity and quality. The major responsibility for improving productivity and quality rests with industry. We are entering a new manufacturing era. Industry needs to take an intensive look at manufacturing operations and aggressively move to replace outdated and inefficient capital equipment.

While the Secretary of Defense was giving the industrialists a pep talk, others were looking for misdeeds. The Pentagon's Inspector General published a "Red Book" in 1984, so named for the color of its cover, to instruct Defense Department officials on how to spot fraud. Product substitution, like that in the cases of parachute cord and armor plate, and cost mischarging were cited as two of the more prevalent forms. Bribery, while not so frequent, was considered to be more serious because it undermined the integrity of the procurement process.

The Red Book defined product substitution as "attempts by contractors to deliver to the government goods or services which do not conform to the contract requirements, without informing the government of the delinquency." When caught, the Red Book said, "contractors frequently argue that the substituted goods or services delivered to the government were 'just as good' as what was contracted for even if specifications are not met and that, therefore, no harm is done the government." But the substitute was usually not so good, the book said, and "its introduction into defense supply channels undermines the reliability of the entire supply system."

The book cited a contractor—none were named—who would allow "random unscheduled inspections of products prior to shipment and then substitute defective parts into the already inspected shipment." Another contractor "would surreptitiously enter a locked area and substitute specially created samples for those the quality assurance inspection personnel had selected." Then the contractor would "move inspection tags to uninspected, substandard goods after the inspectors had left, remove part of the good material after inspection, and add substandard or previously rejected materials." Finally, the contractor would "disguise the true condition of substandard goods with chemicals that the known inspection process would not disclose."

Cost mischarging, the Red Book said, has become common. "Because the government reimburses all costs which are allowable, allocable, and reasonable, the contractor may increase profit by mischarging. If labor costs are mischarged, they may be multiplied by 100 percent to 300 percent in indirect cost allowances." The book added, "Frequently work that is being done by low level technicians is billed as being done by senior scientists or engineers at much higher rates." The book pointed particularly to fraudulent accounting, false labor billing, and faked time cards by defense contractors.

In one instance, a defense contractor was not clever in seeking extra payment through false labor charges. A Defense Department auditor discovered that the contractor had charged work to a high-cost account for a KC-135 aircraft when the contract called for work on a C-130 aircraft. The Red Book said that "based upon the changed charge numbers, a ridiculous number of employees were working on the same aircraft during the same labor shift." In another case, an acoustical research firm shifted costs on both commercial and Defense Department contracts to overhead and allocated the overhead "to those contracts (principally Department of Defense) which provided the best overhead rate." In a third case, a large contractor was caught shifting research and development costs to another contract. The corporation was convicted and paid a fine of $30,000, plus a settlement of $720,000 to the Defense Department and $300,000 in legal costs.

Bribes offered by defense contractors, the Red Book said, are "a very real problem." It noted that "a Navy commander accepted several thousand dollars in money and goods to ensure that the government made purchases from a particular company." In another case, "a Department of Defense employee accepted almost $90,000 over four years to make sure a specific company was awarded contracts." Again, "a corporate sales manager was sentenced to ten years in prison, fined $1,000, and ordered to make nearly $10,000 in restitution after conviction on multiple charges of bribing a Department of Defense civilian employee relating to a scheme of false and inflated billings." Still more: "A member of a corporate board of directors was sentenced to 30 days confinement and fined $1,000 after being convicted of a conspiracy to bribe a civilian employee of the Department of Defense." Finally, according to the Red Book, "A GS-4 file clerk was convicted of receiving approximately $50,000 in bribes from various contractors to provide them inside information used to enhance their bid packages."

A scandal about excessive prices for spare parts erupted in mid-1983 after an Air Force staff sergeant, Charles R. Kessler, objected to having the Air Force pay $1,118.26 for a plastic stool cap that should have cost no more than $10. It began in January 1983 when Sergeant Kessler, a crew chief in the 552nd Airborne Warning and Control Wing at Tinker Air Force Base in Oklahoma, ordered two plastic caps for stools used in airborne warning and control planes, the aircraft with the radar dome atop the fuselage and popularly known as Awacs. The plastic caps were installed to steady a small stool on which the navigator stood when he took readings on stars with a sextant, a navigational device. When Sergeant Kessler saw two of the plastic caps missing, he routinely ordered replacements. Then he noticed the listed price of $1,118.26 each. Together with Billy Manning, a civilian supply specialist, the sergeant decided to challenge the pricing. By March 1984, the Defense Industrial Supply Center in Philadelphia determined that the price was excessive, with an Air Force memo asserting that it "should not exceed $10."

Back in 1979, Boeing, which had built the Awacs planes, had priced the stool cap at $219.18 each in a long list of spare parts the company would furnish for the Awacs. The Air Force did not question the price at that time. By 1981, however, the initial supply of plastic stool caps had run out, and the Air Force ordered more from Boeing. When the service asked for only three caps, Boeing priced them at $2,749.65. That included 75 cents for the plastic itself and $72.61 for other materials. There were 66.71 hours of labor costing $833.49, plus $354.61 for fringe benefits. Overhead came to $1,376.83; profit, taxes and other costs brought the total up to $916.55 per cap. The Defense Industrial Supply Center added a surcharge to cover inflation, transport, packing, obsolescence, breakage, and pilferage to bring the price to $1,086.17, which was paid with no questions asked. One of the three stool caps went to the Awacs wing at Tinker Air Force Base, the other two into storage. When Sergeant Kessler asked for those two, another surcharge brought the grand total to $1,118.26. For his protest, Sergeant Kessler was eventually given a letter of commendation and a bonus of $1,166.40.

About the same time, word came that the Navy had paid $436 for a hammer that could have been bought for $7 in a hardware store. A company called Gould had bought the small sledgehammer for a tool kit furnished to the Navy for $847,000 to repair the flight simulator to train pilots to fly the F-18 fighter. The difference between the $436 and the $7—a legal difference under Defense Department regulations—included $102 for manufacturing overhead; $93 for assembly, including four hours of engineering time; $41 for administrative overhead; $37 for repairs if the hammer should break; $2 for materials handling; and $1 for a box. To that was added 31.8 percent for more administrative costs, $56 as a finder's fee, and $7 for capital costs.

Later, a senior official in the Pentagon's Office of the Inspector General, John W. Melchner, testified before a congressional committee that a naval training center had failed to follow regulations in ordering several parts, also for the F-18 flight simulator. "Rather than requisition them through the supply system," he said, "the center took the expedient approach and procured all items from Sperry," a contractor. That included paying $110 for a 4-cent diode, $44 for a 17-cent lamp, and $122 for a $2.37 microcircuit. After a review, Mr. Melchner said, 348 of 483 items had been found in stock and should have been obtained through the system. "The Naval Training and Equipment Center purchased all items from Sperry and paid $80,204 for what would have cost only $3,658 through the Department of Defense supply system," Mr. Melchner said. "There is absolutely no difference in the item purchased at Sperry and the item already in the supply system." Two naval officers were reprimanded, and a refund was obtained from Sperry.

In a similar case, Mr. Melchner told the committee that McDonnell Douglas, builder of the F-18, had proposed charging the Naval Air Systems command $3,155,498 for parts that could have been provided by the supply system for $638,854. "We immediately advised Navy personnel to obtain the items through the supply system," he added drily. Likewise, the Senate Committee on Governmental Affairs, led by Senator William V. Roth, Republican of Delaware, asserted that General Dynamics had marked up prices on spare parts for the F-16 fighter an average of 34 percent in one batch of contracts. The company, for example, bought a seal from Sunstrand for $38 and sold it to the Air Force for $389, a markup of 1,000 percent.

With the publicity given those and other "horror stories" about spare parts, the Inspector General, Mr. Sherick, told the Senate Appropriations Subcommittee on Defense in August 1983, "There is no doubt that something is wrong here." But he was of mixed mind about the extent of the ill. "I do not think these are just random mistakes that occur in any major procurement as some suppliers would have us believe," he said. "Neither are they rampant throughout the system." A review of prices of 30,000 items, mostly spare parts for aircraft and engines, showed that 15 percent were overpriced; Mr. Sherick later revised that to 36 percent. The causes of that excessive pricing, he said, were several, with the faults in both the defense industry and the Pentagon:

In the past, we have not made all of our procurement and inventory management personnel sufficiently price conscious. . . . Procurement personnel often go through a clerical process giving little thought to price comparison with previous buys and, therefore, to what items should cost.

Pentagon agreements with defense contractors allowed them to "redetermine" the price they should charge for a spare part long after the initial order had been placed. Mr. Sherick said that practice removed "contractor risk and incentive to control costs." He continued, "Some supply and procurement officials have been reluctant to seek competition because it is deemed faster, easier, and safer to buy sole source," or from one supplier. The system lent itself to added costs.

Far too frequently, contractors from whom the Department of Defense purchases spare parts do not manufacture the items. Rather, they purchase the item from another company, who may have purchased the item from yet another company and so on. Each contractor adds handling costs, plus overhead and profit, to the price. . . . We have to change that attitude and let both the responsible government officials and the contractors know that it is no longer business as usual.

Nonetheless, the horror stories continued. By mid-1984, dozens of reports of excessive prices charged by companies in the defense industry had come from the Pentagon, the General Accounting Office, and the Congress. The Center on Budget and Policy Priorities, a private organization critical of military spending, compiled those reports into a catalog comparing prices set by contractors with those in hardware stores. The list was devastating: General Dynamics had asked $9,609 for a 12-cent hexagonal wrench and $7,417 for a 2-cent alignment pin; Hughes Aircraft had priced a $3.64 circuit breaker at $2,543, a $547 circuit card at $1,315, and a 48-cent fuse at $512; Gould Simulator Systems asked $489 for a $3.39 circuit tester, $729 for a $3.96 crimping tool, and $599 for a $1.69 drill set.

The catalog compared prime contractor prices with those in the government supply system, subcontractor prices with those charged by prime contractors, and the price when a part was ordered by the Defense Department with the price when it was delivered. In each case, the Defense Department was charged substantially higher prices. Reviewing the entire catalog, the Pentagon claimed that it had discovered the higher prices and either had refused to pay them or had obtained a refund. But government officials did not deny that the defense industry had sought to charge exorbitant prices.

A new wrinkle in the spare parts issue arose in mid-1984, when the Air Force discovered that it had been throwing away spare parts in the belief they were no longer needed, then turning around and ordering new parts of the same type for far higher prices. The cause was an automatic disposal system in which spares were junked or sold for scrap when no order came in for a given period, such as a year. The Pentagon declared a moratorium on the disposal of excess materials until the situation had been straightened out. What that cost the taxpayers could not be determined. There seemed to be no way to find out what had been thrown out and to measure that against what had been bought to replace it.

Perhaps most symbolic of wasted money was the $7,622 coffee brewer installed in the Lockheed C-5 air transport. It came to light in the summer of 1984 when a young airman first class, Thomas Jonsson, testified before a congressional committee. Called a "hot beverage unit" by the Air Force, it was sold by Weber Aircraft of Burbank, California, and defended by the Air Force as being able to make, besides coffee, soup for the crew and to survive a crash if the plane was shot down in combat.

Another shortcoming of the American defense industry, and one that could cripple the United States, is the inability of most companies to surge into high rates of production in the event of war. The armed forces have only limited stockpiles of ammunition, supplies, extra weapons, fuel, and equipment. It would be up to industry, in a conventional conflict, to replace everything consumed in battle. In earlier conflicts, except the Korean War, American industry had time to see a war coming and to tool up for expanded production. But sudden hostilities, perhaps like the North Korean surprise attack that began the Korean War, have become the most likely of the possible conventional conflicts today. The inability of American industry to shift swiftly to wartime production means that American forces might be forced to stop fighting because they had run out of ammunition or weapons and supplies. That inadequacy, called a "war-stopper" by military officers, means that an enemy need only outlast American forces, not defeat them in battle.

In a comprehensive survey in 1984, the Air Force concluded that the defense industry would be unable to accelerate production to meet the demands of a surprise attack or to mobilize for wartime production even if signs of a coming conflict were visible. While the study concentrated on aircraft, missiles, and weapons for the Air Force, it looked at the needs of the other services and found the conclusions applicable across the board. The study was done by senior Air Force officers along with executives from General Dynamics, Hughes, McDonnell Douglas, Grumman, Sperry, and Westinghouse. Together, they found an absence of government planning to overcome the industrial weakness despite the emphasis given to the industrial base by the Reagan Administration.

After postulating different contingencies, the Air Force study found, "The aerospace industrial base cannot fully meet any of the mixed surge situations. Tactical missiles and some large aircraft cannot surge without the initiation of extraordinary measures." The study continued, "The ability of the industrial base to accelerate production rates and to sustain those rates initially is severely limited." The reasons: "Both prime and subcontractors are constrained from mobilizing by the availability of skilled manpower, capital equipment, material, tooling and test equipment, and real property." While the situation for each company, and for each weapon, was different, the Air Force said the shortcomings were common throughout industry.

The study said the potential shortage of skilled labor was most critical. "Competition between contractors for a finite amount of skilled manpower resources, plus the likely demands of military conscription, will severely tax the manpower reservoir in critical skill areas." Moreover, the study said, "the loss of foreign sources, especially for electronic components and critical strategic materials, will severely hamper industry's ability to mobilize if corrective measures are not taken." Having the right machinery was a genuine problem. "Current lead-times of 12 to 24 months, coupled with a significant increase in demand, raise questions of the ability of the machine tool industry to respond," the report said. "Timely buildup of machining capability will be a factor in the rate of production acceleration."

The Reagan Administration's Pentagon, under Secretary of Defense Weinberger, has had a mixed record in curbing the excesses of the defense industry. Mr. Weinberger took office with no visible plan and made his way with a series of seemingly unrelated actions. Some were his initiatives, while others were responses to pressures from Congress, whistleblowers, and news reports. It was a long, slow process that combined jawboning, negotiation, an effort to stimulate competition, barring work for errant contractors, and prosecuting alleged criminals. But Mr. Weinberger's Pentagon was perceived to have moved too slowly against the defense industry, and that perception contributed heavily to the erosion of support in Congress for President Reagan's expensive program of military buildup. Mr. Weinberger's efforts were weakened by a lack of continuity in Deputy Secretaries, as the Pentagon had three different men occupy that position in four years. The Deputy Secretary has customarily taken charge of managing the department's business. Mr. Weinberger's case was weakened by his repeated claims of credit for misdeeds discovered and corrected that were, in fact, revealed by others. In addition, Mr. Weinberger repeatedly blamed the Congress, critics, and the press for distorting news of his accomplishments.

On the other hand, the problem confronting Mr. Weinberger and his associates was enormous. "The Department of Defense spends about $600 million each and every day of the year—Saturdays, Sundays, and holidays," said Mr. Sherick, the Inspector General. "In fiscal year 1984, the department placed 15 million contracts worth $146 billion involving over 60,000 prime contractors and hundreds of thousands of other suppliers and subcontractors." He told reporters: "You know, this is a big operation. We are not running a hot dog stand."

It was difficult for the Defense Department to crack down too hard on defense contractors because of an inherent problem—the Pentagon had no place else to go for many weapons. Only the Electric Boat division of General Dynamics had the shipyard to build Trident nuclear-powered ballistic-missile submarines. Only Newport News Shipbuilding could construct a 90,000-ton aircraft carrier. To invest in another shipyard or plant and to tool up for a second source of many weapons would be prohibitively expensive. "I have to say," Mr. Sherick acknowledged, "that the Department of Defense couldn't operate a half hour without contractors."

The leader of a drive to get more competition into defense contracting was John Lehman, the Secretary of the Navy. He forced Grumman, builder of the A-6 Intruder attack bomber for the Navy, and McDonnell Douglas and Northrop, producers of the F-18 that doubled as a fighter and bomber, into a price war. He was able to get both producers to come down by telling one that he would buy more planes from the other if prices didn't drop. Mr. Lehman did the same by pitting General Electric and Pratt & Whitney against each other in aircraft engines.

Mr. Lehman's most effective moves were directed at the shipbuilders, already hurting from foreign competitors who had taken away nearly all of their commercial business. Mr. Lehman's main tactic was to split contracts by giving more work to the better bidder but enough to the other bidder to keep the shipyard in operation—and hungry enough to come back the next year with a more productive bid. Mr. Lehman awarded a contract to Newport News Shipbuilding in late 1984 to build three nuclear-powered attack submarines while giving Electric Boat, in Groton, Connecticut, a contract for one even though that shipyard had been the principal builder. Similarly, Mr. Lehman awarded a contract to Bath Iron Works in Maine to build two Aegis cruisers, which feature advanced electronic apparatus to detect and shoot down attacking aircraft. But Ingalls Shipyard, which had been the primary builder of Aegis ships in its yard at Pascagoula, Mississippi, got a contract for only one. The Secretary of the Air Force, Verne Orr, adopted the same tactic in early 1985, splitting an engine contract 54/46 between General Electric and Pratt & Whitney.

To root out waste and fraud, Mr. Weinberger appointed as Inspector General the irrepressible Mr. Sherick, a street-smart man from a tough neighborhood in Philadelphia who had spent forty years in military procurement. Under Mr. Sherick, the Defense Contract Audit Agency was expanded by 400 people to 4,100, the Defense Criminal Investigative Service was set up, and the Defense Department joined with the Justice Department to establish the Procurement Fraud Unit to prosecute alleged violators of the law. A "hot line" was revitalized to permit Defense Department employees or the general public to phone in with allegations of wrongdoing. Along with the Red Book to alert officials on spotting fraud went classes of instruction on related issues. By the end of 1984, Mr. Sherick claimed that "corrective actions" had reaped $8.1 billion in "monetary benefits" to the taxpayers. Broadly defined, those benefits included money retrieved from contractors who had overcharged, money saved when a potential overcharge was discovered, and savings from the campaign to find waste and fraud.

Until June 1983, many military officers were privately critical of the defense industry and the shoddy equipment that was delivered to the services but did not to speak out for fear of reprimands from their civilian superiors or members of Congress. That criticism was uncorked after Paul Thayer, then Deputy Secretary of Defense, told a gathering of defense industrialists that shoddy workmanship added as much as 30 percent to the taxpayer's bill. That was a signal to civilian and military officials that going after waste or fraud would be supported by the Pentagon's top managers. For the most part, the revelations of the spare parts scandal, the halting of payments to Hughes Aircraft, General Dynamics, and other contractors, and the prosecution of criminal violations came after Mr. Thayer had addressed the issue in public.

In the campaign against waste, the Pentagon claimed in late 1984 that it had received refunds from over 250 contractors. To avoid going to court, Chromalloy American Corporation, of St. Louis, agreed to pay back $4 million it had gotten by manipulating catalog prices. The Flying Tiger Line, an air cargo carrier, agreed to return an overpayment of $262,494 that came from sending a bill twice to the Air Force. The Navy got back $94,128 from several suppliers of spare parts. The Pentagon started giving bonuses to employees who spotted fraud or found other ways to save money. Mark Oppilla, a contract negotiator at the Navy Aviation Supply Office in Philadelphia, got $1,000 for saving the Navy $1.8 million by finding more competitive suppliers of refueling nozzles. The Air Force, arguing that inflation had dropped, negotiated a $439 million price reduction with Lockheed on a $7.8 billion contract to buy fifty C-5 cargo planes.

In an effort to restrain contractors from adding unnecessary features to their products, Deputy Secretary Taft instructed the services and the Defense Logistics Agency to challenge "requirements that are not cost-effective, particularly in weapons systems and replacement items already in the field." Addressing defense contractors, he pleaded: "Help us identify these gold-plated items. They are giving both the Defense Department and the defense industry a black eye."

Lastly, Mr. Weinberger asserted that much of what the Defense Department had done under his supervision had gone well:

While the Department of Defense did buy a diode for $110, we also bought 122,000 diodes for less than 3 cents each, and we were repaid for the $110 one. While we bought a $435 claw hammer, we also bought 87,244 hammers for 6 to 8 dollars each, and received a refund for the over-priced hammer. While we were refusing to pay for two pairs of over-priced pliers from one of our prime contractors, we were buying over 3,500 of the same type of pliers for $3.10 each.

He said that 43 percent of all dollars spent on procurement went into contracts for which there had been competition; another 29 percent had been spent for additional orders under contracts that had previously been subjected to competition. Only 28 percent, Mr. Weinberger asserted, had been noncompetitive in fiscal year 1984.

On the other side of the ledger, the first Deputy Secretary of Defense, Frank Carlucci, issued in the spring of 1981 a set of thirty-two initiatives intended to get Pentagon procurement in hand. It called for putting realistic prices on weapons, for careful projections of inflation, for building weapons faster so that the economies of scale could cut the cost of each unit, and for eliminating marginal programs. A key initiative was multiyear procurement, in which an order for tanks would be placed for, say, three years at a fixed price to give the program stability. The government could count on a known cost, and the producer, with a known rate of production, could more efficiently order materials, streamline his labor force, and keep overhead costs down.

Four years later, however, few of those initiatives had been fully adopted. Instead of realistic pricing, Mr. Weinberger, under budget pressures from Congress, suddenly came up in the spring of 1985 with a $4.6 billion dividend that he said could be cut without harming national security, claiming that inflation had been not so high as projected. Weapons programs were stretched out, few programs were cut, and multiyear contracts were scarce. Not all of that could be laid at the door of the Pentagon, because Congress had been lukewarm. The effect of those changes would have been to reduce dollars spent in election districts. "We saw it more as a statement of aspirations to which we could all subscribe than as a radical new game plan," an unnamed military officer told *The Wall Street Journal*. "There were some pretty good things in the initiatives, but they tend to puff and hype it too much. Not much has really changed."

The Defense Procurement Fraud Unit, the joint venture between the Justice and Defense Departments, didn't accomplish much. After a year of operation, it had recovered only $3 million, peanuts considering the size of the military budget. Part of the problem, said Richard A. Sauber, the thirty-three-year-old head of the unit, was the difficulty in proving a violation of the law. "For the most part, when there's disclosure as to what the price will be, but we go along, it's not a crime," he said. "It may be stupidity, laziness, or bad management, but it's not a crime when we pay too much for something." After three years, the unit had obtained only nineteen convictions for bribery, false claims, and labor mischarging. Half of those were related to one investigation of a supply yard in Philadelphia. Senator Charles E. Grassley, Republican of Iowa and a sharp critic of military procurement practices, called that "a spit in the ocean." But Mr. Sauber argued that

$7,600 coffee pots and $600 toilet seats generally don't amount to criminal cases because there's no deception, no fraud, no misrepresentation about what's involved. There are some very gray cases where it's really not clear that the government didn't know or at least acquiesce in what was going on.

By 1985, Mr. Sauber had left the Justice Department for private practice, where he represented Litton Industries and other defense contractors.

After the scandal over spare parts erupted, Mr. Weinberger issued a ten-point set of new rules to govern the procurement of those items.

Included were incentives to increase competitive bidding, discipline for officials who were negligent, strengthened controls on pricing, and insistence on refunds where possible. But Mr. Melchner, the senior official in the Inspector General's office, reported in 1985 that an audit "showed that the parts control program was not working the way it should." He said in a memorandum that "reported program results and cost avoidance benefits from the program were significantly over-stated." He reported that recommendations were not being implemented, that the number of parts entering the supply system was not being minimized, that some parts did not meet design requirements.

During the political season of 1984, Mr. Weinberger sought to deflect criticism of military spending by insisting that abuses by defense contractors had been uncovered by the Defense Department. That, however, was only partly true. The discovery of the $110 diode, the $200 switch, and the $243 circuit breaker were found "in response to a Congressional inquiry," according to Derek J. Vander Schaaf, a senior official in the Inspector General's office. The $1,118.26 plastic stool cap was exposed by an Air Force sergeant to Congress. The $7,622 coffee brewer was brought to public attention by an Air Force airman, also before Congress. The Securities and Exchange Commission uncovered some of the allegations against General Dynamics as did a House subcommittee led by Representative John Dingell, Democrat of Michigan. The House Operations Committee staff discovered the $659 ashtrays sold to the Navy by Grumman. The Defense Department took two years to crack down on Hughes Aircraft, despite repeated warnings. The General Accounting Office, an arm of the Congress, found the Sidewinder and Sparrow missiles that were unserviceable, as well as the excessive profits at Newport News Shipbuilding and three other companies, and Lockheed's overcharges for replacing wings on the C-5 transport. A newspaper reporter uncovered the faults with the Bell helicopters that caused so many crashes. The Pentagon did uncover some wrongdoing, mostly in response to outside pressures, but it had a good bit of help along the way.

For the defense industry, it has been a sorry performance. The relentless pace of revelations of misconduct in recent years has done as much as anything to crack the already fragile consensus supporting national defense. The disclosures, and the failure of the Pentagon to impose standards and controls on the industry, have undermined the efforts of the Reagan Administration to renew American military strength. Part of the fault lies with the companies in the defense industry and with the Pentagon. Unless either has been forced to confront a shortcoming, as with Hughes Aircraft in Tucson, they have passed off problems as isolated instances. Both the defense industry and the Defense Department have been more concerned with images than with realities. But the fault lies as much with the situation of monopoly and monopsony, and the absence of real checks on that incestuous relationship. The Pentagon has made some effort to introduce competition to regulate the industry, but that competition has been artificial at best. All in all, it has been a grand opportunity for greed, incompetence, inefficiency, arrogance, and complacency to flourish.

On the back of the door into his office, Mr. Sherick tacked up a poster showing the late comedian W. C. Fields peering suspiciously over cards held close to his chest. "It reminds me," Mr. Sherick said, "of the kind of people I have to deal with." While his charter ran across most operations of the Defense Department, he concentrated on the procurement of weapons for the same reason that Willie Sutton gave for robbing banks: "That's where the money is." Mr. Sherick was sometimes criticized for going after too many small contractors, but he justified that by saying "the money is spent in a lot of small pieces." When he cited cases that had been referred to law enforcement or administrators for prosecution or sanction, he was asked whether that was just the tip of the iceberg. Mr. Sherick was not one to recoil from mixing a metaphor. "Well, I keep turning over rocks," he said, "and each one I turn over, I keep finding things."

CHAPTER 7

"WE'RE STRETCHED THIN"

AMID the palm trees of MacDill Air Force Base in Tampa, Florida, sits a beige box of a building that is the headquarters of the United States Central Command, known in military jargon as CENTCOM. The command evolved from the Rapid Deployment Force formed in 1980 and was led until late 1985 by General Robert C. Kingston, a gruff Boston Irishman who relished his GI nickname, Barbwire Bob. The general took pride in having led troops in battle as a platoon leader, company commander, battalion commander, and brigade commander in the years since he enlisted in the Army in 1948.

General Kingston and his successor, General George B. Crist of the Marine Corps, had the toughest assignment of any field commander in American military service. Central Command is responsible for defending American national interests, primarily access to oil, in a vast region around the Persian Gulf, an area larger than the continental United States. It covers nineteen nations, from Egypt and the Sudan in the west to Pakistan in the east, from Jordan and Iraq in the north to Kenya in the south. The command's task is made more difficult by the crunching fact that its headquarters is 7,000 miles from the Straits of Hormuz at the southern end of the Persian Gulf, the most critical point in its area of responsibility. If the Suez Canal from the Mediterranean through Egypt to the Red Sea were to be closed, it would be 12,000 miles around the tip of South Africa from Tampa to the straits.

Most difficult, Central Command has no combat forces permanently assigned. It is a headquarters, and little more. The command has a force list of four Army divisions, seven Air Force tactical fighter wings and two strategic bomber wings, three Navy aircraft carriers and a battleship, and four Marine Corps amphibious brigades, plus supporting forces, for a total of about 300,000 people. But that is for planning only. Army, Navy, Marine Corps, and Air Force units that

210

might be placed under its operational control must come from another command in the United States, Europe, or the Pacific.

To add to the command's burdens, air and sea transport available to move troops, weapons, and supplies is limited. A battalion of 800 paratroopers and a squadron of twenty-four fighter planes could be deployed into the region by air within forty-eight hours of an order to move. But it would take more than a month by sea to get an Army or Marine division of 16,000 to 18,000 troops on the ground with their arms, including tanks and artillery, and to bring in more Air Force fighters to provide air cover. It would take three months to bring in two more divisions, seven to ten Air Force fighter squadrons, plus the logistic support of engineers, transport, and supply units the force would need.

Another complication is a lack of bases and the reluctance of nations in that region to be allied with the United States. The United States has negotiated agreements with Egypt, Somalia, Kenya, and Oman that give American forces limited access to their military bases, but those agreements are tenuous at best and, given the volatile politics of the region, nothing on which to rest a solid policy.

Central Command thus underscores the extent to which the United States has committed itself to police the world. The command has been ordered to fulfill commitments made by American political leaders to nineteen of the sixty nations to which the United States has pledged some form of military alliance since World War II. But the command's lack of forces, transport, bases, and allies also underscores the dismal fact that the United States does not have in existence, nor anywhere on the horizon, enough military power to fulfill those commitments.

Beyond that, the forces assigned to commands in the Atlantic, Pacific, and European theaters have been spread out in peacetime and would be stretched more in a crisis—whether to the breaking point can only be conjectured. On any given day, 35 percent of the men and women in the armed forces are on duty outside the continental bounds. That does not include soldiers and airmen on temporary duty abroad or sailors and marines based in the United States but away at sea; the Navy generally has one-third of its ships at sea all the time. In sum, rarely in history have the military forces of a nation been so far-flung as those of the United States today. The Romans, the Mongols, and the British, in their heydays of empire, have been among the few that compare.

The Reagan Administration in recent years has stretched the armed forces even more by devising an ambitious military strategy that seeks not only to contain the Soviet Union but to confront the Russians and to roll back their power. The objective has been to regain American military superiority over the Soviet Union, although the administration has denied that. But a secret document called *Defense Guidance* showed the Reagan Administration's military strategy to be perhaps the most ambitious since the document known as NSC-68 laid out the doctrine of containment of 1950. Signed by Secretary of Defense Weinberger in March 1982, *Defense Guidance* called for a full array of nuclear, conventional, and unconventional forces. Those forces would be capable of every possible military action in nearly every place, from fighting a protracted nuclear war to mounting an antiterrorist operation. Where earlier administrations had rejected "rolling back" Russian power as too dangerous in a nuclear world, the Reagan Administration sought opportunities to do so, as in the invasion of Grenada in 1983. In the event of hostilities with the Soviet Union, *Defense Guidance* said, the administration planned to strike not only at the point of attack but at other places in "geographic escalation" or "horizontal escalation." Under an assumption of a nuclear standoff between the United States and the Soviet Union, American armed forces were instructed to prepare to fight a prolonged war around the globe with conventional arms. "Our long-term goal," Mr. Weinberger said in public, "is to be able to meet the demands of a worldwide war, including concurrent reinforcement of Europe, deployments to Southwest Asia and the Pacific, and support for other areas."

The nation's military leaders, however, warned their political superiors that the strategy was too ambitious for the forces on hand and those planned. Senior officers argued in the councils of government, and sometimes outside, that the United States needs either a more powerful military force or a lower level of commitment. In the jargon of the Pentagon, the imbalance between commitments and military power has been called the "strategy-force mismatch." After General David C. Jones of the Air Force retired in 1982 as Chairman of the Joint Chiefs of Staff, he cautioned that "the mismatch between strategy and the forces to carry it out is greater now than ever before because we are trying to do too much." A retired Army colonel asserted that the United States had reversed the dictum of Theodore Roosevelt, who said, "Speak softly but carry a big stick." Today, said the irreverent colonel, "We are shooting our mouths off and carrying a twig."

Moreover, the Reagan Administration has failed to make the armed forces ready for sustained battle at levels above that needed to invade Grenada, despite the largest peacetime military budgets in American history. Nor, according to projections made by the administration itself, would the forces be ready until the end of the decade—and in some sectors, not then. The armed forces have serious deficiencies in transport, ammunition stockpiles, supplies of spare parts, reserves of wartime matériel, and combat medical care. Those are what military officers call "war-stoppers," or shortages so severe that American forces might have to stop fighting because they had run out of ammunition or could not treat the wounded. The Reagan Administration's program to "rearm America" has made heavy investments in new weapons at the expense of mundane items like ammunition, and has thus lacked balance. Consequently, an American President trying to repel a conventional attack could be confronted rather quickly with an awful choice: to surrender or to resort to nuclear arms.

General Wallace H. Nutting, the Commander in Chief of Readiness Command who was responsible in 1985 for preparing Army and Air Force units in the United States to move to Europe or other war zones, singled out transport as an example of a potential war-stopper:

Strategic mobility—the capability to project and sustain decisive military power—is the cornerstone of our military posture in support of our national strategy. No matter how combat-ready our forces are, they represent a paper tiger without the ability to deploy rapidly to various crisis zones worldwide when and where our vital national interest is threatened.

In addition, the mismatch between commitments and forces has been exacerbated by the failure of allies to bear a proportionate share of the military and economic burden for the collective defense. By almost any measure of national population, wealth, and national interests, the United States carries far more of the relative burden for the common defense than do any of its allies, collectively or singly. Perhaps most striking, the United States in 1983 spent $911 to defend each American citizen while West European governments, collectively, spent only $265 per person, according to Defense Department figures. Britain spent $426 per capita, France $398, Germany $360, and Italy $167. Japan spent only $101 per person. A NATO calculation based on different exchange rates came up with $962 for each American, which was more military spending per person than any two European nations combined.

The combination of extended commitments, the dichotomy between strategy and forces, the cost of deploying forces around the world, the lack of readiness for sustained battle, and the lag in allied efforts have led to calls for retrenchment. Those calls have come from diverse Republicans and Democrats, and from academicians, editorialists, and defense intellectuals. The extent of American military commitments around the world has thus become a critical issue in the national debate over the security of the United States.

After a century of avoiding entangling alliances, American commitments abroad began with the annexation of the Philippines in 1898. President McKinley justified the departure from the tradition set by President Washington by proclaiming a moralistic tone that continued into the future. "No imperial designs lurk in the American mind," President McKinley declared. "If we can benefit those remote peoples, who will object?"

American commitments expanded in World War I but contracted later when the Senate rejected United States participation in the League of Nations. The United States, however, insisted on being considered one of two major powers in the treaty that limited naval forces in 1922. Moreover, marines were dispatched in the 1920s and 1930s to prevent a leftist takeover in Nicaragua and to bring order to anarchic Haiti. The Army's 15th Regiment was posted to Tientsin in China; 5,000 marines were later dispatched to protect American interests there; and Navy gunboats patrolled the Yangtze River until World War II.

After World War II, American commitments expanded swiftly as the Cold War with the Soviet Union took shape. Allied occupations of Germany and Japan led to American pledges to protect those nations from the Soviet Union. President Truman set a precedent in 1947 with the Truman Doctrine. In a message to Congress asking for economic aid for Greece and Turkey, the President said, "I believe that it must be the policy of the United States to support free peoples who are resisting attempted subjugation by armed minorities or by outside pressures." Later that year, the United States signed the Inter-American Treaty of Reciprocal Assistance, better known as the Rio Pact, in which twenty North and South American nations agreed that "an armed attack against an American state shall be considered an attack against all the American states" and that each signatory "undertakes to assist in meeting the attack." For the first time, the United States pledged itself, before the outbreak of hostilities, to use military force to aid an ally.

That same year, an article in the magazine *Foreign Affairs* signed only with an *X* but soon discovered to be the work of George Kennan, a diplomat and acute observer of the Soviet Union, became the intellectual foundation for the doctrine of containment. That policy sought to prevent the expansion of Russian power beyond the Soviet Union and its Eastern European satellites. Containment was codified in 1950 by President Truman's National Security Council in a document known as NSC-68. That document said the United States should reject isolation, appeasement, and preventive war, but opt for building a relatively large standing military force and adopting political and economic actions intended to contain the Soviet Union. The top-secret appraisal, later declassified, said:

We must, by means of a rapid and sustained build-up of the political, economic, and military strength of the free world, and by means of an affirmative program intended to wrest the initiative from the Soviet Union, confront it with convincing evidence of the determination and ability of the free world to frustrate the Kremlin design of a world dominated by its will. Such evidence is the only means short of war which eventually may force the Kremlin to abandon its present course of action and to negotiate acceptable agreements on issues of major importance.

Initially, the policy of containment did not envision a long-term deployment of American military forces abroad. Another document from the National Security Council, NSC-82, said, "it is hoped that the United States will be able to leave to European nation-members the primary responsibility of maintaining and commanding such a force." Later, Senator Bourke Hickenlooper, Republican of Iowa, asked Secretary of State Dean Acheson whether the United States would send troops permanently to defend Europe. "The answer to that question, Senator," Mr. Acheson replied, "is a clear and absolute 'no.'"

But the outbreak of the Korean War in June 1950 made Europeans fear a similar attack, which led to the stationing of more American forces in Europe and elsewhere. That deployment has expanded by fits and starts ever since. Forty years after the end of World War II, the United States has sizable forces in Western Europe, Korea, Japan, and the Philippines, plus smaller contingents in the Middle East, the Indian Ocean, and, lately, Central America. The strategy of posting forces abroad is called forward deployment, or forward defense.

Interwoven with forward deployment has been the policy of forming alliances into a coalition against the Soviet Union, often with the United States pledging to defend a nation in return for the right to station forces there. With the inauguration of the North Atlantic Treaty Organization, or NATO, in 1949, the United States again pledged, before the outbreak of hostilities, that an attack on one member of the pact was to be considered an attack on all. After NATO came the Central Treaty Organization, or CENTO, which included Iran and Pakistan along the southern border of the Soviet Union, and the Southeast Asia Treaty Organization, or SEATO, which was intended to keep China and North Vietnam in check. Both CENTO and SEATO are defunct, but American commitments to some of their members, such as Pakistan and Thailand, remain intact. The Australia–New Zealand–United States treaty founding ANZUS pledged the United States to help defend those nations. Treaties committed the United States to the defense of the Philippines, Japan, and Korea. Equally important, although not legally binding, were political commitments made to other nations, especially to Israel and later to Egypt.

President Eisenhower extended American commitments by signing a law in 1957 that was the basis for the Eisenhower Doctrine. It authorized the use of American military forces against communist aggression "to secure and protect the territorial integrity and political independence of nations who requested such aid." President Kennedy, in his inaugural address in January 1961, reinforced that with a fiery political declaration: "Let every nation know, whether it wishes us well or ill, that we shall pay any price, bear any burden, meet any hardship, support any friend, oppose any foe to assure the survival and the success of liberty."

The objective of the American involvement in Vietnam was to contain a North Vietnam considered the surrogate for the Soviet Union in Southeast Asia. The widespread disillusion following the war in Vietnam led President Nixon to move away from containment. In the Nixon Doctrine, he said the United States would gradually shift the burden of frontline defense to other nations, with the United States providing the nuclear umbrella and the strategic reserve of conventional forces for the free world. Mr. Nixon fostered détente and arms control with the Soviet Union, opened relations with Communist China, and reduced military spending during his truncated second term. Those policies were largely continued by President Ford and President Carter.

The Soviet invasion of Afghanistan in December 1979 reversed détente. President Carter, saying he had been stunned by the Soviet action, committed the United States to the use of military force about as far from the continental United States as it is possible to go. "Any attempt by any outside force to gain control of the Persian Gulf region," Mr. Carter proclaimed in early 1980, "will be regarded as an assault on the vital interests of the United States of America, and such an assault will be repelled by any means necessary, including military force."

By the time Ronald Reagan became President on January 20, 1981, the United States had experienced three decades in which American commitments had been made to nations around the world and military forces dispatched to ever farther reaches. His administration was to expand both.

Mr. Reagan arrived in the White House without a comprehensive military program beyond the campaign pledge in the Republican platform to achieve military superiority over the Soviet Union. Mr. Reagan's first national security adviser, Richard V. Allen, scoffed at calls for a new strategy. "All we need to do," he said in an interview, "is to set priorities and start building." During the early months of 1982, however, the President turned to military policy because of unrest in Central America, attacks on his defense budget, and disarray among his advisers on national security. Mr. Reagan brought in Thomas C. Reed, a former Secretary of the Air Force, to conduct an intensive review of national security policies that ended with the President signing a top secret National Security Decision Directive to set his strategy in place. The military component of that directive was drawn from *Defense Guidance*, which provided the strategic underpinning for the military budget for fiscal year 1984 and for military planning for the following four years. *Defense Guidance* has been refined each year since but, according to senior officials in the Reagan Administration, has remained constant in its fundamentals.

Defense Guidance revealed in great detail the military ambitions of the Reagan Administration and the strategy by which it would seek to achieve military superiority over the Soviet Union. It drew an aggressive portrait of the Soviet Union and outlined, albeit in turgid language, the administration's military plans throughout the world in peace and in war.

Claiming that the Soviet Union had a comprehensive strategy "for projection of military power and a long-term policy to expand a global network of military facilities," *Defense Guidance* said,

United States forces might be required simultaneously in geographically separated theaters. . . . United States conventional forces, in conjunction with those of our allies, should be capable of putting at risk Soviet interests, including the Soviet homeland, and defeating Soviet and Soviet-inspired aggression in many regions.

That would include Europe and the lines of communication to it, the Eastern Mediterranean and its littoral, the Persian Gulf, Northeast Asia, Southeast Asia, and Latin America. "Counteroffensives will be directed at places where we can affect the outcome of the war," *Defense Guidance* said. "If it is to offset the enemy's attack, it should be launched against territory or assets that are of an importance to him comparable to the ones he is attacking."

Regionally, *Defense Guidance* seemed to foreshadow the invasion of Grenada, saying that American armed forces must be prepared to "counter Soviet and Cuban supported terrorism, military influence, and destabilizing actions in the Caribbean basin"; "reverse Communist gains in El Salvador, Nicaragua, Grenada, and other areas of Latin America"; and "seek close military ties with Panama, Honduras, Jamaica, the Dominican Republic, and other Central American and Caribbean countries." After the invasion of Grenada, instructions to the armed forces in the 1984 *Defense Guidance* were sharpened with orders to seek more combined maneuvers with "indigenous military forces" in Latin America. National security was said to be jeopardized by threats to the Panama Canal, the Soviet and Cuban presence in Nicaragua, and the effect of developments in Central America on Mexico. "Central America, therefore, is critical to our mid-range efforts in the region," the document said. The armed forces were instructed to foster "regional political-military relationships with key Latin American countries in the areas of regional territorial and air defense, security of vital lines of communication, and facilitation of sea and air movement."

In Europe, *Defense Guidance* emphasized efforts to get allies to acquire stockpiles of ammunition, fuel, and supplies for nonnuclear war. Improvements were necessary "to assure that forward deployed NATO forces would not be overwhelmed in the earliest stages of a high intensity war." The document called for building up defenses in Norway on the northern flank and in Turkey on the southern flank and for finding "more effective linkages with the people of East Europe so as to deny Soviet confidence in the reliability of her allies."

Defense Guidance linked United States and allied forces in Western Europe with the security of the Persian Gulf. The policy would be to "urge allies to contribute to security in Southwest Asia, specifically, by providing military and economic assistance, access to transit facilities for United States forces deploying to Southwest Asia, and military contingents as feasible." Most Europeans have resisted American efforts to connect the security of Western Europe with that of Southwest Asia, considering the latter an American responsibility even though Europe is more dependent on oil from the region than is the United States. The armed forces were instructed to "give particular attention to the close strategic connection of the southeastern forces of NATO with the Persian Gulf region by providing forces that can be used both in the direct defense of NATO and in the defense of allied interests in Southwest Asia."

In the Middle East and Southwest Asia, *Defense Guidance* went beyond the doctrine of President Carter.

Our principal objectives are to assure the continued access to Persian Gulf oil and to prevent the Soviets from acquiring political-military control of the oil directly or through proxies. To achieve these goals, we must allocate a disproportionately larger investment to this region, and we must upgrade our capabilities to project forces to, and operate them in, the region. We should also urgently increase and improve the capabilities of friendly indigenous forces.

It is essential that the Soviet Union be confronted with the prospect of a major conflict should it seek to reach oil resources of the Gulf. Because the Soviets might induce or exploit local political instabilities, their forces could be extended into the area by means other than outright invasion. Whatever the circumstances, we would be prepared to introduce American forces directly into the region should it appear that the security of access to Persian Gulf oil is threatened.

With instructions similar to those for Central America, the 1984 *Defense Guidance* directed the armed forces to build up "as substantial a land presence as can be managed" in Southwest Asia. "We remain committed to acquiring the capability to conduct a sustained defense of the region as far forward as possible, including Iran," the document said. It said "the military weakness of friendly regional states, the lack of infrastructure to sustain a large military force, and the long distance from the United States necessitate a continued large investment to upgrade our capabilities to project, operate, and sustain forces in the region."

In East Asia and the Pacific, *Defense Guidance* said, the foremost objective "is, in conjunction with our regional friends and allies, to prevent the Soviet Union and Vietnam from expanding their influence." To achieve that, the United States would maintain sufficient strength on the Korean peninsula. The United States would seek to "transform our relationship with Japan into an active defense partnership in which Japan significantly increases its defense capabilities to be able to provide for its own defense, including sea lines of communication protection to 1,000 miles." The cohesion of the Association of Southeast Asian Nations, or ASEAN, would be fostered to counter Vietnamese expansion and "to support the projection of United States power from the Western Pacific to the Indian Ocean and Persian Gulf." A "strategic relationship" with Communist China would be sought "by supporting measured increases in its military capability without threatening our Asian allies and friends." (Curiously, for a Republican administration that vowed not to abandon the Nationalist Chinese government on the island of Taiwan, there was no mention of Taiwan in the *Defense Guidance*.)

Beyond the geographic objectives, *Defense Guidance* set out the administration's military strategies for peacetime, crises, and wartime. One paragraph illuminated the extent to which the administration intended to keep American forces abroad in peace:

Overseas basing of United States forces will continue in Europe, the Western Pacific, Latin America, and, when circumstances permit, in Southwest Asia. Naval and air forces will provide for a continuous presence of combatant forces in the North Atlantic, Caribbean, Mediterranean, Western Pacific, and Indian Ocean/Southwest Asia regions. Selective deployments of significant forces will be made to South America, Africa, Southeast Asia and the Southwest Pacific. Ground and air deployments will periodically be made to Southwest Asia, as political considerations permit.

For crises not involving the Soviet Union, *Defense Guidance* said that the United States would avoid provoking Moscow but that "the posture and deployment of United States forces will present evidence of the intention and the capability of the United States to meet its security and political objectives." The document emphasized the role of special operations forces, such as the Army's Green Berets, that have been trained in commando raids, guerrilla warfare, and other unconventional tactics. Such forces "will be employed during a crisis, where the use of larger, conventional forces would be premature, inappropriate, or infeasible, to conduct low-intensity surgical operations and to control the situation or terminate the crisis on favorable terms."

If the United States engaged in a conventional conflict that did not involve Soviet forces, *Defense Guidance* said, the United States would seek a swift solution to the conflict: "The United States will seek," it said, "to limit the scope of the conflict, avoid involvement of Soviet forces, try to curtail Soviet support to the enemy's side, quickly end United States military involvement, and ensure that United States military objectives are met."

In the event of Soviet attack, *Defense Guidance* said, "United States forces will be employed against the Soviet forces to compel the Soviets to cease the aggression and to retreat." If the Soviet attack took place where the United States had an advantage, the United States would seek "to terminate the conflict decisively and, as much as possible, inflict a permanent setback on the Soviet Union to deter aggression elsewhere." If the attack should come at a place not to the American advantage, the United States would prepare measures "that threaten Soviet vulnerabilities critical to their prosecution of the war and prepare for the possibility of a global United States–Soviet war." While preparing for counteroffensives on other fronts, *Defense Guidance* cautioned, with masterly understatement, that geographic escalation should be carefully controlled "since the Soviet Union enjoys war-widening options at least as attractive as ours." In the global war, the United States would also "neutralize rapidly Soviet and other hostile forces in the Caribbean and Latin America," meaning that Russian forces in Cuba and Cuban forces would come under attack.

Defense Guidance said the priority in Central Europe would be "to stop the initial Warsaw Pact thrust with minimal loss of territory, then to gain the strategic initiative." Then, "emphasis will be given to offensive moves against Warsaw Pact flanks to force diversion of Pact resources from the central front." To disrupt the enemy's rear, "special operations forces will conduct operations in Eastern Europe and in the northern and southern NATO regions."

In Southwest Asia, the document continued:

Special operations, naval, and air forces will assist regional states in impeding a Soviet advance into the region until United States ground forces can be introduced. United States forces will be rapidly projected into the region to directly confront the Soviet attack and assist regional allies in the defense of the oil fields and the Arabian Peninsula. The United States will establish naval and air superiority in the region and provide logistic support to the air and ground forces of friendly regional states.

In the Pacific, the strategy gave priority to defending Alaska and Hawaii. Next came controlling the sea lanes through the South China Sea to the Indian Ocean and Persian Gulf, assisting allies, and encouraging Chinese military operations, "that would fix Soviet ground, air, and naval forces in the USSR's Far Eastern territories." *Defense Guidance* said: "Forces will conduct offensive operations designed to exploit Soviet vulnerabilities critical to the prosecution of the global conflict and tie up Soviet forces in defensive roles. Opportunities for counteroffensives against North Korea, Vietnam, and Soviet coastal areas will be exploited."

To end a war, *Defense Guidance* said in classic Pentagon jargon, "The United States will seek to effect conflict termination at the earliest practical time" with the integrity of American and allied territory secured and "unimpeded Free World access to oil and other essential strategic resources." To do that, it would be necessary to destroy "the war-fighting capability of the Soviet Union and its allies to the point that the United States and its allies cannot be coerced" and to bring about "the economic exhaustion of the Soviet Union." Mr. Reed, who led the national security review in 1982, was more direct. "We should hope to prevail," he said. "There's nothing wrong with winning." General Vessey, then chairman of the JCS, was blunt. He told a gathering of sergeants major at Fort Bliss in Texas that the strategy was designed "to restore peace—or what in Washington the word-mongers call 'restoring peace on favorable terms.' Now, that means to me, in soldier language, that we win the war."

From the beginning, however, the nation's senior military officers told the administration that the strategy was too ambitious for the forces available. The Joint Chiefs of Staff drew up a list of forces they said would be needed to execute the administration's long-range plan. It called for expanding the active Army from its 16 divisions to 23 divisions. The Marine Corps would be expanded by 1 marine amphibious force to 4 such units, each with 58,000 marines. The Navy would need 24 aircraft carriers, instead of 13 in the fleet and 2 ordered, each with 6 or 8 escort ships. Air Force tactical fighter wings would be expanded from 24 to 44. The Air Force said it would need 499 bombers instead of the 364 on hand. To provide the airlift and sealift, the chiefs said, long-range air transport must be more than tripled, from 304 aircraft to 1,308.

The Joint Chiefs told their civilian superiors, in addition, that the stategy was too ambitious for the funds the Reagan Administration expected to get from Congress. The administration had a five-year plan that was to have cost $1,500 billion, or $1.5 trillion. The military chiefs said the services would need another $325 billion to bring the forces up to a peacetime level that would provide an effective deterrent and that would be able to put out brush fires. To fight a prolonged conventional war or to wage a protracted nuclear war if deterrence failed, the chiefs said still another $325 billion, or a total of $750 billion, would be needed.

Some military officers cautioned obliquely but in public that the nation was overcommitted for the forces at hand. General Meyer, Chief of Staff of the Army in 1981, defined the "strategy-force mismatch" as "a gap between what our military forces in being are able to do and the enunicated national strategies." The general, in a speech in Boston to the World Affairs Council, said, "There has, and was, and continues to be a differential between the strategy we've announced for the nation and the capabilities of the forces we have to respond to that strategy." From a soldier's standpoint,

The Reagan Administration's strategy proposed a more global approach to our responsibilities. Secondly, it envisions the need for a capability to engage in a war of more indeterminate length rather than just one of short and violent exchange. And third, it accepts the need to take action under a period of tension.

This framework obviously requires that you have adequately sized forces ready across the full spectrum of warfare from counter-terrorism all the way through strategic nuclear exchange. That key linkage between our force capabilities, the forces in being, and the strategy is one of very real concern, and is one that must be brought into order. Otherwise, we will have the President and the leadership of our nation proposing ways in which they will go about national security without the military strength to back it up.

General Meyer's successor, General Wickham, agreed. "I guess traditionally we've had the range of contingency needs that probably exceed the force capabilities that we've been able to generate," he said. "That probably applies now." He went on: "So we are stretched to maintain our commitments. We are stretched in terms of resources to meet commitments." The Commander in Chief of American forces in the Atlantic region, Admiral McDonald, testified before the Senate Armed Services Committee in 1984 that "our current fleet deployments demonstrates how our forces can be stretched to the geographic extremes." The Atlantic Command's forces operate in a vast triangle whose points are the Caribbean, the edge of the Mediterranean, and the Arctic. Some ships are temporarily assigned to the fleet in the Mediterranean, which is a separate command. "In this context," he said, "I must tell you that our forces continue to be very heavily committed around the world, and stretched so thin that very little surge capability exists for rapid response to additional crises."

A voyage by the battleship *New Jersey* made Admiral McDonald's point. She left home port at Long Beach, California, on June 9, 1983, for a three-month cruise in the western Pacific. While taking part in an exercise near Thailand in July, she was ordered to steam across the Pacific to Central America as part of a show of force. Passing through the Panama Canal, *New Jersey* sailed out of the Caribbean and across the Atlantic and the Mediterranean to the coast of Lebanon, where she provided gunfire support for marines in Beirut. The ship returned to Long Beach on May 5, 1984, ending 322 days and 76,000 miles at sea, among the longest deployments in United States Navy peacetime history.

The deployment of *New Jersey* reflected the constant drills by the armed forces around the world. Each year, the Army and Air Force practice reinforcing the 350,000 Americans in Western Europe in an exercise codenamed REFORGER, which stands for "return of forces to Germany." In REFORGER 84, Army units from Fort Polk in Louisiana, Fort Hood in Texas, and Fort Lewis in Washington were airlifted to Germany, along with 51,000 tons of equipment aboard two ships. The 17,000 soldiers joined American troops and allied forces in Europe for a simulated response to an attack by the Warsaw Pact. The Air Force sent 1,200 airmen in a parallel drill called CRESTED CAP. Another move took American land, naval, and air forces from the United States and from bases in the western Pacific to South Korea, where the United States already had 29,000 soldiers and 11,000 airmen. In TEAM SPIRIT, they train in repelling an invasion from North Korea. Every other year, Central Command deploys forces for BRIGHT STAR to nations such as Egypt, Somalia, Kenya, and Oman. In other years, those forces train in the desert in the western United States in GALLANT EAGLE. In Central America, exercises like BIG PINE, which are shows of force intended to discourage Nicaraguan military expansion, appear likely to continue.

Elsewhere, the Strategic Air Command's bomber and missile crews practice for nuclear warfare every year in GLOBAL SHIELD. Squadrons from the Tactical Air Command "surge" to Europe for exercises or to train with ground forces. In COBRA GOLD in Thailand, EASTERN WIND in Somalia, ADVENTURE EXPRESS in Turkey, TEAM WORK in Norway, and TANGENT FLASH in the Philippines, the forces practice amphibious landings. At sea, the Navy holds mock battles with an annual FLEETEX in the Pacific, a READEX in the Atlantic, OCEAN VENTURE in the Caribbean, UNITAS around South America with ships from Latin American navies, and RIMPAC in the Pacific with the Japanese, Canadian, Australian, and New Zealand navies.

The aircraft known as Awacs and officially called Airborne Warning and Control Systems have often been assigned to show the flag, much as gunboats did in an earlier day. Home base for the thirty planes, which are Boeing 707s packed with electronic sensors and communications apparatus and mounting radar domes on their backs, is Tinker Air Force Base, Oklahoma. During a typical period in 1983, four Awacs were in Saudi Arabia, where their radar watched Iraqi and Iranian airspace as those nations fought. Two Awacs took part in

BRIGHT STAR in Egypt, and another two were sent to the Sudan to look for Libyan planes that might attack Chad. Three Awacs were flying from Iceland watching the North Atlantic and three were posted to Okinawa in the western Pacific. Back home, one Awacs was on duty with the North American Aerospace Defense Command. Eight were training with fighters from the Tactical Air Command, or training new Awacs crews of twenty-eight pilots, navigators, radar operators, communicators, and electronic specialists, or helping law enforcement officers run down drug smugglers. Three were in depot maintenance for thorough checks, two were having routine maintenance done on the flight line, one was having its radar calibrated, and another was set aside for training maintenance crews.

The Navy deploys aircraft carrier battle groups that comprise a carrier, a cruiser, several destroyers and frigates, replenishment ships, and two to four submarines. In a given period, the carrier *Midway*, whose home port is Yokosuka, Japan, was in the western Pacific. The carrier *Vinson* was in the Indian Ocean, *Eisenhower* in the Mediterranean, *Coral Sea* in the Atlantic on the way to the Caribbean, and *Ranger* in the Pacific off the coast of Nicaragua. *Constellation* was in a long overhaul at Bremerton, Washington, and the other six were in port or training off the East and West Coasts.

The Army in 1986 had the equivalent of five and a half divisions in Europe, one in South Korea, and a brigade in Panama. The Marine Corps had most of a division on Okinawa. Because the United States lacks air transport to move large units in a hurry, four light Army divisions of 10,000 soldiers have been formed. Those divisions, whose troops came from the standing ranks, were intended to make the United States better able to respond to crises.

Altogether, the United States has 360 installations overseas, some of them small radar stations keeping a lonely watch, recreation areas, or warehouses. But others are large operating bases like the Yokosuka Naval Base in Japan, Clark Air Force Base in the Philippines, the Stuttgart Army headquarters that is one of 176 posts in Germany, and Holy Loch submarine base in Scotland. In addition, the United States , on any given day may have twenty or more training teams of 3 to 100 people abroad teaching or advising military forces of other nations. More teams handle sales of military equipment, among the largest of which is the 500 Americans from all four services in Saudi Arabia, where they are helping to build a modern Saudi military service. Elsewhere, battalions of 800 soldiers rotate in and out of the Sinai desert every six months as part of a peacekeeping force.

Sometimes the military services have forces deployed so widely that a war game must be postponed. In the summer of 1983, President Reagan ordered American forces to maneuver in Honduras to signal Nicaragua and Cuba that the United States was serious about halting the expansion of leftist influence in Central America. But the President caught the Defense Department by surprise. Senior officers protested that commitments of troops and sea and air transport to other operations, plus a lack of funds, would prevent them from dispatching forces to Honduras until November, after the new fiscal year began. They also planned exercises smaller than the President envisioned so they could carry out the President's orders without canceling other operations.

A senior officer on the staff of the Joint Chiefs, asked about the delay and the substitute plan, sighed, "We're stretched thin."

The forces are spread so thin that General Nutting, the commander of the Readiness Command responsible for deploying troops from the United States to points overseas, told Congress in 1985, "We today do not have a single soldier, airman, or sailor dedicated to the security mission within the United States." Even forces stationed in the United States have been committed to overseas deployments in the event of hostilities. General Nutting raised the possibility of a threat from the Soviet Union's *Spetsnaz* forces, which he said have been trained "to operate far behind enemy lines for extended periods of time and to be capable of operating throughout an enemy's homeland."

Because the forces have been stretched, military officers have been anxious to avoid a new commitment in Central America, although they are quick to say that the decision is the President's and that they will obey his orders. But they would prefer that American leaders seek political and economic solutions. Moreover, they see the services, particularly the Army, as having just recovered, emotionally and materially, from the war in Vietnam. They want to avoid burning up that newly won health in another jungle. An intervention in Central America would almost certainly require a revival of the draft, a move many officers believe would cause dissent. Some officers believe that measured pressure must be kept on the Sandinista government in Nicaragua to make it behave, but think an invasion of Nicaragua would be a costly mistake. Similarly, many American military officers were critical of the British for fighting with Argentina over the barren Falkland islands, far in the South Atlantic, with few people and flocks of sheep. American officers scorned a venture that took British ships away from the North Atlantic patrol and took funds that might have been spent improving the British Army on the Rhine in Germany.

The high cost of sending forces abroad, plus the investments made by the Reagan Administration in new weapons, has held back improvements in military readiness and the capacity to sustain battle. Moreover, when Congress has cut the budget, it has reduced appropriations for ammunition, spare parts, and wartime supplies rather than slice into weapons programs that produce jobs in home districts. Yet it is the ammunition, fuel, and medical supplies that combatant commanders say they must have to prepare for what they call the "come-as-you-are" war.

Consequently, if the United States were called upon to help deter an Iranian invasion of the oil fields of Saudi Arabia, it would most likely be unable to move sufficient forces there in time to be credible. If the United States found it necessary to respond to a surprise attack in South Korea, it would be unable to sustain forces for more than a few weeks. If NATO had to repel a Soviet invasion of Western Europe, the forces would lack ammunition to fight for more than a month or six weeks.

Transport requirements beyond a small-scale operation like the invasion of Grenada are immense. In the campaign for the Falkland Islands, the British needed nearly 100 ships to transport troops, weapons, ammunition, food, fuel, and supplies. Weapons and equipment for one American mechanized infantry division of 16,000 soldiers weigh nearly 30,000 tons. The Army figures it would take 1,443 flights of C-141 transports to fly such a division to the Persian Gulf, and that would take more than twelve days.

A congressional study determined that, to fulfill military obligations, the armed forces should be able to move by air sixty-six million ton-miles a day, a calculation that combines the weight of equipment to be moved with the distance and the time required. The head of the Military Airlift Command, General Thomas M. Ryan Jr., told Congress in 1984 that the capacity of air transport was 33.6 million ton-miles a day. Defense Department projections said if the trend continued, only fifty million ton-miles a day would be available in 1990 and the goal of sixty-six million ton-miles would not be reached until 1996.

Even more marked were shortcomings in shipping, which would be the way most American troops, weapons, and supplies would go to war. Airlift is good for getting people and things someplace in a hurry, but it is expensive and limited in what it can carry. Sealift is good for getting many people and things someplace in not such a hurry and for far less money; it would move 90 to 95 percent of all military cargo during a conflict. The Defense Department has estimated that the nation should have the shipping capacity to move 4.6 million tons within thirty days. In 1981, that capacity was 3.1 million tons, which expanded to 3.8 million tons by 1984. Capacity was projected to grow to 4.1 million tons by 1990, but it would take until 1996 for the 4.6-million-ton goal to be reached.

Even if they could get there, forces would lack ammunition to sustain the battle. The Joint Chiefs of Staff told Congress in their annual report in 1985, "Ammunition shortfalls are the critical issue in matériel sustainability," which is Pentagon jargon for the ability to continue fighting. "Commanders continue to identify inadequate ammunition stockpiles as the most significant constraint on their combat capabilities." The Commander in Chief of Atlantic forces, Admiral McDonald, told Congress in 1984 that inadequate supplies of munitions "remain the most serious detriment to current war-fighting capability." The admiral came back in 1985 to say, "Correcting ordnance deficiencies is my number one priority."

General Rogers, commander of American forces in Europe, reported in 1984 that his command would not be able to sustain combat for long because it did not have "manpower, ammunition, and war reserve matériel to replace losses." General Rogers's deputy, General Richard L. Lawson of the Air Force, elaborated: "Some munition stocks, most notably air-to-air missiles, naval munitions, high-technology munitions, are well below our required stockage, to the point where they could be classified as war-stoppers." General Rogers held to that line the next year. "The stockage levels of major end items of Army equipment and war reserve kits for the Air Force are too low," he said. "Exhaustion of their supply, as well as of selected munitions items, could be termed a war-stopper."

The Pacific commander, Admiral Crowe, said in 1984 his prime concern was whether "we have enough ammunition, enough spare parts, enough oil in the right places, enough consumables and sustainables for a protracted conflict out here." The following year, he said "shortages of essential warfighting items still remain to be addressed." The admiral, named Chairman of the Joint Chiefs of Staff in 1985, added, "Expense and manufacturing capacity are limiting factors in air-to-air missile buys and it will be several years before we are well."

The General Accounting Office, an agency of the Congress, reported in 1984 that the Navy could send into battle only eight of its fourteen aircraft carriers, compared with six of thirteen when the Reagan Administration came into office. The rest would be short of missiles, bombs, and critical supplies. The Chief of Naval Operations,

Admiral Watkins, admonished subordinates to give priority to buying tactical missiles when they drew up the 1985 budget. The Navy was "cross-decking" missiles and other ammunition, which required a ship returning from overseas to transfer its munitions to the ship leaving the United States. Submarines could carry a full load of torpedoes when they went to sea, but they would find no second load when they returned to port.

The armed forces' lack of readiness in battlefield medicine approached scandal. Dr. William Mayer, the Pentagon's chief medical officer, told Congress in 1984:

Current estimates of our wartime medical readiness reveal that, should the U.S. become involved in a fullscale conventional conflict overseas, we have sufficient medical capability to care for only 20 percent of the estimated casualties. Military line commanders have called this situation a "war-stopper"—our forces would be unable to sustain an action for an extended period of time.

A year later, Dr. Mayer raised that estimate to three in ten, with the other seven being left on the battlefield, possibly to die. The military services lack doctors, nurses, corpsmen, operating facilities and instruments, beds in hospitals, transport, and almost everything else to treat men wounded in battle. General Rogers agreed. "If war were to break out in Europe in the near future," he told Congress, "we could not cope with the anticipated casualties."

Within the Reagan Administration, a few voices have been raised about military readiness, but they have gone largely unheeded. The foremost spokesman was Lawrence J. Korb, an Assistant Secretary of Defense until he resigned in 1985, who repeatedly cautioned the Defense Resources Board, the Pentagon's executive committee, that they were neglecting readiness. Nevertheless, Secretary of Defense Weinberger claimed, in his 1984 annual report to Congress, that "39 percent more of our major military units are categorized as fully or substantially ready for combat" than when the administration took office in 1981.

Mr. Korb, in a memorandum to Mr. Weinberger, urged caution. "Any time one tries to simplify and summarize a subject as complex as defense readiness, he is vulnerable to challenge," he said. "This problem exists in spades with our 39 percent statistic." Mr. Korb said the number was correct but pointed out that it was a combination of increases and decreases:

Naval ship and aircraft unit readiness improved substantially during this period, largely because of dramatic improvements in personnel readiness. Air Force and Army readiness—as measured by unit reports—actually declined. . . . Both the Army and Air Force declines were averaged in with the Navy improvements to yield a succinct summary statement of change in defense readiness.

Mr. Korb also asserted, "We must recognize that all of our readiness-related programs are not fully funded despite our pronouncements about the high priority we accord to readiness in defense resource allocation." In an interview later, he said the services had enough ammunition, supplies, fuel, and other wartime necessities on hand in 1981 to fight for fifteen days. By 1984, that had been raised to thirty days, plus a little more with older munitions. By the end of the decade, the administration planned that it would again double to a sixty-day supply.

The administration's *Defense Guidance*, however, said the stockpile of ammunition, fuel, spare parts, and the other items consumed in battle should be enough to enable the forces to fight for 180 days. The 180-day goal was set because it would take that long for industry to begin turning out ammunition and supplies faster than they were being used against a well-armed, durable enemy. *Defense Guidance* laid out a doctrine for conventional war that was based on two assumptions: (1) that the nuclear standoff between the United States and the Soviet Union would prevent either nation from resorting to nuclear weapons; (2) that the Soviet Union, with its large conventional forces, might try to outlast the United States, fighting until American forces ran out of ammunition. For those reasons, *Defense Guidance* called for large stockpiles of munitions and supplies and the expansion of the munitions industry so that it would surge into high levels of production when a crisis arose. But by 1986, there was no indication that either the stockpile or the industrial capacity was anywhere in sight.

Investigators on the staff of the House Appropriations Committee looked into military readiness over an eighteen-month span in 1982 and 1983 and found, in a 376-page report made public in 1984, that "the United States Army cannot be sustained in combat for any extended period." The report, written by the staff of a committee controlled by Democrats during a Republican Administration, questioned the ability of the Navy "to sustain full combat air and surface operations for more than a week's duration." It asserted that navies of

Soviet surrogates and those Third World forces who, while not capable of defeating the United States Navy, could inflict damage tantamount to a national disgrace. . . . The United States Air Force is not capable of conducting sustained conventional war operations against the Soviets. . . . While combat forces are capable of initiating a response, the forces do not have the war reserve matériel and the combat service support to sustain wartime operations. Shortages in aircraft and equipment spare parts, personnel, fuel storage capacity, casualty care, communications, and munitions continue as severe limitations in the capability to sustain war against Soviet forces.

Specifically, the investigators said "serious shortcomings are found which encompass the entire spectrum of United States combat service support for a NATO contingency." Units available to the Central Command, which would be responsible for protecting United States interests in the region around the Persian Gulf, "all indicated serious readiness problems." If hostilities broke out in Northeast Asia, the report said, "United States forces in Korea will have to sink or swim on their own" as they could not be reinforced. The investigators said increases in operations and maintenance funds in recent years "have not demonstrably improved the readiness of the existing force." The Army alone, they contended, would need $164.6 billion to buy the weapons, equipment, ammunition, and supplies to sustain combat for 180 days. Like Dr. Mayer, the investigators found medical facilities to be inadequate. The chief of the United States naval hospital in Yokosuka, Japan, said that 60,000 American casualties could be expected if war broke out on the Korean peninsula. But his hospital had only 350 beds, while two Army field hospitals of 1,000 beds each were in storage.

After the report became public, Mr. Weinberger called a news conference to denounce

the serious and potentially dangerous nature of the misstatements and the errors in the interpretation of this House Appropriations staff work. . . . The potential danger is that people, our foes and some of our friends, will get a wrong and incorrect impression of both our capabilities and our resolve. That, in this kind of world where that's an essential part of deterrence, is, I think, a dangerous disservice to the United States.

But Mr. Weinberger did not dispute the facts. The Pentagon had reviewed the investigative report before it was made public and had commented that "most of the data on which the staff conclusions were drawn, while not specifically verified, appear correct." The Pentagon said that the report "highlights long-standing and well-recognized deficiences which this Administration inherited and has moved vigorously to correct" and that later data "provide a much more optimistic view of our combat capabilities."

The Pentagon's own projections, moreover, showed that the services would have deficiencies in readiness for many years. A booklet entitled *Improvements in U.S. Warfighting Capability* reported that the Army's stockpile of munitions would reach 95 percent of its objective by 1990, but the Navy would have only 70 percent of its needs by then and the Air Force only 60 percent. Only the Marine Corps, the smallest of the services, would have filled its munitions stockpile by 1990.

In sum, the Reagan Administration had spent billions of dollars on weapons and warships and aircraft. But the program lacked balance; the administration had bought plenty of guns but not enough beans and bullets and bandaids to field a force nearly so ready as it should be.

American forces are spread thin partly because allies in Western Europe and Japan have refused to acquire military power in proportion to their wealth and needs. Two pertinent facts: The United States has a smaller population but more wealth than the combined European members of NATO, which includes Canada. The population of the United States in 1983, the latest year for which most comparative figures on military forces are available, was 234.5 million, compared with the 394 million in the other fourteen members of NATO. (These figures include France, which is a member of NATO but does not take part in its military structure, and Spain, the newest member of NATO.) The gross domestic product of the United States, which is the total of the goods and services produced in a nation, for that year was $3,288 billion, compared with $2,896 billion among the other NATO nations. In per capita gross domestic product, Americans were far ahead, at $14,023 each, compared with $7,352 in Western Europe.

Even so, *The Economist*, a prominent journal in Britain, observed in 1984:

Future historians will scratch their heads when asked to contemplate the fact that the United States, with fewer people and less government spending than Western Europe, nevertheless provides most of Europe's nuclear protection, a large chunk of its non-nuclear defenses, and almost all of the men, ships and aircraft which guard the Gulf oil that European industry depends on while Europe provides no reciprocal service for the United States.

The differences in military spending between the United States and the allies is vivid. The United States, according to comparative calculations by the Defense Department, spent $214 billion, or 6.6 percent of gross domestic product, for defense in 1983, the latest figures available in a pattern that has seen few recent changes. That included spending for the nuclear deterrent and for American forces spread around the world. The other fourteen nations in NATO spent $104 billion, or 3.6 percent of their combined gross national products.

In manpower, according to Defense Department figures, the United States had 3.3 million military and civilian people within the Defense Department compared with 4.2 million in similar positions in Western Europe. That was 1.40 percent of the American population, compared with 1.19 percent in Europe. The United States thus had relatively more people involved in defense, even with a volunteer force, than did the Europeans, most of whom raise armies through conscription.

In conventional weaponry, according to the Defense Department, the United States provides more than a proportionate share—63 percent of the naval tonnage and 53 percent of the principal surface combatants, 42 percent of the tactical fighters and 39 percent of the ground forces. The United States, as *The Economist* noted, deploys almost all of the forces intended to protect the oil resources for the industrial world in the Persian Gulf, even though Western Europe is more dependent on that source than is the United States.

In a vital but often overlooked category, American forces had, as 1985 began, about thirty days of ammunition and other wartime stocks to sustain the battle in a major conflict. While no American military officer said that was enough, the Europeans had on hand five to ten days' worth of ammunition and war supplies. A Defense Department report said in 1984:

The lack of adequate capability to sustain combat operations for long with manpower, munitions, and war reserve equipment to replace losses is one of NATO's most critical and persistent shortfalls. In war, such shortages would force commanders to curtail operations to avoid running out of critical consumables, and the price of such rationing would be measurable directly in lives and kilometers lost. In turn, those losses would increase the pressure on NATO to escalate to nuclear weapons.

General Rogers, the American commander in Europe, told *The Wall Street Journal* the lack of ammunition and weapons to replace those lost in battle meant that "I have to request the release of nuclear weapons fairly quickly after a conventional attack. And I'm talking about in terms of days, not in terms of weeks or months." Similarly, he told *The Boston Globe*, "If you take the amount of [European] ammunition that is needed and the amount produced each year, there's a hell of a disparity between the two." Lord Carrington of Britain, the Secretary General of NATO, called the imbalance "ludicrous."

In response, defense ministers of NATO agreed in late 1984 to begin a six-year program that would cost $7.85 billion to improve ground equipment, build more aircraft shelters, and to acquire a thirty-day stock of ammunition.

Over the years, the Europeans have been willing to rely on the United States for a good part of their defense and yet have criticized American military ventures elsewhere. Few Europeans contributed to the American struggle in Vietnam, and most have opposed American involvement in Central America, sometimes couching that criticism in political or moral terms. But the real, underlying fear is that the United States will become so tied down that its contribution to the security of Western Europe will be eroded.

After President Reagan ordered the invasion of Grenada, Prime Minister Thatcher contended that the United States should not have used military force "to walk into other people's countries." That comment was in some contrast to the material and moral support Mrs. Thatcher's government received from the Reagan Administration a year earlier during the war over the Falklands. The West German foreign minister, Hans-Dietrich Genscher, announced that "we would have advised against the intervention" into Grenada, while the government of France voted in the United Nations to deplore what was labeled a "flagrant violation of international law." The conservative columnist of *The New York Times*, William Safire, commented, "The lesson is that our NATO partners are interested exclusively in having the United States defend Europe and are resentful of any action the U.S. takes elsewhere to protect its own security."

On the other side of the world, the United States has disparate military relations with Japan, Korea, the Philippines, and China. Unlike NATO, where much of the relationship is multilateral, each American military tie with a nation in Asia is bilateral. Little holds the nations of that region together, militarily, politically, or economically.

With Japan, America's most important ally in Asia, the United States has a mutual-security treaty that requires the United States to defend Japan but requires Japan only to permit the United States to base forces there. In recent years, the Japanese have often been accused of enjoying a "free ride" in defense because they spent less than 1 percent of their national wealth on defense each year. That came to $12 billion in 1983, the lowest by far of any major nation. Only 0.2 percent of the Japanese population serve in their small, underequipped military force, which lacks ammunition and supplies for more than a few days of combat.

Successive Japanese prime ministers, under pressure from the United States, have agreed to acquire the ships, submarines, and aircraft that would enable Japan to defend itself and the sea lanes for 1,000 miles from Japanese shores. If that goal was achieved, American military officials said, the United States would be able to shift forces to the south to protect the lines of communication from the Pacific through the South China Sea and the Straits of Malacca to the Indian Ocean and the Persian Gulf. Japan, which Prime Minister Yasuhiro Nakasone once called "an unsinkable aircraft carrier," would guard Northeast Asia, watching the Soviet navy with it base at Vladivostok. In a conflict, Japan would try to close the straits through which the Soviet navy could exit to the Pacific Ocean.

Japan, however, has given few signs that it intends to acquire the forces to which it has agreed. Japanese leaders cite the famous Article IX of their constitution as a leading reason for not building an adequate military force. Article IX stipulates that Japan has forsaken the use of military force and will not maintain land, naval, or air forces. But Article IX, in reality, was abrogated in the mid-1950s when the Japanese, at American insistence, formed what is euphemistically called the Self-Defense Force. Since then, it has been government policy and public opinion, not constitutional law, that has restrained the expansion of Japanese military forces. In moments of private candor, some Japanese political leaders have acknowledged that they have a good thing with the Americans providing their defense and that Japan will resist a military buildup as long as possible.

In South Korea, the United States has 40,000 troops, including an infantry division and several squadrons of fighter aircraft. They have been there under a mutual-security treaty, although in reduced numbers, since the end of the Korean War in 1953. Both Korean and American military officers have long said, privately, that the South Koreans are well enough manned, armed, and trained to defend themselves, with American air and possibly naval help. South Korea does its full share of military spending, although a Pentagon audit showed that the Koreans have resisted paying their share of the costs of combined operations with the United States.

The United States has 15,000 military people in the Philippines, mostly at Clark Air Force Base and the naval station at Subic Bay. But those bases have been threatened by the internal instability and leftist insurgency of the Philippines, as well as by a thinly disguised form of rent paid to the government of former President Ferdinand Marcos. Mr. Marcos once told visiting American Congressmen that if they did not like a $900 million economic aid package that had been negotiated with Washington, he might seek a deal with the Soviet Union. He got his $900 million. (The Greeks have suggested they would turn to the Soviet Union if the United States did not provide military aid against their archenemies, the Turks, who are also members of NATO. But what was once a favorite ploy against the United States has gone out of fashion because most American governments have recognized it as bluff.)

The United States and New Zealand got into a diplomatic tiff in 1985 when the new government in Auckland refused to permit American warships to call at New Zealand ports unless the United States guaranteed that the ships were not armed with nuclear weapons. It has been standing policy that the United States does not confirm or deny the presence of nuclear weapons in any specific place. The challenge could not be overlooked, as it would most likely have had repercussions elsewhere. If New Zealand got away with its demands, leftist student and political groups in Japan might have been aroused to make similar demands, possibly upsetting the "transit agreement" between the United States and Japan. Under that secret accord, the United States may bring nuclear arms temporarily into Japan aboard ship or plane but may not store the weapons there. Similarly, the Greens and antinuclear groups in Europe seeking to block the deployment of Pershing II and ground-launched cruise missiles might have gained an argument to use against their governments. The Reagan Administration, therefore, told New Zealand that military and intelligence cooperation would cease.

The United States and China, which fought each other in the Korean War, have engaged in a military minuet in recent years. After President Nixon reopened American relations with China in 1972, the Carter and Reagan Administrations sought to begin military relations with China to encourage the Chinese to keep more than fifty Russian divisions tied down along the 5,000-mile border between the two nations. The Chinese have resisted those overtures, saying they oppose efforts by either superpower to gain what they call "hegemony" over Asia.

The Chinese, whose army is large but poorly trained and badly equipped, have set a low priority on modernizing their forces and have been more interested in acquiring American technology and economic aid to strengthen their faltering economy. Moreover, Americans and Chinese share little in political values. Despite exchanges of visits by political and military leaders it seems likely that military relations will develop neither fast nor far. When Secretary of Defense Weinberger visited Peking in September 1983, he sought Chinese cooperation against the Soviet Union. But the Chinese government was decidedly cool. The defense minister, Zhang Aiping, told Mr. Weinberger that "we will not attach ourselves to any big power or bloc of powers." In late 1985 the Chinese agreed to buy $98 million worth of technology with which to make artillery fuses and projectiles and, in April 1986, agreed to buy $550 million worth of aviation electronics over six years to improve the fire control and navigation systems in F-8 fighter planes.

Because the United States lacks the forces and the readiness to fulfull its commitments around the world, and because allied nations have failed to bear a fair share of the burden for collective defense, the cry "Yankee, go home" is being heard once again. Now, however, it is coming from the Americans. Senior officials of the Reagan Administration have repeatedly urged the allies to contribute more in forces and funds to the common defense. But other voices have counseled a fundamental contraction in the far-flung deployment of American forces by the year 2000 as the structure of security built in the 1950s is no longer suitable.

Secretary Weinberger, on trips to Europe during his first year in office, told the Europeans that they must increase their military spending and modernize their forces. "Our people will not want to march alone," he told the NATO defense ministers in Bonn. "If our effort is not joined by all who are threatened, by all who face the common danger, we in the United States could lose at home the critical public support for which we have labored long and hard."

The American ambassador to NATO, David M. Abshire, lamented the different perceptions of the Warsaw Pact's military capabilities and intentions. "The alliance does not possess," he said, "a comprehensive, politically agreed upon assessment of comparative NATO/ Warsaw Pact military capabilities." The supreme commander of allied forces in Europe, General Rogers, was more direct:

A lot of people in Western Europe are damn comfortable with the social gains they've made since World War II and don't want to give them up. We've ballyhooed the success of NATO for thirty-five years as the greatest peace movement in history. That's true, but there is a hell of a lot of wishful thinking going on.

On the other side of the political fence, Harold Brown, who was President Carter's Secretary of Defense, touched on the same issue in his book *Thinking about National Security*:

The United States cannot be expected to maintain its commitments and forces in defense of a Western Europe that is not prepared to maintain its own

defense efforts. The unwillingness of some Western Europeans even to acknowledge the existence of a major military threat from the Soviet Union
hardly encourages the United States to spend added billions to preposition
more division sets of equipment in Europe or to plan for added airlift and
sealift to Europe.

Senator Nunn, the senior Democrat on the Armed Services Committee, introduced a measure into Congress in June 1984, calling for
the withdrawal of 90,000 American troops from Europe within five
years unless the Europeans increased military spending. The proposal
was defeated, 55 to 41, after which a milder measure introduced by
Senator William Cohen, Republican of Maine, was adopted by a vote
of 94 to 3. Mr. Cohen's bill did not call for the withdrawal of American
forces but admonished the Europeans for not carrying more of the
burden. Later, Senator William V. Roth Jr., Republican of Delaware,
said after a meeting with European leaders, "I came away with little
reassurance that the situation is likely to improve soon." Representative Lee H. Hamilton, Democrat of Indiana, agreed that "the allies
need to be persuaded to do more" but disagreed with the tactics. "It
is one thing to seek to persuade a partner in private discussions to do
something," he said, "it is another to bully him through open threats."

Senator Carl Levin, Democrat from Michigan and member of the
Armed Services Committee, was especially critical of the Japanese,
whose automobiles competed with those made in his home state. Pointing to the low levels of Japanese military spending, he said Japan
deserved harsh criticism for "abusing its alliance relationship with the
U.S. and taking unreasonable advantage of our nation." He asserted
that "unless Japan substantially improves its burden-sharing performance in the near future—unless it begins to meet its willingly agreed
to commitments—Congress may well have to consider legislative proposals affecting our Pacific troops levels."

Mr. Nunn's proposal and other voices of criticism sent a message
that disturbed many Europeans, who took pains to defend their military efforts. Manfred Woerner, the West German Defense Minister,
expressed his displeasure when he visited Washington. "Threatening
is not a method with which you can treat an ally," he said. "If you
threaten us with the withdrawal of part of your troops, to whose benefit
is that? The Soviet Union's. It is entirely the wrong signal to send to
the Soviets." Mr. Woerner, who is fluent in English, said: "We are
sovereign states in Europe. We are partners, allies, friends. We want
not to be put under pressure. We ought not to be threatened with a
stick." He contended that "all along the way, I've heard that melody

of Europeans not taking a fair share of the defense burden. That's a wrong impresssion. It is unjustified as far as my country is concerned." Mr. Woerner rattled off figures, such as Germany providing 50 percent of the land forces in Europe, to make his point. He asserted that Americans overlooked what he called "the heavy political and psychological burden our country bears." There were 400,000 foreign soldiers in West Germany who went on 5,000 maneuvers each year outside the confines of military training bases, disrupting the lives of German citizens, he said. Beyond that was the constant roar of jet aircraft and the danger of crashes in which civilians could be killed.

Prime Minister Thatcher added her voice, telling visiting American journalists that Britain has increased military spending to 5.5 percent of gross domestic product, that Britain had forces in Belize, the Sinai, Lebanon, Cyprus, Gibraltar, Northern Ireland, Hong Kong, Diego Garcia (a British island in the Indian Ocean), the Persian Gulf and, as trainers, in Zimbabwe. "After your good selves," Mrs. Thatcher said,

we are the top spenders in NATO both in absolute terms and in proportion of GDP [gross domestic product, an economic measure similar to gross national product]. And, along with the U.S., we are the only country that has troops on the Central Front [in Germany] though we are not part of the mainland. We have 65,000, including our Air Force, and apart from the U.S. we make the biggest naval contribution to NATO. So we, in fact, have done our stuff.

General Rogers sided with the Europeans on the question of withdrawing American troops; he was adamantly opposed to using that as a threat to persuade the Europeans to make a greater effort in defense. "U.S. troops are not here in Western Europe merely out of motives of Christian mercy," he told the German magazine *Stern*. "They are here for the vital interest of the U.S.A., whose fate is inextricably bound with that of Europe." He asserted: "You can't get the Europeans to do more if the U.S. is doing less. The U.S.A. must lead, and not threaten, blackmail, or penalize its allies."

But voices calling for a withdrawal have become more vigorous all along the political spectrum. Former Secretary of State Henry Kissinger, certainly no isolationist, wrote an essay in *Time* magazine in which he asserted that "by 1990, Europe should assume the major responsibility for conventional ground defense," with a European officer replacing the American as supreme commander of allied forces. The United States would "emphasize highly mobile conventional forces capable of backing up Europe and contributing to the defense of, for example, the Middle East, Asia, or the Western Hemisphere." He said that "a gradual withdrawal of a substantial portion, perhaps up to half, of our present ground forces, would be a logical result." Mr. Kissinger set a condition: "Any withdrawal would make sense only if the redeployed forces were added to our strategic reserve; if they were disbanded, the effect would be to weaken the overall defense."

Similarly, Zbigniew Brzezinski, President Carter's national security adviser, told *The Washington Times* that the United States should reduce its ground forces in Europe over the next ten years. He said Europe should become more conscious of its identity, "which will not take place if Western Europe remains indefinitely dependent on the United States and an extension of American power. . . . Europe needs to achieve some level of independence from Washington." He asserted: "We should make the Europeans do more and reduce their military complacency and cultural hedonism. The Soviets won't withdraw unless we do. Since a Soviet withdrawal is unlikely to be agreed fundamentally, some gradual movement on our side is necessary."

Two specialists at the Institute for Foreign Policy in Washington, Jeffrey Record and Robert J. Hanks, went further:

The time has come for the United States to begin withdrawing most of its ground forces from Europe, and to adopt a global strategy based on sea power and the ability to project power from sea to shore. Such a course is dictated by two developments: the steady political disintegration of the North Atlantic Treaty Organization as an instrument capable of mustering an adequate defense of Europe, and the emergence of a host of new threats to vital American security interests in Southwest Asia and other areas outside of Europe where the United States does not enjoy politically secure military access ashore.

Laurence Radway, professor of government at Dartmouth College, entered what he called "a plea" to remove all ground, naval, and air personnel, together with their conventional and nuclear weapons from the continent, the Mediterranean, and Britain. "If Western Europe were subsequently attacked," Professor Radway said, "the United States military response would have to be launched from offshore positions." He contended:

The prospective withdrawal of American troops will force Western Europe to a serious reassessment of its need for conventional and strategic forces. The United States should encourage this development on the sound principle that those who are closest to the Soviet Union must decide how great a threat they think it poses and what they are prepared to do about it.

Addressing those who contend the Europeans would reach an accommodation with the Soviet Union, Mr. Radway doubted they would "accept Soviet authoritarianism with its doctrinal rigidity, secret police, fumbling economy, and bumbling, hamhanded bureaucracy."

Vermont Royster, the gifted editorialist of *The Wall Street Journal*, recalled the drafting of the Truman Doctrine and cited President Truman, who wrote in his memoirs, "This was, I believe, the turning point in America's foreign policy, which now declares that <u>wherever</u> aggression, direct or indirect, threatened the peace, the security of the United States was involved." Mr. Royster agreed, but after the wars in Korea and Vietnam, the engagements in Lebanon and Grenada, and the continuing worldwide deployments of forces, he wrote: "It's no wonder then, I think, that the American public grows uneasy." He concluded. "Simply put, it is how much of the world order can the U.S. carry on its own shoulders. What are the limits on our strength? Whatever anyone may think, 'wherever' is a very big place indeed."

For four decades, the United States has taken upon itself the task of policing the world. Even after the war in Vietnam, which caused so much soul-searching about the military role of America in the world, the United States has continued to shoulder the burden of defending not only Americans but vast numbers of other people on every continent. Under President Reagan, as could be seen in *Defense Guidance*, the United States has adopted an ambitious strategy that would have the nation meet opponents in almost every clime and place. Yet American military power has not expanded sufficiently to achieve the strategic aims laid down by the administration. The United States lacks the forces, the transport, and the warmaking supplies to execute the tasks laid on the armed forces. That gap, called the strategy-force mismatch, had been made worse by the reluctance of allies to carry a proportionate share of the load. The sum total has led to demands that American military commitments and forward deployments be scaled back to bring them within the capabilities of the forces now and in the near future. Those voices seem to be echoing the advice of two sages, one Eastern, the other Western:

"Contributing to maintain an army at a distance," said the Chinese statesman, Sun Tzu, "causes the people to be impoverished."

"He who defends everything," said Frederick the Great, "defends nothing."

CHAPTER 8

~~~~~~~~~~~~~~~~~~~~~~~~~~~~~~~

SEVEN CARDINAL SINS

TO PROVIDE FOR the nation's military power, American tax-payers put up $300 billion a year, a sum that almost defies comprehension. If a football field, including both end zones, was to be covered with $20 bills laid tightly side by side, $300 billion would pile up into a mound thirty-three feet high, and weigh 15,000 tons. The Bureau of Engraving and Printing produces $60 billion in currency a year, in denominations of $1 to $100. If all that money were given to the Defense Department, it would take the bureau five years to turn out what the Pentagon gets in a year.

From that enormous sum of money arise two critical but separate and distinct questions:

- Can the American economy, over a long period, support that level of military spending without serious damage to the nation's standard of living?
- Have American taxpayers been getting their money's worth in military power and national defense from that amount of annual military spending?

The answer to the first is clearly yes. The $300 billion is about 7 percent of the national wealth, or gross national product. The historical record during modern American military history, beginning in 1950, shows that the economy has supported much higher levels of military spending in both peace and war. As a portion of the federal budget, the $300 billion is about 30 percent; as a part of all federal, state, and local governmental spending, it is about 20 percent. Such percentages are higher than those during the period after the war in Vietnam, but lower than the percentages during and between the wars in Korea and Vietnam. Moreover, military spending in the last two decades has risen at a much slower rate than that for social welfare and other governmental spending. Consequently, how much the nation spends on military power is less a question of economic capacity than an issue of political will.

The answer to the second question—has the money been well spent?—is just as clearly no. One of two things is wrong with the $300 billion military budget:

- It is $100 billion too much. The military budget could be cut by one-third and leave the United States with the same number of troops, tanks, aircraft, and warships the nation has today. To accomplish that, some of the burden would have to be shifted to the allies, forward deployments would be contracted, and wrenching reforms would be needed in Congress, the defense industry, the Defense Department, and the military services.
- It is $100 billion of wasted spending. The taxpayers, with a rationalized military budget, could spend that $100 billion to pay for an expanded force with more troops, more and better aircraft and ships and tanks, more effective training and operations, more air and sea transport, adequate combat medical support, and larger stockpiles of supplies to be ready for war if necessary.

Wading through the quagmire of military budgets is not easy. It is a bewildering morass of terms—budget authority, appropriations, outlays. It is a confusing swamp of one-year and five-year plans, of budgets broken into Army, Navy and Marine Corps, and Air Force components, then into categories of procurement, personnel, operations and maintenance, research and development, military construction. The military budget is a bog of functions such as nuclear forces, conventional forces, air- and sealift, training, communications and intelligence, and administration. The numbers are stupefying. Families think of budgets in hundreds and occasionally thousands of dollars, corporations in hundreds of thousands and millions of dollars. But discussion of military spending is in hundreds of millions, or billions, and often tens of billions of dollars.

The military budget, however, is more than an abstract jumble of huge numbers. It is the fundamental plan, the blueprint of an administration's program for defending the nation. It is the starting point for military policy and reflects the military values and aspirations of the United States. The military budget is a signal of American intentions to friend and foe alike and thus has a profound effect on the political standing of the United States in the international arena. At home, military spending exerts a pervasive, although not overwhelming, influence on the course of the national economy, including employment, and on the state of the federal government's budget, including the federal deficit.

Today, however, the military budget is out of control. The poli-

ticians and military officers who draw it up plunge ahead from year
to year without anyone in the executive or legislative branches of
government examining the fundamentals of what funds are needed
and why. Rarely are searching questions asked about the purposes
and consequences of approving or disapproving each item. Each annual budget is put together on the basis of the last and is thus only
an expansion or revision of the budgets that were approved by Congress before.

Why the budget is out of control is reasonably clear, as will be
detailed below. How much it is out of control, or how much it costs
the taxpayer in excesses and waste, is more difficult to determine. But
there is a body of evidence compiled over six years from officials in
the Defense Department, members of Congress and their staffs, officials in other government agencies, executives in the defense industry, private businessmen, specialists on military spending in think
tanks and universities, and military officers that makes possible credible conclusions. These conclusions are no more than estimates, but
they are derived from evidence that consistently points in the same
direction.

The categories of excessive or wasteful military spending could be
called the Seven Cardinal Sins:

- Unequal Burden Sharing. The allies of the United States in Western Europe and Japan fail to carry a fair share of the financial
  burden for the common defense. They rely on the United States
  to provide not only the nuclear umbrella but a large portion of the
  front-line conventional ground, naval, and air forces, plus the strategic reserve forces for the alliance. Estimated excessive annual
  cost: $40 billion.
- Strategy of Forward Deployment. The deployment of United States
  military forces on every continent and sea, either on permanent
  duty or temporarily on maneuvers far from the United States, adds
  about 10 percent to the yearly defense bill. Estimated excessive
  annual cost: $30 billion.
- Congressional Pork Barrel. The Constitution mandated to the Congress the obligation to raise and support armed forces. But few
  representatives or senators consider the national interest when voting for military expenditures. The prime consideration is what is
  in the bill for the congressman's district or state. Estimated excessive annual cost: $30 billion.
- Inefficient Defense Industry. Inefficient and uneconomic production of arms and equipment by American defense contractors, cost

overruns, poor engineering and shoddy workmanship, lack of reliability in their products, and the defense industry's abuse of its monopoly adds another 10 percent. Estimated excessive annual cost: $30 billion.

- Poor Pentagon Management. A failure to formulate a realistic strategy, and to relate military spending to that strategy, the reluctance to streamline the Defense Department, the escalation beyond inflation in the cost of weapons add to costs. So do bloated civilian and military bureaucracies and a lack of qualified people to supervise the defense industry. Estimated excessive annual cost: $15 billion.
- Lack of Interservice Coordination. Civilian officials and military leaders of the Army, Navy, Marine Corps and Air Force are so intent on serving the interests of their own services and bureacracies that they lose sight of what is needed to serve the nation. Estimated excessive annual cost: $15 billion.
- Personnel. The United States, to its credit, pays men and women in the armed forces a living and competitive wage. But the cost of retired pay, the equity of the retirement system, and the loss of invaluable skills and experience has come increasingly into question. Estimated excessive annual cost: $5 billion.

Not included here are savings that might be realized through an agreement on arms control with the Soviet Union, or with other potential adversaries. Agreements like that, by definition, can happen only when both sides, or several nations, come to an understanding. Consequently, the costs considered here are only those that could be controlled by the United States, or by the United States and its allies in Western Europe and Japan.

Altogether, the excessive costs of the Seven Cardinal Sins amount to $165 billion, more than half of the annual military budget. But what could be saved would depend mostly on how the savings were achieved. If, for instance, the allies began to pick up their share of the financial burden, and thus added to their forces, Americans would be saved little if the United States kept the armed forces at their present size. On the other hand, the high cost of the American strategy of forward deployment could be cut substantially if those forces were brought home, thus reducing the cost of operating overseas. Reform in Congress, the defense industry, and the military services could save enormous sums. But it would be too much to expect, in the best of worlds, for those institutions to be rationalized to the extent of cutting all waste or getting every dollar's worth of more national defense.

Even so, there is a persuasive case to be made that one-third of the military budget, or $100 billion, could be cut or put to better use.

United States military budgets have undulated since World War II. In the last year of that war, the budget to prosecute the conflict to the end was the equivalant of $625 billion as measured in 1986 dollars, with the effect of inflation removed. (Military budgets in this discussion are in 1986 dollars unless otherwise noted.) During demobilization, military budgets plummeted to $75 billion in 1949, then started up when the Korean War began in 1950. The peak of military budgets in that conflict came in 1952, when President Truman's budget was $325 billion. Following the Korean War, President Eisenhower's military policy was based on the threat of massive retaliation, which relied on nuclear forces that were less expensive than conventional arms. Defense budgets fluctuated between $170 billion and $190 billion during the Eisenhower Administration.

With the election of President Kennedy in 1960, military budgets increased as he shifted to a strategy of flexible response that called for more conventional forces. With their reliance on manpower, arms, and equipment, those forces were more expensive. That change in emphasis, plus the Cuban missile crisis of 1962 and the United States response to Soviet advances in nuclear weapons, brought the military budget up to $215 billion in 1963. Then began a buildup for the war in Vietnam, the peak of which came in 1968 at $261 billion.

At the same time, a new element entered the equation. President Johnson's program for social welfare known as the Great Society began to consume ever-larger portions of federal spending. Actual outlays of funds for social and economic programs in 1964 were $45 billion, compared with $55 billion for military expenses, in what dollars were worth then. By 1971, social and economic expenditures had more than doubled and by 1976 doubled again. In 1985, that spending peaked at $554 billion, as measured in 1985 dollars, then dropped slightly to $531 billion. In contrast, actual outlays of funds for military programs climbed to a much lower peak of $286 billion in 1986.

A long, slow slide in military budgets started as the United States withdrew from Vietnam, urged allied nations under the Nixon Doctrine to look more to their own defenses, and entered a period of détente with the Soviet Union. President Nixon's policies were continued for most of the administrations of Presidents Ford and Carter. The low point in the military budget came in 1975, under President

Ford, when it was $178 billion. President Carter, despite campaign pledges to cut defense spending, began a gradual buildup and brought the military budget to $197 billion in fiscal year 1980, his last full fiscal year in office.

Since then, military budgets under President Reagan have leaped. Shortly after taking office, Mr. Reagan asked the Congress to amend the military budget to increase it to $222 billion in 1981 and to $249 billion in 1982, as measured in 1986 dollars. In 1983, President Reagan's military budget surpassed the peak year of the Vietnam War and reached $268 billion. For the fiscal year 1986, which began on October 1, 1985, the military budget, at $297 billion, was larger than any since World War II, save the peak year during the Korean War. Mr. Reagan contended that those budgets were necessary to replace what had been lost in Vietnam, to overcome what he called the "decade of neglect" in the 1970s, and to acquire enough military power to encourage or force the Soviet Union to negotiate on arms control.

The trend in outlays, or actual spending, lagged behind because of the congressional process of appropriating funds. A large sum may be authorized in a particular year for, say, an aircraft carrier, but the funds are spent over the following five to seven years. Thus outlays peaked during the last year of the Korean War in 1953 at $234 billion and again during Vietnam in 1968 at $263 billion. Under President Reagan they have shot up, with the $286 billion estimated during 1986 the highest since World War II, including the Korean and Vietnam wars.

In key economic indicators, the budget for national defense took 90 percent of the federal budget toward the end of World War II and consumed almost 40 percent of the gross national product. During the three years of the Korean War, budgets for national defense hovered just below 70 percent of the federal budget and between 13.5 and 14.5 percent of the gross national product. Between Korea and Vietnam, military budgets slid slowly from 60 percent of the federal budget down to 43 percent and from 11 percent of gross national product down to 7.7 percent.

During Vietnam, military budgets took only a bit more of the federal budget, about 45 percent, and slightly less than 10 percent of the gross national product. As spending for social welfare continued to climb during the Johnson, Nixon, Ford, and Carter Administrations and the first Reagan Administration, military spending as a portion of national wealth and of the federal budget began to slide. Military spending as a percent of GNP and the federal budget dropped to a low point during the last year of President Carter's administration, when national defense took 22.7 percent of the federal budget and only 4.9 percent of gross national product.

Under President Reagan, the share of the gross national product and the federal budget dedicated to defense have gone up. In 1986, the defense budget was projected to take 29 percent of the federal budget and 6.8 percent of gross national product. While President Reagan's military budgets have been large when compared with other peacetime military budgets or even with budgets during the Korean and Vietnam conflicts, they have not been excessive in relation to the national economy or the federal budget. In a slightly different calculation produced by the Treasury and the Office of Management and Budget in the White House, national defense spending in 1986 was projected at $267 billion. Spending for Social Security and Medicare was estimated to be $268 billion; another $150 billion was allocated for health and income security.

George F. Brown, Jr., vice-president of Data Resources, a research organization in Washington, argued before Congress that the American economy was able to support the military spending needed for national security:

From today's base or even considerably expanded levels of defense spending, it is clear that the nation can afford the levels of defense deemed necessary on national security grounds. Current and proposed levels of defense spending can be accommodated without threatening the long-term health of the United States economy. . . . While defense spending has important and notable impacts on various dimensions of economic activity, it is in no way a pivotal element within today's economy. Defense spending influences economic growth, employment, inflation, the deficit, and numerous other measures of national economic activity, but does not dominate any of them. The challenge facing the Congress and the Administration remains in reality, as philosophically it should, that of determining what levels of defense activity are necessary to meet the nation's national security objectives.

Harold Brown, who was Secretary of Defense in the Carter Administration and who had a firm grip on the economics of defense, wrote after leaving the Pentagon that democratic nations could afford to pay for their defense. "It is clear that the Western countries have, in economic terms, the ability for substantial further increases in their military expenditures and capabilities," he said. Mr. Brown asserted, moreover, that the level of the military budget is more an issue of political will than economic capacity. "In terms of the will to do so," he said, "and the very serious political difficulties that would be entailed in a program for such an expansion, the answer is quite different." The key question, Mr. Brown said, is "whether the economies of the industrialized democracies can in practical political terms sustain a build-up of their military expenditures and efforts in reply to the expansion of Soviet military capabilities."

During the first Reagan Administration, the political will was evident for two years, then waned. Until fiscal year 1985, the Congress debated the President's budget proposals vigorously but approved 97 percent of the sums requested. Then the mood in Congress changed. The shift was caused by the rising deficit in the overall federal budget, a perception that the administration had no military strategy, and repeated horror stories of abuse by the defense industry. Republicans and Democrats in Congress and the public started to question the large sums, to ask whether they were in proper ratio to welfare and other domestic needs, and to criticize the allies for not carrying their share of the financial burden for collective defense. Consequently, the Congress held President Reagan's proposed military budget to the same level as the year before.

Without a doubt, another fundamental reason for the change in mood has been the awakening perception that American taxpayers have not gotten their money's worth for the $1 trillion spent by the Congress and the Reagan Administration on the military forces. The size of the armed forces has grown but little and lags far behind that of 25 years ago. The readiness of the forces for war, which is measured in training, ammunition, and spare parts, has not made the progress promised. The ability to sustain conventional battle on the scale of a Korean or Vietnam war, to say nothing of a conflict with the Soviet Union, thus avoiding the need to resort to nuclear weapons, has improved only a small amount since 1980. Modern equipment is being fielded, but at a price that makes large numbers impossible. A grim joke in the Pentagon holds that if present trends continue, sometime in the twenty-first century the entire defense budget will be needed to buy one gun, one ship, and one airplane.

Two disparate studies have concluded that the nation has experienced less improvement in its military forces than it should have for the large sums spent. One was done by George W. S. Kuhn, a consultant to the Heritage Foundation, a conservative research organization that has vigorously supported President Reagan. The other was done by Franklin C. Spinney, a cost analyst in the Department of Defense considered by Secretary of Defense Weinberger and his associates to be a maverick. Mr. Kuhn wrote:

Our defense establishment has stagnated. Its structures and practices now soak up even sizable funding increases with negligible results. Instead of achieving decisive increases in fighting power needed to best a very real threat, our forces require all the currently available funds, and more, just to maintain inadequate strength levels. The trends in force structure, readiness, and overall fighting capability are, in the best cases, only marginally improved; on the whole, they are stable at low levels or still declining.

The increased spending secured by President Reagan should afford significant improvements in force size. It does not. . . . If anything, the readiness account is tighter than acquisition. It is falling further behind actual readiness needs as more complex systems come on line. . . . The Reagan budget increases have not changed the unhealthy trends in United States defense capabilities.

Finally, in a prediction that turned out to have been right on the mark, Mr. Kuhn wrote in 1983: "The pressure to reduce defense spending is mounting. A military program that demonstrates tangible progress toward decisive improvements will retain public support. One that gains public support and then fails to translate its added resources into added strength will lose that support."

In the second analysis, Mr. Spinney contended that "a growing force that is more expensive to operate and is projected to operate at an increased tempo implies an increasing rate of growth in the operating budget over the long term. However, the five-year defense plan projects a decreasing rate of growth in the operating budget." He asserted with a touch of sarcasm that "the assumption that we can decrease the rate of growth in the operating budget while increasing the size, complexity, and readiness of the force appears optimistic."

Mr. Spinney noted that, despite soaring military budgets, the number of aircraft in the Air Force had dropped by 63 percent between 1957 and 1984, the number of ships in the Navy was down by 50 percent, and the number of people on active duty in the Army had shrunk by 22 percent. "We are under constant pressure," he concluded, "to reduce readiness, slow rates of modernization, and ultimately shrink the forces size—even when the budget is increasing."

Despite the contention in the political arena, few Americans have focused on the key issues of military spending. Debates during the 1984 presidential election campaign were superficial, as have been the annual debates in Congress and much of the coverage in the press and on television. Most of the time, the debate has centered about the rate of growth in military spending, whether it should be 10 percent or 5 percent or zero. It has featured arguments over specific programs, such as President Reagan's Strategic Defense Initiative, better known as Star Wars, or whether to build 50 or 100 MX ballistic missiles, or whether one large aircraft carrier would be better than several smaller carriers. Outside Congress, advocates of increased military spending, such as the Committee on the Present Danger, or those opposed, such as Common Cause, have looked at single trees and lost sight of the forest. Just as the Reagan Administration has thought that military weakness could be turned into military strength by spending money, so the critics have argued that problems could be solved by cutting weapons programs.

Altogether, there has been for many years little penetrating examination of the fundamental issues by officials that compared with the thought behind the document known as NSC-68 produced under President Truman's direction. It set basic goals, defined genuine threats, determined ways to confront those dangers, and suggested the real costs of defense. Each administration since has done its own survey of national security, but there has been no searching inquiry into why the United States should spend $300 billion a year for military power, no effort to specify the national interests and the nature of the threat to those interests that might make $300 billion seem like a reasonable insurance premium. There has been little effort to examine the military forces that might be needed to protect the national interests from the perceived threat and to relate American forces to those of the allies. There has been little discussion of the relation of military spending, and the power it should buy, to diplomacy, international economic policy, and the other elements that provide for national security.

The failure of America's allies to carry a fair share of the burden for the collective defense is a leading reason for excessive American military spending. For forty years, American taxpayers have stood in the breach, each paying more than his share of the cost of defending the free world. Altogether, American taxpayers have paid for a military force that is relatively larger than those of any ally. Successive administrations in Washington have pleaded with allies in Europe and Japan to increase their military spending, both to build more military power and to relieve some of the burden on the United States. But no American administration has been willing to go to the mat with the allies, mostly for fear that pressure might damage the alliance or even cause it to fall apart.

A measure of a nation's contribution to collective security is the amount of money it spends on military power relative to its national wealth. Each year, the Department of Defense submits to Congress a *Report on Allied Contributions to the Common Defense*. In 1985, the

Pentagon reported that in 1983 the United States had 44.5 percent of the gross domestic product, a measure similar to gross national product, of the loosely defined alliance that includes the European members of the North Atlantic Treaty Organization, Japan, and the United States itself. But the United States provided 64.7 percent of the alliance's military spending to assemble, arm, and train the American armed forces. In contrast, the European members of NATO collectively had 39.2 percent of the wealth but contributed only 31.6 percent of the total military budget. Japan, which is not a member of NATO but has a bilateral security treaty with the United States, had 16.3 percent of the wealth but lagged far behind in providing only 3.7 percent of the military spending. Those ratios have remained constant over the last fifteen years, save that the share of the United States dropped slightly after Vietnam.

The total in actual military spending, as differentiated from budgeting, for the alliance in 1983 was $330 billion, according to the Defense Department's report. Had that been divided according to relative shares of national wealth, the American portion would have been $146.8 billion, or $66.8 billion less than the $213.6 billion American taxpayers paid that year. NATO's share would have gone up from $104.4 billion to $129.3 billion while Japan's share would have more than quadrupled from $12 billion to $53.9 billion.

The disparity between American spending for military power and that of allied nations is sometimes recognized abroad, even if governments in other capitals don't want to admit it in public. To examine the differences in military spending, a journal called *International Defense Review*, which is published in Switzerland, compiled figures from the International Institute of Strategic Studies and the World Almanac. Although the figures were slightly different from those in the Defense Department report, the pattern was the same. The journal reported that in 1984 each Briton spent $450 a year for defense, each Frenchman $330, and each German $307. Altogether, the Europeans averaged $240 a year, with poorer countries such as Turkey and Portugal and smaller countries such as Luxembourg pulling the average down. That $240 was only 3 percent of the average European per capita income of $8,002. In contrast, each American paid $920 a year for defense, which was 10.7 percent of his or her yearly per capita income. The journal commented:

The data, for Europeans, are rather disturbing. The United States government spends four times as much on defense, per head of population, as the average European government which is a full fledged member of NATO (i.e., excluding France). When we look to see what this means in terms of how hard it hits the average citizen where it hurts most, in his pocket, we find that defense spending per American represents 10.7 percent of his annual income. For his NATO European counterpart, on the other hand, it represents the allocation of a mere 2.8 percent of his annual income.

Try explaining that to the average U.S. voter who tends to see the East-West confrontation in the most straight-forward terms. Clearly, the four-to-one ratio of United States defense expenditure to European is out of proportion, even allowing for America's global commitments.

Even if the Europeans and Japanese picked up a full share of the burden, the potential savings of $66.8 billion to the United States would be overstated. The United States provides the nuclear umbrella, and it is clearly in the American national interest that the United States continue to control those nuclear arms. The United States maintains a large navy, both to protect American national interests around the world and to contribute sea power to the alliance, and that is expensive. The United States relies on a volunteer army, as does Britain, while other nations have conscription, which in some instances is less costly.

The United States could cut military expenditures by an estimated $40 billion without the alliance's losing collective strength, if the West Europeans and the Japanese increased their military spending. Those savings would be realized, however, only if the United States reduced the size of its forces or scratched plans for expanding the forces. Each ship built by the British, for instance, would mean one fewer ship the United States need build. A new German infantry battalion would replace a similar American battalion facing East Germany. A new Japanese air squadron would eliminate the need for an American squadron to patrol the skies around northern Japan. The total amount of allied military power would remain the same. If, however, the United States continued to build more ships, retained the same number of infantry battalions, and kept the air squadron on active duty, overall allied military power would increase. That would not save money for the American taxpayer, but it would lessen the relative share of the burden he carried.

The cost of forward deployment, or forward defense, is directly connected to the commitment of the United States to the defense of other nations in the free world. Where spending as a contribution to the collective defense relates to the size of the armed forces, spending for forward deployment concerns the disposition or stationing of those forces. The cost of forward deployment is the difference between the cost of stationing forces abroad compared with the cost of keeping them at home. It assumes that the size of the force and the state of training and readiness would be the same in either case.

The cost of maintaining and operating an American armored division in Germany, for instance, is more than that for a similar division in Texas. The price of fuel in Europe is higher, as is the price of food. Transporting people, supplies, spare parts, mail, and countless other items from the United States to Europe adds to the cost. Housing for troops and families, plus schools, commissaries, hospitals, and recreational facilities must be provided. The Air Force, which has tactical fighter squadrons in Europe and Asia, has costs similar to those of the Army, plus the additional expense of running the Military Airlift Command to serve American forces abroad.

For the Navy, extra costs arise from operating far from home ports and at a high tempo. At any one time, the United States may have 100 ships at sea in the Caribbean and South Atlantic, in the Eastern Atlantic and the Mediterranean, in the Pacific or the Western Pacific, or the Indian Ocean. They maintain a swift tempo of operations not only to train but to caution the Soviet Union or other potential adversaries, and as reassurance to allies. Battalions of marines are afloat in amphibious assault ships in two oceans most of the time.

Steaming an aircraft carrier and her six or eight escorting cruisers, destroyers, and submarines in the Indian Ocean, as opposed to the Atlantic Ocean off the east coast of the United States, costs an extra $450,000 a day, according to the Navy. That includes the cost of sailing from the United States to the Indian Ocean and operating there at a higher tempo than would be necessary to maintain security closer to home. The wear and tear on machinery caused by warmer water makes coolers work harder; the grit in the air wears out equipment faster when the ships are within 200 miles of the coast, which is often. Transporting people, supplies, spare parts, and mail from the United States to the ships adds to the cost. To support that and other American military efforts in the oil region around the Persian Gulf, the United States spent $90 million in 1984 for construction of a base on the British island of Diego Garcia in the Indian Ocean. Another $22.4 million was spent in 1985, and $48 million was planned for 1986, for a total of $160.4 million in three years on one small base alone.

Still another cost arises from what the armed forces call the "rotation base" in the United States, which trains and provides forces for duty in Europe and Asia. For instance, when a sergeant trained as a tank commander at Fort Hood, Texas, is ordered to Germany to replace a tank commander whose three-year overseas tour has finished, he leaves a void at Fort Hood. The sergeant in Germany does not go to Fort Hood to replace him; he is promoted to a new assignment elsewhere, or goes to an advanced school, or leaves the Army. Therefore a new tank commander must be trained at Fort Hood. When that is multiplied several ten thousands of times a year, the Army experiences what it calls "turbulence," meaning a constant turnover of people caused by the need to provide a flow of trained soldiers to divisions overseas. If those divisions were at home, there would still be promotions and transfers, but the absence of a demand that soldiers be sent overseas for set lengths of time would bring more order to the process.

Every year, the United States dispatches forces for short periods to points all over the globe for training exercises—REFORGER to Europe, TEAM SPIRIT to Korea, BRIGHT STAR to the Middle East, BIG PINE to Central America. In such maneuvers, forces are trained to move quickly to trouble spots or to reinforce American troops overseas. But those moves are costly—in 1985, the Military Airlift Command paid chartered airlines 5.5 cents a passenger-mile to move troops and Defense Department people. For a battalion of 800 soldiers to fly 16,000 miles from the United States to South Korea and back cost $700,000. In addition, the United States has about 360 bases abroad. The armed forces were authorized to spend $1.2 billion on base construction outside the United States in 1984, $1.1 billion in 1985, and planned for $1.4 billion in 1986. Moreover, some governments, such as those in the Philippines and Greece, demand rent for the use of bases within their territory. On the other hand, many nations spend considerable sums to help the United States bear the burden. The government of Japan, for instance, spends $2 billion a year in rent, security, and logistic support for American bases there.

Another cost to the American economy is the drain on the United States international balance of payments. The dollars the American government spends in Europe and Japan, as well as personal expenditures of American military people and their families, are spent in the German or British economies rather than at home. That causes an outflow in the balance of payments, which is the difference between payments Americans make to other nations and payments received from them. The net deficit in military transactions, which is the difference between foreign military sales and other receipts on the income side and the costs of stationing and operating forces abroad on the spending side, was $1.6 billion in 1984.

In calculating an overall cost of forward deployment, the Defense Department measures such costs in several ways. Each is defined differently, according to a report to Congress. The incremental cost of maintaining American forces in Europe in 1985 amounted to only $2 billion. That included additional costs of housing, schools, and overseas cost-of-living allowances. But if those expenses, plus the additional costs of fuel and other operating expenses were counted, the Pentagon said, the sum would be $15 billion. In another calculation, the Pentagon estimated that it cost $55 billion a year to station forces in Europe if the cost of new equipment, training in the United States before deployment to Europe, logistics, research and development programs, and administrative costs were added. The report went on to say that the total cost of those forces, plus forces in the United States pledged to the defense of Europe, cost $90 billion annually. A similar study by the General Accounting Office, the congressional investigative agency, said about 56 pecent of the annual outlays for military forces could be attributed to United States forces in Europe and those committed to the reinforcement of Europe.

Of all those calculations, the $15 billion figure is the most applicable to the difference between having the forces in Europe and having them at home. The other calculations assumed that certain payments, such as those for new equipment, logistics, and research and development, would not be needed in the United Sates, where the withdrawn forces would be demobilized. On the premise that forces withdrawn from overseas would remain on active duty, only those incremental costs directly associated with the forces abroad should be counted. If the cost to maintain forces in Europe is an extra $15 billion a year, that should be doubled to cover the cost of forward deployment in the rest of the world, including Korea, Japan, the Philippines, the Indian Ocean, the Caribbean, Central America. Thus, the estimate of an incremental cost of the worldwide forward deployment of American forces is $30 billion a year.

Members of Congress like to give the impression that they are the watchdogs of the public treasury, keeping a jaundiced eye on the profligate tendencies of the Defense Department. But the impression is at variance with the actuality, for Congress does not reduce the cost of defense. Congress adds to it, substantially, every year. Congress does so by approving spending for weapons, armories, barracks, trucks, furniture, child care centers, and even shelters for the homeless—all items for which no one in the administration or the Defense Department has asked. In the committee hearings and on the floor of each house, members of Congress go through a long-standing and long-winded ritual of questioning the military budget of the administration, whether Democratic or Republican, supposedly looking for places to trim. Instead of cutting, however, the Congress in 1983 added $2.6 billion for programs not requested by the administration. In 1984, that figure went to $4.8 billion, and it was over $6 billion in 1985. In most cases, the sole purpose of the addition was to spend federal funds in the electoral district of a powerful or persuasive member of Congress. It had little to do with national defense.

In addition, Congress rarely permits the Defense Department or the defense industry to operate efficiently. The Reagan Administration has been eager to buy weapons through multiyear procurement, giving a defense contractor a guaranteed order for, say, aircraft for two or three years. With that assurance, the manufacturer could plan ahead, buy materials in economic lots, rationalize the labor force, stabilize overhead, and generally put his mind to efficient production. But Congress has balked in many cases because too many political levers would be lost. Members of Congress want to be able, each year, to extract something from the Pentagon or from other members of Congress in return for supporting the defense program.

The administration proposed in 1982 that thirty-four weapons programs be put under multiyear contracts, which were generally viewed as more economical and efficient. Congress approved only half of those, for a saving of $2 billion over the lives of the contracts. Paul Thayer, the Deputy Secretary of Defense in 1983, told Congress the appropriations bill had "so many restrictions on multiyear procurement that our contracting personnel are discouraged from including it in their acquisition strategy." He said the 1984 act "approved only 7 out of 14 multiyear candidates we submitted. The taxpayer lost potential savings of over $1 billion."

Similarly, Congress has often refused to permit the Pentagon to buy arms at an economical rate. If the administration and the Congress have agreed that a large quantity of a particular weapon is to be bought, it would be more economical to buy in large batches at a steady rate. According to Mr. Thayer, the administration obtained the approval of Congress to adjust eighteen programs for economical production in 1983 and 1984, only to have Congress reduce seventeen of those programs in 1984 to offset the earlier savings.

About the same time, Richard D. DeLauer, the outspoken Under Secretary of Defense in charge of developing weapons from 1981 through 1984, criticized Congress for failing to scrutinize military policies. He said too many congressmen involved themselves in specific decisions solely to protect their political interests. "It seems that, over the years, Congress has digressed from an oversight role in which it would participate in the establishment of policy objectives and measure progress toward achieving the policy goals," he said. "Unfortunately, Congressional oversight has become far too detailed to provide policy makers or the public with a coherent view of our accomplishments or our needs." Mr. DeLauer contended that congressional oversight had become an annual exercise in "line item management," asserting that most congressmen were motivated by "the parochial interests of constituencies and the increase in size and diversity of Congressional staffs."

Admiral James D. Watkins, the Chief of Naval Operations until mid-1986, contended that congressional intervention was especially noticeable in research programs. Parochial interests run high in those projects because congressmen hope that research may lead to lucrative contracts for production of arms. Admiral Watkins complained in a congressional hearing that the House had made 147 changes in the Navy's 319 research programs while the Senate had changed 129. By the time the measure came out of a House-Senate conference in which differences in the two versions had been reconciled, only 173 programs had survived as submitted.

A presidential commission led by J. Peter Grace, chairman of the W. R. Grace company, asserted that the taxpayers could be saved $2 billion a year if the Defense Department was permitted to consolidate military bases. For several years, the Defense Department asked Congress to permit it to pull together helicopter training for all services at the Army's aviation school at Fort Rucker, Alabama. The Pentagon reasoned that the basics of flying Army, Navy, Marine, and Air Force helicopters are alike. But the Navy enlisted the congressional delegation from Florida to resist because the Navy wanted to continue training pilots at the Naval Air Station in Pensacola, Florida. The congressional delegation wanted to keep the business the helicopter school brings to Pensacola.

Senator John Tower, the Republican from Texas and former chairman of the Armed Services Committee, spent much of his last year in Congress criticizing it for interfering in the execution of defense policy. Mr. Tower testified before the Budget Committee in 1984 that

the Congress—occasionally including my own committee—is engaged in too much micro-management at the expense of the broader review of defense requirements and priorities. Moreover, Congress itself is often the source of the restrictive rules, regulations and guidelines that prevent the efficient use of taxpayer dollars. The Defense Authorization and Appropriation Acts contain over one hundred general provisions, many of which tell the Department of Defense what it cannot do to spend defense dollars wisely.

Congressional action on individual defense programs can also be a primary cause of increased costs. We have stretched out programs, and even continued those for which there is no longer a valid military requirement. In some cases, we have promoted dual-sourcing where the real demand is barely sufficient to support one producer, or insisted upon sole-sourcing where competition would be excluded.

Many military officers, executives in the defense industry, and specialists on military budgets agree that large sums could be saved or spent more effectively if the congressional pork barrel could be eliminated. Lawrence J. Korb, an Assistant Secretary of Defense in the Reagan Administration, once said the pork barrel cost "the tax-payer at least $10 billion a year in things we don't want, things we don't need, but are there to protect a vested interest." Mr. Korb asserted that the special interests, in forcing extra spending on the Pentagon, "come at you in droves." Frank C. Carlucci, who was the first Deputy Secretary of Defense in the Reagan Administration, ac-cused Congress of adding $20 billion a year to the cost of arms and supplies because of irrational budgeting. "The key to efficient pro-curement is budget stability," he said. Representative Les Aspin, the Democrat from Wisconsin who was elected chairman of the House Armed Services Committee in 1985, has several times turned his guns on Congress. "Ten to fifteen percent of the Defense Department budget is in there because some constituency insists on it," he told *The Wash-ington Times*. "It is too expensive in terms of heartburn to take it out. . . . There are a number of things that are there because the amount of money saved is not worth the screams of anguish that would ac-company taking them out."

Altogether, the accumulative evidence suggests that 10 percent of the annual military budget, or $30 billion, is the amount of excessive or ineffective military spending caused by Congress.

The defense industry's contribution to the excessive cost of military power has become easier to document in recent years because military and civilian leaders in the Defense Department have been more willing to criticize the industry in public.

General Mullins, the head of the Air Force Logistics Command whose address to business executives was cited earlier, said the Air Force alone could save $1,238 billion over thirty years, or $41 billion a year, if those who produced aircraft and other weapons would make them more reliable. "Just try to imagine how much less our entire defense program would cost over a 30 year period if we could only get a handle on logistics dependency with increased reliability," the general said.

Imagine the cost reductions in maintenance. Imagine the potential savings in airlift requirements, from transport to flying hours. Imagine what it would mean if we didn't have to recruit, train and deploy as many maintenance technicians. . . . Across the board, we wouldn't need all those maintenance facilities. We wouldn't require all that equipment. We wouldn't have to buy all that material.

He gave what he called "some very conservative dollar savings" that would accrue if better reliability reduced the need for spare parts and support equipment by 75 percent. "That alone would represent a savings of over $6 billion in the fiscal year 1984 Air Force budget, and almost $8.25 billion in the fiscal year 1985 budget," he said. "Then there would be substantial savings in operations and maintenance costs, about $7.5 billion this year and almost $9.5 billion in fiscal year 1985." Those savings, when coupled with savings in civilian personnel, "could easily free up 20 percent of the entire Air Force budget to be used in more productive and meaningful ways," he said. "Over a 30-year weapon systems life-cycle period, assuming just a 5 percent inflation rate, the savings would amount to 1 trillion 238 billion dollars," the general asserted. Moreover, that didn't include "the costs of military personnel, construction, research, development, test, evaluation and the wide spectrum of miscellaneous procurement expenses that would result from the fact that our weapons systems are reliable."

In another measure, Deputy Secretary of Defense Thayer asserted that 10 to 30 percent of the cost of weapons could be saved if defense contractors made things right the first time. The savings would work out to $10 billion to $30 billion a year. A defense industry executive, Al Lovelace, vice-president for quality assurance at General Dynamics, estimated that the nationwide cost of scrap and rework was 15 percent of annual military procurement, or $15 billion a year. A. Ernest Fitzgerald, the "whistleblower" in the Department of the Air Force, testified before Congress in 1984 that $30 billion was being wasted in buying weapons. "Too many of our procedures and too much of our activity in the acquisition-management business is aimed at cost and budget justification instead of cost reduction," he said. "Too many of the administrators in this end of our business instinctively react to protect budgets and the interests of big contractors."

The cost of depot maintenance, which means repairs done by skilled technicians in facilities with advanced machines and tools, is rising at a rate faster than the rate of military spending, according to the Defense Department. In 1980, depot maintenance cost $7.4 billion. By 1983, that was up to $11.8 billion. The estimate for 1985 was $14.9 billion. Much of that was due to weapons made poorly in the first place.

The absence of competition, especially among small companies that sell parts and supplies to the Defense Department, was blamed for adding to costs. The executive vice-president of a group representing 14,000 small companies estimated that the Defense Department could save $4 to $5 billion a year by relying on competitive bids instead of a single source for spare parts. William E. Hardman, of the National Tool & Machining Association, said only 10 percent of the 3.9 million spare parts bought each year was obtained through competition. "Study after study has demonstrated that lead times are reduced and costs cut nearly in half when procurements are switched from sole source to a competitive basis," he said in testimony before a congressional committee. "By application of the percentages, it is apparent that $5 to $6 billion could be saved each year by switching those procurements from sole source to open competition." After subtracting the costs of making the changes, he said, "the net savings could be as much as $4 to $5 billion each year."

The ever-expanding secret budget, sometimes called the "black budget," is in some dispute. In that budget are sensitive programs—such as developing the Stealth bomber, intended to evade detection by radar—in which the government seeks to protect newly developed technology. The Pentagon has justified hiding Stealth costs from public scrutiny on grounds that an estimate of spending could help the nation's adversaries. Some knowledgeable officials argue that classified projects are run more efficiently and economically than those in the open because they are unfettered by red tape, congressional pork barreling, and unrealistic demands for testing. But others assert that it is a potential source of waste. William W. Kaufmann, who helped to prepare Pentagon budgets for many years, has estimated that a $300 billion budget may have $18 billion worth of hidden programs. "The problem is that there's no public debate on any of this stuff," said Mr. Kaufmann, an economist at the Massachusetts Institute of Technology. "And when you have no public scrutiny, things can go wrong." David C. Morrison of *The National Journal* presented a persuasive argument in 1986 that the black budget had risen to $22 billion.

Setting aside the question of the black budget, the accumulation of evidence suggests that the defense industry drains off $30 billion a year that could be saved or put to better use.

After an eighteen-month study of the organization and operation of the federal government, the Grace commission reported to President Reagan and then came out to meet the press. "The government," J. Peter Grace declared, "is run horribly."

In the letter to President Reagan that accompanied a report on the commission's findings in January 1984, Mr. Grace said savings "can be achieved without raising taxes, without weakening America's needed defense buildup, and without in any way harming necessary social welfare programs." He argued that the government could save $424.4 billion over three years, of which $104.5 billion could be saved in the Defense Department. Mr. Grace, in a book entitled *Burning Money— The Waste of Your Tax Dollars*, said later that the inefficiencies in the Defense Department could be eliminated "without costing us a single important weapons program, without dismantling any of our defenses, and without foregoing new weapons systems."

Mr. Grace's task force reported that "almost 40 percent of the recommended savings can be derived from improving management of the weapons acquisitions process." It found functions in the Department of Defense overlapping with those in the Departments of the Army, Navy, and Air Force that "make the process of acquiring major weapons more costly and more time consuming than necessary." The report said $7.2 billion could be saved by requiring common parts in weapons and another $7.2 billion by stabilizing weapons programs for five years and having more multiyear contracts.

The task force advised the Army to "stabilize the design of a weapons system earlier in its life" because "repeated schedule and quantity changes add billions to the price tags for major weapon systems." The Army wasted money by moving people around too much, the task force said. The Navy was advised to seek more competitive bids and to have two or more sources for its ships and arms, a practice the Navy had begun. The task force saw deficiencies in Navy storage and supply operations, including problems with inventory control, security, receiving, and shipping. Like the Army, the Navy was advised to stabilize programs. "Frequent revisions in guidance for planning and budgeting phases," the report said, "result in massive expenditures of staff effort to cope with the changes." The Air Force was advised to make more use of multiyear procurement and dual sourcing to enhance competition, to rely more on contracting out commercial and industrial activities to the private sector, and to manage consultants better.

The difficulties of determining the true cost of weapons became apparent in the differing views of the Defense Department and the

General Accounting Office over the effect of inflation. Coping with inflation is a critical management issue because of the long time between the design of a weapon and the end of production fifteen to twenty years later. John R. Quetsch, a senior career official in the Pentagon comptroller's office, told a congressional committee that "unanticipated inflation was the single major factor contributing to cost growth in major weapon system acquisitions during the late Seventies and early Eighties." In a review of weapons programs, Mr. Quetsch said, the Pentagon found that inflation caused 57 percent of cost growth in 1977, 85 percent in 1979, and 81 percent in 1982. With the Reagan Administration's success in holding down inflation, he said, recent estimates on the long-term cost of a weapons program have been closer to the mark.

But the General Accounting Office, an investigative agency of the Congress, contended that "inflation is not the central cause of cost escalation." Rather, the agency said in a report, the practice of focusing on highly complex weapons and underestimating actual costs were the culprits. "Budgeting practices are unrealistic in their attempts to plan for and manage cost escalation," the agency's report said. "Cost projections are consistently understated."

Mr. Quetsch pointed to the F-15 Eagle aircraft, the Air Force's premier fighter, built by McDonnell Douglas. In 1970, he said, "we estimated that this program of 749 aircraft would cost $6 billion." Inflation over the planned life of the program would add $1.4 billion for a total of $7.4 billion in constant dollars. The number of aircraft to be produced was increased by 627 planes, which added $3.6 billion to the program plus $12.9 billion for inflation. On top came changes in engineering, scheduling, and support equipment that added another $3.3 billion in costs and $8.5 billion for inflation. Finally, Mr. Quetsch testified, "unexpected changes in the price level index since the baseline was established have added another $2.5 billion in inflation." Thus a program that was projected to cost $7.4 billion in 1970 was estimated to cost $38.1 billion in 1984. After adjusting for changes in the number of aircraft to be produced, the real cost growth was 35 percent, and the inflated cost growth 60 percent, Mr. Quetsch said.

The General Accounting Office drew a different portrait with a review of the Army's M-60 tank, blaming much on new technology intended to improve the tank. In constant dollars, each tank cost $580,000 at the start. An improved turret in 1963 cut the price to $564,000. A new air cleaner in 1971, a stabilizing device in 1972, and an improved track in 1974 brought the cost up to $657,000. A new engine and a better electrical system were added in 1975, making the cost of each tank $854,000. Then began a series of changes, including new gun sights, a deep-water fording kit, a new machine gun, a new smoke grenade launcher, an engine smoke generator, a laser range finder, a solid-state computer, and a thermal sight. By 1983, the cost was up to $1.4 million, just short of the $1.5 million price for the Army's newest tank, the M-1 Abrams.

In the long run, both the Pentagon and the General Accounting Office have been right, since inflation and erroneous cost estimates have added to the Defense Department's expenditures. Add to that the findings of the Grace commission, and an estimate of $15 billion as the excessive cost of defense caused by mismanagement in the Pentagon is within reason.

The cost of the lack of coordination among the four services, popularly called interservice rivalry, is most obvious in developing and buying different weapons to perform the same mission. The Air Force developed the MX intercontinental ballistic missile while the Navy was developing the Trident II submarine-launched ballistic missile. They have nearly the same range, accuracy, and explosive power. Yet in fiscal years 1984 through 1986, the Air Force planned to spend $11 billion for the MX and the Navy $6.7 billion for the Trident II. If the missile developed by the Air Force, for instance, had been eliminated and the Navy's missile adapted to the needs of the Air Force, large sums could have been saved during those three years.

Similarly, the Navy and the Air Force separately developed the high-powered F-14 Tomcat fighter and the F-15 Eagle fighter, whose missions and capabilities in fending off enemy air attack are much the same. Yet the Navy planned to pay $3.4 billion between 1984 and 1986 to buy 66 F-14s while the Air Force was budgeting $6.4 billion to buy 126 F-15s during the same period. In lighter fighter aircraft, the Air Force budgeted $9.8 billion to buy 474 F-16s during the three-year period; the Navy put down $8 billion for 252 F-18s; the Marine Corps asked for $3.1 billion to buy 105 AV-8B Harriers during the same period. The Harrier, a "jump jet" that can take off in a very short runway, is a different kind of airplane but performs much the same mission as the other two. In air defense missiles, the Army planned to buy 1,456 Patriots for $3.3 billion, the Navy 3,890 Standard missiles for $2.4 billion, and the Marine Corps 1,400 older Hawk missiles for $420 million during those three years. Must the taxpayers buy two kinds of airplanes and three types of missiles when one of each might have done the job?

On the other hand, there are exceptions. The Air Force and the

Navy have been working together to develop an advanced tactical fighter aircraft to replace current planes when they become obsolete. All services buy the Stinger surface-to-air short-range air defense missile. The Army and the Marine Corps buy the same TOW-2 antitank missiles. Other examples arise where the services work together to achieve economies of scale in the weapons they develop.

But those are less frequent than the separate programs. The Army and the Marine Corps, for instance, have been unable to develop the JVX tilt-wing aircraft, a hybrid between a helicopter and a fixed-wing aircraft. The wing of such an aircraft would rotate the blades of its rotor upwards so that the aircraft could take off like a helicopter, then rotate the wings forward so that the blades would be like the propeller of a fixed-wing aircraft. The Marines want a large plane that can carry more troops from ship to shore in an amphibious assault; the Army wants a smaller version to disperse troops and make them less vulnerable during fast-moving battles on land.

In combat medical care, each service has insisted on having its own equipment and doing things its own way. Each of the three services—the Navy takes care of the Marine Corps—has a combat medical service that, until recently, bought everything from scalpels to bedpans to its own specifications and from different suppliers. The cost, and the inadequate medical care that each of the services would have rendered to its wounded, has forced them to consider buying things together so that their dollars stretch further.

Less tangible losses come from flaws in joint operations. The price of inadequate air and sea transport to carry Army and Marine Corps forces from home stations to faraway battlefields in time to be effective is hard to gauge. What the four services lose in buying different radios that make it impossible for soldiers and marines, sailors and airmen to talk to each other is immeasurable.

In sum, it is hard to be precise in citing an annual excessive cost of interservice rivalry. But the evidence leads to a conclusion that it adds about 5 percent, or $15 billion, to the annual bill.

In the last category, the cost of people, the military retirement system is the main culprit in adding to military spending. Unlike other retirement systems in the government or in many private industries, the cost of retirement is carried in the annual budget, not as a separate item with separate funding.

Today's military retirement program was started after the Civil War and modified over the years to provide an old-age pension for those who had served for thirty years. In recent years, however, the majority of officers and noncommissioned officers have been permitted to retire after twenty years of service, about the age of forty-three for officers and thirty-nine for noncoms. They have then gone on to second careers. What was once intended to take care of military people in their old age has become, in effect, a lucrative plan for deferred compensation.

The cost of retirement has soared in the last fifteen years. Between 1968 and 1982, the number of retired military people doubled, from 644,855 to 1,313,433. Of the officers, 377,523 had left the service after twenty years, while 39,994 retired at the end of thirty years. In the same period, the amount of retired pay went up sevenfold, from $2.1 billion in 1968 to $14.9 billion in 1982. By 1985, it was up to $18 billion and was headed to $25 billion, in constant dollars, by 1990.

Perhaps more important to the national defense, the practice of retiring after twenty years of service has caused an additional loss in the training, experience, and mature judgment that officers and noncommissioned officers take out of the service with them. Given modern living conditions, medicine, and food, a person in his or her early forties is in the prime of life and has a life expectancy of thirty more years. Losing that person costs the taxpayers not only the price of retirement benefits but the time and money to replace the retiring officer or noncommissioned officer.

For the average officer, a lieutenant colonel or Navy commander who retired after twenty years of service, the annual pension in 1986 was $21,100, to which would be added a cost-of-living increase each year. For an Army or Marine master sergeant, a Navy senior chief petty officer, or an Air Force senior master sergeant, all in the second-highest enlisted grade, retired pay after twenty years of service was $11,200. Retired pay is calculated on one-half of base pay while on active duty; other allowances are not included in the computation. But the retired officer and noncommissioned officer is eligible for medical care, has access to commissaries and clubs, and can buy gasoline at stations on military posts where taxes are not assessed.

Those who favor the system acknowledge that it has become deferred compensation but argue that military service is a hazardous profession and that those who undertake it deserve special treatment. They point to sacrifices of military families with the constant moving and the disruptions with separations while the husband and father is away at sea or on duty abroad. They argue that the working wife must give up her job and find another whenever her husband moves. Advocates contend that the prospect of a good retirement is important in persuading middle-ranking officers and noncoms to stay for twenty years.

Savings could be gained by lengthening the normal career beyond twenty years to twenty-five years, plus delaying the age at which a retired person could draw his or her full pension, and slowing down the cost-of-living adjustments. Estimates made by the Defense Department, the Grace commission, staffs in Congress, and associations supporting retired persons run between $4 billion and $6 billion a year. An estimate of $5 billion, therefore, would be in the ballpark. Congress took a step in that direction in 1986 by cutting retired pay after twenty years of service to 40 percent of base pay, rising to 75 percent after thirty years, for those who joined after July 1986.

Altogether, devising a way to take $100 billion out of the defense budget without cutting into military muscle, or to use that $100 billion to buy more military muscle, is within economic reach. Persuading allies to.pick up a greater share of the burden for common defense could save American taxpayers money if those allies expanded their forces and so relieved the United States of that expense. A reduction in the forward deployment of American forces would bring real savings in operating costs. Sizable savings could be had by getting Congress out of the pork barrel and by ensuring, with stringent penalties if necessary, that defense contractors operate efficiently. Reducing friction among the military services would not only save money but would improve military posture. Wringing the bloat out of the Pentagon's civilian and military bureaucracies would do the same. Lastly, small but important savings and improved readiness could be obtained by gradually lengthening time that career people serve before retiring.

Over the long run, a saving of one-third, or an increase in military power by one-third, seems within reach and reason. This estimate, and it is just an estimate, is not intended to have the precision of a skilled cost accountant's assessment. Indeed, the issue of the defense budget is so complicated that maybe even a sophisticated cost accountant would have a hard time nailing down the excesses. But the accumulated evidence adds up to an inescapable conclusion. Moreover, the real issue—whether the special interests could be forced to make sacrifices for the common good in getting control of military spending—is more political than economic. The record of the last thirty years on that score is not promising.

CHAPTER 9

PROTRACTED NUCLEAR WAR

PRESIDENT REAGAN sat before the fireplace in the Oval Office of the White House talking with Hugh Sidey of *Time* magazine about a Soviet attack with nuclear missiles. "Think of it," the President said, gesturing across the room.

You're sitting at that desk. The word comes that they're on their way. And you sit here knowing that there is no way, at present, of stopping them. So they're going to blow up how much of this country we can only guess at, and your only response can be to push the button before they get here so that even though you're all going to die, they're going to die too.

Mr. Sidey wrote that Mr. Reagan left hanging the question of whether he could push that button. "Reagan does not know the answer," Mr. Sidey asserted. "Nobody does."

The President's ruminations and Mr. Sidey's comment underscored the only certainty about nuclear war: None of us really knows what he or she is talking about. Nuclear war would be so much more murderous than anything known to history, so much more devastating in its destruction, so deeply plunging mankind into terror that it is beyond human comprehension. Everything spoken or written about nuclear war, including what follows in these pages, should be viewed with skepticism. Speculation abounds, but no one knows how nuclear weapons would be used for the first time since the atomic bombings of Hiroshima and Nagasaki in 1945. No one can predict whether the victim of nuclear attack would react with deliberation or panic or paralysis. No one can foretell whether the war would be over in one spasmodic exchange or would be fought for weeks or even months in an artillery battle writ large. No one can foresee how the war could be ended. And no man knows the fate of the earth after that.

The inability to comprehend nuclear war may be among the few things about which nuclear thinkers agree. A conservative, Fred C. Iklé, who as a scholar and government official has specialized in questions of nuclear policy since 1955, described what he called the "psychological paradox" of nuclear arms. "A conventional war, experienced by Europe twice in this century, is all too vivid a disaster," said Mr. Iklé, who was born in Switzerland in 1924.

It can be visualized in detail as an unfolding, protracted calamity, its horrors lucidly remembered. Nuclear war, by contrast, is an abstract idea. Its instantaneous terror is so unfathomable that people tend to think about it in all-or-nothing fashion; either no nuclear weapons will be used, or aggressor and defender will be totally destroyed.

After he left the Pentagon, Harold Brown, a moderate and the nuclear physicist who was President Carter's Secretary of Defense, wrote a chilling passage about nuclear war:

The destruction of more than 100 million people in each of the United States, the Soviet Union, and the European nations could take place during the first half-hour of a nuclear war. These deaths would be caused by the blast and the heat of the fireball, and the ensuing fires and collapse of buildings. Many tens of millions of additional casualties would be caused thereafter by nuclear fallout. . . . Such a war would be catastrophe not only indescribable, but unimaginable. It would be unlike anything that has taken place on this planet since human life began.

Similarly, two antinuclear activists, William A. Arkin and Richard W. Fieldhouse, of the Institute for Policy Studies in Washington, wrote that the arcane art of planning for nuclear war is based on untested assumptions that masquerade as scientific precepts. "The lack of any real experience with nuclear war means that assumptions form the basis of all justification, structuring, and criticism of nuclear forces," they wrote. "The assumptions are far removed from the roots or the ultimate effects of the war that would occur if the scenarios were to become reality."

But there may be a glimmer of hope amid this ignorance and despair, a hint that maybe, just maybe, fear of the unknown and unknowable will stay the hand of the politician or warmonger tempted to launch a nuclear strike. Michael Howard, an Oxford don who is among the West's leading military historians and thinkers, told *U.S. News & World Report* that Hiroshima and Nagasaki were only a glimpse of a nuclear catastrophe that would surpass anything that has struck mankind:

The prospect of this happening is a profound and unprecedented deterrent against making war. I think the development of nuclear weapons has given us a chance for the indefinite future of preventing the outbreak of major war, at least between the powers armed with nuclear forces. . . . Wars have become more discrete, finite, managed, deliberate, still used by states for the attainment of political objectives, but increasingly rarely. . . . One cannot rule it out as a possibility, but our very dread of nuclear war makes it a highly remote possibility.

Given the unknowns, nuclear doctrine may seem a venture into a never-never land of concepts divorced from reality. But nuclear doctrine is the starting point from which war plans are derived. It is the justification for choosing which arms are to be acquired and for spending vast sums to produce nuclear arms and to deploy nuclear forces. Nuclear doctrine is driven by the march of technology and seeks to provide coherence as the accuracy, range, and diversity of nuclear arms has developed. It reflects the thinking of political and military leaders who might decide, God forbid, when and how to employ those forces. Nuclear doctrine is shaped by the institutional imperatives of the Air Force, the Navy, and the Army, and the compromises among them as each has sought a place along the nuclear spectrum. It is nuclear doctrine that molds the fundamental perceptions the superpowers have of themselves and of each other as nuclear states, and that influences their approaches to arms control. Perhaps most important for American citizens, nuclear doctrine is needlessly wrapped in abstract concepts and obscure jargon. It has become a theology that, were it Christian, would be the province of Jesuits or, if Jewish, the arena of Talmudic scholars. Because it concerns the very survival of the human race, it ought not be left to the nuclear theologians, but should be brought into the public forum to be dealt with by thinking citizens.

Since the beginning of the nuclear era in 1945, American leaders from President Truman through President Reagan have pondered war plans for nuclear arms. The presidents have been influenced by their own views about these weapons, by the thinking of senior military commanders like General Curtis LeMay of the Air Force, Admiral Arleigh Burke of the Navy, and General Maxwell Taylor of the Army. The presidents and their military advisers have been influenced, in turn, by nuclear thinkers, the earliest of whom was Bernard Brodie, a political scientist at Yale University. Although those strategists number but a few hundred today, they are sprinkled across the nation at influential posts in the government and military services, private think tanks, consulting firms, and universities.

President Truman, who approved the atomic bombings of Hiroshima and Nagasaki, came out of World War II convinced that atomic weapons were to be employed in the future only as a last resort, to terrorize a desperate enemy into surrendering. He avidly sought and succeeded in establishing the close civilian control over the weapon that persists today. He also presided over the development of the thermonuclear bomb, which was even more powerful than the atomic bomb.

A different view was held by Bernard Brodie, who thought that nuclear weapons would revolutionize the reason for having military forces. Nuclear arms were so powerful, he thought, that they could be used only to threaten an enemy with retaliation, thus deterring him from attacking. "Thus far the chief purpose of our military establishment has been to win wars," he wrote shortly after the bombings of Hiroshima and Nagasaki. "From now on, its chief purpose must be to prevent them. It can have almost no other useful purpose." In turning from warmaking to deterrence, Brodie said, "The first and most vital step in an American security program for the age of atomic bombs is to take measures to guarantee to ourselves in case of attack the possibility of retaliation in kind."

But the leadership of the Air Force, then being split off from the Army, saw the atomic bomb as an extension of the conventional bomb, only far more efficient. In the bombing of Japan, they had accomplished with two sorties what had taken thousands of sorties only weeks before. In the first atomic war plan, HARROW, the Air Force in 1946 listed twenty Soviet cities as targets for attack by fifty atomic bombs. A year later, they upped that in TROJAN to seventy cities to be hit with 133 atomic bombs in thirty days.

A committee that analyzed TROJAN in 1949 said that while it would severely damage the Soviet Union, the war plan would not defeat the Soviet government, which had just detonated its first atomic device. The Air Force therefore devised DROPSHOT, a war plan listing four types of targets: Soviet plants producing atomic bombs, the stockpile of those bombs, and the airfields of planes that would carry the bombs; government and military control centers; military targets such as lines of communications, supply depots, troop and naval bases; and industry that would support wartime operations.

With the outbreak of the Korean War in June 1950, the Air Force drew up still another war plan, assigning first priority to BRAVO missions that would blunt the Soviet ability to wage nuclear war, second priority to ROMEO attacks intended to impede Soviet forces, and third priority to DELTA assaults on Soviet industry. Later that year, the Air Force asked Bernard Brodie to review the target list. He recommended that targets be selected for the loss their destruction would have on the ability of the Soviet Union to make war and that the Air Force plan to avoid bombing cities.

But General LeMay, the flamboyant bomber pilot and leader of the Strategic Air Command, thought DROPSHOT too ambitious, calling on pilots to find too many targets spread over too much unknown terrain. Having devised the firebombing of Japanese cities built of wood and paper houses, he urged a return to urban-industrial targets hit in massive air raids. His view prevailed, and urban-industrial targets predominated in the next war plan, OFFTACKLE.

President Eisenhower entered the White House in 1953 with a view of atomic weapons opposite to that of his predecessor. The former General of the Army, perhaps the best informed about nuclear weapons of all the presidents, saw them as weapons of first, not last, resort. In his view, the United States would not start a war, with any weapon. But if attacked, the United States would respond with a mighty force that could include nuclear weapons. That was the doctrine of massive retaliation. In his 1954 message to Congress on the State of the Union, President Eisenhower said the United States intended to deter aggression by having "a massive capability to strike back." He suggested to the Congress that nuclear weapons would be the least expensive way of deterring attack because so much explosive power could be bought for relatively little money.

The Secretary of State, John Foster Dulles, crystallized the policy of massive retaliation. To deter an attack, he said, the United States would "depend primarily upon a great capacity to retaliate, instantly, by means and at places of our choosing." Those words triggered an angry reaction. James Reston of *The New York Times* observed that massive retaliation meant "in the event of another proxy or brushfire war in Korea, Indochina, Iran or anywhere else, the United States might retaliate instantly with atomic weapons against the U.S.S.R. or Red China." In response, Mr. Dulles toned down the rhetoric, saying "the main reliance must be on the power of the free community to retaliate with great force by mobile means at places of its own choice." Mr. Dulles left the policy a bit vague. But Samuel F. Wells Jr. of the Woodrow Wilson International Center for Scholars in Washington has written that President Eisenhower was "never as unsubtle as commonly believed." The President, Mr. Wells said, "desired this result. He was perfectly aware of the advantages of studied ambiguity in public foreign policy statements, especially those concerning the possible use of American military forces."

David Alan Rosenberg, a historian at the University of Houston, has sifted through once secret documents and concluded that President

Eisenhower's preference "for targeting military capability rather than the urban-industrial base marked the beginning of a serious effort to contain escalating force and weapons requirements." But military planners contended that more effective strikes could be mounted against cities and industry. "With great reluctance, Eisenhower at last accepted the conclusion," Professor Rosenberg has written, "that the U.S. could, if it choose, deliver a decisive war-winning blow against Soviet cities, and began to question the necessity of trying to maintain a complete counter-force capability as well." ("Counter-force" is jargon for hitting bomber airfields, missile silos, and nuclear depots that would enable the Soviet Union to wage nuclear war.)

During President Eisenhower's term, preventive war was discussed among strategic thinkers as a way to destroy the Soviet nuclear threat while the United States had overwhelming superiority. But President Eisenhower ruled out preventive war. "The United States and its allies," he said in a policy paper, "must reject the concept of preventive war or acts intended to provoke war." On the other hand, another policy paper said nuclear weapons "will be used in general war and in military operations short of general war as authorized by the President." That paper said the national objective was "to prevail if general war eventuates."

If preventive war was out, a pre-emptive strike was not. The difference between them is timing. A pre-emptive strike intended to blunt a Soviet attack could be mounted after an unmistakable warning of a Soviet attack had been seen. By early 1954, General LeMay and the Strategic Air Command had prepared a war plan in which 735 bombers would hit the Soviet Union from all directions at the same time, with top priority given to the BRAVO mission of taking out Soviet nuclear forces.

In the North Atlantic Treaty Organization, smaller nuclear arms were seen as a way to defend Western Europe without paying for the large conventional forces thought necessary to turn back a Russian invasion. By the mid-1950s, the advance of technology had made nuclear weapons less cumbersome than the unwieldy bombs dropped on Japan, one of which had been called "Fat Man." Brigadier General Robert C. Richardson III, a retired Air Force officer who was on the NATO planning staff in the 1950s, has written that tactical nuclear weapons—meaning artillery, short-range missiles, and bombs dropped from fighter planes—were to be employed to defend Europe with minimum force. He said "if anywhere near the expected nuclear firepower would be expended, then the war would not last very long."

Under President Eisenhower, the Air Force was given 47 percent of the military budget during fiscal years 1954 through 1957 to build not only bombers but the first United States intercontinental ballistic missiles. For ballistic missiles, the trajectory and target are determined at the time of firing by the force, speed, and angle with which they are launched, with corrections made along the way by sensors, computers, and guidance mechanisms on board. The Army got into the nuclear game by acquiring nuclear artillery. The Navy, which had already put small nuclear bombs aboard aircraft carriers, made the biggest advances with Polaris submarines armed with missiles that could be launched from beneath the seas. The first Polaris submarine, the USS *George Washington*, put to sea in 1960 as President Eisenhower's term was drawing to a close.

By then, the Air Force, Navy, and Army had built nuclear stockpiles, with the Air Force's by far the largest. The United States had accumulated an estimated 18,000 nuclear bombs and warheads of varying sizes. There was, however, little coordination among the three services, much to the dismay of President Eisenhower. The Air Force wanted operational control of all long-range nuclear forces, but the Navy resisted. To reduce duplication, the services finally worked out, for presidential approval, a Single Integrated Operational Plan (better known by its acronym, SIOP) to parcel out targets. The target list of 2,021 aiming points included sites for Soviet intercontinental ballistic missiles, bomber and air defense bases, government control centers and military command posts, nuclear weapons facilities, naval bases, and 131 industrial plants in cities.

About the same time, a new theory appeared in Herman Kahn's book *On Thermonuclear War*. Mr. Kahn, a physicist who made his career thinking about the unthinkable, contended that a nuclear war need not be limited to one spasmodic exchange but could be fought and won in other ways. Nuclear war would not be catastrophic, he argued, if a nation was prepared. That included devising a war-fighting strategy, particularly in hitting first; acquiring the weapons and communications to fight that war; preparing a civil defense for the nation's population; and planning to rebuild cities and industry when the war was over. "If proper preparations have been made," he wrote, "it would be possible for us or the Soviets to cope with all of the effects of a thermonuclear war in the sense of saving some people and restoring close to the previous standard of living in a relatively short time."

When President Kennedy took office in January 1961, the world was fifteen years into the nuclear era. But the young President seemed not to hold particular views on nuclear arms and left most of the doctrine to his cerebral Secretary of Defense, Robert S. McNamara. By that time, three options had taken shape. One was the minimum deterrence of Bernard Brodie, in which a small number of nuclear weapons aimed at critical Soviet industries was thought to be enough to prevent Moscow from attacking the United States. A second was the massive retaliation of John Foster Dulles. The third was the controlled war-fighting of Herman Kahn.

Shortly after arriving at the Pentagon, Mr. McNamara was briefed on the SIOP, or nuclear war plan, that called for one massive strike. He was disturbed by the rigidity of the plan and ordered a review of United States nuclear posture, asking the Joint Chiefs of Staff to see whether controlled responses, with pauses for negotiating, were feasible. In September 1961, Mr. McNamara drafted a memo for President Kennedy in which he said the United States should plan on striking "Soviet bomber bases, missile sites, and other installations associated with long-range nuclear forces in order to reduce Soviet power and limit the damage that can be done to us." He urged that the United States hold nuclear forces in reserve for use, if necessary, to destroy Soviet cities "in a controlled and deliberate way."

That became public policy when Mr. McNamara addressed the graduating class at the University of Michigan in June 1962. He thought nuclear strategy should be approached in much the same way as conventional operations. "Principal military objectives, in the event of a nuclear war stemming from a major attack on the alliance," he said, "should be the destruction of the enemy's military forces, not of his civilian population."

The Cuban missile crisis of October 1962 began when the Soviet Union deployed nuclear missiles in Cuba, putting to a test the ability of the American government to control the application of military power. At the time, it was seen as a nuclear confrontation. But twenty years later, several key participants said conventional military forces were more important in resolving the crisis. In 1982, Mr. McNamara assessed that episode with Dean Rusk, the Secretary of State during the crisis; Roswell L. Gilpatric, the Deputy Secretary of Defense; George W. Ball, the Under Secretary of State; McGeorge Bundy, President Kennedy's national security adviser; and Theodore Sorensen, special counsel and close friend of President Kennedy. "The decisive military element in the resolution of the crisis was our clearly available and applicable superiority in conventional weapons within the area of crisis," they wrote in an essay in *Time* magazine.

American nuclear superiority was not in our view a critical factor, for the fundamental and controlling reason that nuclear war, already in 1962, would have been an unexampled catastrophe for both sides. . . . The Cuban missile crisis illustrates not the significance but the insignificance of nuclear superiority in the face of survivable thermonuclear retaliatory forces. It also shows the crucial role of rapidly available conventional strength.

Separately, General Maxwell Taylor, the military officer whose advice was most prized by President Kennedy during the crisis, agreed:

Our great superiority in nuclear weapons contributed little to the outcome of the Cuban crisis. In this situation, the stakes involved were far too small for either party to risk a resort to nuclear weapons. . . . Nuclear superiority is of little use in coping with an adversary similarly armed, whereas conventional superiority at the right place is likely to carry the day.

After the crisis, Mr. McNamara brought the policy of "flexible response" into the nuclear lexicon along with the deployment of 1,000 new Minuteman intercontinental ballistic missiles. "Our forces can be used in several different ways," he said.

We may have to retaliate with a single massive attack. Or, we may be able to use our retaliatory forces to limit damage to ourselves, and our allies, by knocking out the enemy's bases before he has time to launch his second salvos. We may seek to terminate a war on favorable terms by using our forces as a bargaining weapon—by threatening further attack. In any case, our large reserve of protected firepower would give an enemy an incentive to avoid our cities and to stop a war.

When Lyndon Baines Johnson became President after President Kennedy had been assassinated in November 1963, Mr. McNamara continued as Secretary of Defense and maker of nuclear policy. He leaned more toward the concepts of Bernard Brodie in what came to be known as the doctrine of mutually assured destruction, or MAD. As the Soviet Union built up its nuclear force, especially intercontinental ballistic missiles, Mr. McNamara saw the enormous cost of trying to build a nuclear force to maintain American superiority and the ability to launch different kinds of nuclear assaults. In 1965, he said in a congressional hearing that the objective of American nuclear forces was "assured destruction," which he explained was "the capability to destroy the aggressor as a viable society, even after a well-planned and executed surprise attack on our forces." Specialists on Soviet nuclear strategy, however, have asserted that Moscow has never subscribed to the MAD doctrine, which may mean that it is useless.

President Nixon, who came to the White House in 1969 better

versed than most in foreign and military policy, went back toward the policy of flexible response. In his annual review of foreign policy in early 1971, President Nixon said an American President must not be "limited to the indiscriminate mass destruction of enemy civilians as the sole possible response to challenges." He said the President must have "the plans and the command and control capabilities necessary to enable us to select and carry out the appropriate response without necessarily having to resort to mass destruction." An echo came a year later from Secretary of Defense Melvin Laird. "To maintain needed flexibility," he told Congress, "we design our forces so that we have strategic alternatives available for use depending on the nature or level of provocation."

President Nixon's next Secretary of Defense, James R. Schlesinger, fleshed out the doctrine of measured response. In 1974, Mr. Schlesinger announced a change in nuclear strategy, saying the United States would acquire "the forces to execute a wide range of options in response to particular action by an enemy, including a capability for precise attacks on both soft and hard targets, while at the same time minimizing unintended collateral damage." (In the jargon of nuclear theologians, a "soft target"—such as a naval base or a railroad yard—has not been fortified against nuclear explosions. A "hard target" is a military command post or a missile silo that has been strengthened with steel and concrete, or built underground, to withstand nuclear blast. "Collateral damage" means killing civilians.) "What we need," Mr. Schlesinger said, "is a series of measured responses to aggression which bear some relation to the provocation, have prospects of terminating hostilities before general nuclear war breaks out, and leave some possibility for restoring deterrence."

Mr. Schlesinger's doctrine was codified in National Security Decision Memorandum 242, signed by President Nixon in early 1975. It called for deliberate control in a nuclear war as the United States sought to limit damage to itself by destroying Soviet nuclear missiles before they could be launched. Secondly, the doctrine required a secure reserve force, meaning submarines, bombers, and missiles certain to survive a nuclear attack and to be available for retaliatory strikes. In a third element, NSDM 242 looked beyond early nuclear exchanges to say that the secure reserve force would fire at Soviet industry to cripple Soviet efforts to recover from a nuclear war. The object of NSDM 242 was to leave the United States in a position to prevail as it recovered from the war.

With the Watergate scandal and the resignation of President Nixon, NSDM 242 was not fully implemented. The necessary command and communications apparatus that would survive an attack and be available for the control of a response was not built. But the policy, in theory at least, remained in force during President Ford's short tenure.

President Carter brought some knowledge of nuclear weapons with him to the White House in January 1976, having been a naval officer qualified in nuclear-powered and nuclear-armed submarines. But the President appeared to have little interest in nuclear doctrine and relied on Secretary of Defense Harold Brown to draw up a strategy for nuclear arms. President Carter retained the doctrine set forth by President Nixon and President Ford in NSDM 242 but initiated a full review of nuclear strategy that led to a new Presidential Directive, known as PD-59, in 1980.

Leon Sloss, the Pentagon official who directed the analysis of nuclear targeting for Mr. Brown, wrote that policymakers in the Carter Administration came to share a view held by some students of Soviet military strategy: "Namely, that Soviet decision-makers considered victory to be possible in nuclear war and that they were actively preparing to achieve such a victory, should nuclear war occur." Mr. Sloss said their study focused on the possibilities of a protracted nuclear war, which led to a redefinition of the secure reserve force envisioned previously by Mr. Schlesinger. The review put new emphasis on a command and communications apparatus that would endure repeated nuclear strikes and thus would permit the President to order the nuclear forces to respond with a variety of measured, controlled strikes.

In another shift in emphasis, Mr. Sloss said targets were chosen with the intent of "destroying logistics and industries providing immediate support to the enemy war effort" rather than of impeding economic recovery. Increased emphasis was given "to the targeting of enemy military forces and political-military leadership," Mr. Sloss wrote. In addition, he said, the distinction between long-range and medium-range nuclear forces was blurred as "it was becoming clear that nuclear forces ought to be considered as a continuum."

President Carter signed PD-59 in July 1980, and Secretary Brown made public its key points in an address at the Naval War College in Newport, Rhode Island, asserting that it was a "refinement" of earlier policy. "The fundamental premises of our countervailing strategy," Mr. Brown said, "are a natural evolution of the conceptual foundations built over the course of a generation by, for example, Secretaries McNamara and Schlesinger." ("Countervailing" meant the United States would retaliate by striking a Soviet target of equal value to the target the Soviet Union had struck in the United States.)

"In our analysis and planning," Mr. Brown went on, "we are necessarily giving greater attention to how a nuclear war would actually be fought by both sides if deterrence fails." He said the new strategy emphasized "being able to employ strategic nuclear forces selectively, as well as by all-out retaliation in response to massive attacks on the United States." The United States, if attacked, would seek to "exact an unacceptably high price in the things the Soviet leaders appear to value most—political and military control, military forces both nuclear and conventional, and the industrial capability to sustain war." In addition, "we have, and we will keep, a survivable and enduring capability to attack the full range of targets, including the Soviet economic base, if that is the appropriate response to a Soviet strike."

According to William Beecher of *The Boston Globe*, the target list in PD-59 included 700 underground shelters for Soviet leaders, 1,400 silos housing intercontinental ballistic missiles, which is the primary muscle in the Soviet nuclear force, and 600 bunkers, storage sites, and airfields for bombers. In addition, there were 3,000 military units, supply depots, transportation centers, and similar military targets. Lastly, he said, the list included 200 to 400 factories producing arms and matériel.

Along with PD-59 went two other Presidential Directives, one providing for the continuity of government in a nuclear conflict, the other establishing a national security telecommunications policy to support a protracted nuclear war. To preserve the continuity of government, the first directive specified the line of succession in the military chain of command, which is not the same as the constitutional line of succession through the Vice-President, the Speaker of the House, and the President pro tem of the Senate. Designating military successors was intended to enable the United States to carry on if the President had been killed or incapacitated. That chain of command ran from the President to the Secretary of Defense but did not include the Vice-President, to preclude the remote temptation that a Vice-President might one day try to seize control of the armed forces to stage a coup. Precisely where the chain of command went after the Secretary of Defense was a carefully guarded secret, so that an enemy could not know for certain who should be a target. It presumably included the Chairman of the Joint Chiefs of Staff, the Commander in Chief of the Strategic Air Command and his bomber and missile commands, and the Chief of Naval Operations and his captains of submarines armed with ballistic missiles.

The telecommunications directive called for acquiring radio, telephone, telex, and other communications that could endure a nuclear conflict and thus provide connections between the President and the Secretary of Defense, or their successors, and the commanders of the nuclear forces.

In his address at Newport, however, Secretary Brown expressed skepticism that the countervailing strategy could be executed in the deliberate fashion that PD-59 dictated. "We are also not unaware of the immense uncertainties involved in any use of nuclear weapons," he said. "We know that what might start as a supposedly controlled, limited strike could well—in my view, would very likely—escalate to a full-scale nuclear war."

President Reagan took the oath of office in January 1981, with less exposure to the arcane world of nuclear arms than any of his predecessors in the thirty-five years of the nuclear era. Nor did his Secretary of Defense, Caspar W. Weinberger, have any particular expertise in nuclear matters. Their guidepost was the Republican campaign platform, which called for "military and technological superiority over the Soviet Union."

Nonetheless, the President and the Secretary of Defense, relying on specialists they brought into the administration, have presided over a new evolution in nuclear doctrine. In particular, their doctrine has emphasized fighting a nuclear war and prevailing. In its first *Defense Guidance*, the annual plan that set the strategic underpinning for the military budget, the administration laid out its strategic objectives:

The primary role of U.S. strategic nuclear forces is deterrence of nuclear attack on the United States, its forces, and its allies and friends. Should such an attack nevertheless occur, United States nuclear capabilities must prevail even under the condition of a prolonged war.

To reach that goal, the Reagan Administration formulated the most ambitious program for acquiring nuclear weapons the nation had seen in twenty-five years. By the end of the first term, the objectives were clear:

• To regain nuclear superiority over the Soviet Union. Senior officials muted that theme in public, but private conversations and documents left little doubt that they saw nuclear superiority as the best way to deter the Soviet Union. Robert Jastrow, a physicist at Dartmouth College and supporter of the President's nuclear strategy, reflected the thinking of the administration. "The destructive power of the Soviet nuclear arsenal," he wrote in 1983, "is now more than twice as great as that of the United States." Mr. Jastrow quoted the Russian writer Aleksandr Solzhenitsyn on how that power could lead to Soviet blackmail. According to Mr. Solzhenitsyn, the Soviet Union would declare, "Attention. We're marching our troops to Europe, and if you make a move, we will annihilate you." The Russian continued, "and this ratio of three to one, of five to one, will have its effect: you will not make a move." Professor Jastrow argued that was the reason nuclear superiority mattered. "He who can blow up the world three times," he contended, "has more power than he who can blow it up only twice."

- To be able to fight and win a nuclear war, whether limited, protracted, or all-out, if deterrence fails. The rhetoric of the Reagan Administration denied that any nuclear war was "winnable." But *Defense Guidance* made clear that every form of nuclear war had been contemplated. Secretary Weinberger was quoted more than once saying, "You show me a Secretary of Defense who is not planning to prevail and I'll show you a Secretary of Defense who ought to be impeached." In a letter on nuclear policy to seventy newspapers in 1982, he said, "We must have a capability for a survivable and enduring response—to demonstrate that our strategic forces could survive Soviet strikes over an extended period." In a speech at the Army War College, he said: "We must have a capability for a 'protracted' response to demonstrate that our strategic forces could survive Soviet strikes over an extended, that is to say, protracted period. Thus, we believe that we could deter any attack."

- To exploit technology so the Soviet Union would spend money, time, and energy to counter it. A senior official in the Pentagon said that aim was among the reasons the administration would accelerate development of the Stealth bomber, which was designed to evade radar. If the plane worked, it would make the vast Soviet radar network obsolete and would most likely force the Russians to seek a new radar that could detect the Stealth bomber. The official said the administration would rather see the Soviet Union spend money on radar, which cannot attack the United States, than on new missiles. In a wider sense, the technical strategy called on American scientists to compete with the Soviet Union by designing weapons that would render obsolete the accumulated Soviet stocks of equipment. It would impose costs on the Soviets by making uncertain their ability to defend air space, to protect command centers and communications lines, or to ensure that nuclear submarines would survive.

- To entice or force the Soviet Union into negotiations on arms control. From the beginning, President Reagan and Mr. Weinberger said the United States should enter negotiations on arms control with the Soviet Union only after they had begun to "rearm America," particularly in modernizing the nuclear forces. At the beginning of Mr. Reagan's second term, the Soviet Union agreed to renew talks on arms control, which prompted officials of the Reagan Administration to assert that their strategy had been correct.

Among the nuclear thinkers brought into the Administration was Mr. Iklé, the Under Secretary of Defense for Policy. He led a review that concluded with an endorsement of the Carter Administration's doctrine expressed in PD-59, then supervised the drafting of National Security Decision Directive 13 (NSDD-13) for President Reagan's signature in October 1981. Mr. Iklé took charge of drafting *Defense Guidance*, which Secretary Weinberger approved in March 1982. In a covering statement to the 1982 document, Mr. Weinberger said this "first complete *Defense Guidance*" was the "foundation stone" for rebuilding the nation's defenses.

Those documents provided the rationale behind a costly program to acquire forces and weapons to execute the nuclear strategy. A professor of government at American University in Washington, Jeffrey Richelson, wrote an analysis of PD-59 and NSDD-13 in which he said both set forth doctrines for fighting a protracted nuclear war if deterrence failed. But the Reagan Administration's directive went beyond that of the Carter Administration, Mr. Richelson said. NSDD-13 "suggested the need for a revised acquisition strategy—both in terms of increasing acquisition and creating procedures with which strategy and acquisition could be coordinated."

The nuclear doctrine enunciated in NSDD-13 was laid out in more detail in *Defense Guidance*. The 1982 version, a document that was classified secret and modified only slightly in subsequent years, set missions for long-range missiles, bombers, and submarine-based missiles that could attack Soviet political, economic, and military targets. Fuller passages than those in 1982 press reports are cited here to provide context, to give the flavor of official thinking, and to illustrate the arcane language of nuclear war. *Defense Guidance* set six missions for strategic, long-range nuclear forces:

- "Promote deterrence by being convincingly capable of responding to a first strike in such a way as to deny the Soviets (or any other adversary) their political and military objectives." ["First strike" in this instance meant a Soviet pre-emptive attack intended to destroy the nuclear forces of the United States before they could be employed.]

- "Minimize the extent to which Soviet nuclear threats could be used in a crisis to coerce the United States and our allies." ["Crisis" is that condition between peace and open conflict usually described as rising tensions.]
- "Maintain the capacity to support Alliance commitments." ["Alliance" meant the North Atlantic Treaty Organization, but included Japan and other nations to which the United States has commitments.]
- "Should deterrence fail, deny the Soviet Union (or any other adversary) a military victory at any level of conflict and force earliest termination of hostilities on terms favorable to the United States." [A turgid, roundabout way of saying "we mean to win."]
- "Limit damage, by active and passive measures, to the United States and its allies." ["Damage limitation," in this instance, meant a quick reaction to a Soviet strike to prevent more missiles from being fired at the United States.]
- "Maintain in reserve, under all circumstances, nuclear offensive capabilities so that the United States would never emerge from a nuclear war without nuclear weapons while still threatened by enemy nuclear forces." [This is the heart of deterrence, the ability to take a severe hit but to have enough nuclear forces survive and be able to retaliate so effectively that the Soviet Union would quit.]

Defense Guidance sought to break down in the minds of nuclear planners a previous distinction between strategic, or long-range, forces such as bombers and intercontinental ballistic missiles, and theater, or medium-range, weapons such as fighter-bombers and cruise missiles. The long-range forces are based mostly in the United States, the medium-range forces in Europe or at sea. "Our nuclear forces—both strategic and theater—must be governed by a single, coherent doctrine," the document said. "It is important, therefore, that we do not rely on an artificial dividing line between different categories of nuclear weapons. Theater nuclear forces are an essential link between conventional forces and strategic nuclear forces."

According to *Defense Guidance*, medium-range weapons "should be capable of responding flexibly," meaning Pershing II missiles stationed in West Germany could be aimed at targets in the Soviet Union, not just East Germany. Similarly, long-range weapons, such as bombers, "capable of executing theater nuclear options may be tasked for those missions." Moreover, a Russian nuclear attack at sea might cause an American nuclear attack on the Soviet homeland: "It will be U.S. policy that a nuclear war beginning with Soviet nuclear attacks at sea will not necessarily remain limited to the sea."

Defense Guidance laid out strategies for nuclear weapons in peace, crisis, and war. In peacetime,

"U.S. forces sufficient for retaliation will be maintained and operated under all conditions of war initiation to survive a Soviet first strike. Plans will be prepared to attack a wide range of potential targets, including those which may emerge in the course of a conflict, and will be drawn up in such a manner to permit appropriate responses to any level of aggression. . . . Those plans will provide the National Command Authority the maximum degree of flexibility in executing employment options. Plans and forces will be structured so that the U.S. would never be without nuclear offensive forces as long as U.S. enemies shall possess such forces.

(National Command Authority is Pentagon jargon for the President, Secretary of Defense, and the senior officials they designate as immediate subordinates.)

"The United States will forward deploy theater nuclear forces to those areas where our allies accept them and where they enhance deterrence and support the military strategy," the document said.

Planning should recognize that release will neither be immediate nor automatic. Plans for the first use and possible follow-on uses of theater nuclear forces should be developed which give the National Command Authority the flexibility to use theater nuclear forces at a variety of levels.

(The "release" of nuclear weapons meant that they would be fired only on the authority of the President or the Secretary of Defense, if that authority had been delegated to him. "First use" meant the United States might not wait for the Soviet Union to strike with nuclear weapons but would keep open the option of using them in an attempt to repel an invasion of Western Europe by conventional Soviet forces.) Because American nuclear forces are usually on alert, not much would change in a crisis. "Conventional forces, theater nuclear forces, and strategic nuclear forces will be brought to, and maintained at, the state of increased readiness required to demonstrate resolve and prepare for military operations."

In the section on fighting a nuclear war with the Soviet Union, *Defense Guidance*, although repetitious, gave the fullest exposition of the Reagan Administration's nuclear doctrine. The passage suggested that the doctrine was more demanding than those of earlier administrations, calling on United States nuclear forces to be ready to attack thousands of military, economic, and political targets. *Defense Guidance* appeared to put almost equal emphasis on the targets to be struck, unlike the varying emphases set down by earlier administrations, and set victory as the national objective: "The United States must prevail and be able to force the Soviet Union to seek earliest termination of hostilities on terms favorable to the United States."

Defense Guidance outlined the nuclear forces envisioned by the administration as a blueprint for officials who would develop and acquire those forces and for officers who would fashion the intricate war plans that nuclear weapons demand.

Planning officers were instructed to design war plans that would cause the "decapitation" of the Soviet Union. In nuclear parlance, an attack intended to kill large numbers of political and military leaders, thus crippling an enemy's political apparatus, is called "decapitation." *Defense Guidance* said war plans must make sure that

U.S. strategic nuclear forces can render ineffective the total Soviet (and Soviet-allied) military and political power structure through attacks on political/military leadership and associated control facilities, nuclear and conventional military forces, and industry critical to military power.

At the same time, war planners were instructed to "provide for limiting damage to the United States and its allies to the maximum extent possible." ("Limiting damage" refers to efforts to destroy Soviet nuclear forces before they attack.) The United States has kept open the option of "launch on warning" or "launch under attack," which means a retaliatory strike might be launched when unmistakable evidence shows the Soviet Union has launched missiles, but before the warheads hit the United States. The response would be aimed at missiles still in the Soviet Union and at command centers controlling them.

Defense Guidance said American nuclear forces must be able to maintain, throughout a protracted conflict, the ability to attack Soviet industry, transport centers, power-generating stations, and cities to deter a Soviet attack on American cities. The document asked for war plans intended "to inflict very high levels of damage against the industrial/economic base of the Soviet Union and her allies, so that they have a strong incentive to seek conflict termination short of all-out attack on our cities and economic assets."

Vital to the conduct of a protracted nuclear war would be enduring communications among the President, his senior advisers, the commanders of the nuclear forces, and missile, bomber, and submarine crews. Intelligence on what enemy weapons had been launched and on the damage they had caused would be equally vital. So would assessment of the damage that American strikes had caused in the Soviet Union. *Defense Guidance* said the network of sensors and communications must enable the President to control "nuclear counterattacks over a protracted period while maintaining a reserve of nuclear forces sufficient for trans- and post-attack protection and coercion." ("Trans-attack" meant during a Soviet nuclear attack, "post-attack" after it was over.)

Finally, *Defense Guidance* instructed planners to refurbish defenses against bomber attacks, which had long been neglected because the Soviet Union's nuclear forces had been built largely around long-range missiles. The document instructed planners to prepare defenses against cruise missiles, which are new on the nuclear scene. The war planners were asked to integrate medium-range nuclear forces with conventional forces "to achieve theater campaign objectives."

Defense Guidance further specified a United States nuclear force in which "greater emphasis will be placed on the multiplicity of strategic systems and basing modes to strengthen" the existing triad of long-range bombers, intercontinental ballistic missiles, and submarine-launched ballistic missiles. The purpose would be "to complicate Soviet defense and attack planning, to create synergism among our strategic force elements in attack planning and execution, and to hedge against unforeseen degradations in individual force elements." ("Synergism," a favorite word of nuclear planners, meant that each of the different weapons, such as bombers and missiles, reinforced the others so that the sum was greater than the total of the parts.) For the Russian war planner, attacking American bombers, land-based missiles, and sea-based missiles would generate different demands. Launching a missile attack against American missile silos in the Midwest, for instance, would warn American bombers to make emergency takeoffs from their alert bases. Firing short-range submarine missiles at bomber bases in the United States could trigger a massive salvo of long-range missiles aimed at Soviet missile silos. Coordinating those strikes, according to the thinking behind *Defense Guidance*, was made more complicated for the Soviet war planner by the differences in American weapons, especially their basing.

Even as his nuclear doctrine was being fashioned, President Reagan set out to achieve a greater "multiplicity" of nuclear weapons. The administration inherited a nuclear force that comprised 315 B-52 bombers, 1,000 Minuteman intercontinental missiles, and 41 Polaris and Poseidon submarines armed with ballistic missiles. In addition were medium-range aircraft, such as the FB-111, that can carry nuclear bombs; Pershing I medium-range ballistic missiles, with Pershing II missiles under development; artillery, land mines, and antisubmarine weapons for tactical nuclear warfare; and cruise missiles under development for launch from air, sea, or land.

The administration began an expansion of that force shortly after the President took office. In the summer of 1981, the President approved production of the neutron warhead, sometimes called the advanced radiation warhead. President Carter had ordered components of the neutron warhead manufactured but had forbidden assembly into a weapon. The neutron warhead generates less blast than other nuclear weapons, but more radiation. Militarily, it is considered useful against concentrations of tanks or artillery, as neutron detonations would kill enemy soldiers with less damage to surrounding buildings. Secretary of Defense Weinberger said the neutron warhead could "neutralize or pretty well balance by its very presence . . . a tremendous preponderance of armor and men that is definitely on the side of the Soviets in the central front" of Europe.

Within a few weeks came the administration's biggest program for nuclear weapons. Amid considerable fanfare, President Reagan and Mr. Weinberger in October 1981 announced a five-part program that would cost $180 billion over the coming five years. The President decided to cut the proposal to build long-disputed MX intercontinental ballistic missiles from the 200 missiles in President Carter's plan to 100 missiles. The President dumped the Carter plan to keep the missiles in motion on "race tracks" in the deserts of Utah and Nevada. But he and Mr. Weinberger left open the question of where the missiles would eventually be deployed and asked a commission of experts to find a way to base them. President Reagan revived the plan to build 100 B-1 bombers (a plan canceled by President Carter) and instructed the Air Force to press ahead with the Stealth bomber, which is designed to evade radar. He ordered the Navy to accelerate development of the Trident II, or D-5, submarine-launched ballistic missile, intended to be more accurate and more powerful than the Trident I missile. The Reagan program called for refurbishing air defenses against bomber attack. Finally, it called for $20 billion to improve communications connecting the President, the Secretary of Defense, and senior military commanders with bomber, missile, and submarine crews.

Although the decision on MX captured the headlines at the time, the most important element was the plan to revitalize the command and control system to fight a nuclear war if deterrence failed. The program included improved sensors to detect the firing of Soviet nuclear missiles or the movement of bombers and submarines; better command posts and computers to evaluate information; protected places for leaders who would make decisions in fighting a nuclear war; and radio, telex, and telephone communications that could not be disrupted by repeated nuclear assaults.

The existing apparatus included satellites over the Soviet Union and the Atlantic and Pacific oceans to detect the launch of land-based or submarine-based missiles. Giant radar stations in England, Greenland, and Alaska could pick up the trajectory of missiles as they rose above the horizon. Other radar stations in North Dakota and on both seacoasts would track the warheads as they approached targets in the United States. Primary evaluation would be done at the North American Aerospace Defense Command's center deep inside Cheyenne Mountain, near Colorado Springs. But other evaluations would be made at the Strategic Air Command near Omaha in Nebraska, the National Military Command Center in the Pentagon, and the Alternate National Military Command Center at Fort Ritchie in Maryland, near the presidential retreat at Camp David. A large fortified bunker had been constructed underground in Mount Weather in northern Virginia, west of Washington, in which the President and other senior officials could take refuge if they had sufficient warning to flee from Washington before a nuclear attack. In addition, nearly 100 bunkers called the Federal Relocation Arc were scattered around the District of Columbia, Maryland, Virginia, West Virginia, and Pennsylvania to house federal officials so they could continue to function after a nuclear attack.

Of two airborne command posts, one was always aloft. The National Emergency Airborne Command Post, whose acronym NEACP is pronounced "knee-cap," was aboard one of four Boeing 747 airliners crammed with electronic and communications gear for the President or his designated subordinate, and sitting on alert at an airbase in the Middle West. Always aloft was one of several C-135 aerial transports similarly equipped for the Commander in Chief of the Strategic Air Command and codenamed Looking Glass. But the radio, telephone, and telex lines, switching gear, and computers could be knocked out with a high aerial burst of a nuclear warhead, producing an electromagnetic impulse and a surge of electricity that could burn out electrical equipment over half the United States. Explosions like that could make the nation blind, deaf, and dumb.

Planned improvements included new satellites and radar for detection. Among them was the Integrated Operations Nuclear Detection System, scheduled to go up late in the 1980s to detect nuclear explosions in the atmosphere and in space. New sensors on satellites watching the Soviet Union were planned to detect missile launches. The warning system of radar stations in Britain, Greenland, and Alaska was to be improved with more modern equipment, as would be the radar stations on the east and west coasts and those looking south.

The Air Force satellite communications system became operational in 1984. A program to modernize the Defense Satellite Communication System that transmits missile warnings to command centers was begun. New satellites were planned for Milstar, a network of seven satellites scheduled to be in operation by 1990 to provide worldwide, jam-resistant communications. Satellites were mounted atop Minuteman missiles ready for launch into space to replace satellites damaged in a nuclear war. Others were launched into deep space where they have been "parked" until they might be needed, when they would be recalled into lower, operating orbits. To protect satellites from discovery, some will be coated with new composite materials that do not register on radar. Others will be encased in materials that would resist radiation from nuclear explosions in space. Still others will have small rocket motors to escape threats.

On the ground, work was begun on the Ground Wave Emergency Network, or GWEN, of 300 to 500 relay stations. It was designed so at least part would endure a nuclear attack and be ready to switch messages through whatever stations survived. New message terminals were to be installed in bombers, communications to newly deployed missiles in Europe were laid down, and work began on the Extremely Low Frequency, or ELF, antenna buried in northern Michigan and Wisconsin to transmit messages through the earth to submarines in the depths of the oceans. Work was begun on a new mobile command post for the President. At the Strategic Air Command, a truck loaded with communications gear and computers was called HERT, for Headquarters Emergency Relocation Team. The Air Force also deployed a mobile unit at Norad called RAPIER—Rapid Emergency Reconstitution—to take over if the missile warning complex inside Cheyenne Mountain were destroyed.

To provide the President and other authorities a refuge more protected than those in existence, the Air Force began studies of a command post deep underground. Direction for that project came from the 1983 *Defense Guidance*, which instructed that "an enduring command center" be ready in the early 1990s. The reason given in public for the deep underground base was a possible haven for a secure reserve force of intercontinental missiles. But Defense Department officials said it was also under consideration as a command post. Borrowing technology and experience from submarines, in which crews remain submerged for months at a time, the Air Force found ways for crews to live underground for long periods, providing their own recycled air, electric power, water, and waste disposal.

In weapons, the Trident II, or D-5, ballistic missile to be carried in submarines got less attention than the MX but was probably more important to the Reagan Administration's nuclear strategy because submarines have the best chance of surviving a nuclear attack. The Trident II's schedule of deployment was advanced to make it operational in 1989. The new missile's range of 5,000 miles is the same as that of Trident I but its payload of 135,000 pounds in warheads is twice that of Trident I, and its accuracy is estimated at 400 feet (meaning a warhead was expected to land within 400 feet of its target) compared with 1,500 feet for its predecessor. Thus Trident II was said to be capable of destroying the most heavily fortified military targets in the Soviet Union.

Seven of the 18,000-ton Trident submarines, the first of which was named for the state of Ohio, were at sea by mid-1986. The Reagan Administration planned to build at least fifteen more over the next ten years. Each submarine has twenty-four tubes, for a total of 480 missiles, and is capable of staying at sea for seventy days and roaming under 40 million square miles of water, or 30 percent of the earth's oceans. With less time in port needed to switch crews—each ship has two—and to take on provisions, officers estimated that 66 percent of the Trident fleet could be on patrol at any given time, making it a formidable force.

In the air, a fleet of 100 B-1 bombers, which are improved versions of the aircraft designed in the 1970s, are scheduled to be in operation by 1988. The new bomber was designed to carry bombs and air-launched cruise missiles, with emphasis shifting to cruise missiles in the 1990s as Soviet defenses improve and the need for a "standoff" weapon increase. The second bomber, the Stealth aircraft, featured new technologies, such as rounded contours, hidden engine exhausts, composite materials for the skin of the aircraft, radar-absorbent coatings, and radar-suppressing electronics. That technology, which was a closely guarded secret, was intended to reduce the radar "signature" of the aircraft, or its appearance on a radar scope, to practically nothing. Contrary to a general impression, the Stealth bomber was intended to be a companion, not a successor, to the B-1. In a nuclear war, the B-1s would attack less protected targets while Stealth bombers would be sent against targets with formidable radar and missile defenses. Both would go after mobile targets and those that had escaped warheads from missiles. Stealth bombers were scheduled to be operating in the early 1990s. The B-52s would continue in service, largely as cruise-missile carriers that would stand off 1,500 miles from their targets to launch missiles.

Easily the most disputed element of the President's nuclear program was the MX missile, which the administration called Peace-keeper. At nearly fifty tons, it had been designed to carry ten warheads 7,000 miles. Each warhead should hit within 300 feet of its target and would be able to destroy a missile silo, command center, or base that had been hardened with steel and concrete.

The controversy over MX was less with the missile itself, although many liberal and leftist groups opposed it, than with its base. Some thirty-five different land, underground, sea, submarine, and aerial bases were rejected for various military, cost, or political reasons. The underlying issue was this salient fact: No unprotected, stationary missile base in the United States could survive a heavy nuclear attack, given the increasing numbers, explosive power, and accuracy of Soviet missiles. Even those who favored a buildup of American nuclear forces expressed doubts about spending enormous sums of money on missiles that could not survive an attack. By the end of 1985, after years of wrangling, the Congress and the Reagan Administration agreed that fifty of the MX missiles would be deployed in Minuteman silos unless the administration could come up with another base acceptable to the Congress. Those fifty missiles were in marked contrast with the 200 originally envisioned by the Carter Administration.

One method of protected land basing, however, remained possible, and that was deep underground. (With the penchant of the Pentagon to assign acronyms to nearly everything, this project was quickly, if informally, called Deep Underground Missile Basing, or DUMB.) In the summer of 1984, the Air Force completed a series of tests, then advised the Secretary of Defense in a top-secret memorandum that a deep underground base was feasible technically and militarily. The Air Force said the deep base could house the missiles of the secure reserve force specified in *Defense Guidance* to survive a nuclear attack and be ready for retaliation or to fight a prolonged war.

The underground base would look like a 400-mile rectangular network of subways built 2,500 to 3,500 feet below the surface, probably under a desert in the southwestern United States, and would be able to survive for a year without supplies from the surface. The mission of the base's crew would be to wait out a nuclear barrage on the surface, then dig out with tunneling machines like those used to build subways. The initial legs of the exit tunnels would already have been started; even so, it would take many days, or even weeks, to bore a shaft to the surface. The shafts would be on a shallow angle, up which a missile would be driven to the surface on a transporter. There, from a known point from which to calculate, the missile would be fired. The Air Force said the base could be completed by the mid-1990s.

In addition, the uncertainties over MX caused a presidential commission led by a retired Air Force officer, Lieutenant General Brent Scowcroft, who had been national security adviser to President Ford, to recommend development of a small, mobile intercontinental ballistic missile. Dubbed Midgetman, the missile would probably carry only one warhead for 6,000 miles, making it less destructive than MX. But the fifteen-ton missile would be launched from a mobile transporter that could be kept in motion on a large expanse of government territory, or hidden in the side of a mountain from which it would "dash" to one of several designated firing points on warning of an attack. Midgetman could be based, either by itself or in a mix with MX missiles, in the deep underground base, according to the Air Force. Testing was due to be completed in 1988, with production to begin in 1990 and the missiles to be operational by 1992.

In another program, the United States began deploying to Europe in 1984 new Pershing II medium-range ballistic missiles under an agreement reached with West Europeans by President Carter. Many Europeans, particularly West Germans, wanted a more visible sign of the American nuclear commitment. President Carter agreed to replace Pershing I missiles with 108 Pershing II missiles, which have a range of 1,500 miles, compared with 460 miles for the earlier version. Equally important, the Pershing II has a smaller warhead with much greater accuracy, making it a more lethal weapon. Deployment of the Pershing IIs to West Germany was completed before the end of 1985.

Still another set of missiles were cruise missiles, the production of which was increased early in the Reagan Administration, that could be launched from ground, the sea surface, below the sea, or the air. A cruise missile is a flying torpedo about eighteen feet long, with stubby wings and a small jet engine. Once launched, the cruise missile flies several tens of feet above the ground, steering itself through the terrain. Sensors "read" the ground below and compare it with a map stored in the missile's computer. If the missile strays from its prescribed course, the sensors advise the computer to order a correction. At launch, ground-launched cruise missiles immediately pick up known points of reference and begin tracking their course. Air-launched and sea-launched cruise missile are guided by inertial navigation systems measuring speed, direction, and wind drift until they reached a known point, when the sensors pick up the terrain features and guide the missile to the target. The key feature of the cruise missile is its flat trajectory close to the ground, where it can move through a radar beam so quickly that it will have come and gone before air defense units on the ground can react.

The United States deployed the first of 464 ground-launched cruise missiles to Europe in conjunction with the Pershing II missiles in 1984, with deployment scheduled to be completed by 1988. At the same time, submarines began taking on Tomahawk cruise missiles; later, the Navy planned to arm four battleships being brought out of retirement with even more cruise missiles. The Air Force began carrying the first version of air-launched cruise missiles aboard converted B-52 bombers in 1982. Two years later, the Reagan Administration switched to an advanced missile made with Stealth technology to make it even more difficult to detect. The air-launched cruise missiles are operationally tested with a B-52 flying to the far north of Canada, turning south and launching the missile over the Canadian tundra, which resembles Siberia. The missiles, which fly over sparsely inhabited regions to land in a base at Cold Lake in the province of Alberta, were said to be very accurate. "From 750 miles away, if it carries a bigger, conventional warhead, we can put it into RFK stadium," said a Pentagon official. "From 1,500 miles away, with the smaller nuclear warhead, we can fly it through the goalposts."

The ambition, strategy, and cost of the Reagan Administration's nuclear program has drawn criticism from many quarters. To the chagrin of some conservative supporters, the administration proceeded without having set forth its nuclear policy to justify its programs to the American public. Colin Gray, president of the National Institute of Public Policy, a private research organization near Washington, accused the Reagan Administration of acting without thinking:

The Administration chose to announce its strategic forces modernization program on October 2, 1981, before it delivered a comprehensive policy story that would explain the relevance of these weapons to the problems it identified and before it announced a politically attractive arms control policy. Because of this, the Administration appeared to be favoring weapons that had no strategic-policy meaning. It also appeared to be more interested in building weapons than in containing the pace and scope of the arms race. So, while the Reagan Administration has not been indifferent to strategy or arms control, it has appeared as such.

Mr. Gray said if the administration believed the United States should be able to limit the damage it might suffer in nuclear war, it should say so. "The public can and should be told," Mr. Gray asserted, "that to plan for victory in nuclear war is to plan for the United States to accomplish its policy purposes, whatever they may be at the time."

A contrary, but equally critical, view came from Paul Bracken, a political scientist at Yale and onetime member of Herman Kahn's Hudson Institute. "There is a pervasive sense among both critics of nuclear weapons and strategists inside the security establishment that questions of how nuclear weapons would really be used are questions of irremediable insanity," he said in his book *The Command and Control of Nuclear Forces* in 1983.

What passes for a strategic debate is little more than construction of a facade of nuclear logic to permit getting on with the day-to-day job of deterrence. The most that can be said for this practice is that creating a veneer of rationality in the discussion of nuclear strategy is a ritual used to convince opponents that we are serious about deterrence. In many instances, the motivation is even harder to identify, serving only as a psychological defense mechanism against what is, at bottom, an issue of madness.

Widespread skepticism inside and outside the government focused on the question of whether the administration's nuclear strategy could be executed, no matter how much money was spent and how many weapons were acquired. There was serious question that anyone would survive a nuclear exchange to be in charge of fighting a subsequent war, given the likelihood of a decapitating strike. In particular, there was strong doubt that the communications system would survive to transmit orders to the forces over a period of days or weeks.

The General Accounting Office, surveying the nuclear force after President Carter's PD-59 had been signed but before President Reagan launched his nuclear program, concluded that existing forces "will not provide all the capabilities needed to fully carry out the strategy." In a 1981 report, the GAO said, "While weapons systems need to be improved, improvements to the command, control, and communications network must be given a high priority if the United States is to implement counter-vailing strategy."

After it became known in 1982 that the Reagan Administration's policy was to prepare for protracted nuclear war if deterrence failed, General David C. Jones of the Air Force, who was about to retire as Chairman of the Joint Chiefs of Staff, scoffed. "If you try to do everything to fight a protracted nuclear war," he told a group of military correspondents, "then you end up with the potential of a bottomless pit." He supported plans to protect weapons and communications so they could survive an initial nuclear strike, but he said, "I don't see much chance of a nuclear war being limited or protracted" without "a tremendous likelihood of it escalating" into a full exchange. "In defense, we are in the priority business," he added. "We can't do everything. I personally would not spend a lot of money on a protracted nuclear war."

For the last twenty years, according to Alan J. Vick, a specialist in nuclear doctrine at the Rand Corporation, the California think tank, students of defense "have focused on command and control survival as the most profound problem among the operational necessities of nuclear war." He wrote that "the current communications system was predicated upon the belief that nuclear war would consist of one exceptionally destructive attack and one equally total retaliation. The demands placed upon a system that has only to function once, then crawl in a corner and die, are quite straightforward. Current strategy, however, demands a more robust system, one capable of surviving and operating under nuclear conditions for weeks." Four years after President Reagan pronounced his plan to modernize the nuclear force, Mr. Vick said, elements of the command system "are few, large, and inherently vulnerable to nuclear effects."

Doubts that a nuclear exchange could be limited to deliberate strikes came from Barry R. Schneider, an analyst at the National Institute for Public Policy:

The danger of decapitation attacks would seem to make a mockery of the idea of fighting limited nuclear wars, or protracted nuclear wars. Even if the U.S. leaders somehow survived a first-wave Soviet attack, our command and control network is so perishable in a nuclear environment that a slow, tit-for-tat "walk" up and down the escalation ladder seems unlikely. . . . The command, control, communications, and intelligence technology simply is not there.

He said that even if large sums were spent to modernize the network, it was not likely to be effective: "The problems of adequately protecting the network and the leadership simply dwarf the available near-term solutions. Once begun, a nuclear exchange between the superpowers is likely to be massive and virtually uncontrollable."

Bruce G. Blair, a research associate at the Brookings Institution in Washington, wrote a book called *Strategic Command and Control* in 1985, then joined the Defense Department to work on those issues. He ticked off seven shortcomings in the Reagan Administration's nuclear strategy:

First, the existing command structure cannot begin to support a doctrine of extended nuclear flexible response. Second, standard calculations of a Soviet advantage in protracted counterforce exchanges bear no relation to actual circumstances because they presuppose a command structure that does not exist. Third, the technological and procedural foundations of such a structure have scarcely been defined, much less conceived. Fourth, procurement of such a structure has not been funded, is bound to be costly, and would compete with force modernization programs for scarce resources. Fifth, preparing forces and command networks for protracted intercontinental nuclear war is not palatable to significant segments of the defense community, a fact that dims the outlook for financial authorization. Sixth, even if the large outlays required for extensive command modernization are ultimately approved, the investment would surely stimulate aggressive Soviet development of countermeasures. A final point, and of key significance, is that pressures for preemptive attack or immediate retaliation would remain strong even if substantial improvements in the versatility, survivability, and endurance of the command structure were realized.

Testimony on flaws in communications came from General Robert T. Herres, Commander in Chief at Norad, who told Congress in 1986: "The Soviets possess a substantial capability to jam our communications resources. Fixed and mobile jammers can impact virtually every frequency band our communications systems use. Additionally, high-altitude nuclear weapons could be used to disrupt our present satellite and radio networks." General Herres, an Air Force officer, said Norad relied primarily on commercially leased communications to transmit warning messages from Norad's underground center in Cheyenne Mountain in Colorado to Washington or to SAC headquarters in Omaha. "But they are not hardened against nuclear weapons effects nor the threat from electronic jamming," he said. Norad also used the Air Force satellite communication system, known as AFSATCOM, and a jam-resistant system in the defense satellite communication system called JRSC. "That's all we have today," he said, "commercial circuits, AFSATCOM, and JRSC. . . . We do not have enough capability on each system to cover all Norad and U.S. Space Command missions."

Skepticism about protracted nuclear war in the workaday world came from an insider, Colonel Richard L. Walker of the Air Force, who held impressive credentials. He had advanced degrees in nuclear engineering and applied science; served in the Strategic Air Command on the Joint Strategic Target Staff, which continually revises target lists for the nuclear forces; and worked in the Defense Nuclear Agency. While a research fellow at the National Defense University, a senior

military educational institution in Washington, Colonel Walker wrote
a treatise entitled *Strategic Target Planning: Bridging the Gap Between
Theory and Practice*. He stated this question: "Are the policymakers
who are responsible for developing and refining strategy aware of the
basic limitations that become fully apparent only in the practical-
estimate mode of strategic analysis?"

He asserted that nuclear war–fighting imposed a burden on the
targeting staff "simply from the vast number of calculations required.
. . . As increased flexibility is introduced, the burden increases at least
in a linear fashion." Colonel Walker said relying on computers was
unwise. "The man-in-the-process approach cannot be sacrificed to
meet rising calculational demands," he contended. "An attempt to
replace the analyst with a programmed decision-making 'black box'
is not an acceptable solution." He said executing a nuclear attack plan
"is extremely involved and requires many discrete, unique decisions
that often rely on military judgment." He suggested that bomber crews
who had been briefed on flight plans, routes, and targets would find
it difficult to shift to new plans selected at the last minute. Similarly,
submarine crews could not change the guidance in their missiles from
targets that had already been programmed. Those were "basic limitations on the degree of flexibility attainable in strategic target planning.

"The most critically deficient aspect of the U.S. strategic posture,"
the colonel wrote, "is the command, control, communications, and
intelligence system. Already overstressed, the system appears inadequate for the evolving threat." In the arcane language of the nuclear
world, he wrote:

The key element in the strategic force must be a system of hardened command, control, communications, and intelligence facilities that can provide
a lasting battle management function. A system capable of reacting to strategic
warning with rapid retargeting could provide the force multiplication needed
to permit increased flexibility without excessive increases in the size of the
strategic arsenal.

For people not schooled in nuclear jargon, the colonel's thesis
meant the system of sensors to provide warning must be reliable. The
system must have command centers and protected communication
lines that could survive a nuclear blast. Enduring communications
would permit the President and senior military leaders to control
nuclear forces as the battle unfolded. Such a system, moreover, must
be able to react quickly to new warnings and to select new targets. If
the system was adequate, the majority of the bombers, missiles, and

submarines could survive an attack and be available for retaliatory strikes. Increasing the number and kinds of nuclear weapons therefore would not be needed to ensure that a sufficient number would survive for retaliation.

Colonel Walker's final admonition, however, was crystal clear: "Strategy designed in ignorance of real limitations is likely to fail."

CHAPTER 10

~~~~~~~~~~~~~~~~~~~~~~~~~~~~~~~~~~~

STAR WARS, SILENT SERVICE

I T IS the year 2003.

For the past fifteen years, relations between the United States and the Soviet Union have become increasingly antagonistic. In 1988, the Russians, frustrated by their inability to win the guerrilla war in Afghanistan, tripled the size of their force from 100,000 to 300,000 and crushed the Afghan freedom fighters. The United States and West European nations denounced Moscow in the United Nations but did little else. A year later, the Americans, equally frustrated by the running sore of the Sandinista government in Nicaragua, invaded and toppled the leftist regime in a six-month campaign that took 100,000 troops and a large support contingent.

Soviet leaders protested that the United States had resumed its nineteenth-century imperialist intervention in Latin America, but refrained from other action. The Soviet Union, unable to stamp out the drive for freedom led by the Solidarity movement in Poland, finally sent in several tank divisions in 1993 in a heavy-handed move reminiscent of earlier occupations of Budapest and Prague. The United States, buoyed by its victory in Central America, had the Central Intelligence Agency instigate rebellion among anti-Castro groups in Cuba. The Soviet Union, having steadily enlarged its intelligence operation in Mexico City, fostered guerrilla hit-and-run raids from Mexico across the border into Texas. After the turn of the century, the United States helped to arm and finance Chinese incursions into the Soviet Union along the 5,000-mile border between the giant nations. In 2001, the long-running arms negotiations in Geneva collapsed as the United States refused to give up the Strategic Defense Initiative started by President Reagan back in 1983. The Soviet Union, despite pledges to observe the SALT I and SALT II pacts banning the deployment of new missiles, had fielded new generations of mobile intercontinental ballistic missiles along the Trans-Siberian railway; both the missiles, the SS-29 and SS-30, carried ten warheads that could hit any target in the United States with pinpoint accuracy.

Meantime, the United States made steady progress in developing, testing, and deploying the antimissile shield built by the Strategic Defense Initiative Office in the Pentagon and known popularly as Star Wars. The basic research phase neared completion in 1991, and full-scale development began on sensors, protected communications lines, laser generators, and mirrors off which beams would bounce in space. Most important, designing and building computers with enormous capacities for ultra-high-speed calculations moved ahead faster than expected. As the mind and nervous system of strategic defense, those computers were intended to absorb great streams of information about large numbers of missiles and warheads launched into space, to determine trajectories in split seconds, to calculate aiming and firing orders for the weapons, and to transmit those orders. The computers were ready by 1996. Despite continuing political opposition, Congress voted sufficient funds in fiscal years 1997, 1998, and 1999 for the initial deployment of new sensors amid much ceremony in January of the year 2000. Over the next three years, more sensors were lofted into geosynchronous orbits in which the satellites moved at the same speed as the earth's rotation, thereby staying over one spot. Modern radar stations were constructed across an arc from England through Greenland and Canada to Alaska. Laser weapons were placed in bunkers sunk into western deserts of the United States where cloudy weather would least interfere with them. Others were dispersed through the central plains, but away from the silos housing Minuteman and MX nuclear missiles.

Two redundant computer sites were built, one deep in the Rocky Mountains away from the Norad warning center and the other deep inside a mountain along the Appalachian Trail in Pennsylvania. By early 2003, the system reached what military officers called "initial operating capability" and began what strategic thinkers called the transition phase. Star Wars was intended to defend missile silos in the Middle West, bomber fields along the northern tier of states, and bases for missile-bearing submarines at Kings Bay in Georgia and Bangor in the state of Washington. Priority was given to protecting the White House and other key government offices in Washington, plus bunkers built deep underground near Camp David for the President and his senior advisers, and selected military bases around the country. But the system lacked sufficient capacity yet to defend industry or cities from nuclear attack.

Beyond the scientific and technical progress, another generational change had taken place in both Soviet and American politics. In Moscow in the year 2003, the General Secretary, the top official in the

Communist Party and Soviet government, is a career party official who has risen through the ranks of the party and the bureaucracy in the provinces and then in the capital. He is sixty-one years old, having been born in 1942, and thus has no personal memory of World War II, which the Russians call the Great Patriotic War. But he had been thoroughly schooled from his earliest days on the heroism of the Soviet people and the Red Army in repelling the armies of Nazi Germany. Similarly, the Chief of the General Staff, the nation's top soldier, is fifty-nine, having been born in 1944. He, too, has no memory of the suffering of World War II, when the Soviet Union lost 20 million people. Nor has he served in battle except for a brief tour in Afghanistan.

In the United States, the leaders are a bit younger but still of the same generation. The President, born in 1947 and now fifty-six years old, never knew World War II, does not remember the Korean War, and escaped the draft during the war in Vietnam as a college and then law student. The Chairman of the Joint Chiefs of Staff, a Navy admiral of the same age, is a destroyerman who has heard only a few shots fired in anger and built his reputation in the Navy as an advocate of a maritime strategy.

Senior Soviet military officers watching the Americans deploy the antimissile shield have become, by the beginning of 2003, extraordinarily nervous. Paranoid to begin with, they have visions of the United States mounting a pre-emptive nuclear strike against Soviet missile bases. When the new antimissile defense is in place, they fear, the United States could hit the Soviet Union with reasonable certainty that Americans would suffer only moderate damage in return. Put the other way around, the United States was moving into a position in which it would be able to negate the threat of Soviet missiles. The Americans could be reasonably sure that few Soviet warheads, even if launched in a surprise attack, would penetrate the antimissile shield. Politically, the Americans could almost ignore the Soviet nuclear force.

The Chief of the General Staff in Moscow decided, therefore, that a "now or never" situation had evolved. He instructed a handful of his most experienced nuclear war planners to draw up a secret scheme for a pre-emptive strike against the United States. He told them the objective was to destroy the Star Wars weapons and computer centers, to decapitate American political leadership by destroying Washington and key military command posts, and to obliterate the military communications of the United States. After their calculations, the planners informed the Chief of General Staff that 50 percent of their warheads could get through the antimissile shield. They recommended firing

1,000 missiles with 10,000 warheads in the first salvo; with half getting through, that would put 5,000 warheads on targets. Of the 10,000 warheads, 5,000 would be aimed at the 1,000 American missile silos; 2,000 would be directed at Washington, military command posts, and communications centers; 1,000 would be aimed at submarine bases, airfields, and supply depots that support the nuclear forces; the final 1,000 would barrage likely operating areas for American ballistic missile submarines. Even though not all of the American nuclear forces would be wiped out, the Chief of the General Staff was certain the Americans, confronted with that destruction, would surrender rather than retaliate. In addition, he reasoned, the attack would sever communications between the President and the nuclear forces, making the situation so confusing the Americans could not respond.

The Chief of the General Staff and his planners briefed a cautious and skeptical Politburo for many weeks but finally obtained their approval. Every effort was made to mask preparations for the attack, but that was impossible. The exodus of Soviet leaders from Moscow, even though spread out and at night, was noticed by American diplomats in Moscow and by intelligence satellites that eavesdropped on Russian telephone conversations. Information from photographic satellites noted that Soviet ballistic-missile submarines failed to return to port on schedule, remaining hidden at sea. Other submarines left port earlier than had been routine. Still other satellite reports showed the transport of missiles along the Trans-Siberian railway to have picked up. Electronic intercepts indicated that radio message traffic had increased, especially lateral transmissions among nuclear units as they coordinated firing plans. Soviet forces in the western Soviet Union and in Eastern Europe dispersed to the field.

In the Norad warning center inside Cheyenne Mountain in Colorado, those warning signs were noted in a steady stream of intelligence reports. The warning center always operated at a high state of alert; now no one had to be told to pay special attention. Thus the Air Force lieutenant colonel in charge of the missile warning section at 3:47 one morning was almost unsurprised when the monitors lit up, lights flashed, and the klaxon sounded. When the first of the 1,000 Soviet missiles broke through the cloud cover over Siberia, they were picked up by American heat-seeking sensors in space. As the screen filled with missile traces, the lieutenant colonel conferred quickly by telephone with counterparts at the Strategic Air Command headquarters in Omaha and the National Military Command Center in the Pentagon. They immediately agreed they had all seen the same thing. The lieutenant colonel decided not to wait for confirmation from radar that would see the missiles as they rose over the horizon. He picked up a telephone that went directly to the four-star general in command of Norad, who was at home asleep. The insistent buzz—no gentle ring— woke him immediately.

"Sir," said the lieutenant colonel, "this is no drill. I repeat, sir, this is no drill. We show 1,000 missiles incoming at 1 minute 30 seconds. Confidence in the report is high. Request permission to activate Star Wars I." That was the informal code name for setting the strategic defensive system into action. Until Star Wars came along, Norad's function was to warn of an attack; only the President had the authority to order the Strategic Air Command to fire back. But the need to activate Star Wars immediately after a Soviet attack had been launched was imperative, as every second counted. The commanding general at Norad had thus been given the authority to initiate the defensive system. The general asked what the monitor screen looked like. "Sir, there is no mistake," the lieutenant colonel replied. "The screen is nearly full." "Very well," said the general, "execute. I will call the President and the Pentagon." The lieutenant colonel pulled a lever before the telephone was back on its cradle.

High in space, the sensors in satellites watching the Soviet Union transmitted a stream of data on speed, altitude, and headings of the missiles to the world's most advanced computers deep underground. The computers sorted out those data, set up a firing order, and instructed the laser guns to fire streams of energy into space. The streams struck mirrors controlled and aimed by the computers, and ricocheted off in the direction of the rising missiles. Tiny adjustments in milliseconds bounced thousands of streams at the missiles, 300 of which were blown up during the last minute of the rocket boost stage. The 700 missiles that escaped the first layer of the strategic defense launched their "buses" or containers with ten warheads each; the containers radiated enough heat for the sensors to track. A second round of streams from the laser guns showered down on the buses, knocking out 550.

The remaining 150, however, dispensed their 1,500 warheads along with 4,500 decoys, giving the radar that had picked up their tracks in space an enormously difficult task of sorting out the real from the fake. But this mid-course phase of about half the thirty-minute flight was the longest, by far, allowing the computer to order the firing of 5,000 small rockets, each carrying five small projectiles equipped with radar sensors. They formed a wall across the path of the incoming warheads and decoys that smashed into them like rocks in space, shattering on impact. Even so, 500 Soviet warheads survived and began their descent into the atmosphere, accelerating and dodging as they came down. A fourth defensive layer of particle beams, like electronic bullets, and more rockets thrown into space got all but 100 of the warheads. A close-in, point defense of the missile silos of ultra-fast-firing "Gatling" guns guided by radar knocked off forty more.

But sixty of the warheads got through. They destroyed thirty-five of the 1,000 Minuteman and MX missiles in silos sprinkled across the prairies of the Middle West. They knocked out the submarine base at Kings Bay in Georgia, the Norad warning center in Cheyenne Mountain in Colorado, and bomber bases in upstate New York, northern Michigan, and North Dakota. At sea, three of the twenty-four Trident submarines armed with ballistic missiles were lost when Soviet target officers guessed where they were operating. Nationally, about a quarter of the communications network was taken out. Cities were not targets, but some warheads were deflected off course by the battle in space, while others were inaccurate. Omaha, site of the headquarters of the Strategic Air Command, survived, but warheads exploded in a line to the west, turning Fremont, Wahoo, and Lincoln into ash. A warhead aimed at Colorado Springs fell short and detonated over the airport in Denver, incinerating every living thing in a circle a mile across. A warhead blown off course exploded in the middle of downtown Minneapolis, turning it into a wasteland of rubble and fire; another made the residential suburbs west of Chicago into an inferno; a third landed north of St. Louis near the junction of the Missouri and Mississippi Rivers, sucking tons of water into the sky, then spraying radioactive rain for miles around.

Altogether, the number of immediate deaths on and around the military bases and in the devastated cities came to nearly 20 million. Several million more were to die within days or weeks, most of them because medical care was totally inadequate and because everything, from electrical power to food distribution, came to a standstill in the areas that had been hit. The 20 million dead were thirty-five times more than all of the American dead in every war since the Revolution. It was 7 percent of the nation's population of 280 million people. It was the same number of people, military and civilian, who were killed in the Soviet Union during the six years of World War II.

But the nation's political leaders in Washington had survived. So had more than 90 percent of the land-based retaliatory missile force, 60 percent of the bombers, and most of the submarines armed with ballistic missiles. In addition, attack submarines armed with cruise missiles survived within range of the Soviet Union. Enough communications endured to permit the authorities in Washington to estimate what had happened and to be able to communicate with most of the nuclear forces. The President and his senior advisers gathered in a bunker built within a five-minute helicopter flight of the White House. During the attack, the President had ordered all forces to hold their fire.

With the damage assessments in shortly after the initial wave of the attack, the President asked for recommendations on the next move. The Secretary of State was belligerent. "All-out attack on the Soviet Union, Mr. President," he said. "They still have 12,000 warheads left." The Secretary of Defense was cautious. "Mr. President, I suggest an attack about the same size as that we have just taken," he said. "They do not have the strategic defenses we have, and will suffer more, and will quit." The admiral who was Chairman of the Joint Chiefs of Staff took a different tack. "I advise a strike to decapitate the political leadership, Mr. President," he said. "Once we have taken them out, the Soviet Union will collapse." The national security adviser suggested a slight modification. "Mr. President, I think we should add to that more shots at Moscow, Kiev, and a few other places so the Soviet leaders who do survive will know we have the upper hand both offensively and defensively," he said. "They will know they miscalculated and will quit." The Vice-President shook his head. "There is no way out of this except mutual suicide, Mr. President," he said. "We have more than 90 percent of our people still alive, and the Soviets will attack the cities if we fire back. But the Soviet Union cannot occupy us. Let's negotiate and stop this madness."

The President turned away to ponder, then turned back to the advisers standing in a semicircle around him. "Thank you, gentlemen, for your thoughtful advice," the President said. "I have decided that we will. . . ."

Fiction? Of course. Plausible? That's what the Star Wars dispute has been about since 1983.

Missiles were brought into the nuclear forces of the Soviet Union and the United States in the late 1950s. From that time until today, there has been little defense against them. Both the Soviet Union and the United States experimented with antiballistic missile defenses in the 1960s but set them aside when they signed the Anti-Ballistic Missile, or ABM, treaty in 1972. An exception was the one system the Soviet Union was allowed to build around Moscow. The United States decided against the single system it was allowed. Since then, deterrence has rested on the capacity of each nation to threaten the other with devastating retaliation if an attack was launched. That balance has been called Mutual Assured Destruction, or MAD.

President Reagan sought to change that balance on March 23, 1983, when he placed defense against nuclear missiles back on the national agenda. In a televised speech, the President startled the nation, and not a few of his own advisers, with a radical proposal:

What if free people could live secure in the knowledge that their security did not rest upon the threat of instant U.S. retaliation to deter a Soviet attack, that we could intercept and destroy strategic ballistic missiles before they reached our own soil or that of our allies? . . . I clearly recognize that defensive systems have limitations and raise certain problems and ambiguities. If paired with offensive systems, they can be viewed as fostering an aggressive policy, and no one wants that.

The President asked the nation's scientists "to give us the means of rendering these nuclear weapons impotent and obsolete." In the government, he directed that a comprehensive effort define a long-term research program, the ultimate goal of which would be to eliminate the threat posed by nuclear missiles. "We seek neither military superiority nor political advantage," the President asserted. "Our only purpose—one all people share—is to search for ways to reduce the danger of nuclear war."

Politically, the surprise was a blunder. The speech itself was vague and abstract. Few listeners knew what the President was talking about. It quickly became evident that the President and his advisers had not thought through the proposal and were not prepared to explain what it meant. For months afterward, officials in the administration gave markedly different versions of what they intended to do. Chief among those was Secretary of Defense Weinberger, who insisted that the aim was to provide a "thoroughly reliable" defense that would stop all incoming missiles and would protect not only military forces but cities and people. Others in the administration admitted that no defense was perfect but that the effort would be worthwhile because millions of lives could be saved and the nation's nuclear forces strengthened. Some officials suggested openly it would take even longer than the President had suggested before anything resembling an effective defense could be made to work. A senior technical official in the Pentagon said that the theory of strategic defense was known but that many of the practical applications were dubious and, in any event, would be enormously expensive. "We know the physics," he added, "but the engineering . . ." His voice trailed off.

The bigger political mistake of administration officials so eager to have their surprise was their failure to prepare the American public or to explain what the President's proposal was all about. That lapse cost the administration the initiative and the derisive nickname of Star Wars pinned on the proposal by political opponents. Overseas, the administration failed to consult with allies or even to inform them of what was coming. The reaction was quickly hostile, for many Europeans feared the defensive shield would protect America but abandon Europe to invasion, nuclear blackmail, or nuclear destruction.

In an attempt to bring order out of the continuing confusion around the President's policy, the White House published in January 1985 a pamphlet to define the objective of what had been belatedly given the official title of Strategic Defense Initiative. "The combined effectiveness of the defense provided by the multiple layers need not provide 100 percent protection in order to enhance deterrence significantly," the booklet said. "It need only create sufficient uncertainty in the mind of a potential aggressor concerning his ability to succeed in the purposes of his attack." Not a month later, Secretary of Defense Weinberger contradicted that statement. "The goal is clear and unchangeable," Mr. Weinberger said in his annual report to Congress. "It is to secure a thoroughly reliable defense against all incoming Soviet missiles, either intermediate or long-range, and to destroy, by nonnuclear means, those missiles before they get near any target."

Finally, in May 1985, the National Security Council drafted a National Security Decision Directive, NSDD-172, in an effort to get administration officials in harmony on the Strategic Defense Initiative, or SDI. "There are people inside the government with different concepts of what this thing is supposed to do, and people with different agendas of what they'd like it to do," an official explained. "From now on, anyone who speaks out on S.D.I. will have his speech cleared, his briefing cleared, his interview cleared. His text will be checked and he'd better stick to it."

NSDD 172, however, did not clear up the confusion. On SDI's objectives, it was almost silent. "It is too early in our research program," it said, "to speculate on the kinds of defensive systems— whether ground-based or space-based, and with what capabilities— that might prove feasible and desirable to develop and deploy."

The long road to President Reagan's speech in 1983 began in 1967, when he was the first Governor of California to visit the Lawrence Livermore National Laboratory, a leading center of research into nuclear technology. Edward Teller, the physicist who helped develop the hydrogen bomb, showed Mr. Reagan through the lab. Later, during the 1980 presidential campaign, Mr. Reagan visited the Norad missile warning center inside Cheyenne Mountain in Colorado and was reported to have said:

I think the thing that struck me was the irony that here, with all this great technology of ours, we can do all of this yet we cannot stop any of the weapons that are coming at us. I don't think there's been a time in history when there wasn't some kind of thrust, even back in the old-fashioned days when we had coast artillery that would stop invading ships.

The Republican platform that year called for "vigorous research and development of an effective antiballistic missile system, such as is already at hand in the Soviet Union, as well as more modern ABM technologies."

When the Reagan Administration came to office, officials began to show interest in defense against nuclear attack. Mr. Weinberger openly criticized the antiballistic missile treaty and suggested the administration might abrogate it. After the President disclosed his plan in 1981 to modernize the offensive nuclear forces, Mr. Weinberger linked it with research on defense.

Research and development for antiballistic missile defenses will be increased and the program accelereated. Our efforts will not be directed toward creating an effective city defense, which we continue to believe is not technically feasible. Ultimately, any ground based scheme may require such a defense, but we are unwilling to commit to ballistic missile defense today because of uncertainties of cost and effectiveness.

In the administration were officials such as the Under Secretary of Defense for Policy, Mr. Iklé, and senior military officers who thought a defense against missiles should be developed. *Defense Guidance* in 1982 contained some inkling of their thinking. "Research and development efforts will be accelerated on ballistic missile defense systems which could provide defense for our strategic forces," the document said. "In the longer term, our force posture must include surviving and enduring air defenses able, as part of our overall capability, to withstand a protracted conflict."

The next *Defense Guidance*, prepared during the winter of 1983, went considerably further. For the first time, it called for strategic defensive forces and a combination of defensive measures, which were not specified, that would "limit damage and contribute to the survival of the United States and Canadian populations." It further called for measures, again unspecified, that would "limit damage to retaliatory forces and critical command, control, and communication nodes from bomber or cruise missile attacks." In addition, research and development in ballistic-missile defenses was to be aimed at protecting the MX missile.

In another first, the 1983 *Defense Guidance* gave instructions on developing directed-energy weapons, such as lasers and particle beams, which were to become an integral part of President Reagan's missile defense plan. The objectives set forth for the next five years were "to expand the technology base toward identifying new concepts and applications that could yield marked increases in the capabilities of directed energy weapons." Researchers were to ascertain whether they could proceed to develop prototype weapons. Each service was to delve into specific directed-energy weapons, with the Air Force made responsible for the majority. In one program, the Air Force was to work toward a demonstration of lasers in space and in another to evaluate ground-based lasers "in high payoff strategic applications," meaning against Soviet nuclear missiles.

In the meantime, Dr. Teller, who had long advocated a defense against nuclear missiles, came to have more influence on President Reagan's thinking. Dr. Teller met with a group of scientists, businessmen, industry executives, and members of Mr. Reagan's kitchen cabinet at the Heritage Foundation, a conservative think tank in Washington, where they discussed national defense. That gathering was led by Karl R. Bendetsen, an industrialist and overseer of the Hoover Institution on War, Revolution and Peace at Stanford in California. Another prominent member was Lieutenant General Daniel O. Graham, a retired Army officer, former head of the Defense Intelligence Agency, and a strong advocate of missile defense.

Eventually, the group divided over avenues of approach. A faction led by Mr. Bendetsen and including Dr. Teller advocated research into advanced technology. General Graham formed a group centering around his concept of "High Frontier," asserting that a defense against nuclear missiles could be built quickly with known technology. The first group met with the President in January 1982. General Graham was not included, but the following month he issued a 175-page report on High Frontier to take his case to the public. Later in 1982, the President met again with Dr. Teller and, in early 1983, with the group led by Mr. Bendetsen. The Joint Chiefs of Staff, at the urging of General Meyer, the Army's Chief of Staff, and Admiral Watkins, the Chief of Naval Operations, discussed progress in missile defense with the President in February 1983. But the chiefs had no intention of urging the President to take the matter to the public and vigorously

tried to dissuade Mr. Reagan from doing so. They thought it premature because the technology was still so uncertain.

The President, however, decisively overruled all objections and
brought into public view the sweeping proposal for a defense of the
homeland against nuclear missiles in his speech in March. The President couched his proposal in high moral terms, saying the objective
was to rid the world of nuclear arms. But there was a chasm between
the rhetoric and the reality. Mr. Reagan, in effect, asked the nation
to buckle on a nuclear shield that, together with the nuclear sword
he was burnishing, would give the United States clear military superiority over the Soviet Union. The President sought to change the
nuclear equation from parity between the United States and the Soviet
Union to superiority for the United States. A defense that would blunt
the Soviet nuclear threat, even if imperfect, when coupled with a
strong nuclear offensive force, would amount to superiority whether
intended or not. Put another way, a soldier carrying a rifle and wearing
a helmet and a flak jacket to protect his body would be superior to
an equally well-trained and identically armed soldier lacking the helmet and flak jacket.

Shortly after the President's address, the White House set up two
panels to examine the proposal. James C. Fletcher, a former head of
the National Aeronautics and Space Administration, headed the Defense Technologies Study Team of scientists. It eventually urged research on a three-tier system that could stop 30,000 warheads and
could be built in the late 1990s. A Future Security Strategy Study
headed by Fred S. Hoffman, a military analyst, included specialists
on weapons who reported that a defensive system "may prove unat-
tainable in a practical sense against a Soviet effort to counter" it. The
Hoffman panel suggested concentrating on defending missile silos.
The White House did not choose formally between them but proceeded to develop technology to defend United States nuclear forces
first and possibly cities later.

More immediately, the Defense Department began to devise a war
plan and a command structure that would integrate the nuclear sword
with the antimissile shield in a new war-fighting posture. That effort
grew out of the administration's plans for protracted nuclear war if
deterrence failed, as outlined in its *Defense Guidance*. Mr. Iklé, under
whose supervision the plan was drafted, said the plan was intended
to establish "a good, coherent posture." He said the project was intended "to update nuclear employment plans and guidance for the
transition from offense to defense in the 1990s." The weapons to be

included were the Strategic Air Command's long-range missiles, bombers, and aircraft carrying cruise missiles; the Navy's submarines armed with ballistic missiles and cruise missiles; the Navy's surface ships on which cruise missiles had been mounted; the Army's Pershing II intermediate-range missiles; and the Air Force's ground-launched cruise missiles in Europe. If a nuclear war broke out, all would be employed in coordination with the defensive shield.

By 1986, *Defense Guidance* had elevated the Strategic Defense Initiative to the same top priority as the President's plan to modernize the nuclear forces. "The highest priority," the document said, "is assigned to the President's strategic force modernization program. . . . SDI shares this priority." In response to criticism that SDI could not defend the nation against medium-range missiles with lower trajectories or against bombers and cruise missiles, *Defense Guidance* said "research on defense against tactical ballistic missiles should be conducted as a hedge against Soviet tactical ballistic missile accuracy." Further, the document ordered "research on defense against air-breathing attacks . . . to provide options for complementing a future deployment of ballistic missile defense." ("Air-breathing" is Pentagonese for bombers and cruise missiles, both of which are powered by air-breathing engines.)

Even with the euphemisms in NSDD-172, the directive intended to end confusion over SDI, the Reagan Administration's objective was clear. Despite disclaimers that "the aim of the Strategic Defense Initiative is not to seek superiority," the directive said "our basic reliance on nuclear retaliation provided by offensive forces, as the essential means of deterring aggression, has not changed." Further, the document said in an unclassified version, "the Soviet Union recognizes the potential of advanced defense concepts—especially those involving boost, post-boost, and mid-course defenses—to change the strategic situation.

"The existing NATO strategy of flexible response must remain fully valid for the alliance as long as there is no more effective alternative for preventing war," NSDD 172 said, referring to the policy of holding open all options to counter a Soviet invasion of Western Europe. "The goal of our research is not, and cannot be, simply to protect our retaliatory forces from attack" (a carefully crafted sentence that actually said part of the reason for building a missile defense would be to protect offensive forces). "If a future President elects to move toward a general defense against ballistic missiles," the document continued, "the technological options that we explore will certainly also increase the survivability of our retaliatory forces." In sum, "For the foreseeable future, offensive nuclear forces and the prospect of nuclear retaliation will remain the key element of deterrence."

NSDD 172 hinted at another reason for pursuing missile defense, which was to force the Soviet Union to spend money, energy, and human talent to match it or attempt to overcome it. That would be part of the same technological strategy that stimulated development of the Stealth bomber to evade radar, thus making the Soviet radar network obsolete. Soviet funds poured into research on a new defensive system meant that those funds could not be used for weapons that would threaten the United States. In another euphemism, NSDD 172 said an objective of the Strategic Defense Initiative was "to channel long-standing Soviet propensities for defenses toward more stabilizing and mutually beneficial ends." In the thinking behind the initiative, NSDD 172 said, "we seek defense options which provide clear disincentives to attempts to counter them with additional offensive forces." To carry that idea to its logical conclusion, it wouldn't make much difference whether the American defense worked or not, so long as the leaders of the Soviet Union thought it worked. As NSDD 172 asserted, that belief could enhance deterrence and force an additional burden on the already strained Russian economy. If, instead, the Soviet Union put more funds and materials into building more rockets, that would increase the danger to the United States marginally since the added missiles would be mainly overkill. But the strain on the Soviet economy would be similar.

The Strategic Defense Initiative Office established by the President in 1984 had, by mid-1985, sorted out the research schedule of the program. Lieutenant General James A. Abrahamson, the Air Force officer in charge, said in a report to Congress that a phased approach was envisioned. A decision point was to be reached in the early 1990s, when the initial research should have been completed. At that time, the President would have to decide whether the defensive system was feasible, whether it was worth the billions it would cost to deploy the actual system, and whether to proceed. That could well be the most critical point in the program, and will require a strong political will, especially to halt the program if the technology has not proved out. Weapons programs, once begun, build constituencies supported by special pleadings from defense contractors and congressmen who like jobs in electoral districts. As in the law of physics, a weapons program set in motion tends to stay in motion.

Assuming a decision is made to go ahead, the development of

sensors, weapons, communications, and computers would take place through the 1990s. "A transition phase," General Abrahamson said, "would be a period of incremental, sequential deployment of defensive systems." He said deploying each piece would be designed to "enhance deterrence and reduce the risk of nuclear war." The final phase, in the next century, would be a period "during which deployment of highly effective, multi-phased defensive systems would be completed."

A layered defense of at least four stages was envisioned. In the first, exotic weapons would attack missiles during the "boost" phase of about three minutes, when missiles fired from their silos were rising into the atmosphere. During the second, or "post-boost" phase, after the rockets had burned out and fallen away, those same weapons would shoot at containers, or "buses," loaded with warheads as they moved into trajectory. Hitting as many missiles or buses as possible during the first and second stages would take top priority, as ten warheads could be destroyed in one shot. In the third stage, those warheads would separate from the bus and disperse onto their own trajectories along with numerous decoys. Every warhead, instead of every ten warheads, would then become a small, cold, single target. But that mid-course stage would last fifteen minutes, giving the defense more time to shoot. The final stage, lasting only two minutes, would occur when the warheads would dip into the atmosphere and speed toward their targets. But defensive weapons need only fire at short ranges.

Battle management is the most important piece of research in the Strategic Defense Initiative, particularly into computers that could handle 10 million instructions and be completely reliable. Those computers would take information from sensors, sort it out, and decide which weapons should engage what targets—when the targets might number in the tens of thousands and the battle be over in less than thirty minutes. Asked whether a limited system could be ready by 1995, General Abrahamson said "the problem is being able to put together the command and control by that time," meaning the sensors, transmission lines, computers, and communications through which the President and his senior civilian and military subordinates could direct the battle in space. "The long pole in the tent is the command and control structure," the general said. "That is the important element in the research program that we have to move forward."

What Star Wars would cost no one would know until the early 1990s. General Abrahamson said the five-year research bill would be $26 billion. George A. Keyworth, the President's science adviser until 1986, said the cost could be contained within the 15 percent of the annual military budget devoted to nuclear weapons, or $45 billion. John E. Pike, of the American Federation of Scientists, and Gordon Adams, of the Center on Budget and Policy Priorities, both critics of Star Wars, estimated between $70 billion and $100 billion by 1993. Professor Robert Jastrow, the physicist at Dartmouth who was a keen supporter of the program, thought it would eventually cost between $100 billion and $200 billion. Richard DeLauer, the Under Secretary of Defense for Research and Engineering during the first term of the Reagan Administration, said it would cost eight times as much as the Manhattan Project, which built the atomic bomb. Factoring in inflation, that would bring the estimate to $160 billion. The Council on Economic Priorities, another opponent of the project, contended it would cost $400 billion to $800 billion. James Schlesinger, who had served as Secretary of Defense, Director of Central Intelligence, and Chairman of the Atomic Energy Commission, said it would cost $50 billion a year to build and operate. A full defense that included defenses against bombers and cruise missiles, he said, would cost "well over half a trillion and probably will exceed a trillion."

The President's Strategic Defense Initiative split the ranks of scientists, strategic thinkers, and politicians. The division was due in part to the ineptitude of the administration, which failed to explain its plan to the public, to brief the Congress on what was going on, and to present a rigorous technical approach to scientists. Many critics feared the plan would intensify an arms race with the Soviet Union and cause the abrogation of the Anti-Ballistic Missile Treaty, or ABM Treaty, which they regarded as among the most solid arms control agreements with the Soviet Union.

As with other military programs, the leading salesman for the administration was Secretary of Defense Weinberger. He asserted that among the "prospective benefits" would be complicating enemy calculations, thus making him think twice before attacking. "Moreover, an effective defense would not need to be leak-proof to create this uncertainty," Mr. Weinberger said, contradicting earlier statements that the objective would be a thoroughly reliable defense against all warheads. He argued that failure to pursue research would risk a Soviet breakthrough. The plan would be a prudent hedge against Soviet deployment of an antimissile defense, to which they seem to be heading in violation of the 1972 Anti-Ballistic Missile treaty, he argued. Strategic defense would be "an insurance policy" against accidental Soviet launch of a missile, or missiles fired from some other nation.

Outside the administration, support for strategic defense came in a prescient article by Stephen Peter Rosen, of the Center for International Affairs at Harvard. In the spring of 1981, two years before President Reagan's address, Mr. Rosen laid out cogent arguments for a strategic defense in more detail than did the administration in 1983 and after. The need for a policy trying to minimize, rather than maximize, the cost of nuclear war had become urgent, Mr. Rosen said. "America will be spending a sizeable amount of additional money on its strategic forces in the 1980s. It would do better to buy live Americans than dead Soviets."

The group led by General Graham naturally supported the President. "Any search for a 'technological end-run' on Soviet military advantages leads inexorably to space," said a High Frontier booklet. Changes in weaponry on land, sea, and air would be "product improvement," the booklet argued. "It is in the area of space technology where the U.S. advantage can be decisive." Speaking for the other group of advocates, Mr. Teller contended a strategic defense would make "obsolete all their weapons and force them into very costly expenditures." He told Congress that any defense should place aggressors in a disadvantageous position. "This means that counteracting the defense should be more expensive than the defense itself," he said. "Aggression will be effectively deterred by doubt that it can succeed."

Among those in public life who endorsed the President's plan, perhaps the most surprising was Zbigniew Brzezinski, a Democrat who had been the national security adviser to President Carter, Mr. Reagan's political opponent in the 1980 election. But Mr. Brzezinski was a hardliner on the Soviet Union before, during, and after his tenure in the White House. He contended a strategic defense "would inhibit a first strike" and "would enhance arms control." Mr. Brzezinski joined Professor Jastrow and Max M. Kampelman, the Washington lawyer who headed the American delegation at the arms control negotiations in Geneva, in advocating the President's plan. In a long article in *The New York Times Magazine*, they argued that strategic defense was technically feasible, strategically desirable, and politically possible. They suggested replacing the policy of mutually assured destruction, in which the United States and the Soviet Union would blow each other off the face of the earth, with what they called the "Strategy of Mutual Security." "The combination of defense against space missiles with retaliatory offensive weapons in reserve enhances deterrence," they contended.

On the other side, the array of opponents against Star Wars was extensive. Among the leaders was the Union of Concerned Scientists that published a book entitled *The Fallacy of Star Wars* and called the plan "the political fantasy of Ronald Reagan." Among key scientists criticizing the technical feasibility of strategic defense were Hans A. Bethe, a Nobel laureate in physics; Kurt Gottfried, professor of physics and nuclear studies at Cornell; Henry W. Kendall, a physicist at the Massachusetts Institute of Technology; Richard L. Garwin, a researcher for International Business Machines; and Carl Sagan, professor of astronomy and space studies at Cornell. Noel Gayler, a retired Navy admiral, was another vocal critic, as was Sidney Drell of Stanford. Drell told Congress he had "grave doubts, both on technical and strategic grounds, that significant acceleration or expansion of ABM research and development is either warranted or prudent."

William J. Perry, Under Secretary of Defense for Research and Engineering in the Carter Administration, found the President's program technically not feasible because it would be impossible to render Soviet nuclear forces "impotent." Jonathan Jacky, a specialist on computers at the University of Washington School of Medicine, cautioned that critical computer software would not be reliable because "all large programs contain undiscovered errors and omissions that come to light only after prolonged experience in actual use." Cory Coll of the Lawrence Livermore National Laboratory, which was doing research on missile defense, questioned the reliability of computer software. "It's hard to imagine a half-dozen people understanding enough of the program," he said, "to be able to understand the whole thing and make sure that there aren't some quirks or errors introduced in just the software." Kosta Tsipis, a physicist at MIT, asserted: "Nuclear weapons are so destructive that either you have a perfect defense or you don't have anything. And a perfect defense is impossible." Ashton B. Carter of Harvard wrote an analysis for the Congressional Office of Technology Assessment asserting that prospects for the antimissile shield were "so remote that it should not serve as the basis of public expectation or national policy about ballistic missile defense."

Among those influential in public policy, Harold Brown—a nuclear physicist, former Secretary of the Air Force, and former Secretary of Defense—initially urged President Reagan to "give up his objective of trying to substitute defense of the American population for deterrence by the threat of retaliation." He asserted that "the combinations of limitations—scientific, technological, systems engineering, cost— and especially the potential countermeasures make the prospect of a perfect or near-perfect defense negligibly low." Later, however, Mr. Brown appeared to soften his opposition, at least on technical issues. He wrote in *Foreign Affairs* in 1986 that, by the year 2000, developing space-based kinetic energy weapons appeared to be technologically feasible: "These chemically propelled rockets would intercept the of-fensive missile during the boost phase and destroy the target by impact or by detonation of an exploding warhead." Space-based directed energy weapons, such as particle beams and chemical lasers, could be deployed shortly after 2000, he said. A terminal defense was techni-cally feasible. The computer software to manage the battle in space, costing between $500 million and $5 billion, could be freed from errors in the codes "through automated software production and through aritificial intelligence." In sum: "The near-term prospects for ballistic missile defense capabilities are reasonably well known. Technically, they appear cost-effective for defense of some kind of strategic retali-atory forces. For defense of populations against a responsible threat, they look poor through the year 2010 and beyond."

Other influential skeptics included Lieutenant General Brent Scowcroft, a retired Air Force officer and chairman of President Rea-gan's commission to examine the MX missile. He supported research into strategic defense but contended that the concept had not been thought out. Even more skeptical was Mr. Schlesinger, the former Secretary of Defense and a Republican, who scoffed: "The heart of Reagan's speech was the promise that someday American cities might indeed be safe from nuclear attack. There is no serious likelihood of removing the nuclear threat from our cities in our lifetime or in the lifetime of our children."

Vigorous criticism came from former Secretary of Defense Robert S. McNamara; George F. Kennan, the former Ambassador to the Soviet Union; McGeorge Bundy, national security adviser to Presi-dents Kennedy and Johnson; and Gerard Smith, chief of the American delegation to the Strategic Arms Limitation Talks (SALT I). "What is centrally and fundamentally wrong with the President's objective is that it cannot be achieved," they said in a joint statement.

The overwhelming consensus of the nation's technical community is that in fact there is no prospect whatever that science and technology can, at any time in the next several decades, make nuclear weapons "impotent and ob-solete." . . . The notion that nuclear weapons, or even ballistic missiles alone, can be rendered impotent by science and technology is an illusion.

Separately, former Secretary of State Dean Rusk said "we should make a maximum effort with the Soviets to prevent this space war concept before it begins." He asserted: "The idea of getting some kind of unilateral advantage seems rather futile. We'll come out of it with expenditures that will boggle the mind without any appreciable ad-vantage." Mr. Rusk, who served under Presidents Kennedy and Johnson, said Americans should be able "to look up at heaven and see the handiwork of God, not the folly of man."

Polls at the time indicated a deep split among Americans over the wisdom, feasibility, and cost of SDI. *The New York Times* found that 62 percent of the people thought the proposed system would work but only 48 percent thought developing it would make arms negotiations with the Soviet Union easier. Men and women split over the issue of the arms race, 54 percent of the men thinking the Strategic Defense Initiative would make it more dangerous while only 42 percent of the women thought so. Only 40 percent of the people thought it would be worth the cost. In another poll, the *Los Angeles Times* found that 56 percent thought Star Wars threatened the Soviet Union and 55 percent were against spending money for research into strategic defense. Perhaps most important, slightly less than half said they had heard little or nothing about the proposal.

Over the next several years, public opinion shifted toward a lukewarm acceptance of the President's plan. A poll in late 1985 was taken by Penn & Schoen, a firm that had worked for both Republicans and Democrats, for the Committee on the Present Danger, a conservative group that supported the SDI. The poll found that 41 percent of the people who responded favored the plan while 37 percent were unfamiliar with it; 78 percent favored going ahead with research and 73 percent favored using it in the United States if it could be developed. For the long run, 46 percent said they thought it would make the world safer while 36 percent said it would make little difference and 12 percent thought it would be less safe. A large majority, 77 percent, rejected bargaining SDI away in negotiations with the Soviet Union. Other polls reflected the same opinions: The *Los Angeles Times* reported that 58 percent of those the newspaper had queried thought that SDI should be developed, but 59 percent thought it would cost too much. A Gallup poll found that 61 percent favored the program, while 44 percent thought it would make the world safer.

Americans at first may have been unsure in what they thought of Star Wars; the Russians were not. Only four days after Mr. Reagan's speech, General Secretary Yuri Andropov asserted that the United States was seeking the capacity to fire a pre-emptive first strike. He contended that Mr. Reagan sought to render the Soviet Union incapable of mounting a retaliatory strike and therefore was seeking "to disarm the Soviet Union in the face of the U.S. nuclear threat." Soviet diplomats in Washington were eager to explain why their government opposed Star Wars. They saw it as primarily offensive, not defensive, with the United States attempting to gain a decisive advantage over the Soviet Union. "We will never let you get ahead of us again," said one Russian diplomat. To match or to counter the strategic defense would cost the Soviet Union tremendous sums of money. "We have better things to do with money," a Soviet diplomat acknowledged. They said Moscow would probably invest more in offensive missiles than in defensive technology to counter the United States. "We know how to build rockets," said a Soviet diplomat, "We know we are good at that. But we don't know as much about the other things."

In their effort to disparage the Star Wars proposal, Soviet scientists floated a curious paper to American scientists and journalists in 1984 and 1985. Written in English and packed with scientific formulas, it was entitled "A Space-Based Antimissile System with Directed Energy Weapons: Strategic, Legal, and Political Implications." "We have reason to regard the prospective United States SBAMS [spaced-based antimissile system] as a means of insuring a first-strike capability," the paper said. "The assertions coming from the Reagan Administration that the new antimissile defense systems spell salvation from nuclear missiles for mankind are perhaps the greatest ever deception of our time." The paper issued by the Committee of Soviet Scientists for Peace against the Nuclear Threat asserted that the strategic defense could be knocked out by small ballistic missiles, space mines in orbit, lasers based on the ground, and clouds of chaff. Launching dummy missiles would cause the defense to react and use up stocks of fuel.

Vladimir V. Shcherbitsky, a member of the ruling Politburo, visited Washington in March 1985 to say that Moscow would respond with both offensive and defensive measures if President Reagan went ahead with the strategic defense plan. "Neither side can or should strive to achieve military superiority no matter what name it is given, an antimissile shield or strictly defensive 'shield,' or anything else," he said. "Such an aspiration is simply chasing illusions."

On the other hand, Nikolai Basov, of the Soviet Academy of Sciences, said the Soviet Union would have no difficulty in matching the defensive plan of the United States. Mr. Basov had won the Nobel Prize in 1964 for work in quantum physics and was a leader in Soviet efforts to build a strategic defense. American officials said repeatedly that the Soviet Union had been working on such defenses for fifteen years and had built a new radar deep in Siberia for antimissile defense.

Lord Chalfont, who had often represented Britain at disarmament conferences, contended in an article in *The Times* of London that the Soviet Union could not have it both ways.

Either the Strategic Defense Initiative is dangerous, provocative, and destabilizing or it is useless, expensive, and easily neutralized; either it is technologically unfeasible or it is well within the reach of Soviet military scientists. Indeed, what appears to be a baffling contradiction in Soviet attitudes to strategic defense is easily explained if one simple proposition is accepted—namely that the Soviet Union has been engaged for many years on a secret program of research into space-based defense, and that it now fears it may be overtaken by a similar program that has all the weight of Western technology, industrial infrastructure, and economic resources behind it.

The reaction to the Strategic Defense Initiative among America's allies was mostly negative at first. Only Prime Minister Margaret Thatcher of Britain and Prime Minister Yasuhiro Nakasone of Japan gave cautious approval. West European leaders were miffed at not having been informed that the proposal was coming. They saw it as an attempt by the United States to return to an isolationist "Fortress America," leaving Europe to fend for itself. Many Europeans saw it, according to David S. Yost, an associate professor at the Naval Postgraduate School in Monterey, California, as "technologically naive." And, like critics in the United States, they feared the ABM Treaty would be abandoned and the arms race quickened. "At the heart of European concern," wrote William J. Broad, a science reporter for *The New York Times*,

lies a key technical consideration—the short time in which Soviet warheads can reach Europe—and the military judgment that many of these weapons would slip underneath the most elaborate shield that the United States could place in space.

As with American public opinion, however, European opinion seemed to shift toward a lukewarm acceptance of the SDI. The Reagan Administration seemed to persuade European governments that a defensive shield could help to protect Western Europe. More important, perhaps, was an offer to European manufacturers to take part in lucrative contracts to develop the system. Britain and West Germany took advantage of the offer while France, true to the Gaullist tradition, sought to lead Europe into an independent version of the SDI.

Below the proposed strategic defensive shield would be not much else to protect the United States from nuclear attack until well into the 1990s. The United States in early 1986 was in the early stages of developing antisatellite weapons intended to knock out Soviet intelligence, reconnaissance, and communications satellites. Defenses against bomber attacks had been neglected since the 1960s. Finding a defense against air-launched or sea-launched cruise missiles had only just begun. There was a growing awareness of the threat of nuclear terror, but not much had been done to prevent it. Nuclear war by accident was worrisome but, in reality, a very remote possibility. Only the Navy had mounted a powerful campaign intended to put it into a position to knock out Soviet submarines armed with ballistic missiles, but that was a chancy proposition at best.

The main antisatellite research in recent years has been in an F-15 fighter plane armed with a rocket to which has been attached a homing device, sometimes called the "tomato can" for its size and shape. The F-15 flies to a high altitude to fire the rocket into a low orbit where it launches the homing device toward the target. When the homing device reaches the target, it destroys the satellite with kinetic energy, which is a fancy way of saying the device and the target collide at high speeds and shatter each other. In the simplest terms, the F-15 pilot throws a rock at the satellite and smashes it. Another possibility for making an antisatellite, or ASAT, weapon would be to load a satellite with explosives and loft it into orbit near the satellite that is the target. The space mine could then be detonated on order. But finding the target and staying with it is not easy, despite advanced radar and other sensors. "Space," as one Pentagon officer put it, "is a very big place."

President Reagan's Strategic Defense Initiative aroused interest in finding a way to defend the nation against cruise missiles, the flying torpedoes that can be launched by aircraft, surface ships, and submarines. The Soviet Union has deployed cruise missiles at sea, including those in an entire class of nuclear-powered submarines. Current cruise missiles fly slower than the speed of sound but so low they are hard to spot by ground-based radar. They can be spotted by airborne radar that "looks down," but building enough fighter planes and keeping them on patrol to look for cruise missiles would be expensive and complicated. Secretary of Defense Weinberger has suggested that cruise missiles could be destroyed by laser or particle-beam weapons similar to those envisioned for strategic defense.

A related problem is stopping submarine-launched ballistic missiles fired along what is known as a depressed trajectory. Normally, a submarine attacking the United States with ballistic missiles would stay far off shore and fire its missiles into space from which they would drop on targets here. To achieve a depressed trajectory, the submarine would come close to shore and lob the missile on a path that would rise only a few miles, with the missile taking only six to eight minutes to come down on its target. How to stop a missile fired that way can only be conjectured, with hope that something could be derived from the technology of Star Wars.

In the 1950s, when the main United States nuclear force was the fleet of long-range bombers, an air defense was assembled on the belief that the Soviet Union would acquire a similar fleet. The Distant Early Warning, or DEW, line was built across Greenland, northern Canada, and Alaska to warn of Soviet bombers flying across the Arctic. All-weather interceptor aircraft intended to shoot down invading bombers were acquired. The Soviet Union, however, emphasized interconti-nental ballistic missiles. Thus, American air defenses were considered unnecessary and allowed to become obsolete.

Recently, however, the Soviet Union has built what NATO calls Backfire and Blackjack bombers with enough range to threaten the United States. Added to that has been the prospect that President Reagan's strategic defense might reduce the ability of Soviet missiles to strike the United States, thus turning the Soviet Union to bombers. The Reagan Administration has therefore started to rebuild the air defense network. A new North Warning System of more than fifty radar sites costing $2 billion is to be erected in conjunction with Canada across the northern reaches of that nation and Alaska to watch for bombers. In addition, long-range radar that can see over the horizon is to be built in the United States to look for bombers coming in low from the east, west, or south. The F-106 jet interceptors built in the 1960s are to be replaced by F-15 jet fighters. The Canadian gov-ernment plans to buy more light F-18 jet fighters and to base them farther north. But it will be into the 1990s before all of that has been accomplished.

Specialists in the study of terrorism and of nuclear arms say the chances of terrorists' using a nuclear weapon have increased in recent years. Bernard J. O'Keefe, an industrialist who has been involved with nuclear issues since the bombing of Hiroshima, told a conference in Washington that "there is very little that can be done to prevent a skilled, determined, well-organized terrorist organization from setting off a nuclear detonation in United States territory." Mr. O'Keefe and other specialists pointed to the spreading knowledge of nuclear tech-nology and materials and said that assembling a rudimentary nuclear device is within the reach of some terrorists. While nuclear weapons themselves are closely guarded, nuclear materials for military and commercial use are in transit all the time and are vulnerable to theft. Breaking into a nuclear power plant and threatening to blow up the reactor, thus releasing radiation into the air, would not be difficult for dedicated terrorists. Even a hoax, in which terrorists assert they have a nuclear device when they don't, could cause panic and chaos.

On the other hand, the chances of a nuclear weapon being fired by accident are infinitesimal. The nuclear age has not been without accidents—planes inadvertently dropping nuclear bombs, planes loaded with nuclear bombs crashing, nuclear-powered submarines lost at sea with all hands, a Titan missile having its thin skin ruptured by a dropped wrench and exploding to throw its warhead out of the silo (without detonating). But the safeguards are extensive. Nuclear bombs are no longer carried aloft on airborne alert. Ballistic-missile forces, while on alert, are not in a hair-trigger posture. Crews must receive authenticated orders, must remove locks intended to prevent unauthorized firing, and must turn at least four keys. The Norad warning center relies not on one sensor but on a variety of data to ascertain whether the Soviet Union has launched a missile. Nor does Norad or any other agency have the authority to order weapons fired—that belongs to the President, his designated subordinates, and the separate Strategic Air Command. Perhaps most important, few strategic thinkers believe that a Soviet attack would be a "bolt-out-of-the-blue," that is, an attack without warning and without a long slide toward military hostilities. American authorities presume that leaders of the Soviet Union have similar safeguards, controls, and attitudes.

In contrast to the futuristic Star Wars and the uncertainties of defenses against cruise missiles and bombers, the United States Navy has mounted a relentless campaign to detect and track Soviet submarines armed with ballistic missiles. The effort by what the American Navy calls the "silent service," for its secrecy and way of operating beneath the sea, is very much in the here and now, with continuing improvements based on known technology planned out to the twenty-first century. American undersea technology is believed to be well ahead of that of the Soviet Union, even though the Russians have been straining to catch up. The submarine campaign is aimed at putting American submarines into position to destroy Soviet submarines before their nuclear missiles can be fired. Once the missiles are flying, American submarines cannot stop them.

The Soviet Union has been deploying missile-bearing submarines in at least three echelons. Older submarines known in NATO terminology as, curiously, the "Yankee" class are armed with relatively short-range missiles and are stationed 500 to 1,000 miles off the Atlantic and Pacific coasts. Their missiles are within easy range of the nation's capital in Washington; of important naval bases in Norfolk, Virginia, and Charleston and Kings Bay, Georgia; and of naval bases at San Diego in California, Bangor in Washington, and Pearl Harbor in Hawaii. Other submarines cruise the Baltic and Norwegian seas west of the Soviet Union and the Sea of Japan and the Okhotsk and Bering Sea to its east. They are believed to have intermediate-range missiles aboard aimed at Western Europe, Japan, and China.

In the third group are the newest submarines—the Delta I, II, III, and IV classes and the Typhoon, at 30,000 tons the world's largest undersea vessel—which have the range to roam far into the Pacific and Atlantic. But they have generally been held in waters closer to home from which their missiles can still hit most targets in the United States. Those submarines, the strategic reserve of the Soviet nuclear force, can be guarded by land-based aircraft, surface ships, and Soviet attack submarines more easily in those northern bastions than on the high seas.

To detect and track those Soviet submarines, the United States has deployed a vast network of sensors and weapons. When a Soviet ballistic-missile submarine leaves its base at Polyarny, near Murmansk on the Barents Sea, or from Vladivostok on the Sea of Japan, or from Petropavlovsk on the Kamchatka Peninsula opposite the Aleutian Islands, it is seen by an American satellite. As the Russian submarine submerges and is lost to the satellite, it can be picked up by an American fast-attack submarine (to American submariners, "fast attack" is one word) that may trail it throughout its voyage. To remain undetected, American submariners listen on passive sonar, which emits no signal, rather than active sonar, which sends out a "ping" that hits a target and bounces back to measure range and direction—but gives away the presence of the submarine that sent out the ping. When a Soviet submarine sails into the Atlantic through the channels between Greenland, Iceland, and Norway or the United Kingdom, it is heard by an array of hydrophones called SOSUS, for sound surveillance system, that has been strung across the bottom of the sea. The same would be true of a Russian submarine entering the Pacific across the array of hydrophones strung from the Aleutians to Japan. If a Soviet submarine has not been picked up in the Arctic Sea, American fast-attack submarines lurking in the Atlantic near the gaps begin trailing the Soviet ship as it enters the Atlantic.

Navy P-3C Orion aircraft, the military version of the Lockheed turboprop Electra, patrol the Atlantic from Iceland to Britain and from Bermuda to the Azores; the Mediterranean from bases in Spain, Italy, and Greece; the Pacific from the Aleutians, Okinawa, Guam, and the Philippines; and the Indian Ocean from the British island of Diego Garcia to Kenya and the Omani island of Masira. Those planes, which are loaded with sensors and fly for fourteen hours 200 to 500 feet above the water, drop sonobuoys that listen for sounds emitted by Russian submarines. Whatever the sonobuoy picks up is transmitted to the plane to give location, depth, direction, and speed of the Soviet submarine. Warships on the surface towing arrays of hydrophones pick up the same information. American fast-attack submarines add more information from Soviet submarines they are trailing, or those they come across in chance encounters beneath the sea. A new class of ocean surveillance ships called TAGOS tow arrays of hydrophones behind them to fill the gaps, particularly listening for sounds in the valleys between ridges rising from the sea bottom where Russian submarines might try to hide. All of that, plus information from antisubmarine patrols run by Canadian, Norwegian, British, and Dutch ships, is fed into a watch room at Task Force 24 in Norfolk and a similar center in Hawaii. There, minute-by-minute plots of Soviet submarines are kept. Altogether, the United States Navy usually knows exactly where every Soviet submarine is in the Atlantic. Keeping track in the Pacific is harder because the ocean is bigger and natural choke points fewer. In the northern seas, the task is even more difficult.

In many cases, American submariners know which submarine they are tracking, and sometimes who the Russian captain is. Every submarine has a "signature," a combination of distinct sounds from propellers, generators, and pumps that register in earphones and on sonar screens and are recorded on tape. When contact with a Soviet submarine is made and its particular signature heard, the tape is run through a computer aboard the American carrier or ship or submarine to identify the submarine being hunted.

In the early 1980s, one Russian submarine captain was known as "Crazy Ivan." Unlike other Soviet submariners, who were predictable and steady, and maybe a bit unimaginative, "Crazy Ivan" was full of antics. It is a standard tactic for submariners of any navy to "clear the baffles" periodically. Because of the noise from the ship's own engine and screws, sonarmen cannot hear in a cone behind their own submarine. Thus, frequently, the captain orders a sharp turn to the left or right so that sonarmen can direct their attention to the area that was immediately behind them. But "Crazy Ivan" was not satisfied with routine maneuvers. Instead, after a period of calm sailing, he suddenly ordered his submarine to dive, then rise close to the surface, turn left, turn right, dive again, gyrating left and right until he finally settled down on a steady course again. Crazy Ivan, of course, was not crazy at all, just different. But that identified him.

Most important, behind each Soviet missile submarine in the Atlantic and Pacific, at a range of a few thousand yards, is an American attack submarine with torpedo tubes loaded and ready to shoot. The rules of engagement, which tell an American submarine captain the circumstances under which he is to attack a Russian submarine, are a closely held secret. Presumably, he has been instructed to sink the Soviet submarine on order from his operational headquarters, or when he is certain that the Soviet submarine has fired a missile, or if he has unmistakable evidence that the Soviet submarine has opened its missile hatches and prepared to fire. None of that would be done in isolation but after tactical warning that hostilities were about to begin or had already begun.

The Secretary of the Navy, John Lehman, told an audience of Nordic specialists at Harvard in 1985 that if the Soviet Union begins a war, American fast-attack submarines would immediately try to sink Russian missile submarines. Even if the Soviet Union confined its attack to conventional weapons and did not escalate to nuclear arms, the American Navy would go after Soviet submarines as quickly as possible wherever they were. Mr. Lehman, never known for reticence, said American submarines would attack "in the first five minutes of the war" in an effort to eliminate the Soviet Union's strategic nuclear reserve. In 1986, Mr. Lehman and the Chief of Naval Operations, Admiral Watkins, made that policy public in articles about the administration's maritime strategy.

With that prospect, and the American antisubmarine campaign in the Atlantic and Pacific, the Soviet high command has increasingly sent its ballistic-missile submarines under the protective cover of the Arctic ice. They are safe there from the prying eyes of American satellites and aircraft. But that move has confronted the United States with a new need to send fast-attack submarines under the ice to find the Soviet missile ships, a requirement that has been given high priority. The Navy has "hardened" the towers and diving planes of some fast-attack submarines so they can punch their way through thin layers of ice that can be found in the Arctic. Other problems, however, have been formidable. Passive sonar can be effective in the steady temperature of Arctic water, but the sound of ice grinding and moving on the fringe of the Arctic ice pack can pound the ears of sonarmen. Navigation close to the North Pole and away from navigation satellites can be a nightmare. Communication from headquarters to a submarine under the ice is difficult. Soviet submarines have been reported hard to detect when they hide between the jagged keels of ice that protrude several hundred feet below the surface layer. But senior naval officers said the United States cannot concede the Arctic to the Soviet Union and thus has been learning to operate there as well as in the open seas.

While American submariners believe their technology is ahead of that of the Soviet Union, they are in an unending race to stay ahead. The Reagan Administration has embarked on a program to build a fleet of 100 modern fast-attack submarines capable of putting the Soviet ballistic-missile fleet constantly at risk. The American nuclear-powered submarine force in 1985 consisted of thirty-three submarines of the 6,900-ton Los Angeles class, thirty-seven submarines of the 4,400-ton Sturgeon class that have been "hardened" for Arctic operations, thirteen submarines in the Thresher class of 4,300 tons, and submarines of assorted older classes to bring the total to ninety-seven. Only four older diesel-electric boats remained in the fleet.

The Navy began building a new class of submarines in 1985 with four ships modeled on the Los Angeles class. But they incorporated quieter propulsion, extensive developments in quieting machinery, and special hull coatings to reduce the sonar "signature" as well as to improve the submarines' passive listening ability. The new class will be equipped with an advanced combat system to coordinate sonar, navigation, and weapons control and will be armed with advanced torpedoes and Tomahawk cruise missiles. Those missiles can be tipped with either conventional or nuclear warheads and are designed to attack military targets on land rather than at sea. Also under development has been a new antiship missile intended to attack vessels on the surface or underwater when they are out of torpedo range. The missile would be fired from a torpedo tube, rise to the surface, fly to the target, and finally zero in on the surface ship or plunge back into the sea to seek its submerged target.

For the next century, the Navy is designing the SSN-21, a new attack submarine. The schedule calls for requesting the first construction funds from Congress in 1989 and for the first SSN-21 to join the fleet in 1995. The new submarine is to have the latest in quieting techniques, speed, and endurance, plus advanced sonar, navigation, and fire controls. Some of that technology is being incorporated in the submarines modeled on the Los Angeles class.

To improve the detection of Russian submarines, especially newer and quieter ships armed with ballistic missiles, the Navy is developing a new undersea sensor that is a filament made of fiber optics. The code name of the program is Ariadne, after the daughter of King Minos of Crete who gave Theseus a thread so that he could find a way out of the Minotaur's cave. The fiber optic thread is to be strung along the bottom of the sea in addition to present arrays of hydrophones. The thread would be laid covertly by submarines across known routes through which Soviet submarines exit from port; across choke points between Greenland, Iceland, and Norway in the North Atlantic; and in areas in which Soviet missile submarines operate, includng the Arctic. The Indian Ocean, which is not covered with sensors on the sea bottom now, would be a likely area for deployment.

The training of American fast-attack submarines continues for the day no one wants. In the Bahamas, along the east coast of Andros Island, lies a deep underwater range seventy-five miles long and fifteen miles wide where fast-attack submarines practice detecting, tracking, and sinking Soviet submarines. Range boats on the surface launch torpedoes programmed to run courses and to emit sounds like those of a Russian submarine. The American submarine in training uses its sonar to detect the Russian "submarine," employs underwater tactics to track the target without being detected, and fires an exercise torpedo to hit the moving target. Altogether, the training is the nearest thing possible to the real world.

On a summer day, the fast-attack submarine *City of Corpus Christi* (SSN 705), commanded by Captain F. L. "Skip" Bowman, glides slowly at 300 feet below the calm surface of the range in an area known as the Tongue of the Ocean for its shape. Over the ship's intercom comes the order: "Battle stations, battle stations." In the hushed control room, darkened except for the red glow of navigation gauges and the green glow from tracking monitors, Captain Bowman sketches a quick scenario aloud so that all hands understand his plan of attack. From the sonar room just forward of the control center, Sonarman Second Class Donald Cox reports a bearing on the Russian submarine. From the navigation table, Quartermaster Second Class Ronald Peterson suggests a course change. Captain Bowman's orders are crisp: "Helm, right full rudder, steady course two four zero." The helmsman, in accord with standing practice, repeats the order: "Right full rudder, steady course two four zero, helm, aye." Fire control technicians begin tracking the target on consoles on the right side of the control room while an officer at a plotting board seeks to determine the range to the target.

In the darkened alley that is the sonar room, sonarmen watch the squiggly vertical lines flowing like slow waterfalls down the screens of monitors to represent noises in the ocean, constantly adjusting cursors to refine the sounds coming through the headsets. The bearings they take are fed continuously to the attack center and to plotting boards in the control room. At the attack center, fire control technicians labor to triangulate on the target. After the captain runs the submarine on several different legs to give the sonar different bearings on the target, an officer announces, "We have a solution," giving a bearing to the target and an approximate range. The captain checks to see whether weapon and ship are ready, then orders, "On generated bearing, shoot." Chief Petty Officer C. P. James turns a handle to the right to fire a torpedo from a tube three decks below. In the torpedo room, there is a "pop" as a valve opens, a "thump" as the torpedo is expelled from the tube, and a "hiss" as the pressurized air dissipates.

Back in the attack center, Fire Control Technician First Class Thomas Clouthier watches the trace of the torpedo. That information is sent back to the submarine's attack center through the thin wire that the torpedo pays out as it races to the target. "Active search," announces fire control. Then: "Detect, detect, detect." But the torpedo, which has a homing device aboard, loses the target for a minute, with fire control announcing again: "Active search." A low groan comes from the thirty submariners in the control room. Then, again: "Detect, detect, detect." After a long breath-holding pause: "Homing, homing." Finally, over the radio from the range officer monitoring the practice run: "Bullseye."

The control room, led by the captain, exhales: "Yaah." To evade retaliation from another Soviet submarine, the captain orders a steep dive. As the submarine plunges into the deep, Petty Officer Second Class William Urban, manning a plotting board, draws an X across the target, scribbles "die, commie," and rolls up the paper to get ready for the next run.

CHAPTER 11

~~~~~~~~~~~~~~~~~~~~~~~~~~~~~~

BOLD CHANGES

THE ARMED FORCES of the United States have been stricken with a split between field and flagpole that has left them capable of applying only minimal military power in pursuit of American national interests. In the field, American soldiers, sailors, airmen, and marines are motivated, well led at the combat level, and well trained. But around the flagpole in Washington, political and military leaders muddle along out of step with one another, permit costly abuses by the defense industry, pursue policies that are beyond the capacity of the forces to execute, and allow enormous waste in military spending. In nuclear forces, the number and mix of weapons is adequate but the pursuit of a doctrine of protracted nuclear war approaches folly. Seeking a defense against nuclear missiles in the Strategic Defense Initiative, or Star Wars, is feasible so long as it is done with caution. But its advocates should play straight with the American public on what the program is intended to achieve.

To defend the nation, bold changes are needed. A sweeping overhaul is necessary to bring cohesion to the military establishment, to foster quality and economy in the production of arms, to bring policies into line with realities, and to get military spending under control. The changes advocated here would comprise the most drastic revisions in the history of the Defense Department. In recent years, there have been several changes and dozens, if not hundreds, of studies urging reform. For the most part, however, they have amounted to tinkering at the margin and have failed to go to the root of the problems.

To give the armed forces the ability to accomplish the missions assigned by the President and the Congress, the nation's leaders should:

- Streamline the Department of Defense by abolishing the anachronistic Departments of the Army, Navy, and Air Force and several offices within the Pentagon in favor of a consolidated, centralized department under the clear-cut authority of the Secretary of Defense. In effect, the unification begun in 1947 should be carried to its logical conclusion.

- Provide for coherent, consistent military plans and operations by abolishing the anomalous Joint Chiefs of Staff and replacing it with a single operational Chief of Military Staff supported by a Joint Military Staff drawn from all services. A new Military Advisory Council to render advice to the President and the Secretary of Defense would comprise the Chief of Military Staff, his deputy, and the chiefs of staff of the military services.

- Make the forces more combat-ready by giving commanders of the unified combatant commands undisputed authority over the forces assigned to them. Make those commanders more effective by redrawing the lines marking geographic areas of responsibility to give each commander control over contiguous regions of land, sea, and air.

- Foster cohesion in the services by realigning them into a ground force of the Army and Marine Corps; a Navy; a Tactical Air Force of present Air Force, Navy, and Marine Corps fighters; and a new Strategic Nuclear Force of bombers, missiles, and submarines. Consolidate logistics, transport, and communications into a new Military Support Service. Continue the volunteer force, reserve the draft for wartime, but consider universal military training.

- Return Congress to its constitutional role of oversight by adopting a two-year military budget, prohibiting congressional additions to the defense budget but retaining the right of Congress to cut each item, and revising the committee structure to make it parallel the new organization of the Pentagon.

- Generate quality and economies in the defense industry, whose companies do not operate in a free market as private enterprises, by regulating it as a public utility under the scrutiny of an independent commission like those watching trade or the markets for securities.

- Reaffirm treaties with allies and political commitments to friendly nations, but insist that they bear a fair share of the military and financial burden of collective security, including an increase in the size of their military forces. Should any nation fail to do so, the United States would be free to withdraw from the treaty or commitment.

- Make United States forces more flexible and less costly by withdrawing most American troops from abroad but retaining them on active duty to provide a strategic reserve for the free world. Small forces would remain overseas as symbols of American commitments but the nation would rely on the Navy, plus newly built air and sea lift, to project power around the rim of the Eurasian continent and elsewhere.

- Freeze the defense budget for at least five years to bring military spending under control and to force the defense establishment to rationalize, allowing only for inflation and one-time expenditures to achieve revisions without cutting into training and operations.
- Revise nuclear doctrine to restrain plans for protracted nuclear war and to shift the emphasis from static land-based to mobile, airborne, and sea-based weapons; continue research into Star Wars defensive weapons but with careful checks to ascertain that they work before producing them; limit defense to military installations.

The most glaring weakness in the military power of the United States today is the legacy of Vietnam. The national consensus on the use of military force as an instrument of national policy, always fragile, was shattered by the war in Southeast Asia. Since then, the support of the armed forces by the American public and the confidence of Americans in their government's ability to apply military power wisely have not been restored. Moreover, building a new consensus has been sorely neglected by the Reagan Administration, despite the sometimes overblown rhetoric of senior officials.

Paradoxically, the great strength of American military power today is the quality of the people in the armed forces. The ranks of the forces are filled with competent men and women who are among the best ever to wear the uniform of the United States. In large part, the young people who enlist are educated and willing to learn; noncommissioned officers have renewed pride and ability; the officer corps is professional. Combatant commanders are impressive; ship captains, squadron commanders, battalion commanders, and senior noncommissioned officers are able leaders. The forces that stand watch at home and around the world train hard, perform well in operations, and have been infused with new weapons and equipment. They do a good job of guarding the nation's interests.

In vivid contrast, the establishment that comprises the President, the Secretary of Defense, the Secretaries of the Army, Navy, and Air Force, the Joint Chiefs of Staff, the Congress, and other government agencies is rent with discord. The division among them is exacerbated by bloated civilian and military bureaucracies, contorted chains of command, and interservice and intraservice contention over roles, missions, and money. The political and military leadership, moreover, countenances a defense industry, supposedly the arsenal of democracy, that is riddled with incompetent management, shoddy workmanship, waste, deception, and sometimes outright fraud.

American forces are stretched thin around the globe and are inadequate to fulfill the military commitments made by American political leaders who have allowed those pledges to grow almost mindlessly since the end of World War II. Not since 1950 has there been a searching re-examination of national interests and strategy, although President Nixon started down that path with the Nixon Doctrine, which called on other nations to provide for their own defense while the United States provided the nuclear umbrella and the strategic reserve. But because of Vietnam and Watergate, the Nixon Doctrine was not fully developed. Nor have political leaders scrutinized the commitments to allies and other nations even though it has become clear that most have not been carrying a proportional share of the military and economic burden for the common defense.

When the costs of the disarray in the high command, the abuses of the defense industry, the excessive military commitments, and the shirking of allies are added up, the bill for national defense is one-third higher than it should be. In addition, the armed forces will not be ready for anything much larger than the invasion of Grenada for the rest of this decade despite the $1 trillion spent during President Reagan's first term. The administration has failed to provide the forces with sufficient transport, ammunition, spare parts, all sorts of mundane supplies, and combat medical facilities. In sum, the taxpayers are not getting their money's worth.

In the nuclear arena, the forces of the United States seem adequate to deter a Soviet attack, although the only certainty about nuclear warfare is that no one really knows much about it. The Reagan Administration has moved ahead with its plan to modernize the nuclear deterrent, building a fleet of 100 B-1 bombers, converting the majority of the 240 B-52 bombers to carriers of cruise missiles, and made progress in developing the Stealth bomber designed to evade radar. Deployment of fifty MX, or Peacekeeper, intercontinental ballistic missiles has begun, the Minuteman force of 950 missiles is being refurbished, the small mobile long-range missile is being developed, Pershing II medium-range missiles and ground-launched cruise missiles have been deployed in Western Europe, and research continues for a deep underground missile base. At sea, Poseidon submarines bearing ballistic missiles continue on patrol while the powerful Trident class has come into the force. The Trident I, or C-4, missiles are operational, and Trident II, or D-5, missiles are due to be operational by 1990. But communications among the President, the civilian and military high command, and the nuclear forces in the field, although improved and hardened against nuclear attack, are inadequate to fight a prolonged nuclear war.

In defense against nuclear attack, President Reagan has sought to change the nuclear equation and military balance with the Soviet Union through his Strategic Defense Initiative, better known as Star Wars. If it works, his plan to build a shield against nuclear missiles with exotic new weapons will be the most far-reaching military development since the atomic bomb in 1945. A workable defense against nuclear missiles would be incorporated into nuclear war-fighting doctrine and would enhance the power of nuclear arms. Together, the antimissile shield and the nuclear sword are intended to give the United States military superiority over the Soviet Union in nuclear conflict, including protracted nuclear war. That may be a goal worth pursuing, but its proponents have been less than honest in advocating it. Instead of leveling with the American people, President Reagan has couched his plan in moralistic terms of reducing nuclear stockpiles and making nuclear weapons obsolete.

In a comprehensive reordering of American military power, the nation's leaders should start with a clean sheet of paper, save what is useful, modify what can be adapted, and eliminate what is outworn or obsolete. These drastic revisions should be guided by a master plan and omnibus legislation, with the parts fitted together, and changes made in sequence toward a known and stated goal. This can be done only with great pain, for most vested interests would be shattered. But the national interest demands a rational, effective, and economic military force that can be applied, when necessary, as an instrument of national policy.

These changes will require vigorous and sustained presidential leadership, the top priority of the Secretary of Defense, and the co-operation of the leaders of Congress and the defense industry. Consultations with allies will be trying. Meantime, the task of defending the nation must go on as usual. Altogether, it will take a minimum of five years to accomplish this reform, more likely ten, and it could well take until the end of the century before a new military structure is squared away.

Perhaps a starting point could be the appointment of a presidential commission, a device that has been successful in recent years for dealing with vexing issues like Social Security, Central America, and the MX intercontinental ballistic missile. A commission outside the administration, but responsible to the administration and the Congress, could command wide support if it included retired senior military officers, former Secretaries of Defense and State, former members of Congress, retired industrial and labor leaders, strategic thinkers, scholars, and prominent men and women not beholden to special interests.

They could be asked to draw up a new strategic charter modeled on NSC-68, that remarkable document of 1950, to define national objectives and a national strategy to achieve them. The new charter would specify the military threats to the nation and lay out a military strategy to protect national interests. The charter would outline the size and type of required nuclear, conventional, and unconventional military forces and would set forth a plan to acquire those forces. It would review the constitutional, legal, and political authority of the President to send forces into hostilities. The commission would estimate the long-term costs of a new military posture so that the taxpayers will realize what would be required.

In 1950, the drafting of NSC-68, which was officially entitled "The Report by the Secretaries of State and Defense on United States Objectives and Programs for National Security," was begun in response to the Soviet Union's first explosion of a nuclear device. But the authors from the State and Defense departments, largely under the guidance of Secretary of State Dean Acheson, went beyond their instructions to reverse the policy of accommodation with the Soviet Union. With the approval of President Truman, they embarked the nation on a policy of building strong alliances with friendly nations and seeking to contain the Soviet Union. NSC-68 provided the intellectual framework within which most diplomatic and military strategy was formulated during and long after the Korean War.

The authors of NSC-68 rejected accommodation with the Soviet Union because "the free world will not succeed in making effective use of its vastly superior political, economic, and military potential to build a tolerable state of order among nations." They shunned isolation. "There is no way to make ourselves inoffensive to the Kremlin except by complete submission to its will," the authors said. "Therefore, isolation would in the end condemn us to capitulate or to fight alone." NSC-68 likewise rejected preventive war as "generally unacceptable to Americans."

The charter, instead, elected a fourth course, which was to deter and contain the Soviet Union by building military, political, and economic strength of the United States and like-minded allies: "We can expect no lasting abatement of the crisis unless and until a change occurs in the nature of the Soviet system," it said. "The resort to force, internally or externally, is the last resort for a free society." Much in NSC-68 remains applicable today. But in at least one respect, NSC-68 would not be a good example for the late 1980s—it was kept secret until 1975. A new charter should be written so that it could be made public, debated, and revised until it musters the widest possible support and is seen as evidence of national unity. As the authors of NSC-68 preached but did not practice:

There are risks in making ourselves strong. A large measure of sacrifice and discipline will be demanded of the American people. They will be asked to give up some of the benefits which they have come to associate with their freedoms. Nothing could be more important than that they fully understand the reasons for this.

A new charter would state fundamental national interests and provide a strong and dispassionate assessment of the threats to those national interests, especially but not exclusively from the Soviet Union. That assessment, drawing on the best factual intelligence the United States can offer, should be free of the cries of "The Russians are coming, the Russians are coming" that have been so prevalent in the national debate in recent years. Americans today need clear, cool, hardheaded analyses, not slogans.

The new charter would outline the comprehensive political, economic, diplomatic, and military strategies needed to repel those threats. Since 1950, the United States has been committed to two wars and innumerable other military conflicts that have brought repeatedly into question the authority of the President to send forces into hostilities. The provisions of the Constitution, pertinent laws, and the War Powers Resolution should be reviewed and a consensus reached as to when and under what circumstances the President may act independently, and when with the advice and consent of Congress.

It would be particularly helpful if a presidential commission could produce a serious and reliable estimate of the ability of the American economy to sustain a military force in peacetime. Much of the debate over national defense in the 1980s has revolved around questions of what America can or cannot afford, a debate marked by considerable emotion, not a small amount of chicanery on many sides, and little solid analysis.

The Pentagon is the obvious place to initiate bold changes. Despite several changes since the Defense Department was established in 1947, the Secretary of Defense is still not the master of his own house. The Pentagon should be rid of feudal domains and the Secretary of Defense affirmed as the civilian official in undisputed charge, responsible to the President and accountable to the Congress for the department's performance. The number of principal deputies to the secretary should be limited to ensure clear-cut lines of authority. The Deputy Secretary would, as now, be the number two in charge and the day-to-day manager of the department.

Four under secretaries would consolidate control over the broad functions of the department. The Under Secretary for Policy and Intelligence would draft the fundamental policies of the department and would assume direction of the Defense Intelligence Agency, the National Security Agency, and some intelligence functions acquired from military departments. The Under Secretary for Combat Forces would be responsible for recruiting, training, equipping, and administering the armed forces. The Under Secretary for Arms Acquisition would supervise the development and purchase of all weapons for the armed forces, with a particular eye to standardizing and eliminating duplication. The Under Secretary for Military Support would be responsible for logistics, transport, and communications of the entire department and the forces. In addition, there would be staff assistant secretaries, including the comptroller, director of program evaluation and analysis, chief legal adviser, director of legislative liaison, and public affairs adviser.

In the new regime, the Under Secretary for Policy and Intelligence would be responsible for ensuring that military strategy and policies were in accord with national strategy set by the President. Much of that Under Secretary's operation would continue as it is today, such as drawing up the annual *Defense Guidance* to provide a rationale for budget decisions. The Under Secretary would continue to maintain liaison with the State Department on political-military matters and to have assistant secretaries who specialized in foreign regional matters. He would be the Defense Department's main liaison with the Central Intelligence Agency. Within the department, all strategic, long-term intelligence functions would come under his purview, as sound intelligence is the basis for realistic policy. Tactical intelligence would remain under the control of combatant commanders and their component forces.

Appointing an Under Secretary for Combat Forces would be among the most far-reaching changes in the Defense Department. It would, in effect, consolidate the functions of the former Secretaries of the Army, Navy, and Air Force, plus those of the Assistant Secretaries of Defense for Health, Reserve Affairs, and Manpower. The Under Secretary for Combat Forces would have four civilian assistant secretaries who would be responsible for land, sea, tactical air, and strategic nuclear forces. Reporting to those assistant secretaries would be the uniformed chiefs of staff of each service. The staffs of each service would be integrated, combining the civilian and military staffs that exist in the military departments today and eliminating duplication. Civilian officials, for instance, might be in charge of recruiting while military officers set policy for training. Peacetime health for service people and their dependents could be the responsibility of a civilian doctor or medical administrator; combat medical care would be the province of a military doctor. Financial matters could be left to a civilian, but military promotions would be the responsibility of serving officers.

The Under Secretary for Arms Acquisition would be in charge of the Pentagon's hardware purchases. Under his control would be consolidated the research, development, and testing of weapons and equipment for all forces. Many of those functions today are scattered among the military services and the Department of Defense. That under secretary would be responsible for the purchase of all arms and equipment, but not of supplies that would be in the domain of the Under Secretary for Support. Among his primary objectives would be to eliminate today's costly duplication. The Under Secretary for Arms Acquisition would be charged, for example, with developing and buying fighter planes that could operate both from land and from aircraft carriers, and missiles that could be used by all services. He would be responsible for obtaining radios with which all services could talk to each other, and medical equipment that Army, Navy, and Air Force doctors alike would use. He would devote much attention to achieving economies of scale in the production of arms so that the taxpayers could buy sixty airplanes of one kind for considerably less than they pay for sixty airplanes of two different types today—or, better yet, buy seventy-five airplanes for the current price of sixty.

Like the other under secretaries, the Under Secretary for Arms Acquisition would be a political appointee. But the procurement bureaucracy serving the Under Secretary would be a corps of permanent specialists. To eliminate the "revolving door" of executives rotating between the government and the defense industry, those specialists would be forbidden after a certain period of government employment, say ten years, from taking jobs in the defense industry. Moreover, the procurement specialists would be civilians, not military officers. To provide operational expertise and advice, military officers from the field would be assigned as advisers, not program managers, to the procurement staff for two or three years. But they, too, would be forbidden from later accepting employment with a defense contractor.

The Under Secretary for Military Support, the fourth of the new under secretaries, would be responsible for pulling together strategic transport, long-range communications, and logistic operations that are now divided among the services. By having a single top-level advocate for these functions, which are neglected in some cases and duplicated in others, the armed forces would have a single voice at the budget table contending for the support they need at a reasonable cost to the taxpayers. Rail transport, for instance, is now the province of the Army, sea movement that of the Navy, and airlift that of the Air Force. But no one is in charge of making sure they work together. The Under Secretary for Military Support would assemble those parts into a cohesive whole. The same would be true of long-range communications, engineering support for bases, and bulk purchases of thousands of routine items such as oil, paper, and shoelaces. Tactical transport, combat communications, combat engineering, and front-line supply systems would remain under the control of local commanders.

A new service, the Military Support Service, would be under the guidance of the Under Secretary for Military Support for training and administration but under the operational control of the Chief of Military Staff and the Commander in Chief of the Military Support Service. It would be a mixture of civilian and military units, each performing a function for which it was best suited. A civilian train crew, for instance, would move tanks to a port where civilian stevedores would load them aboard an attack transport with a military crew for delivery to a combat zone overseas. There the tanks would be unloaded by military stevedores and handed over to Army tank crews. Similarly, civilians could operate, as many do now, centralized supply and maintenance depots in the United States while military personnel could run them overseas in combat zones.

To command the forces raised, trained, and armed by the Defense Department would be the task of the Chief of Military Staff. As the operational commander of United States forces, he would wear five stars as a General of the Army or Admiral of the Fleet and would be the only five-star officer on active duty. His duties would include defining geographic areas of responsibility for commanders in chief, or CINCs, of the combatant commands and deploying forces to them. A primary task would be to supervise the drawing of war plans by

Proposed Organization of the Department of Defense

SECRETARY OF DEFENSE ················ Military Advisory Council

DEPUTY SECRETARY OF DEFENSE

Under Secretary Policy & Intel.	Under Secretary Combat Forces	Under Secretary Arms Acquisition	Under Secretary Military Support
AS-NATO	AS-Army Ch. of Staff	AS-Research	AS-Transport
AS-EA,LA,ME	AS-Navy Ch. of Staff	AS-Development	AS-Commo
AS-DIA	AS-TAF Ch. of Staff	AS-Testing	AS-Logistics
AS-NSA	AS-SNF Ch. of Staff	AS-Procurement	AS-MSS Ch. of Staff

Staff Assistant Secretaries
Comptroller Legal Legislative
PA&E IG Public Affairs

Chief of Military Staff
Vice Chief of Military Staff

Joint Military Staff
—Plans
—Operations
—Budget

CINC SNF	CINC CONUS	CINC South	CINC Atl	CINC Pac	CINC Eur	CINC Cent	CINC MSS

AS = Assistant Secretary; NATO = North Atlantic Treaty Organization; EA = East Asia; LA = Latin America; ME = Middle East; DIA = Defense Intelligence Agency; NSA = National Security Agency; TAF = Tactical Air Force; SNF = Strategic Nuclear Force; MSS = Military Support Service; PA&E = Program Analysis & Evaluation; IG = Inspector General; CONUS = Continental United States.

the CINCs to make sure that the various regional plans fit together. The Chief of Military Staff, who would serve for four years, would supervise joint training exercises and peacetime operations.

In time of hostilities, the Chief of Military Staff would employ the forces and supervise operations, especially when they crossed boundaries separating the combatant commands. The objective would be to conduct coordinated rather than divided operations, selecting forces and assigning them missions according to which unit could do what job best, not just making sure that everyone got a piece of the action. Finally, the Chief of Military Staff would provide the overall, coordinated operational point of view in deliberations over the Pentagon budget, particularly in presenting the views of his immediate subordinates, the commanders in chief of the field commands.

In accord with standard military practice, the Chief of Military Staff would have a deputy ready to take his place when the chief is away or unable to perform his duties. That officer, wearing four stars, would come from another service, would serve for four years, and would be another voice in Washington for the commanders in chief in the field. The director of the Joint Military Staff would be a three-star officer in a billet through which would rotate officers from each service. The ranks of the Joint Military Staff would be filled from officers with field experience and from all services. Officers would serve on the joint staff in three- or four-year tours to bring in fresh operational expertise. But those officers would come under the control of the Chief of Military Staff and his principal subordinates, and their allegiance to the joint staff would be reinforced by having their ratings written by senior officers on the joint staff, not by their services. To make the joint staff a choice assignment that the best and most experienced officers would seek, a tour there, or on the joint staff of a unified combatant command, would be a prerequisite to promotion to brigadier general or rear admiral. Moreover, the Chief of Military Staff would approve all promotions of generals and admirals.

While the Joint Chiefs of Staff as it is now constituted would be abolished, a group to render military advice to the President and the Secretary of Defense should be retained. The chiefs of staff of each service, along with the Chief of Military Staff and his deputy, would be formed into a Military Advisory Council. That council would stay out of the everyday operations of the armed forces and would concentrate on advising the President and the Secretary of Defense on long-term military objectives and policies, including military spending, alliances and treaties, and arms control.

In the structure envisioned here, there would be little chance that the Chief of Military Staff and the Joint Military Staff could endanger American democracy. Two fundamental controls and a deeply in-grained military tradition would prevent undue military influence. First, the President and the Secretary of Defense, the Deputy Sec-retary of Defense, and the four Under Secretaries of Defense, all civilians, would have control over everything except actual military operations. They would exert, in a centralized, clearly defined system, controls that do not now exist. Second, the Congress would retain the power to authorize and appropriate funds; the Secretary of Defense and his principal subordinates would control the expenditure of funds. In any United States government function, control of money is tan-tamount to control of everything else. Third, a strong tradition within the military services of submitting to civilian control has become rooted over the last two hundred years. It is taught in military schools from bottom to top and is preached by senior military commanders who assert that the role of American soldiers, when orders are given by properly constituted civilian authorities, is, "Do as you are told."

Abolishing the military departments, thus eliminating them from operations, would do much to strengthen the authority of the com-manders in chief of the combatant commands in the Atlantic, Pacific, and other regions. So would the establishment of a Chief of Military Staff and the Joint Military staff and a clear-cut chain of command from the Chief of Military Staff to the CINCs. To break the hold of each service on those feudal domains, the officer filling each CINC's position should come, in rotation, from a different service each time a change is made. The European command would no longer be the domain of the Army, the Pacific no longer a Navy fief. A variety of commanding officers would enrich the experience of the staffs of the commands and widen the experience of the top commanders. The joint staffs of the combatant commands should be smaller reflections of the Joint Military Staff in Washington and assembled under the same criteria. Those staffs would assist their commanders in running joint training and peacetime operations, drawing up war plans for approval in Washington, and, should hostilities break out, conducting wartime operations. The CINCs should be asked for their views on basic budget decisions, continuing a practice started during the Reagan Administration.

Because most boundaries marking areas of responsibility for com-batant commands were drawn years ago and because most were in-tended to satisfy service prerogatives more than military needs, they should be redrawn. The Strategic Nuclear Force should be made responsible for the nuclear forces of the United States, controlling both offensive and defensive forces. Another command should become responsible for conventional defense of the United States, a task for which responsibility is divided today. That command's boundaries would be drawn out in the Atlantic and Pacific, and its components would include units from the ground, naval, and tactical air forces. The Southern Command's area should include Mexico, now ignored, and the Caribbean, now part of the Atlantic Command. The European command would be reduced by the withdrawal of large numbers of forces; the Pacific Command's area would be reduced at sea because the Indian Ocean would fall under the control of the Central Command—it is now divided at the high-water mark along the littoral of Southwest Asia.

The armed forces, which are still organized to meet the needs of 1945, should be realigned to meet the needs of the 1990s and the twenty-first century. The objective of a realignment of forces would be cohesive, coordinated operations that would cut down on rivalry and improve combat effectiveness. The management of air space over a battlefield, for instance, is an immensely complicated task, given the numbers of aircraft, their high speeds and agility, and the lethality of their weapons. When the aircraft of a second service are added, the complications more than double because aircraft, tactics, and communications are different. If the aircraft of a third and fourth service are added, the situation can approach chaos, especially if communications are inadequate and joint tactics have not been practiced.

Equally important, the realignment of the military services would reduce interservice squabbling over money and the consequent duplication of staffs and weapons, thus helping to bring military spending into line. Each of the services today suffers from the "not-invented-here" syndrome. The Navy can come up with a good widget, but the Air Force staff, partly out of desire to preserve their jobs and partly out of habit, will ignore it in favor of spending large sums of the taxpayers' money to invent their own widget. The expenditure of billions of dollars by the Air Force and the Navy to develop the MX and Trident II intercontinental missiles is a case in point. With relatively small adaptations, one could have been modified for use by the other. If the nuclear forces had been under one command, it is reasonable to assume the Pentagon would have gotten more for the taxpayers' money by developing only one missile.

In rearranging the forces themselves, it would be tempting to absorb the Marine Corps into the Army as the nation doesn't need and should not be required to pay for two ground forces. But the tradition and esprit of the Marine Corps, which count for much in military operations, are too valuable to be lost. Therefore the Marine Corps should become a corps within the Army, something like the 18th Airborne Corps or the III Corps of armored and mechanized divisions. The Marine Corps headquarters would be abolished and its staff incorporated into the Army staff. But the distinctive Marine uniform, the designation of Marine divisions, and the marine missions in amphibious warfare should be retained and nurtured. (As this is written, there can be heard across the land the sound of muskets being taken down from over mantelpieces, and powder and shot being rammed home. No service is more jealous of its prerogatives and history than the Marine Corps, a jealousy that is understandably rooted in battle-fields from Tripoli to Inchon. But this is precisely the sort of bold change that is necessary to prepare the armed forces for the future and the sort of pain and sacrifice that should be accepted.)

Under this proposal, naval aviation would become part of the new Tactical Air Force. Submarines armed with ballistic missiles would be transferred to the new Strategic Nuclear Force. Transport vessels would be assigned to the new Military Support Service. But the Navy would continue to drive aircraft carriers, warships, amphibious ships, combat auxiliaries, and attack submarines across and under the seas as the main force for American power projection. Those ships, however, would be under the operational control of the commander in chief of the region in which they were operating, not under the orders of the Chief of Naval Operations in Washington as is tacitly the case today.

The Air Force would be reformed as the new Tactical Air Force. The present Air Force's bombers and their tankers, along with its intercontinental missiles, would be transferred to the new Strategic Nuclear Force. Long-range transport aircraft of the Military Airlift Command would go to the new Military Support Service. But medium-range transports such as the C-130 would be absorbed into the new Tactical Air Force to give local commanders tactical mobility. The Tactical Air Force would acquire Navy and Marine Corps aviation, although distinction between land-based air power and sea-based air power would be necessary. Certain numbers of aircraft would still be fitted with tailhooks and landing gear to land on aircraft carriers, and certain numbers of pilots would be required to qualify for carrier landings. But tactical coordination could be accomplished and large savings achieved by cutting down on the number of different aircraft. Moreover, some aircraft would remain in other services. The Army's helicopter gunships are, in reality, flying artillery and would remain with that service. The same would be true for the Marine Corps. Each service has transport helicopters that are flying trucks or jeeps and should remain where they are.

The formation of a Strategic Nuclear Force, with control over all but battlefield nuclear weapons, would be intended to eliminate costly competitive duplication of weapons such as the Air Force's MX and the Navy's Trident II missiles. With one budget, interservice bickering over which service got what weapons would end. In addition, the SNF would make coordinated target planning easier and improve communication and operations among the forces. A variety of weapons gives the President flexibility in responding to attack. Variety also preserves what the nuclear theologians call synergism, meaning the whole is stronger than the sum of the parts. Variety further compounds the difficulties confronting Soviet target planners by forcing them to keep many different targets in view. But proliferation can be carried too far. The Air Force has ground-launched and air-launched cruise missiles; the Navy has surface-launched and submarine-launched cruise missiles; the Army has Pershing II medium-range ballistic missiles. All have similar missions, but planning targets for five sets of crews in three services and maintaining communication among them are horrendously complicated. An SNF would ease that.

Even with this sweeping realignment of the forces, however, interservice rivalry may be so deeply ingrained in the military services that it would continue. A strenuous effort should be made to change those attitudes. The military service, unlike other institutions in American life, has the advantage of being structured and thus able to enforce swift changes, at least on the surface. At West Point, the Naval Academy, and the Air Force Academy, there should be more student exchanges—for summer training, for a semester, for a year—than is the case now. Young officers should have yearlong tours with another service, and more officers should attend middle-level and senior military schools in another service. Officers aspiring to become generals and admirals should serve not only on joint staffs but with another service in a staff or command position. A small but important point: the senior leadership of each service should put out the word that pejoratives about another service will no longer be tolerated.

To man the armed forces, the peacetime volunteer force should be continued because it has been the success story of the 1980s, with the draft held in reserve for wartime. Volunteers make better soldiers and sailors than do conscripts. Raising an armed force with volunteers is fairer than a draft because the taxes to pay the volunteers are assessed across the entire American population.

At the same time, the nation may want to consider universal military training, recognizing that such a program would be costly. It would require a substantial investment to establish training bases and large sums each year to operate. If connected with mandatory service in the reserves, however, such training would provide a trained pool for mobilization in a crisis and should satisfy the demands of those who assert that military service is not being borne fairly by all segments of the population.

Under universal military training, every young man physically, mentally, and morally fit would be inducted, without exemption. He would be given sixteen weeks of basic military training either all at once or over two periods, eight weeks at a time so that schooling would not be disrupted. Each would then be required to serve in an active reserve unit of his choice, in any of the services, for a year to eighteen months, during which he would be trained for that service. After that, the trained people would be placed on an inactive reserve list until they reached their twenty-fifth birthdays.

During basic training, the young men would be paid either the minimum wage or a nominal sum, perhaps $100 a month. But it would be paid equally to all. At the end of basic training, a young man who wished to enter active duty in any service would be permitted to do so, so long as there was an opening. Over the long run, that route would replace recruiting as a source of new people for the services.

The universal military training program would be solely that. It would not provide for people who might want to do community work, enter the Peace Corps, or undertake other civic duties such as volunteering for the police force or hospital aide. A compulsory program would be constitutional only if it was limited to military service, since the Constitution, as interpreted by the Supreme Court, permits a draft to raise armed forces. A broader program would violate the constitutional prohibition against involuntary servitude. Since the Supreme Court has exempted women from the draft, they would be exempt from universal military service. But they would be permitted to volunteer for the armed forces just as now.

The main objective of changes in the role of Congress in the nation's military affairs would be to reduce, as much as possible, the pork barrel of funds voted to enrich electoral districts rather than to enhance the national defense. The taxpayers' money should be spent to build forces, not to provide jobs back home. To do that, Congress should be returned to its function of oversight, setting objectives and determining whether the executive branch reaches them. Congress, which is unable to discipline itself, should be prevented from dabbling in military affairs and interfering with the normal operation of the Defense Department.

Perhaps the single most important reform would be to prohibit Congress from adding to the military budget, inserting into the budget programs not requested by the President, or moving funds from one line or category to another. If the administration asks for 720 M-1 Abrams tanks in a given budget, Congress would not be able to approve 840 just because that would make more jobs in Michigan and Ohio. By forbidding such additions, officials within the Defense Department with private agendas would be precluded from running around the end of the administration to get a partisan supporter on Capitol Hill to slip into the budget funds for the favored project. Getting the Congress to adopt such a practice by law would cause enormous pain. (Like the proposal for moving the Marine Corps into the Army, cries of anguish can be heard as this is written.) But it would be in the national interest and, in effect, would relieve many congressmen of political pressures from home. "The law," a legislator could tell his voters, "won't let me propose funds for a new armory in our district." That would not prevent a congressman from importuning the Pentagon to put his pet scheme into the proposed budget, but such pressures would be easier for an administration to resist.

A second reform, one that has generated increasing support in the Reagan Administration and on both sides of Capitol Hill, is the two-year budget. No matter how much time Congress has been given, the legislature meets effectively only three days a week, from Tuesday through Thursday, and has shown itself unable to consider, amend, and vote on important bills before a new fiscal year starts. Such delays, which are usually covered by continuing resolutions permitting spending at the same level as the previous fiscal year, causes havoc. Changes in programs and new programs must await passage of the new budget. In addition, the one-year budget exacerbates the pork barrel as each congressman feels he must constantly protect the favored project. A two-year budget would ease that pressure.

Under this scheme, an administration would introduce a two-year budget in January of a nonelection year—such as January 1987, for the fiscal period to begin on October 1, 1988, and end on September 30, 1990—to lessen the partisanship of negotiations over the military budget. In a presidential election year, military spending should, of course, be the subject of vigorous debate.

The cumbersome committee structure of Congress should be reformed to reduce the number of committees with oversight of military affairs and to permit those charged with that responsibility to concentrate on their duties. The Budget Committees on both sides of the Congress should set ceilings on military spending in line with the overall federal budget. But the Armed Services and Appropriations Committees, which basically have evolved until they do much the same job, should have their functions combined. A new committee would scrutinize programs submitted by the Defense Department, shape the budget for the fiscal period, and prepare a bill for consideration on the floor in which funds would be both authorized and appropriated. Lastly, the subcommittees of the new joint committee should be organized to parallel the new organization of the Pentagon, with a subcommittee providing oversight for the areas of responsibility under each of the four under secretaries and the Chief of Military Staff.

Curing the ills of the defense industry would be among the most difficult tasks in the reordering of the United States military structure. None of the options is overly appealing. The nation could go on as is, with minor reforms, but that would only continue the production of weapons of poor quality, doubtful reliability, and high price. At the other extreme would be nationalizing the larger companies, turning them into government arsenals. But that would require an immense investment, would be politically and ideologically unpalatable, and would not guarantee efficient operations.

Thus, as a middle-ground compromise, the defense industry should remain in private hands but be regulated as a public utility, which it is. Most large defense contractors are monopolies. On the other side, the Defense Department is a monopsony, the only buyer of most of the arms and equipment turned out by the defense industry. At best, competition can only be artificial and can never regulate the defense industry the way competition regulates normal industrial and commercial enterprises.

An independent public commission with a bipartisan membership should be set up outside the Pentagon as a watchdog over the incestuous relationship between the defense industry and the Pentagon. Members of a Federal Military Procurement Commission would be nominated by the President for terms of three to five years, be approved by the Senate, and be removed only for cause. The commission would function in a quasi-judicial manner, as do other regulatory commissions, and would scrutinize contracts, performance, quality controls, costs, and profits on behalf of the public. The commission would not question the substance of policy or the choice of weapons but the execution of the public's business. The commission, for instance, could insist that contracts known as "cost-plus," in which the government pays the cost of a program plus an agreed fee no matter how well or badly it is run, be used sparingly. It could insist contracts be written so defense contractors share the cost of overruns but benefit from the savings of underruns. In many cases, it could insist on fixed-price contracts, as the Navy has in recent years, in which the defense contractor agrees to a price, and that's it. His profit or loss depends on how well he manages the program.

In the latter half of the 1980s, the temptation to return to the isolation of the 1930s is strong. But the United States has become too much of a world power, has taken on too much responsibility, and has become too much of a target for dangerous adversaries to return to that comfortable era. At the same time, the United States has assumed more than a fair share of the military and financial burden for the common defense of the industrial democracies and should shift that burden so that it is equally distributed. As part of the long-range reordering of American military power, the United States should tell its principal allies in Europe and Asia that they must do more for their own and the common defense. The United States should inform them, in general, that the United States expects to consolidate military spending and the size of American forces at current levels. Expansion of the free world's forces would then be the task of allied nations. The United States should set a deadline between five and ten years hence for reaching those objectives.

The United States should make clear that this is a matter for consultation, not for negotiation. Specifics and timing can be worked out, but the objective should not be open for debate. American leaders should inform allied leaders that a failure to live up to American expectations will cause the United States to reconsider its adherence to the alliance. Surely it is plain that Americans cannot defend people who are not willing to defend themselves. Equally plain, the defense of the United States is weakened when Americans take on the burden of defending people who are unwilling to defend themselves.

The issue of withdrawing American forces from abroad is separate but related in that foreign nations should take up the slack left by the departure of American forces. This change, too, should be made over a period of five to ten years in consultation with allies, but should not be the subject of negotiation. Large numbers of American forces should be returned to the United States to cut costs, to give the United States more flexibility as to where, when, and under what circumstances American forces will be deployed, and to reduce the turbulence caused by rotating people between the United States and bases abroad. Until now, European governments have prevented the United States from moving American forces in Europe to the Middle East or Africa, should they be needed in those regions.

A point to be underscored: All United States forces withdrawn from overseas should be kept on active duty in the force structure; to bring them home and demobilize them would save money but would greatly weaken the national and the collective defense and defeat the purpose of the change.

The United States should withdraw from Western Europe all but one of five divisions, plus smaller ground units, stationed there now. The special Berlin brigade, a symbol of American commitment to that outpost, should remain on duty. All but three of the twenty-two tactical fighter squadrons should be withdrawn. Consequent cuts in supporting forces should be made. American bases should be put into a caretaker status or returned to the host nation. The one or two aircraft carriers routinely deployed in the Mediterranean should be withdrawn and that patrol turned over to the Europeans. American tactical nuclear weapons should be returned to the United States. The Pershing II and ground-launched cruise missiles, both with nuclear warheads, recently deployed to Europe should remain as a bargaining chip in arms control negotiations with the Soviet Union, but with a long-term plan that they be withdrawn. As symbols of the American military commitment, annual exercises such as REFORGER, in which large numbers of American troops are transported to Europe for a month of maneuvers, should be continued and enlarged. Sets of tanks, guns, and other weapons stored in Europe should remain there for American soldiers to pick up after they fly in.

In Asia, the United States should dismantle the United Nations Command in Korea and withdraw all forces, including tactical nuclear weapons, stationed there now. Similarly, American forces stationed in Japan proper should be withdrawn and consolidated on the island of Okinawa, in southern Japan. A Marine Corps regiment should remain on Okinawa, with a battalion rotating for field duty in Korea regularly to show the flag. An air wing should remain on Okinawa, with squadrons rotating for temporary duty to Korea. The aircraft carrier *Midway* and her battle group, for whom Yokosuka in Japan is home port, should be transferred to Guam, the American island in the central Pacific. Two United States bases in the Philippines, Clark

Air Force Base and Subic Bay Naval Base, should be retained with small caretaker forces.

In the Indian Ocean and Persian Gulf, the Central Command should continue as a planning staff for operations in that region. But the patrol should be turned over to the West Europeans and the Japanese since those nations are far more dependent on oil from there than is the United States. At the same time, the United States should make clear to Saudi Arabia, Egypt, other Arab nations, and Pakistan that they cannot count on military help from the United States so long as their critical attitude toward America continues.

While large formations of ground and air forces should be brought home, and the Navy withdrawn from the Mediterranean and Indian oceans, the Navy should continue to patrol the far reaches of the Atlantic and Pacific oceans and in waters closer to home. The patrols of fast-attack submarines, in particular, should continue under every ocean and the seven seas, wherever they must go to accomplish their mission of safeguarding the nation from missile or cruise missile assault.

Without question, the cost of military power is among the most critical issues confronting the nation today, all the more so for the continuing large deficits in the federal government's budget. It is also evident that military spending can be checked and thus contribute to a reduction in the federal deficit. Equally important, military spending can be cut even as the nation's military power is increased. If the military budget were frozen at its current level, military spending would gradually but steadily drop as a percentage of the gross national product and of the federal budget, both of which will continue to expand.

A freeze in military spending should be coupled with the sweeping overhaul of the military establishment. Only by rationalizing would the military establishment be able to maintain or to expand the nation's military power with the allotted funds. The sole exceptions to the freeze should be extra funds to cover inflation, plus funds for one-time expenses, such as refurbishing a camp for a division coming home from overseas and transporting that division to its new home. Those costs would be more than paid off in savings in subsequent years.

The Gramm-Rudman-Hollings measure, which went into effect in 1986, seeks to force the government to balance the federal budget by 1991. It points in the right direction in holding down military spending, but it will do little good for the overall military posture of the

United States if it is isolated from efforts to curb American military commitments, the forward deployment of forces, the pork barrel of congress, the rivalries among the services, and the abuses of the defense industry.

The formation of the Strategic Nuclear Force should lead to rational rather than bureaucratic decisions on nuclear weapons. For example, the congressional prohibition against deploying more than fifty MX Peacekeeper missiles in existing Minuteman III silos should be upheld. No stationary, undefended missile based on the face of the earth can any longer survive a nuclear attack, given the improvements in accuracy and explosive power of incoming warheads. Moreover, missiles based on land cannot be nearly so mobile as those based in the air or at sea. Thus the Midgetman, a small intercontinental ballistic missile with a single warhead, should continue in research but should not be produced and deployed unless a compelling case for it can be made. Similarly, research should continue on the deep underground missile base, but the program should be restrained because the project appears to have limited use.

In contrast, work on the Trident II, or D-5, submarine-launched ballistic missile should be pushed because it has the greatest mobility of any large missile on earth and because American submarine technology is far ahead of that of the Soviet Union. Every effort should be made to maintain that technical lead. Cruise missiles, all based on the same technology, have been deployed on aircraft, submarines, surface ships, and the ground. While such versatility is to be cherished, basing the missiles aboard aircraft and on submarines would seem the most effective; surface deployments, whether on ground or at sea, seem superfluous, and no more should be made. Similarly, the Pershing II medium-range missile adds little to the inventory not already provided by the cruise missiles or the bigger intercontinental missiles. No more should be made.

The B-1 bomber is necessary to replace the B-52 bomber as a penetrating aircraft. But the B-1s would have limited use in a nuclear war, since the bulk of the warheads would be delivered by missile, and the 100 already ordered would seem sufficient for a limited, conventional war. Moreover, the Stealth bomber, designed to evade radar, is scheduled for production in the early 1990s and should be pushed as a companion aircraft because of its technical advances. Even if it works only partly as well as its inventors contend, it would force the Soviet Union into expenditures for new radar defenses, taking funds and engineering talent away from projects that could harm the United

States. But production of the Stealth bomber should be limited because it has limited uses, either in conventional or nuclear war. The day of the bomber is fast passing, its missions being almost completely taken over by missiles.

On protracted nuclear war, the United States should spend the funds needed to ensure that the President could communicate with the nuclear forces in times of crisis and conflict. But the threat of nuclear war is so remote, provided a sufficient deterrent is maintained, and the possibility that it could be conducted like a field campaign during World War II so unlikely that it seems senseless to spend great sums on something that will not happen. Should nuclear war come, the profound panic in a completely new human experience is likely to be so great that the war will be over in a few spasmodic exchanges and the human race will be left with the task of trying to begin civilization again.

Defensively, President Reagan's Strategic Defense Initiative, or Star Wars, is an attempt to generate another swing in the history of war, in which a pendulum has swung back and forth between offense and defense. It is an effort worth pursuing, but it seems a cruel hoax to hold out to the American people, as President Reagan has, the promise of a shield that would prevent the United States from suffering grievous damage in a nuclear war. No shield, no fortress, no Maginot Line has ever been able to do that, and the Strategic Defense Initiative, delving as it is into great unknowns, is even less likely to be impervious.

Thus, work on the Strategic Defense Initiative should proceed, but carefully. It should not be allowed to gallop along with a life and dynamic of its own, regardless of feasibility, as have so many weapons programs in the past. Rather, it should be checked each step of the way. If it works, proceed. But if it doesn't work, be ready to terminate the program. In addition, the Strategic Defense Initiative should be limited to defending military targets such as missile silos, submarine ports, bomber airfields, and headquarters that it would have a reasonable chance of protecting. That would hold the cost in line with the risk. Most important, advocates of the Strategic Defense Initiative should cease the hypocrisy about the program and play it straight with the American people.

Frederick the Great wrote in the eighteenth century that "war is not an affair of chance." In the conduct of war, deliberate leadership, careful planning, and skilled execution culminate in missions that are accomplished efficiently and with the least loss of life. Like war itself, preparing for war in the cause of keeping peace should not be an affair of chance. Rather, to arm a nation so that it may protect its citizens requires the same deliberate leadership, careful planning, and skilled execution as the conduct of military operations. Unhappily, those traits are rare in the making of military policy and the discharge of military responsibilities in the United States.

The nation deserves better. American soldiers, sailors, marines, and airmen who stand guard on the ramparts in a dangerous profession deserve better leadership from their political officials and military commanders. American voters deserve more thoughtful deliberation and closer teamwork from the political leaders they elect and from the civilian officials and military officers whose appointments and commissions accrue from those elections. American taxpayers deserve more careful use of the money that comes from their pockets to pay for American military power. American citizens deserve an all-around better performance in the conduct of their military affairs not only because it is their due but because, absent that, America is in peril.

BIBLIOGRAPHY

BOOKS

Abrahamson, James L. *The American Homefront: Revolutionary War, Civil War, World War I, World War II.* Washington, D.C.: National Defense University, 1983.

Acheson, Dean. *Present at the Creation: My Years at the State Department.* New York: W. W. Norton and Co., 1969.

Adams, Gordon. *The Iron Triangle: The Politics of Defense Contracting.* New York: Council on Economic Priorities, 1981.

Adenauer, Konrad, and the Institute for Foreign Policy Analysis Inc. *The Sixth German-American Roundtable on NATO: NATO and European Security Beyond INF.* Cambridge, Massachusetts, and Washington, D.C.: Institute for Foreign Policy Analysis, 1984.

American Assembly. *Military Service in the United States.* New York: Columbia University, 1981.

Arkin, William M., and Richard W. Fieldhouse. *Nuclear Battlefields: Global Links in the Arms Race.* Cambridge, Massachusetts: Ballinger, 1985.

Aron, Raymond, translated by Ernst Pawel. *The Great Debate: Theories of Nuclear Strategy.* New York: Doubleday and Co., 1965.

Augustine, Norman R. *Augustine's Laws.* New York: American Institute of Aeronautics and Astronautics, 1982.

Barrett, Archie D. *Reappraising Defense Organization.* Washington, D.C.: National Defense University, 1983.

Barrett, Lawrence J. *Gambling with History: Reagan in the White House.* New York: Penguin, 1983.

Berman, Robert P., and John C. Baker. *Soviet Strategic Forces: Requirements and Responses.* Washington, D.C.: Brookings, 1982.

Betts, Richard K. *Soldiers, Statesmen, and Cold War Crises.* Cambridge, Masssachusetts: Harvard University Press, 1977.

———. *Surprise Attack: Lessons for Defense Planning.* Washington, D.C.: Brookings, 1982.

———. *Conventional Forces: What Price Readiness.* Washington, D.C.: Brookings, 1983.

Binkin, Martin, Martin J. Eitelberg, Alvin Schexnider, Marvin Smith. *Blacks and the Military.* Washington, D.C.: Brookings, 1982.

Binkin, Martin, Ire Kyriakopoulos. *Paying the Modern Military.* Washington, D.C.: Brookings, 1981.

Binkin, Martin. *America's Volunteer Military: Progress and Prospects.* Washington, D.C.: Brookings, 1984.

Blair, Bruce G. *Strategic Command and Control: Redefining the Nuclear Threat.* Washington, D.C.: Brookings, 1985.

Blechman, Barry M., and Stephen S. Kaplan. *Force without War: U.S. Armed Forces as a Political Instrument.* Washington, D.C.: Brookings, 1978.

The Boston Study Group. *The Price of Defense: A New Strategy for Military Spending.* New York: New York Times Books, 1979.

Bracken, Paul. *The Command and Control of Nuclear Forces.* New Haven: Yale University Press, 1983.

Braestrup, Peter (ed.). *Vietnam as History: Ten Years after the Paris Peace Accords.* Washington, D.C.: Woodrow Wilson Center for International Scholars, University Press of America, 1984.

———. *Big Story: How the American Press and Television Reported and Interpreted the Crisis of Tet 1968 in Vietnam and Washington.* Boulder, Colorado: Westview Press, 1977.

Brown, Harold. *Thinking About National Security.* Boulder, Colorado: Westview Press, 1983.

Brown, James, and Michael Collins (eds.). *Military Ethics and Professionalism.* Washington, D.C.: National Defense University, 1981.

Bundy, William P. (ed.). *The Nuclear Controversy.* New York: Council on Foreign Relations, New American Library, 1981.

Carnegie Endowment for International Peace. *Challenges for U.S. National Security: Nuclear Strategy Issues of the 1980s.* Washington, D.C.: 1982.

Caputo, Philip. *A Rumor of War.* New York: Holt, Rinehart and Winston, 1977.

Center of Military History. *The War of the American Revolution,* Bicentennial Publication. Washington, D.C.: U.S. Army, 1975.

Chazov, Yevgeni, Leonid Ilyin, Angelina Guskova. *The Danger of Nuclear War, Soviet Physicians' Viewpoint.* Moscow: Novosti Press, 1982.

Chiarelli, Peter W., and Raymond C. Gagnon. *The Politics of Military Reform.* Newport, Rhode Island: Naval War College Center for Advanced Research, June 1985.

Clausewitz, Carl von. *On War,* edited and translated by Michael Howard and Peter Paret. Princeton: Princeton University Press, 1976.

Clark, Asa, Peter Chiarelli, Jeffrey McKitrick, James Reed, (eds.). *The Defense Reform Debate: Issues and Analyses.* Baltimore: Johns Hopkins University Press, 1984.

Cochran, Thomas B., William M. Arkin, and Milton M. Hoenig. *Nuclear Weapons Databook: Vol. 1, U.S. Nuclear Forces and Capabilities.* Cambridge, Massachusetts: Ballinger, 1984.

Cockburn, Andrew. *The Threat: Inside the Soviet Military Machine.* New York: Random House, 1983.

Cohen, Sam. *The Truth About the Neutron Bomb: The Inventor of the Bomb Speaks Out.* New York: William Morrow and Co., 1983.

Collins, John M. *U.S. Defense Planning: A Critique.* Washington, D.C.: Congressional Research Service, 1984.

———. *U.S.–Soviet Military Balance 1980–1985.* Washington, D.C.: Pergamon-Brassey's, 1985.

Comeau, Lois. *Nuts and Bolts and the Pentagon: A Spare Parts Catalog.* Washington, D.C.: Center on Budget and Policy Priorities, August 1984.

Congressional Budget Office. *Defense Spending and the Economy.* Washington, D.C.: Government Printing Office, February 1983.

———. *Reducing the Deficit: Spending and Revenue Options.* Washington, D.C.: Government Printing Office, 1984.

———. *A Review of the Department of Defense, December 31, 1983, Selected Acquisition Report.* Washington, D.C.: July 1984.

Daedalus. *U.S. Defense Policy in the 1980s: Proceedings of the American Academy of Arts and Sciences.* Cambridge, Massachusetts, 1981.

Defense Department. *National Defense Estimates FY 1984, 1985, 1986.* Washington, D.C.

———. *Report on Allied Contributions to the Common Defense.* Washington, D.C.: March 1985.

———. *Report of the DoD Commission on Beirut International Airport Terrorist Act, October 23, 1983.* Washington, D.C.: December 1983.

———. *Going Strong: Women in Defense.* October 1984.

Defense Management Study Group on Military Cohesion. *Cohesion in the Military.* Washington, D.C.: National Defense University, 1984.

Dillard, Walter. *Sixty Days to Peace.* Washington, D.C.: National Defense University, 1982.

Donovan, Robert. *Nemesis: Truman and Johnson in the Coils of War in Asia.* New York: St. Martin's, 1984.

Durch, William (ed.). *National Interests and the Military Use of Space.* Cambridge, Massachusetts: Ballinger, 1984.

Dyson, Freeman. *Weapons and Hope.* New York: Harper & Row, 1984.

Eisenhower, Dwight D. *Crusade in Europe.* Garden City, New York: Doubleday, 1948.

Endicott, John, and Ray Stafford, Jr. (eds.). *American Defense Policy.* Baltimore: Johns Hopkins University Press, 1974.

Fallows, James. *National Defense.* New York: Random House, 1981.

Fitzgerald, Randall, and Gerald Lipson. *Pork Barrel: The Unexpurgated Grace Commission Story of Congressional Profligacy.* Washington, D.C.: CATO Institute, 1984.

Ford, Daniel. *The Button: The Pentagon's Command and Control System—Does It Work?* New York: Simon and Schuster, 1985.

Fullinwider, Robert K. *The AVF and Racial Balance.* College Park, Maryland: Center for Philosophy and Public Policy, University of Maryland, March 2, 1982.

Gabriel, Richard, and Paul Savage. *Crisis in Command: Mismanagement in the Army.* New York: Hill and Wang, a division of Farrar, Straus & Giroux, 1978.

Gansler, Jacques. *The Defense Industry.* Cambridge, Massachusetts: M.I.T. Press, 1980.

Goodwin, Jacob. *Brotherhood of Arms: General Dynamics and the Business of Defending America.* New York: Times Books, 1985.

Graham, Daniel O. *High Frontier: A New National Strategy.* Washington, D.C.: High Frontier Inc., 1982.

Gray, Colin. *Strategic Studies and Public Policy: The American Experience.* Lexington: University of Kentucky Press, 1982.

Grechko, A. A. *The Armed Force of the Soviet Union.* Moscow: Progress Publishers, 1977.

Hackett, John. *The Third World War.* New York: Macmillan, 1978.

———. *The Profession of Arms.* New York: Macmillan, 1983.

Hattendorf, John, Mitchell Simpson III, John Wadleigh. *Sailors and Scholars: The Centennial History of the U.S. Naval War College.* Newport, Rhode Island: Naval War College Press, 1984.

Henderson, Wm. Darryl. *Cohesion: The Human Element in Combat.* Washington, D.C.: National Defense University, 1985.

Hess, Stephen. *The Washington Reporters*. Washington, D.C.: Brookings, 1981.

Heyns, Terry L. *Understanding U.S. Strategy: A Reader*. Washington, D.C.: National Defense University, 1983.

Hudson Institute. *Report by the Committee on Civilian-Military Relationships*. Indianapolis: Hudson Institute, 1984.

Institute for Foreign Policy Analysis. *Security Commitments and Capabilities: Elements of an American Global Strategy*, conference report. Medford, Massachusetts: April 1984.

Jastrow, Robert. *How to Make Nuclear Weapons Obsolete*. Boston: Little, Brown, 1983.

Johnson, James Turner. *Can Modern War Be Just?* New Haven: Yale University Press, 1984.

Joint Chiefs of Staff. *Military Posture FY 1985, 1986, 1987*. Washington, D.C.: Organization of the Joint Chiefs of Staff.

———. *A Concise History of the Organization of the Joint Chiefs of Staff*. Washington, D.C.: Historical Division, JCS, 1980.

Jones, Rodney W. *Small Nuclear Forces*. New York: Praeger and Center for Strategic and International Studies, Georgetown University, 1984.

Kahn, Herman. *Thinking About the Unthinkable in the 1980s*. New York: Simon and Schuster, 1984.

Kaplan, Fred. *The Wizards of Armageddon*. New York: Simon and Schuster, 1983.

Karas, Thomas. *Space Age War: Weapons and Strategies*. New York: Simon and Schuster, 1983.

Karnow, Stanley. *Vietnam: A History*. New York: Viking, 1983.

Kaufman, William W. *The McNamara Strategy*. New York: Harper & Row, 1964.

Keaney, Thomas A. *Strategic Bombers and Conventional Weapons: Airpower Options*. Washington, D.C.: National Defense University, 1984.

Kennan, George F. *Memoirs 1925–1950*. New York: Bantam Books, 1969.

———. *Memoirs 1950–1963*. Boston: Little, Brown, 1972.

Kennedy, Robert F. *Thirteen Days: A Memoir of the Cuban Missile Crisis*. New York: W. W. Norton, 1969.

Kissinger, Henry A. *Nuclear Weapons and Foreign Policy*. Council on Foreign Relations. New York: Harper & Brothers, 1957.

Komer, Robert W. *Maritime Strategy or Coalition Defense?* Cambridge, Massachusetts: Abt Books, 1984.

Kronenberg, Philip S. (ed.). *Planning U.S. Security*. Washington, D.C.: National Defense University, 1981.

Krulak, Victor H. *Organization for National Security: A Study*. Washington, D.C.: United States Strategic Institute, 1983.

Lawrence, T. E. *Seven Pillars of Wisdom: A Triumph*. Middlesex, England: Penguin Books, 1962.

Lefever, Ernest W., and E. Stephen Hunt. *The Apocalyptic Premise: Nuclear Arms Debated*. Washington, D.C.: Ethics and Public Policy Center, 1982.

Leonard, Roger Ashley (ed.). *A Short Guide to Clausewitz on War*. New York: G. P. Putnam's Sons, 1967.

Livingstone, Neil C., and Joseph D. Douglass, Jr. *CBW: The Poor Man's Atomic Bomb: National Security Paper 1*. Cambridge, Massachusetts, and Washington, D.C.: Institute for Foreign Policy Analysis, 1984.

Luttwak, Edward N. *The Pentagon and the Art of War*. New York: Simon and Schuster, 1984.

Martin, Donna. *Defense Procurement Information Papers*. Washington, D.C.: Project on Military Procurement, 1984.

Matloff, Maurice (general editor). *Army Historical Series—American Military History*. Washington, D.C.: U.S. Army Office of the Chief of Military History, U.S. Government Printing Office, 1969.

McCarthy, James R., George B. Allison, Robert Rayfield. *Linebacker II: A View from the Rock*. Maxwell Air Force Base, Alabama: Airpower Research Institute, Air War College, 1979.

McNeill, William H. *The Pursuit of Power: Technology, Armed Forces, and Society since A.D. 1000*. Chicago: University of Chicago Press, 1982.

Millet, Allan R., and Peter Maslowski. *For the Common Defense: A Military History of the United States of America*. New York: The Free Press, a division of Macmillan, 1984.

Nye, Roger H. *The Challenge of Command*. Wayne, New Jersey: Avery Publishing Group, 1986.

O'Brien, William V. *U.S. Military Intervention: Law and Morality*. Beverly Hills: Center for Strategic and International Studies, Sage Publications, 1979.

O'Keefe, Bernard J. *Nuclear Hostages*. Boston: Houghton Mifflin, 1983.

Olvey, Lee, James Golden, Robert C. Kelly. *The Economics of National Security*. Wayne, New Jersey: Avery Publishing Group, 1984.

O'Sullivan, John, and Alan M. Meckler. *The Draft and Its Enemies: A Documentary History*. Urbana: University of Illinois Press, 1974.

Paddock, Alfred H. Jr. *U.S. Army Special Warfare: Its Origins, Psychological and Unconventional Warfare, 1941–1952*. Washington, D.C.: National Defense University, 1982.

Palmer, Bruce Jr. (ed.). *Grand Strategy for the 1980's*. Washington, D.C.: American Enterprise Institute for Public Policy Research, 1978.

———. *The 25-Year War: America's Military Role in Vietnam*. Lexington: University Press of Kentucky, 1984.

Perkins, Stuart L. *Global Demands: Limited Forces: U.S. Army Deployment*. Washington, D.C.: National Defense University, 1984.

Podhoretz, Norman. *The Present Danger*. New York: Simon and Schuster, 1980.

Prados, John. *The Soviet Estimate: U.S. Intelligence Analysis and Russian Military Strength*. New York: Dial Press, 1982.

Pranger, Robert J., and Roger P. Labrie (eds.). *Nuclear Strategy and National Security: Points of View*. Washington, D.C.: American Enterprise Institute for Public Policy Research, 1977.

Quester, George H. *The Future of Nuclear Deterrence*. Lexington, Massachusetts: D. C. Heath, 1986.

Rasor, Dina (ed.). *More Bucks, Less Bang: How the Pentagon Buys Ineffective Weapons*. Washington, D.C.: Fund for Constitutional Government, 1983.

Rearden, Steven L. *The Formative Years, 1947–1950: History of the Office of the Secretary of Defense*. Washington, D.C.: Historical Office, Office of the Secretary of Defense, 1984.

———. *The Evolution of American Strategic Doctrine: Paul Nitze and the Soviet Challenge*. SAIS Papers in International Affairs #4; School of Advanced International

Studies, Johns Hopkins University. Boulder, Colorado: Westview Press, 1984.

Record, Jeffrey, and Robert Hanks. *U.S. Strategy at the Crossroads: Two Views.* Cambridge, Massachusetts, and Washington, D.C.: Foreign Policy Report of the Institute for Foreign Policy Analysis, 1982.

Record, Jeffrey. *Revising U.S. Military Strategy: Tailoring Means to Ends.* Washington, D.C.: Pergamon-Brassey's International Defense Publishers, 1984.

———. *Sizing Up the Soviet Army.* Studies in Defense Policy. Washington, D.C.: Brookings, 1975.

Reed, Robert F. *The U.S.–Japan Alliance: Sharing the Burden of Defense.* Washington, D.C.: National Defense University Press, 1983.

Reinman, Robert A. *National Emergency Telecommunications Policy: Who's In Charge?* Washington, D.C.: National Defense University Press, 1984.

Ridgway, Matthew B. *The Korean War.* New York: Doubleday, 1967.

Scheer, Robert. *With Enough Shovels: Reagan, Bush & Nuclear War.* New York: Random House, 1982.

Schelling, Thomas C. *The Strategy of Conflict.* New York: Oxford University Press, 1963.

Schichtle, Cass. *The National Space Program from the Fifties into the Eighties.* Washington, D.C.: National Defense University Press, 1983.

Scott, Harriet and William. *The Soviet Art of War: Doctrine, Strategy and Tactics.* Boulder, Colorado: Westview Press, 1982.

Spector, Leonard S. *Nuclear Proliferation Today.* New York: Vintage Press, 1984.

Summers, Harry G. Jr. *On Strategy: A Critical Analysis of the Vietnam War.* Novato, California: Presidio Press, 1983.

———. *Vietnam War Almanac.* New York: Facts on File Publications, 1985.

Sun Tzu, translated by Lionel Giles. *The Art of War.* Taipei, Taiwan: Literature House, 1904.

Suvorov, Viktor. *Inside the Soviet Army.* New York: Macmillan, 1982.

Taylor, William J. Jr., and Robert H. Kupperman. *Strategic Requirements for the Army to the Year 2000.* Washington, D.C.: Center for Strategic and International Studies, 1982.

Terry, Wallace. *Bloods: An Oral History of the Vietnam War by Black Veterans.* New York: Random House, 1984.

Tirman, John (ed.), and the Union of Concerned Scientists. *The Fallacy of Star Wars.* New York: Vintage Books, 1984.

Trask, Roger R. *The Secretaries of Defense: A Brief History 1947–1985.* Washington, D.C.: Historical Office, Department of Defense, 1985.

Tyroler, Charles (ed.). *Alerting America: The Papers of the Committee on the Present Danger.* Washington, D.C.: Pergamon-Brassey's International Defense Publishers, 1984.

Uhlig, Frank Jr. (ed.) *The Naval War College Review, Centennial Issue 1884–1984.* Newport, Rhode Island, Naval War College Press, September 1984.

Van Creveld, Martin. *Command in War.* Cambridge, Massachusetts: Harvard University Press, 1985.

Vo Nguyen Giap. *People's War, People's Army.* Hanoi: Foreign Languages Publishing House, 1961.

Walker, Richard Lee. *Strategic Target Planning: Bridging The Gap between Theory and Practice.* Washington, D.C.: National Defense University, 1983.

Webb, James. *Fields of Fire.* New York: Bantam Books, 1979.

Weigley, Russell F. *The American Way of War: A History of United States Military Strategy and Policy.* Bloomington, Indiana: Indiana University Press, 1973.

Weinberger, Caspar W. *Annual Reports to Congress FY 1983–1987.* Washington, D.C.: Department of Defense.

Williams, T. Harry. *The History of American Wars: From Colonial Times to World War I.* New York: Alfred A. Knopf, 1981.

Woodrow Wilson Center for International Scholars. *The National Interests of the United States.* Washington, D.C.: 1981.

Zagano, Phyllis (ed.). *The Nuclear Arms Debate: Volume VI, Number 3.* Hudson River Press: The Book Forum, 1983.

Zumwalt, Elmo R. Jr. *On Watch.* New York: Quadrangle, New York Times Book Co., 1977.

DOCUMENTS AND OTHER PRIMARY SOURCES

Abrahamson, Lt. Gen. James A. The Strategic Defense Initiative. Defense 84, Department of Defense, August 1984.

———. Testimony on the Strategic Defense Initiative. Senate Appropriations Subcommittee on Defense, April 2, 1985.

Abshire, David M. The Atlantic Alliance: The Development of a Resource Strategy. *Signal*, October 1984.

Air Force Academy. Descriptive Characteristics and Comparisons for the Class of 1986, August 1982.

Amlie, Thomas S. US Air Force Memorandum on Cost Reduction. Sept. 14, 1983.

Anderson, Roy A. Improving Defense Procurement. Testimony before the Defense Procurement Subcommittee of the Senate Armed Services Committee, Jan. 30, 1985.

Army, Department of. Survey Results, Professional Development of Officers Study. Washington, D.C., 1985.

Aspin, Les. Manning the Military: The Female Factor. March 5, 1984.

———. Ready or Not. *The New Republic*, Oct. 29, 1984.

———. Speech to Carnegie Endowment, Jan. 17, 1985; reprinted in *Aerospace Daily*, Jan. 18, 1985; pp. 109–113.

———. Interview, *Washington Times*, Feb. 21, 1983.

Atlantic Command. Operation Urgent Fury Report. Norfolk, Virginia, Feb. 6, 1984.

Avco Corporation. John J. Ford Elected Vice President, Government Affairs of Avco Corporation, press release, Jan. 27, 1984.

Bipartisan Appeal to Resolve the Budget Crisis, Presentation to Senate Budget Committee, Feb. 2, 1983.

Brown, George J. The Economic Consequences of Defense Spending: Implications for 1984 and Beyond. Testimony before Task Force on Economic Policy and Growth, House Committee on the Budget, undated.

Brown, Harold. The S.D.I.: Defense Systems and the Strategic Debate, speech at Johns Hopkins University. Washington, D.C., Dec. 14, 1984.

———. Economic Policy and National Security, ORBIS, Summer 1982.

Brown, James R. Testimony before House Appropriations Subcommittee on Defense, March 27, 1984.

Cambridge Reports, February 1985 National Survey on Defense Issues, Cambridge, Massachusetts.

Campbell, David. Speech to DoD Psychologists Conference at Colorado Springs, Colorado, April 18, 1984.

Carter, President Jimmy. Televised Speech to Nation, Jan. 23, 1980.

Center for Strategic and International Studies. Toward a More Effective Defense, Washington, D.C., February 1985.

Clark, William. National Security Strategy; address at Center for Strategic and International Studies, Washington, D.C., May 21, 1982.

Colby, William. Testimony before Senate Committee on Foreign Relations, Jan. 11, 1984.

Committee for National Security. Spending for a Sound Defense: Alternatives to the Reagan Military Budget; Washington, D.C., 1984.

Committee on the Present Danger; National Poll on Strategic Defense Initiative by Penn & Schoen Associates, Washington, D.C., Oct. 24, 1985.

Common Cause. The Role of Congress in Defense Budget Decision-Making: Views of Congressional Staff Members, Washington, D.C., April, 1985.

Comptroller General. Countervailing Strategy Demands Revision of Strategic Force Acquisition Plans, draft, May 1981.

———. DoD Can Combat Fraud Better by Strengthening Its Investigative Agencies, March 21, 1983.

———. Observations Concerning Profit Rates on Selected Navy Contracts, April 12, 1983.

———. Defense Spending and Its Relationship to the Federal Budget, June 9, 1983.

———. Joint Major System Acquisition by the Military Services: An Elusive Strategy, Dec. 23, 1983.

———. How Well Do the Military Services Perform Jointly in Combat? Feb. 22, 1984.

———. The 1978 Navy Shipbuilding Claims Settlement at Litton/Ingalls Shipbuilding—A Final Report, April 4, 1984.

———. Reductions in U.S. Costs to Station Forces in the Federal Republic of Germany and the United Kingdom Are Unlikely, July 31, 1984.

———. Compensation by 12 Aerospace Contractors, October 12, 1984.

———. Ambiguous Federal Regulation Criteria on Defense Contractors' Public Relations Costs, letter to Secretary of Defense Caspar W. Weinberger, Oct. 29, 1984.

Courter, Representative Jim. Newsletter to constituents, August 1983.

———. Military Reform; Remarks to Defense Week Conference; Washington, D.C., Dec. 6, 1984.

Crowe, Admiral, William J., Jr. Navy squaring up to expanding role; interview in San Diego Union, April 8, 1984.

———. Testimony before Senate Armed Services Committee; Feb. 27, 1985.

———. Interview with Armed Forces Journal, May 1985.

DeLauer, Richard D. Statement on Defense Acquisition Management before Senate Armed Services Committee, Nov. 16, 1983.

———. Management of Joint Weapons Programs, statement before Senate Appropriations Subcommittee on Defense, May 16, 1984.

Department of Defense, Office of the Actuary. DoD Statistical Report on the Military Retirement System, FY 1983, Defense Manpower Data Center; RCS no. DDM (A) 1375.

Department of Defense. Narrative Summaries of Accidents Involving Nuclear Weapons 1950–1980, May 10, 1981.

———. Military Manpower Training Report FY 1985, February 1984.

———. Defense Against Ballistic Missiles: An Assessment of Technology and Policy Implications, April 1984.

———. Improvements in U.S. Warfighting Capability FY 1980–1984, May 1984.

———. U.S. Expenditures in Support of NATO (excerpts), June 1984.

———. Point Paper on the 39 Percent Increase in Readiness, undated.

———. The Whole Truth Catalog, August 1984.

———. Report of Allied Contributions to The Common Defense, March 1985.

Department of Defense, Inspector General's Office. Report on the Audit of the DoD Parts Control Program, no. 85–075, January 3, 1985.

———. Semi-annual report to Congress, May 31, 1984.

———. Indicators of Fraud in DoD Procurement, June 1, 1984.

———. Semi-annual Report to Congress, November 29, 1984.

Department of Defense, Public Affairs News Releases

1983

Aug. 11: DoD IG condemns release of draft spare parts price audit.

Aug. 11: Defense contractor sentenced for fraud.

Sept. 12: Former DoD employee sentenced.

Sept. 23: President of Ohio firm sentenced for bribery.

Sept. 28: Former DoD employee sentenced.

Oct. 28: Scrap dealer sentenced in fraud scheme.

Dec. 9: Sperry pleads guilty in fraudulent claims.

Dec. 14: Contractor pleads guilty to substandard parachute cord.

Dec. 21: Defense contractor sentenced.

1984

Jan. 18: Three family members sentenced for $7 million sewer fraud.

March 1: Air Force receives voluntary credit from Flying Tigers Lines.

March 7: National Semiconductor Corporation indicted.

April 16: DoD contractor sentenced for bribery and mail fraud.

May 3: *New Jersey* comes home.

May 4: Former naval officer sentenced.

May 22: Army and Air Force sign agreement.

May 23: $4 million overcharge refunded to DoD.

May 23: Defense contractor sentenced.

July 9: Moratorium on disposal of defense assets announced.

July 17: Reforger 84.

Aug. 7: DoD acts to recover spare parts overcharges.

Aug. 23: Former DoD employee sentenced for accepting bribe.

Sept. 12: Masters of Ocean Sciences candidate selected.

Sept. 25: DoD announces court actions against waste, fraud, and abuse.

Sept. 26: DoD cites progress in combating waste, fraud, and abuse.

Oct. 21: Military manpower strength assessment, FY 84.

Nov. 13: New educational benefits for service members.

Dec. 14: Contractor pleads guilty to substandard parachute cord.

Dec. 26: C-5B contract price reduction.

1985

March 1: New GI bill plus new Army college fund.
April 22: Former Pratt & Whitney employee sentenced.
May 6: DoD contractor sentenced.
Aug. 6: Virginia firm sentenced for fraud.
Aug. 7: Former defense employee sentenced for accepting bribes.
Dec. 9: U.S. military strengths worldwide.
Dec. 21: Defense contractor sentenced.

1986

Feb. 13: Survey of 1985 worldwide drug and alcohol abuse.
Feb. 18: Military manpower strength assessment, first quarter FY 86.
Feb. 27: DoD accepts $5.2 million pricing refund from Boeing.

Department of Defense, Memoranda for Correspondents, Press Advisories:

Dec. 1, 1983: Watkins commends Navy employee.
Dec. 1, 1983: Voluntary refunds from contractors.
March 22, 1984: Ocean Venture 84.
April 2, 1984: Ocean Venture 84.
May 23, 1984: One Stop Motor Parts sentences.
July 17, 1984: Stebbins debarred.
July 17, 1984: Coker Controls debarred.
July 17, 1984: Portsmouth Auto Parts debarred.
Nov. 6, 1985: Snooks sentenced.
Nov. 6, 1985: Bisset, Cowan sentenced.
Dec. 2, 1985: Share sentenced.
Dec. 2, 1985: Kaplan sentenced.

Diamond, Martin. The Military and the Democratic Republic. Speech at Northern Illinois University, Nov. 15, 1976.
Eagleburger, Lawrence. The State of Things, as Seen from State. Interview with *The New York Times*, April 22, 1984.
Eisenhower, President Dwight D. Letter to Everett E. Hazlett; Aug. 20, 1956.
———. Farewell Address, Jan. 17, 1961.
Espionage Act of 1918.
Farris, Major General Jack B. "Army Must Improve Operations with Navy," interview in *Navy Times*, Nov. 5, 1984.
Fitzgerald, A. Ernest. Statement on Reliability and Availability of Agency Information before Senate Judiciary subcommittee on Administrative Practice & Procedure, June 19, 1984.
Gallup Poll. Growing Majority Sees Deficit Threat, Rising Demand Found for Defense Cuts, May 5, 1985.
Gates, Merrill C. Notice of Progress Payments Suspensions, letter to Hughes Missile Systems Group, Aug. 21, 1984.
Goldwater, Senator Barry. "Congressional Oversight of National Defense," speech to Senate, Oct. 1, 1985.
———. "DoD Organization—A Historical Perspective," speech to Senate, Oct. 2, 1985.

———. "The Joint Chiefs of Staff and the Unified Commands," speech to Senate, Oct. 3, 1985.

Grace, J. Peter. Statement to press on the President's Private Sector Survey on Cost Control, June 30, 1983.

Harr, Karl G. Jr. Some Perspectives on the Defense/Space Industry.

Herres, General Robert. Interview *Denver Post*, Nov. 17, 1985.

House Committee on Government Operations. Navy's Political Rating System, Nov. 23, 1983.

Howard, Michael. Nuclear Arms Make Chances of War 'Far More Remote'; interview in *U.S. News & World Report*, April 9, 1984.

Inter-American Treaty of Reciprocal Assistance, Sept. 2, 1947.

Joint Chiefs of Staff. Rescue Mission Report, August 1980.

Jones, General David C. Statement before the Investigations Subcommittee, House Armed Services Committee, April 21, 1983.

Kennedy, President John F. Inaugural Address, Jan. 20, 1961.

Korb, Lawrence J. Testimony before House Armed Services Subcommittee on Military Personnel and Compensation, Nov. 17, 1983.

———. Defense Policy Making: Constraints and Opportunities; lecture at the National Defense University, reprinted in the *Naval War College Review*, Jan. 2, 1984.

———. Memorandum for Secretary of Defense: Readiness, Feb. 17, 1984.

———. Testimony before Senate Armed Services Subcommittee on Manpower and Personnel, March 11, 1985.

La Rocque, Rear Admiral Gene R. Statement to House Committee on the Budget, March 25, 1985.

Lawrence, Vice Admiral William P. Women in the Military, statement to House Armed Services Subcommittee on Personnel and Compensation, Nov. 17, 1985.

Lehman, Secretary of the Navy John. "Let's Stop Trying to Be Prussians," *The Washington Post*, June 10, 1984.

Levin, Senator Carl. Levin Adds $330 Million to Budget for Non-nuclear Defense—Biggest Addition Yet, press release, Nov. 10, 1983.

———. Levin to Reagan: Keep Commitment to Budget More M-1 Tanks, press release, Jan. 13, 1984.

———. Allied Burden Sharing Amendment, speech to Senate, June 20, 1984.

Lind, William S. The Grenada Operation, report to Congressional Military Reform Caucus, April 5, 1984.

Lugar, Richard. The Direction of American Foreign Policy, statement to the Senate, Jan. 23, 1985.

Lyons, James A. Speech before Current Strategy Forum, Naval War College, Newport, R.I., June 19, 1984.

MacArthur, General Douglas. Quoted in NAUS newsletter #47; October–November 1976.

Mahaffey, Lieutenant General Fred K. Press conference for NATO journalists, March 11, 1985.

Marine Corps Development and Education Command; Operational Overview Jan–Mar 1984.

Maroni, Alice, and Robert Foelher. The Defense Spending Debate: Comparing Recent Defense Appropriations with 1981 Projections, Congressional Research Service, May 29, 1984.

Maroni, Alice. Estimating Funding for Strategic Forces, Congressional Research Service, May 31, 1984.

Marquez, Lieutenant General Leo. Statement before the House Armed Services Committee on Spare Parts, Property Retention Initiatives, June 21, 1984.

Marsh, Secretary of the Army John O. Jr. Testimony before House Appropriations Subcommittee on Defense, March 8, 1984.

Mayer, William. Medical Facilities, testimony before House Appropriations Subcommittee on Military Construction, March 8, 1984.

——. Medical Programs. Testimony before House Appropriations Subcommittee on Defense, May 1, 1984.

McDonald, Admiral Wesley L. Status of the Atlantic Command, Testimony before Senate Armed Services Committee, Feb. 23, 1984.

Melchner, John W. On Audit Reports Concerning Overpayments on Spare Parts for the F/A-18 Aircraft Program, statement to House Armed Services Subcommittee on Investigations, July 13, 1983.

——. Memorandum for the Under Secretary of Defense: Report on the Audit of the DoD Parts Control Program, 1985.

Meyer, General E. C. Transcripts of speeches, articles, testimony, correspondence, June 1979–June 1983.

——. Remarks to World Affairs Council, Boston, Sept. 24, 1981.

——. The J.C.S.—How Much Reform Is Needed? *Armed Forces Journal*, March 1982.

——. The Army of the Future, a conversation with American Enterprise Institute, Jan. 27, 1981.

——. Interviews with *The New York Times*, Aug. 14, 1981, June 16, 1983.

——. Interview with defense correspondents, June 9, 1983.

Moskos, Charles C. Jr. Serving in the Ranks: Citizenship and the All-Volunteer Force, Dec. 16, 1979.

——. The Enlisted Man in the All-Volunteer Force, January, 1984.

——. Army Women on Deployment: Report from Honduras, December, 1984.

Mullins, General James. Address to AFA/ESD Symposium at Hanscom Air Force Base, Massachusetts, April 26, 1984.

NSC-68: A report to the National Security Council, reprinted in Naval War College Review, May–June 1975.

Nunn, Senator Sam. The Need to Reshape Military Strategy, speech to Center for Strategic and International Studies, Georgetown University, March 18, 1983.

——. Improving NATO's Conventional Defenses, *USA Today*, May 1985.

——. Congressional Oversight of National Defense, speech to Senate, Oct. 1, 1985.

——. Defense Department Organization, speech to Senate, Oct. 2, 1985.

——. The Unified Commands, speech to Senate, Oct. 3, 1985.

Nutting, General Wallace H. Evolution of the Readiness Command, statement to Senate Armed Services Committee, Feb. 23, 1984.

——. Interview with *The New York Times*, October 1985.

Orr, Secretary of the Air Force Verne. Letter to John E. Welch Jr., General Electric Company, March 15, 1985.

Perry, William. A Critical Look at 'Star Wars' speech reprinted in *SIPI Scope*, January/February 1985.

Pownall, Thomas G. The Defense Industry: What Is It? Where Is It? Why Is It? speech to Town Hall of California, Oct. 15, 1985.

President's Blue Ribbon Commission on Defense Management. An Interim Report to the President, Feb. 28, 1986.

President's Commission on Strategic Forces. Report to the President, April 1983.

——. Report to the President, March 21, 1984.

President's Private Sector Survey on Cost Control. Task Force Report on the Office of the Secretary of Defense, July 13, 1983.

——. Task Force Report on the Department of the Army, July 13, 1983.

——. Task Force Report on the Department of the Navy, July 13, 1983.

——. Task Force Report on the Department of the Air Force, July 13, 1983.

Pustay, Lieutenant General John. The Problem Is Systemic, *Armed Forces Journal*, February 1984.

Quetsch, John R. Testimony before House Appropriations Subcommittee on Defense, June 9, 1983.

——. Major Weapons Systems: Cost Estimating, Reporting, and Control, statement to the Senate Committee on Governmental Affairs, May 24, 1984.

Reagan, President Ronald. Speech on defense, March 23, 1983.

——. Second Inaugural Address, Jan. 21, 1985.

——. Interview with *The New York Times*, Feb. 11, 1985.

——. Peace and National Security, televised address, Feb. 26, 1986.

——. Message to Congress on foreign policy, March 14, 1986.

——. Speech on aid to Contras, March 16, 1986.

——. Speech on Libya raid, April 14, 1986.

Rickover, Admiral Hyman S. Testimony before House Armed Services Subcommittee on Procurement and Military Nuclear Systems, June 16, 1981.

Rogers, General Bernard W. Statement to House Armed Services Committee, March 6, 1984.

Roth, Senator William V. Jr. Letter to Secretary of the Air Force Verne Orr, Jan. 4, 1984.

——. Letter to Secretary of the Army John O. Marsh, Jan. 4, 1984.

Schlesinger, James. Statement before Senate Committee on Foreign Relations, April 30, 1982.

——. Statement before Senate Armed Services Committee, Nov. 2, 1983.

——. Statement before Senate Committee on Foreign Relations, Jan. 11, 1984.

——. Schlesinger warns on uncertain foreign policy trumpet, interview with *The Washington Times*, May 15, 1984.

——. Statement before the Senate Committee on Foreign Relations, Feb. 6, 1985.

Schratz, Paul. War, Morality and the Military Professional, Proceedings of the Naval Institute, September 1983.

Sherick, Joseph. Statement to Senate Appropriations Subcommittee on Defense, Aug. 4, 1983.

——. Press briefing at DoD, Sept. 26, 1984.

——. Statement to House Energy and Commerce Subcommittee on Oversight and Investigations, April 24, 1985.

Shull, C. Blaine. Hughes Tucson Plant Operations, statement to House Armed Services Subcommittee on Investigations, Sept. 20, 1984.

——. Hughes Tucson Plant Operations, statement to Senate Armed Services Task Force for Selected Defense Procurement Matters, Oct. 18, 1984.

Shultz, Secretary of State George. Power and Diplomacy in the 1980s, address before the Trilateral Commission, April 3, 1984.

———. Terrorism and the Modern World, address to Park Avenue Synagogue, New York, Oct. 25, 1984.

———. The Meaning of Vietnam, speech to State Department, April 25, 1985.

Shultz, Secretary of State George, and Secretary of Defense Caspar Weinberger. Shultz versus Weinberger—When to Use U.S. Power, in *U.S. News & World Report*, Dec. 24, 1984.

Spinney, Franklin C. Defense Facts of Life, Dec. 5, 1980.

———. Defense Program Analysis and Evaluation: Is History Repeating Itself? briefing to Congress, March 22, 1984.

Stamper, Malcolm T. Crisis without a Cause, remarks to Aerospace Industries Association, Williamsburg, Virginia, June 1985.

Stark, Representative Fortney H. "Pete". Remarks submitted for the record, House of Representatives, *Congressional Record*, April 22, 1985.

Strategic Defense Initiative Office. Fact Sheet on S.D.I., June 29, 1985.

Summers, Colonel Harry G. Jr. The Astarita Report: A Military Strategy for the Multipolar World, An Occasional Paper from the Strategic Studies Institute, U.S. Army War College, Carlisle Barracks, Pennsylvania, April 30, 1981.

———. The Post-Vietnam Army, paper at U.S. Army War College, Carlisle Barracks, Pennsylvania, undated.

Taft, William H. IV. Remarks to University Club of Chicago, Oct. 16, 1984.

———. Remarks to National Security Industrial Association, Arlington, Virginia, Dec. 6, 1984.

———. Speech to the National Security Industrial Association, Washington, D.C., Dec. 11, 1984.

Taylor, General Maxwell D. Testimony before the Joint Economic Committee of Congress, April 27, 1982.

Taylor, William J. Jr., and David H. Petraeus. The Legacy of Vietnam for the American Military, paper, 1985.

Thatcher, Prime Minister Margaret. Interview in *Defense Week*, July 16, 1984.

Thayer, Paul. Memorandum on Guidance on the Acquisition Improvement Program, June 8, 1983.

———. Statement to House Committee on the Budget, Oct. 26, 1983.

Tower, Senator John. Letter to colleagues, Feb. 1, 1983.

———. Statement before the Senate Committee on the Budget, March 6, 1984.

———. Letter to colleagues, April 3, 1984.

Union of Concerned Scientists, Papers on Strategic Defense, undated.

United States Army Headquarters. Memorandum on Joint Force Development Process with USAF, May 22, 1984.

Vander Schaaf, Derek J. Statement to Senate Committee on Governmental Affairs, Nov. 2, 1983.

Vessey, General John W. Jr. Remarks to Third Annual C3 Conference, Washington, D.C., June 27, 1983.

———. Interview on *Meet the Press*, NBC television, Nov. 6, 1983.

———. Analysis of Lind Report, June 6, 1984.

Warnke, Paul, and Adam Yarmolinsky. An Alternative Defense Budget, *Los Angeles Times*, March 6, 1985

Watkins, Admiral James D. Our Choice: National Power or Paralysis, address to Baltimore Council on Foreign Relations, March 28, 1984.

———. Newsgram for All Flag Officers, Commanders, Commanding Officers and Officers in Charge, Aug. 8, 1984.

Weinberger, Secretary of Defense Caspar W. Press conference, Aug. 10, 1981.

———. Letter to editors of thirty American and forty foreign publications, Aug. 23, 1982.

———. Memorandum on Spare Parts Procurement, July 25, 1983.

———. Interview, *Omni* magazine, September 1983.

———. Remarks to Federal Procurement and Trade Conference, Indianapolis, July 19, 1984.

———. The Uses of Military Power," address to National Press Club, Nov. 28, 1984.

———. Remarks to National Security Forum for Women, National Defense University, June 11, 1985.

Weyand, General Fred C. Serving the People, The Basic Case for the United States Army; *Commanders Call*, Army War College, Carlisle Barracks, Pennsylvania, May–June, 1976.

———. Vietnam Myths and American Realities, Parameters, Army War College, Carlisle Barracks, Pennsylvania.

Wheaton, Warde F. The Real Cost of Quality, speech before Defense Logistic Agency Bottom Line III conference, June 13, 1984.

White House Pamphlet on the Strategic Defense Initiative, Jan. 3, 1985.

Wilkinson, Spenser. The Brain of an Army: A Popular Account of the German General Staff, Archibald Constable & Co., Westminster, 1895.

Wright, Sir Oliver. Speech to the English Speaking Union and Mid-America Committee, June 29, 1984.

ARTICLES

Adams, Bob. "Arms Firms' Lobbyists Work in Secret to Influence Spending," series in *St. Louis Post-Dispatch*, April 17–22, 1983.

Albright, Joseph. "Shooting Down 'Star Wars,' " *The Atlanta Constitution*, Aug. 8, 1984.

Andrews, Walter. "Data rights raise DoD parts costs," *The Washington Times*, June 1, 1983.

———. "Arms Chief seeks more interservice programs," *The Washington Times*, May 17, 1984.

Archibald, George. " 'Irrational' Budget Process Is Said to Boost Defense Costs by $20 Billion," *The Washington Times*, June 14, 1983.

Army Times. "Korb Says Services Fail to Show Loyalty to SecDef," Aug. 29, 1983.

Associated Press. "The Glitter Has Returned to Being Military Brass," *Hartford Courant*, Feb. 28, 1984.

———. "Space Shield Hopes Called Remote," *Baltimore Sun*, April 26, 1984.

Atkinson, Rick, and Fred Hiatt. "F14 Engine Criticized by Lehman," *The Washington Post*, July 19, 1984.

————. "Noisy Medley: Navy Pours Dollars and Sweat into Keeping Key Carriers Ready," *The Washington Post*, July 22, 1984.

Baker, Captain Brent. "National Defense and the Congressional Role," *Naval War College Review*, July–August 1982.

Ball, Desmond. "U.S. Strategic Forces: How Would They Be Used," *International Security*, Winter 1982/83.

Baltimore Sun: "Weinberger Disavows Idea Atomic War Can Be Won," June 4, 1982.

Barnard, Richard. "New Guidance Calls for More Troops in Mid-East, Caribbean," *Defense Week*, March 19, 1984.

————. "Gen. Rogers Says Europe Is Heedless of His Arms Advice," *Defense Week*, July 2, 1984.

Beecher, William. "General Outlines Plan to Avert Nuclear War," *The Boston Globe*, Dec. 16, 1984.

Bernstein, Peter W. "What's Behind the Spare Parts Follies," *Fortune*, Oct. 29, 1984.

Bertram, Christoph. "Europe and America in 1983," *Foreign Affairs*, 1983.

Bethe, Hans A., and Richard L. Garwin, Kurt Gottfried, Henry W. Kendall, Carl Sagan, and Victor Weisskopf. " 'Star Wars' Seen as Unworkable and Dangerous," letter to the editor, *The Wall Street Journal*, Jan. 2, 1985.

Betts, Richard K.: "Misadventure Revisited," *Wilson Quarterly*, Summer 1983.

Biddle, Wayne. "Pushing for Weapons that Work," *The New York Times*, July 8, 1984.

————. "Patriot Missile Delayed by Problems in Tests," *The New York Times*, July 18, 1984.

————. "Rickover Linked by House Panel to Gifts from Ship Builders," *The New York Times*, July 19, 1984.

————. "Navy Expects to Modify Its F-18's to Correct Flaw," *The New York Times*, Aug. 1, 1984.

————. "McDonnell Douglas Says It Will Pay Cost of Fixing F-18 Flaw," *The New York Times*, Aug. 3, 1984.

————. "G.A.O. Aide Warns Many U.S. Missiles Would Be Useless," *The New York Times*, Sept. 19, 1984.

————. "At General Dynamics, the Clouds Linger," *The New York Times*, Sept. 23, 1984.

————. "New Study Finds Inflated Labor Costs on Weapons," *The New York Times*, Oct. 11, 1984.

————. "5 Big Military Builders Paid No Taxes for 3 Years," *The New York Times*, Oct. 16, 1984.

————. "Navy Says Base on S.I. Would Create 900 Jobs," *The New York Times*, Oct. 28, 1984.

————. "How High Will Star Wars Fly?" *The New York Times*, Dec. 30, 1984.

————. "Talking Loudly and Carrying a Big Stick," *The New York Times*, May 7, 1984.

————. "Star Wars Technology: It's More Than a Fantasy," *The New York Times*, March 5, 1985.

Black, Edwin. "The Strategy Gap: A plan to close it for the sake of peace," *The Washington Times*, Oct. 9, 1984.

Blair, Bruce G.. "Command and Control and National Security," *Signal*, March 1985.

Blum, Howard. "At a SAC Base, Living Centers on State of Alert," *The New York Times*, Feb. 21, 1984.

Boening, Suzanne S. "Woman Soldier, Quo Vadis?" *Parameters*, June 1983.

Boffey, Philip M. "Research Success Marks Recent Days of 'Star Wars,' " *The New York Times*, June 18, 1985.

———. "Dark Side of Star Wars: System Could Also Attack," *The New York Times*, March 7, 1985.

The Boston Globe. "Glossary: Star Wars," January 21, 1985.

The Boston Globe Magazine. "War and Peace in the Nuclear Age," Oct. 17, 1982.

Bowie, Robert R. "Heading Off 'Star Wars' and Deficit Disaster," *The Christian Science Monitor*, March 29, 1985.

Bowman, Robert M. "Why the Soviet Union Is So Concerned about 'Star Wars,' " *The Christian Science Monitor*, Jan. 10, 1985.

Bracken, Paul, and Martin Shubik. "Strategic War: What Are the Questions and Who Should Ask Them?" *Technology in Society*, March 1983.

Brinkley, Joel. "Haig Blames Reagan for 'Star Wars' Dispute," *The New York Times*, Feb. 8, 1985.

Brisbane, Arthur S. "Naval Academy's Harsh Attraction," *The Washington Post*, May 19, 1984.

Broad, William. "Reagan Star Wars Bid: Many Ideas Converge," *The New York Times*, March 4, 1985.

———. "Experts Say Satellite Can Detect Soviet War Steps." *The New York Times*, Jan. 25, 1985.

———. " 'Star Wars' Research Forges Ahead," *The New York Times*, Feb. 5, 1985.

———. "Allies in Europe Are Apprehensive About Benefits of 'Star Wars' Plan," *The New York Times*, May 13, 1985.

Brown, Harold. "U.S. Military Leadership Needs Reform," *Newsday*, April 14, 1985.

———. "Is SDI Technically Feasible?" *Foreign Affairs*, Winter 1986.

Brzezinski, Zbigniew, Robert Jastrow, and Max Kampelman. "Defense in Space Is Not 'Star Wars,' " *The New York Times Magazine*, Jan. 27, 1985.

Bundy, McGeorge, George Kennan, Robert McNamara, and Gerard Smith. "The President's Choice: Star Wars or Arms Control," *Foreign Affairs*, Winter 1984–85.

Burton, Barbara. "Poor Quality Cuts Deeply into DoD Budget," *Defense Week*, June 6, 1983.

BusinessWeek. "Good and Bad News for Reagan on Arms," Harris Poll, Dec. 12, 1983.

———. "The Pentagon Steps Up Its War on Shoddy Workmanship," October 15, 1984, pp. 174–78.

Canan, James W. "Up from Nifty Nugget," *Air Force Magazine*, September 1983.

Carpenter, Ted Galen. "Standing Guard Over Europe," *Reason*, August 1984.

Carter, Ashton. "Command and Control of Nuclear War," *Scientific American*, January 1985.

Center for Defense Information. "Militarizing the Last Frontier: The Space Weapons Race," *Defense Monitor*, Vol. XII, Number 5, 1983.

———. "War Games," *Defense Monitor*, Vol. XIII, Number 7, 1984.

Chalfont, Alan. "Moscow's Star Wars Plan: Keeping Facts Under Wraps," *Toronto Globe and Mail*, April 23, 1985.

Chicago Tribune. "How Navy Is Nailed for $436 Hammer," May 20, 1984.

Coates, James. "$16 Million Pratt-Whitney 'Windfall' Told," *Chicago Tribune*, May 2, 1983.

Cohen, Eliot A. "Constraints on America's Conduct of Small Wars," *International Security*, Fall 1984.

Cohen, Samuel T., and Joseph D. Douglass Jr. "Selective Targeting and Soviet Deception," *Armed Forces Journal*, September 1983.

Corddry, Charles. "U.S. Air Commander Faults Manpower Ceiling in Europe," *Baltimore Sun*, Feb. 25, 1984.

———. "Navy, Fearing Defect, Turns Down Warship," *Baltimore Sun*, Oct. 30, 1984.

———. "Spy Satellites Grow Sharper, Expert Reveals," *Baltimore Sun*, Jan. 1, 1985.

———. "Research for 'Star Wars' Is Taking Off," *Baltimore Sun*, March 17, 1985.

———. "Fitting Various Advances into Single System May Be Difficult," *Baltimore Sun*, March 19, 1985.

———. "Many Doubt Strength Rose with Outlays," *Baltimore Sun*, May 19, 1985.

Correll, John T. "Scoping the Spares Problem," *Air Force Magazine*, January 1984.

Cowen, Robert C. "Scowcroft: A 'Star Wars' Defense Leaves World Open to Non-nuclear Aggression," *The Christian Science Monitor*, May 31, 1984.

Current News. "Star Wars: President's Speech on Military Spending and a New Defense," collection of news articles, Department of Defense, May 4, 1983.

———. "Star Wars," Part II, Department of Defense, May 5, 1983.

———. "Secretary Weinberger's National Press Club Speech," collection of news articles, Department of Defense, Jan. 8, 1985.

Davis, Vincent. "Americans and War," *SAIS Review*, Summer–Fall 1984.

de Lama, George. "Aircraft Carrier as Big as Its Name," *Chicago Tribune*, May 15, 1984.

Defense Daily. "GAO Charges DoD Spent Funds Illegally in C-5 Lobbying," Oct. 4, 1982.

———. "Garn Hits Both Media & Congress for Defense Stance," March 4, 1983.

———. "Tower Urges Budget Committee Not to Cut Defense," March 8, 1983.

———. "Elevated Markup Cited for 67% Aircraft Engines Parts Cost Growth," July 18, 1983.

———. "More Competition & Personnel Called Solution to Overpricing," Aug. 5, 1983.

———. "Small Business Group Sees $4–5 Billion Competition Savings," Oct. 31, 1983.

———. "DeLauer Blames Congress for Increased Defense Costs," Nov. 17, 1983.

———. "Navy to Forgo Development of New Fighter/Attack Aircraft," Feb. 9, 1984.

———. "NATO Infrastructure Program: Faces Two-thirds Shortfall," April 2, 1984.

———. "DeLauer Sees End of JTACMS as Joint Program," May 21, 1984.

———. "Contractors 'Stealing' $300–$500 Million in PR Costs—Brooks," July 26, 1984.

———. "National Semiconductor and DoD Settle Differences," Aug. 9, 1984.

———. "Navy Rejects 14 GE F-404 Engines for the F/A-18," Sept. 11, 1984.

———. "DoD Confirms TI Microchip Caused Discovery Delay," Sept. 14, 1984.

———. " 'High Risk' Cited in Penalizing GE for Engine Work," Nov. 2, 1984.

———. "NATO Ministers Agree to $7.5 Million Infrastructure Boost," Dec. 6, 1984.

——. "Lack of Quality Control Seen Boosting Defense Costs," Dec. 7, 1984.

——. "Navy Official Says Defense Profits Steadily Climbing," Dec. 20, 1984.

——. "Making Strategic Defense Cost-Effective Cited as Critical Factor," March 18, 1985.

——. "Lack of Coordination Between Space Commands Charged," March 21, 1985.

——. " 'Incredible Technical Progress' Reported on SDI," April 11, 1985.

——. "Defense Contractor PR Costs," April 16, 1985.

——. "Pentagon Reports to Congress on SDI FY 1986 Objectives," April 22, 1985.

——. "Three Major Critics of SDI Support $1.4–$2 Billion Research," April 23, 1985.

——. "Recent Major SDI Technical Progress Reported," May 3, 1985.

——. "GAO Finds Shortcomings in DoD Industrial Base Planning," May 21, 1985.

——. "Key SDI Systems Can Be Demonstrated This Decade—Keyworth," June 7, 1985.

——. "SDI Can Be Built for $100–$200 Billion—Jastrow," June 7, 1985.

——. "Teller Says Strategic Defense Is Within Our Grasp," June 7, 1985.

——. "Teller on the Technical Status of SDI," June 10, 1985.

——. "Defense IG Lists Major Contractors Under Investigation," June 21, 1985.

——. "Charge: U.S. C31 System Would Be Useless Within 30 Minutes After Attack," Oct. 2, 1985.

——. "Defense Contractors Criticized for Low Taxes Paid," Oct. 15, 1985.

——. "Rockwell International to Be Debarred by Air Force," Nov. 1, 1985.

——. "Rockwell Sets Up Business Standards Compliance Committee," Nov. 20, 1985.

——. "Air Force & Navy Sign ATF/ATA Variant MOU," March 14, 1986.

——. "Plan to Upgrade Attack Warning Communications Approved," April 3, 1986.

Defense Week. "Sharp Words on Protectionism in Military Tech," October 18, 1982.

——. "Lehman Points Accusing Finger at Congress," June 13, 1983.

——. "AF Study Eyes Radical Rein on Defense Profits," Sept. 17, 1984.

——. "Platt Fires Back At 'Monopoly' Charges," Sept. 24, 1984.

——. "DeLauer Warns Industry on 'Crappy' Work," Sept. 24, 1984.

——. "Grenada Pilots Felt Initial Confusion," Dec. 3, 1984.

Dolnick, Edward. "Anti-missile Defense; An Impossible Dream," *The Boston Globe*, March 26, 1984.

Douglas, Joseph D. Jr. "Strategic Planning and Nuclear Insecurity," *ORBIS*, Fall 1983.

——. "SDI: The Hidden Opportunity," *Defense Science 2003 +*, August/September 1985.

Draper, Theodore. "The Western Misalliance," *The Washington Quarterly*, Winter 1981.

——. "Dear Mr. Weinberger: An Open Reply to an Open Letter," *New York Review of Books*, October 21, 1982.

Drozdiak, William. "Conventional Buildup Troubling NATO," *The Washington Post*, November 21, 1984.

Dudney, Robert S. "The New Army with New Punch," *U.S. News & World Report*, September 20, 1982.

Duffy, Michael. "Air Force Study Eyes Radical Run on Defense Profits," *Defense Week*, Sept. 17, 1984.

———. "Hughes' Faults Common within Defense Industry," *Defense Week*, Sept. 17, 1984.

———. "Salaries Soar at Defense Firms," *Defense Week*, October 29, 1984.

———. "Grenada: Rampant Confusion," *Military Logistics Forum*, July/August, 1985.

Dupuy, Trevor N. "Military Reform; The Case for Centralized Command," *The Washington Post*, June 9, 1984.

Eagleburger, Lawrence. "The State of Things, as Seen from State," *The New York Times*, April 22, 1984.

Earley, Pete. "Sherick Seeks to Plug Pentagon Dike," *The Washington Post*, November 26, 1984.

Ebbert, Jean. "Should Women Serve at Sea?" *The Navy Times Magazine*, August 1, 1983.

Evans, David. "A Runaway Pentagon," *The New York Times*, October 3, 1984.

Fein, Esther B. "The Choice: Women Officers Decide to Stay in or Leave," *The New York Times Magazine*, May 5, 1985.

Feron, James; "Service Schools Gain from Applicants' Patriotism," *The New York Times*, April 12, 1984.

Fialka, John J. "In Battle for Grenada, Commando Missions Didn't Go as Planned," *The Wall Street Journal*, November 15, 1983.

Finn, Edwin A. Jr. "Defense Officials Say More Companies May Have Microcircuit Test Problems," *The Wall Street Journal*, Oct. 17, 1984.

———. "Defense Contractors Being Asked by Pentagon to Retest Semiconductor Parts Bought in Future," *The Wall Street Journal*, Dec. 18, 1984.

Finney, John W. "Military Colleges Getting Back to Basics," *The New York Times*, Sept. 15, 1985.

Friendly, Jonathan. "Paper Assailed for Exposing Faulty Army Copters," *The New York Times*, August 5, 1984.

Fromkin, David, and James Chace. "The Lessons of Vietnam?" *Foreign Affairs*, Spring 1985.

Fuerbringer, Jonathan. "Dole Criticizes Reagan Refusal to Cut Military," *The New York Times*, Jan. 26, 1985.

———. "Hatfield Presses for Military Cuts," *The New York Times*, Jan. 30, 1985.

Furlong, Bob. "Are the Europeans Pulling Their Weight?" *International Defense Review*, May 1984.

Gabriel, General Charles A. "Recovering from the 1970s," *AIR FORCE Magazine*, September 1983.

Gaddis, John Lewis. "Containment: Its Past and Future," *International Security*, Spring 1981.

———. "The Rise, Fall and Future of Détente," *Foreign Affairs*, Winter 1983/84.

Gansler, Jacques S. "We Can Afford Security," *Foreign Policy*, Summer 1983.

Garwin, Richard L., Kurt Gottfried, and Donald L. Hafner. "Antisatellite Weapons," *Scientific American*, June 1984.

Gelb, Leslie H. "Is the Nuclear Threat Manageable?" *The New York Times Magazine*, March 4, 1984.

Gellman, Barton. "Saga of the World's Costliest Plastic Cup," *The Washington Post*, Aug. 21, 1983.

Gemperlein, Joyce. "Military's Airlift Decision Pits Pa. and New Jersey," *The Philadelphia Inquirer*, June 5, 1983.

———. "Phila. Airport Wins Bid to Transport Air Force," *The Philadelphia Inquirer*, Feb. 24, 1984.

Gergen, David. "Pentagon Follies," *U.S. News & World Report*, June 3, 1985.

Gerstenzang, James. "Public Backs 'Star Wars,' Hopes for Arms Control," *Los Angeles Times*, Nov. 19, 1985.

Gerth, Jeff. "Pentagon Study Explores Profits for Contractors," *The New York Times*, March 15, 1985.

Getler, Michael. "U.S. Military Favors Lebanon Pullout," *The Washington Post*, Dec. 18, 1983.

———. "Diplomats Are Bold, Pentagon Wary," *The Washington Post*, March 4, 1984.

Glass, Andrew J. "Dole Attacks Weinberger over Pentagon's Hidden Funds," *The Atlanta Constitution*, May 21, 1985.

Gordon, Michael R. "Aerospace Executives Get Help from Pentagon in Bid to Keep Fringe Benefits," *National Journal*, March 17, 1984.

———. "Star Warriors," *National Journal*, July 7, 1984.

Grace, J. Peter. "Defense Dept. Called Ripe for $100 Billion in Trims," *St. Louis Post-Dispatch*, Nov. 21, 1984.

Gray, Colin S. "Defense, Deterrence, and Doctrine," *National Institute for Public Policy*, March 1982.

———. "Nuclear Strategy: A Regrettable Necessity," *SAIS Review*, Spring 1983.

Greenberger, Robert S. "Airman Criticizes Pentagon Programs' Enforcement Efforts," *The Wall Street Journal*, Sept. 20, 1984.

———. "Fraud-busters Save Billions for Defense," *USA Today*, Sept. 27, 1984.

Greider, William. "Birds of a Feather: Hawks and Doves Flock Together for Defense Dollars," *The Milwaukee Journal*, Aug. 12, 1984.

Greve, Frank. "A Report of U.S. Military Ineptness in Grenada," *The Philadelphia Inquirer*, Oct. 21, 1984.

Grier, Peter. "U.S. Public Opinion Generally Favors 'Star Wars'," *The Christian Science Monitor*, Nov. 21, 1985.

Gross, Richard. "The Great Debate: Weinberger's Finest Hour," *Defense Science and Electronics*, May 1984.

Guidry, Vernon A. Jr. "Pentagon Itself OK'd High Costs for Spare Parts," *Baltimore Sun*, Aug. 21, 1983.

———. "Pentagon Aide, Air Force Differ on Special Unit," *Baltimore Sun*, April 1, 1985.

Haberman, Clyde. "Japan Is Delaying Military Buildup," *The New York Times*, May 13, 1984.

Hackworth, David. "Wonder Weapons That Worry Warriors," *The Washington Post*, Sept. 6, 1981.

Hadley, Arthur T. "America's Broken War Machine," *The New Republic*, May 7, 1984.

Hadley, Stephen J. "Thinking About SDI," *FPI Policy Briefs*, March 10, 1986.

Hale, Ellen; "Air Force Denies Overpaying for Parts," *USA Today*, Sept. 14, 1984.

Halperin, Morton, and David Halperin. "The Key West Key," *Foreign Policy*, Winter 1983/84.

Hamilton, Lee H. "US and West Germany: persuading a friend to change," *The Christian Science Monitor*, Jan. 3, 1985.

Harper's. "Should the U.S. Stay in NATO?" April 1984.

Hart, Senator Gary. "What's Wrong with the Military?" *The New York Times Magazine*, Feb. 14, 1982.

Heisbourg, François. "U.S. Defense Cuts Worry French Expert," *The Washington Times*, Dec. 21, 1984.

Heritage Foundation. "Public Opinion and the Defense Debate," February 1983.

Hershey, Robert Jr. "Panel Says U.S. Can Trim Costs by $424 Billion," *The New York Times*, Jan. 13, 1984.

Hewey, Dale. "They Found a Career," *All Hands*, July 1983.

Hiatt, Fred. "Military Academies Enjoying Boom Years," *The Washington Post*, May 10, 1983.

———. "Airmen Say C5A Parts Are Vastly Overpriced," *The Washington Post*, Sept. 20, 1984.

———. "Change Brewing: Case of the $7,400 Coffee Maker," *The Washington Post*, Oct. 6, 1984.

———. "Warplanes Grounded by Navy," *The Washington Post*, Dec. 22, 1984.

———. "Forces Are Shifting in Favor of the U.S., Shultz Tells Senate," *The Washington Post*, Feb. 1, 1985.

———. "Profits Soar in Buildup," *The Washington Post*, April 1, 1985.

Hiatt, Fred, and Rick Atkinson. "Air Force Victory Is Illusory in the Case of $748 Pliers," *The Washington Post*, March 22, 1985.

Hirst, Don. "Blacks: Punishments High, Skills Low," *Army Times*, Dec. 27, 1982.

Howard, Michael. "Reassurance and Deterrence: Western Defense in the 1980s," *Foreign Affairs*, Winter 1982/83.

———. "The Causes of War," *Wilson Quarterly*, Summer 1984.

Howe, Russell Warren. "Brzezinski Urges U.S. Force Cuts in Europe," *The Washington Times*, Jan. 23, 1985.

Iklé, Fred. "NATO's 'First Nuclear Use': A Deepening Trap?" *Strategic Review*, Winter 1980.

Ingersoll, Bruce. "U.S. Grants Limited Immunity to Veliotis in Exchange for Data on Navy Fraud Case," *The Wall Street Journal*, May 11, 1984.

Jacky, Jonathan. "The Star Wars Defense Won't Compute," *The Atlantic*, June 1985.

Jacobs, Sanford L. "Small Defense Contractors Bear the Brunt of Pentagon's New Crackdown on Cheats," *The Wall Street Journal*, Jan. 5, 1984.

Jameson, Sam. "Japan Forces Woefully Weak, U.S. General Says," *Los Angeles Times*, July 9, 1981.

Jastrow, Robert. "Why Strategic Superiority Matters," *Commentary*, March 1983.

———. "Reagan Versus the Scientists: Why the President Is Right about Missile Defense," *Commentary*, January 1984.

Jervis, Robert. "Deterrence and Perception," *International Security*, Winter 1982/83.

Kaplan, Fred. "Military's 'Revolving Door' with Business," *The Boston Globe*, Jan. 15, 1984.

———. "Ploy or Warning, Soviet Studies Stings," *The Boston Globe*, Jan. 13, 1985.

Kegley, Charles Jr., and Eugene R. Wittkopf. "The Reagan Administration's World View," *Orbis*, Spring 1982.

Keller, Bill. "Pentagon Cancels Antiaircraft Gun; 'Not Worth Cost'," *The New York Times*, Aug. 28, 1985.

Kelly, Orr. "The B-1: When Pentagon, Politicians Joined Hands," *U.S. News & World Report*, July 11, 1983.

———. "Behind Deadly Foul-Up of Army's Helicopters." *U.S. News & World Report*, Aug. 27, 1984.

Kennedy, William. "Army and Navy Have Their Own Fiefdoms," *The Philadelphia Inquirer*, Nov. 15, 1983.

———. "What Are U.S. Vital Interests?" *The Christian Science Monitor*, Dec. 26, 1984.

———. "Listen to Some of Your Critics, Cap," *The Wall Street Journal*, Feb. 11, 1985.

Kester, John G. "Logistics Under Siege," *Military Logistics*, September/October 1984.

———. "Thoughtless J.C.S. Change Is Worse Than None," *Armed Forces Journal*, Nov. 1984.

Kinnard, Douglas. "McNamara at the Pentagon," *Parameters*, Volume X, no. 3, 1980.

Kissinger, Henry. "A Plan to Reshape NATO," *Time*, March 5, 1984.

Kittle, Robert A. "Furor Over Pentagon's 'Revolving Door'," *U.S. News & World Report*, April 29, 1985.

Klaidman, Stephen. "The Woman the Brass Love to Hate," *Washington Weekly*, Sept. 24, 1984.

Kling, Bill. "Brzezinski Supports Reagan on 'Star Wars,' " *The Washington Times*, Jan. 21, 1985.

Klurfeld, Jim. "Star Wars Plan Is Modified," *Newsday*, June 14, 1985.

Knickerbocker, Brad. "Reagan Defense Buildup Prompts Strategy Debate," *The Christian Science Monitor*, July 28, 1983.

———. "Defense Budget: $30 Billion Wasted?" *The Christian Science Monitor*, June 26, 1984.

———. "U.S. Forces Abroad: Is Nation's Military Spread Too Thin?" *The Christian Science Monitor*, Aug. 1, 1984.

Kondracke, Morton M. "Les Aspin: Reagan's Friendly Foe," *The Wall Street Journal*, Jan.17, 1985.

Korb, Lawrence J. "The Executive and the Joint Chiefs," *Society*, July/August 1980.

———. "Logistics: The Long Pole in Warfare's Tent," *Defense*, Jan. 1984.

Korb, Lawrence, and Linda Brady. "Rearming America; The Reagan Administration Defense Program," *International Security*, Winter 1984/85.

Kotz, Nick, Nancy Nathan, and Cathryn Donohoe. "Where Have All the Warriors Gone?" *Washingtonian*, July 1984.

Kraus, Melvyn. "Prompting Europe to Better Defend Itself," *The Wall Street Journal*, March 15, 1984.

Kuhn, George W. S. "Ending Defense Stagnation," Heritage Foundation, 1983.

Kurtz, Howard. "Defense Unit Said to Lag in Prosecution," *The Washington Post*, March 24, 1985.

Layne, Christopher. "Ending the Alliance," *Journal of Contemporary Studies*, Summer 1983.

Lemann, Nicholas. "The Peacetime War," *The Atlantic*, October 1984.

Lemnitzer, General Lyman L. "Don't Alter Joint Chiefs," *The New York Times*, June 19, 1984.

Lewy, Guenter. "The Proprieties of Military Intervention," *Parameters*, June 1981.

——. "Some Political-Military Lessons of the Vietnam War," *Parameters*, Spring 1984.

Lodal, Jan M. "Deterrence and Nuclear Strategy," *Daedalus*, Fall 1980.

Los Angeles Times. "Costly, Dangerous Ripoffs," July 3, 1983.

——. "Servants or Masters? Revisiting the Military-Industrial Complex?" special section, July 10, 1983.

Lugar, Senator Richard G. "Foreign Policy Agenda," *Washington Quarterly*, Spring 1985.

Luttwak, Edward. "The Decline of American Military Leadership," *Parameters*, December 1980.

——. "The Operational Level of War," *International Security*, Winter 1980–1981.

——. "The Price of Efficiency," *Military Logistics*, July/August 1984.

Lynn, William. "Sick Pentagon, Sick Defense," *Los Angeles Times*, April 13, 1983.

MacDougall, William, and Gordon Witkin. "At Service Academies, More Emphasis on Brains," *U.S. News & World Report*, Sept. 12, 1983.

Margolick, David. "Single Mothers Join Suit to Enlist in the Military," *The New York Times*, Dec. 25, 1984.

McCartney, James. "Glenn Lashes Out at Weinberger on Patriotism Issue," *The Philadelphia Inquirer*, Feb. 1, 1985.

McComas, Lisa A. "Nobody Asked Me But . . .," *Naval Institute Proceedings*, August 1983.

McCoy, Tidal W. "Who's Really Responsible for Pentagon Waste?" *Human Events*, June 30, 1984.

McFarland, Keith. "The 1949 Revolt of the Admirals," *Parameters*, Vol. XI, No. 2.

Melman, Seymour. "Limits of Military Power for National Security," *USA Today*, July 1981.

Meyers, Dan. "Phila. Airport Gets a New Tenant: The U.S. Military," *The Philadelphia Inquirer*, Sept. 20, 1984.

Middleton, Drew. "NATO Buildup: A Plan to Spur Europe's Contribution," *The New York Times*, Oct. 30, 1984.

Miller, Nathan. "Profiteers and Patriots," *Baltimore Sun*, Oct. 30, 1984.

Minerbrook, Scott. "Grenada Invasion's Down Side," *Newsday*, Aug. 13, 1984.

Mohr, Charles. "Reagan Is Urged to Increase Research on Exotic Defenses Against Missiles," *The New York Times*, Nov. 5, 1983.

——. "Antitank Testing Unrealistic, Some Officials Say," *The New York Times*, May 22, 1984.

——. "Military Price on Coffee Maker Cited as $7,622," *The New York Times*, Sept. 20, 1984.

——. " 'Star Wars': No Sign of Emerging Consensus," *The New York Times*, Feb. 1, 1985.

——. "Former Military Aides Question Space-Based Defense Plans,"*The New York Times*, March 1, 1985.

——. "What Moscow Might Do in Reply to Star Wars," *The New York Times*, March 6, 1985.

——. "General Expects Decision on Space Defense in 1990s," *The New York Times*, March 16, 1985.

Mohr, Henry. "U.S. Should Go Public When Security Threatened," *St. Louis Globe-Democrat*, April 28–29, 1984.

Mollenhoff, Clark R. "Another General Retires to Defense Industry," *The Washington Times*, July 14, 1984.

Morganthau, Tom, and Nicholas Horrock. "The New Warriors," *Newsweek*, July 3, 1984.

Morrison, David C. "Is Japan Bearing Its Defense Burden?" *Newsday*, Nov. 16, 1983.

———. "Pentagon's Top Secret 'Black' Budget Has Skyrocketed During Reagan Years," *National Journal*, March 1, 1986.

Mossberg, Walter. "Military Buildup Cost Underestimated, Study by Pro-Reagan Foundation Finds," *The Wall Street Journal*, Jan. 10, 1983.

———. "Pork-Barrel Politics: Some Congressmen Treat Military Budget as Source for Patronage," *The Wall Street Journal*, April 15, 1983.

———. "A Nuclear Attack Sub Shows Its Capabilities in Long Silent Patrols," *The Wall Street Journal*, May 19, 1983.

Mossberg, Walter, and Edward T. Pound. "How Pratt & Whitney Gains from the Way U.S. Buys Spare Parts," *The Wall Street Journal*, Oct. 3, 1983.

Mydans, Seth. "Soviet Scientific Paper Calls U.S. Space Based Defense Vulnerable," *The New York Times*, Jan. 8, 1985.

The New York Times. "Defense: Is the U.S. Prepared?" series, Sept. 21–27, 1980.

———. "Questions of Quality: Weapons Utility," Sept. 19, 1984.

———. "14 Navy Jet Engines Flawed," Sept. 9, 1984.

———. "Military Contractors Defend Spare-Parts Bills," Sept. 30, 1984.

———. "Survey Indicates a Sharp Contrast in Views on Missile Defense Plan," Jan. 10, 1985.

———. "Senator Blames Congress for High Cost of Military," Jan. 11, 1985.

———. "Non-Academy Graduates Get Top Navy Jobs," Feb. 3, 1985.

———. "2 Analysts Put Cost of Antimissile Program at $70 Billion by 1993," Feb. 12, 1985.

———. "Weapons in Space," series March 3–8, 1985.

———. "Military 'Pork Barrel' Wastes Billions a Year, Official Says," April 1, 1985.

Newsweek. "Why the Generals Can't Command," Feb. 14, 1983.

———. "The Frozen War," Jan. 23, 1984.

———. "The New Warriors," July 9, 1984.

———. "Can We Fight a Modern War?" July 19, 1984.

Norman, Michael. "Rescued from the Budget Ax, Fort Dix Now Picks Up Its Pace," *The New York Times*, Aug. 17, 1982.

Novotny, Joseph. "Class of '87: New Breed of Plebes," *USA Today*, July 7, 1983.

Oberdofer, Don. "Ex-Defense Chief Calls 'Star Wars' Unrealistic," *The Washington Post*, Dec. 15, 1984.

———. "Military Response Planned to Star Wars, Soviet Says," *The Washington Post*, March 8, 1985.

Offley, Ed. "Military Still Short on Interservice Cooperation," *Norfolk Virginian-Pilot*, Feb. 2, 1985.

Okazaki, Hiroshi. "A Strategy for Japan," *Baltimore Sun*, Sept. 29, 1982.

Owens, Mackubin Thomas. "Congress' Role in Defense Mismanagement," *Armed Forces Journal*, April 1985.

Palmer, General Bruce. "Viet Lesson 1: Civilian, Military Chiefs Must Act Together," *The Boston Globe*, April 27, 1985.

Pear, Robert. "Military Investigating Electronics Companies Over Testing of Parts," *The New York Times*, Dec. 27, 1983.

Perlez, Jane. "Connecticut Questions Award of Pact to G.E.," *The New York Times*, Feb. 24, 1984.

Petraeus, David H. "Lessons of History and the Lessons of Vietnam," paper prepared for publication, 1986.

The Philadelphia Inquirer. "Weapon makers' ripoffs expose the system's rot," April 7, 1985.

Philpott, Tom. "Defense Historian Measures Deadlines in Decades," *Army Times*, Sept. 14, 1981.

———. "Nunn Proposal: Symptoms of NATO Split?" *Air Force Times*, July 23, 1984.

Pincus, Walter. "Navy to Keep Troublesome Engine," *The Washington Post*, Aug. 5, 1984.

Podhoretz, Norman. "Proper Uses of Power," *The New York Times*, Oct. 30, 1983.

———. "The Future Danger," *Commentary*, April 1981.

Polmar, Norman. "Our Navy Is Severely Limited in Gulf," *Los Angeles Times*, June 5, 1984.

Poole, Robert W. Jr. "Rethinking NATO—for Real," *Reason*, June–July 1984.

Porro, Jeffrey D. "The Policy War: Brodie Versus Kahn," *Bulletin of Atomic Scientists*, June/July 1982.

Posen, Barry R., and Stephen W. Van Evera. "Reagan Administration Defense Policy," *International Security*, Summer 1983.

Possley, Maurice, and William Crawford, Jr. "Contractor Fraud Infiltrates Military," *Chicago Tribune*, Feb. 19, 1984.

Powers, James H. "The First Term Soldier: A Self Portrait," *Parameters*, Vol. XI, Number 2.

Powers, Thomas. "Choosing a Strategy for World War III," *The Atlantic*, November 1982.

———. "Nuclear Winter and Nuclear Strategy," *The Atlantic*, November 1984.

Pownall, Thomas G. "Restore Trust to Defense Industry," *The New York Times*, Dec. 5, 1985.

Pustay, John S. "The Problem Is Systemic," *Armed Forces Journal*, February 1984.

Quester, George. "Consensus Lost," *Foreign Policy*, Fall 1980.

Radway, Laurence. "Toward the Europeanisation of NATO," *Atlantic Quarterly*, Summer 1983.

———. "U.S. Forces in Europe: The Case for Cautious Contraction," *SAIS Review*, Winter–Spring 1985.

Rathjens, George W., and Jack Ruina. "100% Defense? Hardly." *The New York Times*, March 27, 1983.

Ravenal, Earl C. "Defense Budget: Where's the Bottom Line?" *The Tribune*, Oakland, April 16, 1984.

Record, Jeffrey, and Robert J. Hanks. "Out of Europe and Back to Sea," *Los Angeles Times*, Sept. 13, 1982.

Record, Jeffrey. "Why Our High-priced Military Can't Win Battles. It's Full of Bureaucrats Instead of Warriors," *The Washington Post*, Jan. 29, 1984.

———. "Jousting with Unreality: Reagan's Military Strategy," *International Security*, Winter 1983–84.

———. "Limitless Ends, Limited Means," *Baltimore Sun*, Aug. 3, 1984.

———. "Incompetence and Irresponsibility," *Baltimore Sun*, Oct. 16, 1984.

———. "Can the U.S. Honor Its Military IOUs?" *The Wall Street Journal*, Oct. 25, 1984.

Reed, Fred. "Military Looks Best Far from Pentagon," *The Washington Times*, May 30, 1985.

Reich, Gary. "Quote of the Decade," *Pegasus*, Wertheim & Co., Oct. 4, 1982.

Reston, James. "Holy War, Holy Week," *The New York Times*, March 26, 1986.

Richardson, Rob C. III. "NATO Nuclear Strategy: A Look Back," *Strategic Review*, Volume IX, Spring 1981.

Richelson, Jeffrey. "PG-59, NSDD-13 and the Reagan Strategic Modernization Program," *Journal of Strategic Studies*, June 1983.

Roark, Anne C. "Air Force Academy Flying High," *Los Angeles Times*, Oct. 14, 1982.

Roberts, Steven V. "Political Aims of Lawmakers Bring Military Budget Rises," *The New York Times*, May 17, 1985.

Robinson, Clarence A., Jr. "U.S. Puts Defense Over Arms Control," *Aviation Week & Space Technology*, Aug. 8, 1981.

Rodman, Peter W. "The Missiles of October: Twenty Years Later," *Commentary*, Oct. 1982.

Rogers, General Bernard W. "Supreme Commander Pessimistic on Defense Buildup," *The Wall Street Journal*, June 5, 1984.

Rosen, Stephen Peter. "Nuclear Arms and Strategic Defense," *Washington Quarterly*, Spring 1981.

———. "Vietnam and the American Theory of Limited War," *International Security*, Fall 1982.

Rosenburg, David Alan. "The Origins of Overkill: Nuclear Weapons and American Strategy, 1945–1960," *International Security*, Spring 1983.

Roth, Senator William V., Jr. "Sharing the Burden of European Defense," *The Christian Science Monitor*, Dec. 3, 1984.

Royster, Vermont. "Thinking Things Over, 'Wherever' Is a Big Place," *The Wall Street Journal*, Jan. 11, 1985.

———. "Thinking Things Over, 'Star Wars' or MADness?" *The Wall Street Journal*, Jan. 30, 1985.

Rusk, Dean, Robert McNamara, George Ball, Roswell Gilpatric, Theodore Sorensen, and McGeorge Bundy: "The Lessons of the Cuban Missile Crisis," *Time*, Sept. 27, 1982.

Safire, William. "NATO After Grenada," *The New York Times*, Nov. 13, 1983.

Sanger, David E. "Chip-Testing Problems Abound, Pentagon Says," *The New York Times*, April 16, 1985.

Santoli, Al. "How Good Are Our Military Officers?" *The Washington Post (Parade)*, Nov. 28, 1982.

Schemmer, Benjamin, and Anthony H. Cordesman. "The Failure to Defend Defense," *Armed Forces Journal*, March 1983.

Schemmer, Benjamin. "Does the US Now Have the World's Worst Weapon System Acquisition Process?" *Armed Forces Journal*, September 1984.

———. "*Defense Guidance* Gives SDI Priority Equal to Strategic Force Modernization," *Armed Forces Journal*, February 1986.

Schilling, Warner R. "U.S. Strategic Nuclear Concepts in the 1970s," *International Security*, Fall 1981.

Schlesinger, James R. "Reorganizing the Joint Chiefs," *The Wall Street Journal*, Feb. 8, 1984.

―――. "The Eagle and the Bear: Ruminations on Forty Years of Superpower Relations," *Foreign Affairs*, Summer 1985.

―――. "Rhetoric and Realities in the Star Wars Debate," *International Security*, Summer 1985.

―――. "Maintaining Global Stability," *Washington Quarterly*, Summer 1985.

Schlitz, Wiliam P. "AF-ROTC Bounces Back," *Air Force Magazine*, January 1984.

Schmit, Richard B. "Schlumberger Unit Has Test Problems with Military Parts," *The Wall Street Journal*, Dec. 4, 1984, p. 44.

Schneider, Barry R. "Invitation of a Nuclear Beheading," *Across the Board*, July/August 1983.

Schratz, Paul R. "War, Morality, and the Military Professional," *Naval Institute Proceedings*, September 1983.

Schwerzler, Nancy J. "Weinberger Resists Call to Join Budget Battle," *Baltimore Sun*, Jan. 30, 1985.

Seib, Gerald F. "Pratt & Whitney Overcharged on Engines, Failed to Explain Costs, U.S. Report Says," *The Wall Street Journal*, Feb. 23, 1984.

―――. "Wary of Pentagon Start-Ups," *The Wall Street Journal*, Feb. 24, 1984.

―――. "Overhaul the Military Chain of Command," *The Wall Street Journal*, Aug. 14, 1984.

―――. "Army Is Paying 'Excess Prices' for Divad Guns," *The Wall Street Journal*, Sept. 21, 1984.

Shaw, Robert D., Jr. "Study: Buying 'Direct' Could Save Pentagon $1 Billion on B1 parts," *The Miami Herald*, Nov. 3, 1983.

Sidey, Hugh. "The Alternative Is So Terrible," *Time*, Jan. 28, 1985.

Simon, Philip, and Mark Rovner. "The Role of Congress in Defense Budget Decision Making: Views of Congressional Staff Members," *Common Cause Study*, 1985.

Sloss, Leon, and Marc Dean Millot. "U.S. Nuclear Strategic Evolution," *Strategic Review*, Winter 1984.

Smith, Hedrick. "Schlesinger Says Distrust Hinders Foreign Policy," *The New York Times*, Feb. 7, 1985.

Smith, Paul. "DoD Report Confirms Spare Part Overpricing," *Air Force Times*, June 18, 1984.

Smith, R. Jeffrey. "Weapons Bureaucracy Spurns Star Wars Goal," *Science*, April 6, 1984.

―――. "Crisis Management Under Strain," *Science*, Aug. 31, 1984.

―――. "Schlesinger Attacks Star Wars Plan," *Science*, Nov. 9, 1984.

Smoke, Richard. "Extended Deterrence: Some Observations," *Naval War College Review*, September/October 1983.

Snyder, William. "Officer Recruitment for the All-Volunteer Force: Trends and Prospects," *Armed Forces and Society*, Spring 1984.

Solomon, Jolie B. "TRW Tells Pentagon, Other Customers It Overcharged by Several Million Dollars," *The Wall Street Journal*, Nov. 16, 1984.

Steinbruner, John D. "Nuclear Decapitation," *Foreign Policy*, Winter 1981–82.

―――. "Launch under Attack," *Scientific American*, January 1984.

Summers, Colonel Harry G. Jr. "Clausewitz and Strategy Today," *Naval War College Review*, March/April 1983.

―――. "Lessons: A Soldier's View," *Wilson Quarterly*, Summer 1983.

_____. "Defense Without Purpose," *Society*, November/December 1983.

_____. "Lebanon, Vietnam, and the U.S. Military," *The Wall Street Journal*, Feb. 21, 1984.

_____. "War: Deter, Fight, Terminate; The Purpose of War Is a Better Peace," *Naval War College Review*, January/February 1986.

Szanton, Peter L. "OMB's Defense Cop-out," *Foreign Policy*, Spring 1985.

Taylor, General Maxwell. "A Do-it-yourself Professional Code for the Military," *Journal of the U.S. Army War College*, December 1980.

_____. "Reflections on a Grim October," *The Washington Post*, October 5, 1982.

_____. "Maligning the Military," *The Washington Post*, Feb. 5, 1984.

Teller, Edward. "Nuclear Weapons for Defense?" *Military Science & Technology*, Aug. 9, 1982.

_____. "To Deter a 'Grizzly': Defense Better Than Retaliation," *Defense Science*, October/November 1985.

_____. "Better a Shield Than a Sword," *Defense Science*, October/November 1985.

Thompson, Mark. "Design Flaw Mars Bell Military Helicopters," *Fort Worth Star-Telegram*, March 25, 1984.

_____. "Chronology of Mast Problem," *Fort Worth Star-Telegram*, March 25, 1984.

_____. "Army, Bell Downplayed Copter Flaw," *Fort Worth Star-Telegram*, March 26, 1984.

_____. "Crashes Alarming to Navy," *Fort Worth Star-Telegram*, March 27, 1984.

_____. "Pilot Lives to Describe Helicopter Crash," *Fort Worth Star-Telegram*, March 28, 1984.

_____. "Widows Hope Suits Will Help End Copter Problem," *Fort Worth Star-Telegram*, March 28, 1984.

_____. "Bell Faults Military for Copter Problem," *Fort Worth Star-Telegram*, March 29, 1984.

Thurston, Scott. "NATO War Games Mix Deadly Reality with a Dash of Fun," *The Atlanta Constitution*, Sept. 22, 1984.

_____. "Military Recruitment Not All Rosy, Despite Pentagon Stance," *The Atlanta Constitution*, Nov. 23, 1984.

Time. "West Point Makes a Comeback," Nov. 4, 1985.

Tofani, Loretta. "GE Pleads Guilty in Fraud Case," *The Washington Post*, May 14, 1985.

Toth, Robert C. "Armed Services' Top Brass Not Typical of Officer Corps," *Los Angeles Times*, May 20, 1984.

Towell, Pat. "Spare Parts Create Flap Coming and Going," *Congressional Quarterly News Service*, July 11, 1984.

_____. "Nunn Amendment Galvanizes NATO, Using U.S. Troop Withdrawal As Prod," *Armed Forces Journal*, August 1984.

Treadwell, David. "Americans Unenthusiastic About 'Star Wars' Project," *Los Angeles Times*, Jan. 30, 1985.

Turner, Admiral Stansfield. "A Strategy for the 90s," *The New York Times Magazine*, May 6, 1984.

Urquhart, John. "U.S., Canada Expected to Agree to Share Costs of Modernizing Arctic Radar System," *The Wall Street Journal*, Jan. 24, 1985.

USA Today. "Topic: WHISTLE-BLOWING," Oct. 3, 1984.

U.S. News & World Report. "Can't Anybody Here Run a War?" Feb. 27, 1984.

_____. "Is U.S. Foreign Policy on the Right Track?" Feb. 18, 1985.

Vartabedian, Ralph. "Secret Arms Programs Proliferate," *Los Angeles Times*, April 10, 1985.

Vick, Alan J. "Post-attack Strategic Command and Control Survival: Options for the Future," *Orbis*, Spring 1985.

Vlahos, Michael. "Strategy and Status of Sealift," *Journal of Defense and Diplomacy*, March 1984.

Wainstein, Leonard. "The Problem of the Joint Chiefs of Staff," *International Security Review*, Fall 1982.

The Wall Street Journal. "Advanced Micro Halts Shipments for U.S. Contractors," Dec. 5, 1984.

———. "Use of Cheaper Goods Called No. 1 Abuse In Defense Contracts," March 13, 1985.

———. "GE Agrees to Pay $1 Million to Settle Government Claim," May 10, 1985.

Washington Analysis Corporation. "Defense Industry Profits," Aug. 20, 1985.

The Washington Post. "Gen. Vessey Sees Women as Biggest Military Change," Feb. 3, 1984.

———. "Navy Refuses Faulty Engines," Sept. 8, 1984.

———. "Potential Cuts Cited in Military Parts Bills," Oct. 12, 1984.

———. "DoD and the Toilet Seats (Cont'd.)," April 22, 1985.

———. "Martin Marietta Settles for $200,000," March 13, 1985.

Waters, Robert. "Navy Chief Told Congress Pratt Engine 'Just Terrible'," *Hartford Courant*, June 27, 1984.

———. "Small Cracks Discovered in Part of GE Engine for Jet Fighter," *Hartford Courant*, July 24, 1984.

———. "Air Force Trims GE Money, Cites Quality Control," *Hartford Courant*, Nov. 1, 1984.

Weiss, Seymour. "Why We Must Think About Protracted Nuclear War," *The Wall Street Journal*, Aug. 30, 1982.

Welch, Jasper. "Strategic Mobility: A Tale of Four SecDefs," *Armed Forces Journal*, July 1984.

Wells, Samuel F. Jr. "The Origins of Massive Retaliation," *Political Science Quarterly*, Spring 1981.

———. "The United States and the Present Danger," *Journal of Strategic Studies*, March 1981.

———. "Limits on the Use of American Military Power," *Wilson Quarterly*, Winter 1983.

Werner, Leslie Maitland. "Fraud: Deciding when to Prosecute," *The New York Times*, Nov. 7, 1983.

White, Theodore. "Weinberger on the Ramparts," *The New York Times Magazine*, Feb. 6, 1983.

Whitmore, Richard. "Congress Keeps the Forts Open," *USA Today*, Dec. 20, 1983.

———. "U.S. Builds Command Post Juggernauts," *San Bernadino Sun*, April 1, 1985.

Wieselter, Leon. "The Great Nuclear Debate," *The New Republic*, Jan. 10 and 17, 1983.

Wildrick, Craig D. "Bernard Brodie: Pioneer of the Strategy of Deterrence," *Military Review*, October 1983.

Wilson, George C. "Defense Contractor May Reap Double Intended Profit on Jet," *The Washington Post*, Sept. 25, 1984.

———. "General Urges Reviving Draft," *The Washington Post*, March 2, 1985.

Wood, David. "Watchdog Raises Hackles in Pentagon," *Los Angeles Times*, November 27, 1983.

Woolsey, R. James. "To Help Presidents Get Key Military Data," *The New York Times*, Jan. 5, 1984.

Yost, David S. "European Anxieties about Ballistic Missile Defense," *Washington Quarterly*, Fall 1984.

Zieman, Mark. "Major Shipyard's Image and Morale Damaged by Revelations of Fraud," *The Wall Street Journal*, Aug. 31, 1984.

INDEX